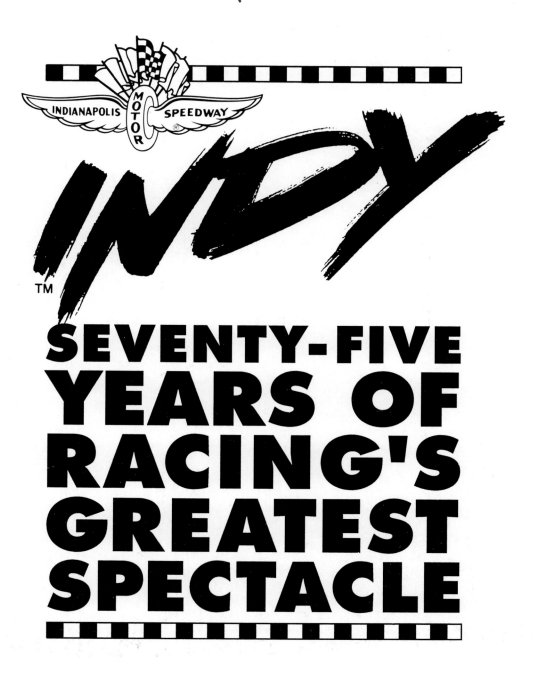

INDIANAPOLIS MOTOR SPEEDWAY

INDY™

SEVENTY-FIVE YEARS OF RACING'S GREATEST SPECTACLE

INDY
™

SEVENTY-FIVE YEARS OF RACING'S GREATEST SPECTACLE

RICH TAYLOR
FOREWORD BY A.J. FOYT, JR.

St. Martin's Press
New York

Indy: Seventy-five Years of Racing's Greatest Spectacle

Book Design by Bob Feldgus

Photos copyright © Indianapolis Motor Speedway unless otherwise credited.

Indy ®, The Indy ®, Indy 500 ®, Indianapolis 500 ®, The Greatest Spectacle in Racing ®,
Home of the 500 ®, Gasoline Alley ®, The Greatest Race Course in the World ®, and the
wheel-wings-flags logo ® are registered trademarks and used under license by Indianapolis
Motor Speedway Corporation.

Taylor, Rich
    Indy: Seventy-five Years of Racing's Greatest Spectacle
    Rich Taylor
    p. cm.
    ISBN 0-312-05447-5
    1. Indianapolis Motor Speedway—History. I. Title.
    GV1033.5.I55T39 1991
    796.7'2'06877252—dc20   90-48934
                                     CIP

First Edition

10 9 8 7 6 5 4 3 2 1

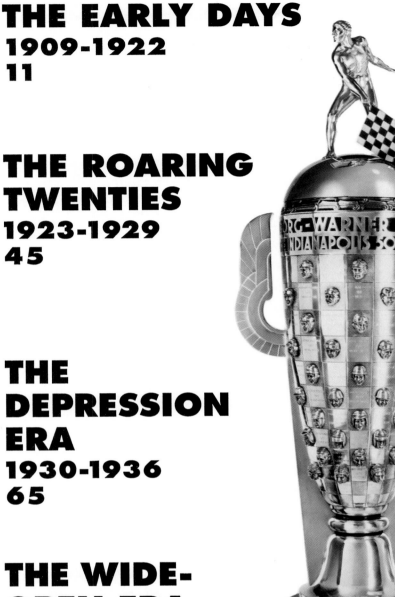

THE EARLY DAYS
1909-1922
11

THE ROARING TWENTIES
1923-1929
45

THE DEPRESSION ERA
1930-1936
65

THE WIDE-OPEN ERA
1937-1941
83

THE ODDBALL ERA
1946-1952
101

THE ROADSTERS
1953-1960
123

THE MID-ENGINE REVOLUTION
1961-1968
149

THE AERO ERA
1969-1978
177

THE INTERNATIONAL ERA
1979-1991
205

THE MONTH OF MAY
243

ACKNOWLEDGEMENTS

A book is like a racing car; one person's name may be on the side, but it takes a whole team to make it go. Bill Donaldson, Vice-President and Director of Marketing at IMS, came up with the idea to publish a history of the Speedway in the first place. He and Kurt Hunt of IMS cheerfully worked overtime to check all the facts and suggest editorial changes. Bob Laycock of IMS supplied the information in the race result tables and read the manuscript for correctness. Donald Davidson, USAC Historian, also fact-checked the manuscript and supplied much of the highlighted trivia information.

Kent Liffick, Director Hall of Fame Museum and Special Events at IMS, coordinated special photography and marketing ideas. Martha Powell, Marketing/Exhibit Coordinator at the museum, cheerfully helped with research and photos. Judy Johnson at the Museum office expedited everything with a smile.

Ron McQueeney, Director of Photography at IMS, and his assistant, Pat Jones, allowed us to take over their photo archives for weeks, supplied photos we'd forgotten and otherwise went out of their way to be helpful.

Mark Ewing, editor of *Sports Car International*, copy-edited the entire manuscript as a personal favor to me. I owe him one. George Witte of St. Martin's Press and Patricia Fogarty also proof-read everything.

Designer Bob Feldgus gave the book its bold and exciting look and stayed up half the night to meet our deadlines. India Cooper and Nancy McCord prepared the index, while Rosemarie Postighone typeset both the race result tables and the index.

Bob McCord put the whole project together and served as the coordinator between IMS, St. Martin's and myself. If any one person deserves credit for seeing this book through to publication, it's Bob.

I'd also like to thank Jack Nerad, editor of *Motor Trend*, who first suggested my name as a possible author, and A.J. Foyt, Jr., for writing the Foreword.

I'd especially like to thank my wife and partner Jean Constantine, who did the layouts and mechanicals, as well as typesetting, copy-editing and historical research. She also endured my creative tantrums with understanding and good humor and met impossible deadlines with grace under pressure. If this book had a dedication page, her name would be on it.

Rich Taylor
Sharon, CT
January 16, 1991

PHOTO CREDITS

All pictures are credited to the Indianapolis Motor Speedway (IMS) or as designated below:
Kevin Alexander, 255 (fan); Steve Baker, 253, center; Mag Binkley, pit stop sequence, 247, 249, 251, 253, 255, 257, 259, 261, 263, 265, 267, 269, 271, 273, 275, 277; 257 top inset (Special Olympics); Dan Boyd, 237, 262; Jean Constantine, jacket flap (author photo); Charles Duffy, 247, top; 256, bottom, right; 257 top inset (Carnegie); Steve Ellis, 246, bottom; Nancy Heck, 252; 266, top; Todd Hunter, 274, bottom; Steve Lingenfelter, 235, bottom; 260; Tom Lucas, 264; Linda McQueeney, 219; Ron McQueeney, 39, top right; 41, top left; 53, center; 61, top right; 186-187, bottom; 200; 205; 214-215, bottom; 215, top; 217; 222, center, top; 223, top, bottom; 229; 235, center; 241; 249, center (2 photos); 254; George Olson, title page; Jim Peterson, 248, top; Tim Peterson, 223, center; Robert Scott, 246, center; Larry Seidman, 258, right; 270; Leigh Spargur, 248, center left (2 photos); 266, top right; Denis Sparks, 233, top; 265, top; Rich Taylor, 69, bottom; Kay Totten Spivey, 262; Bill Stahl, front cover; back cover; 246, top; 257, top (balloons); 257, top; 276; Jeff Stephenson, 259, top right; Steve Swope, 222, bottom; 267, center; 273, top; 274, top; Tobias Studio, IMS Collection (color), 13, 23, 24, 30, 31, 34, 35, 47, 51, 54, 63, 67, 71, 73, 75, 77, 79, 81, 83, 85, 97, 104, 111, 117, 121, 125, 134, 144, 151, 167, 171, 179, 180, 185, 186, 193, 199, 221, 227; Dave Willoughby, 250; Debbie Young, 257, top (Jim Nabors); Loretta Young, 207; 248, bottom right; 263, center.
Special artwork by Carmine Infantino, 25, top; 133, top; 195.

FOREWORD

I remember the first time I came to the Indianapolis Motor Speedway. I was afraid they wouldn't let me in the gate. And they didn't.

That was back in 1956. I'd won a bunch of dirt track races in Texas and driven up to Indy to run in a Midget race on a little oval across the street from the Speedway. The next day was the 500. I went to the Speedway's office to get a pit pass, and they turned me down. I wound up buying a ticket and sitting in Turn One with half the population of Indiana and part of Ohio.

The same thing happened to me the next year, even though I was a two-time feature winner in the USAC Midget division. By then, those fans in Turn One were starting to look like family to me.

The following year, 1958, I had a ride for my first Indianapolis 500 in Al Dean's car. They still wouldn't give me a pit pass, because neither Dean nor his car had arrived yet. "Come back when you've got a car and a car owner," is what they told me. Of course, I finally did get to drive in the race that year, and the rest is history. But the reason I bring this up is that Indy is the one place in the world where every race driver has to prove himself once and for all. He knows it, everybody there knows it, and that's all there is to it.

You know, a lot of people thought Mr. Hulman had lost his mind when he bought the Indianapolis Motor Speedway, weeds and all, back in 1946. But Mr. Hulman sure knew what he was doing and what he wanted—to make the Indianapolis 500 the greatest automobile race in the world. Mrs. Hulman and Mari George, and the late Joe Cloutier, and now young Tony George—they've all been right there, improving the Speedway every year and taking care of Indy's many traditions.

Without Indy, I know my life wouldn't be anything like it is now, and neither would a whole lot of other people's. I've traveled all over the world, and every place I go, the one thing everyone wants to talk about is *Indy, Indy, Indy*. What I tell 'em is, yeah, you got it right—there just isn't anything in the world that's like the Indianapolis 500.

I remember talking to Mario Andretti about Indy one time and he said, "That race is so big now that if you win it, you may not have driven the best race of your life—but it's the one race you'll always remember."

As for me, I don't need credentials to get through the gates of the Speedway any more. Back in those early years, I went from the back seat of my car to the basement of Mari George's home. That's when they started treating me like family, and I've felt like part of the family ever since.

But I'll tell you this: I cannot begin to say how privileged I feel to have won this race four times—and every time I go through one of those gates at the Speedway, I feel every bit as honored as the very first time I did 35 years ago.

INTRODUCTION

Motor racing is the most complicated sport yet invented. Not only is it a contest between men—who are fallible enough—but a contest between machines. And the machines are prone to the most mystifying ailments. Not only is racing a physical contest demanding strength, endurance and reflexes, it is a mental game of strategy, planning and fanatical attention to detail. It is also a battle of psychology, of "will to win," of concentration and self-confidence. Not just for the driver—who is the most visible member of the team—but for all the engineers and mechanics who stand behind him.

This is a story about these people. Some of them are heroes, a few are villains, most of them are extraordinarily bright, dedicated and hard-working. Indeed, some of the most interesting and thoughtful people you're likely to meet in this life are involved in motor racing in one way or another.

Why would such accomplished individuals spend their fortunes and their careers chasing phantom tenths of a second. Certainly not for the glory. Racing is mostly hard, dirty work, punctuated by moments of sheer panic and only occasionally rewarded by fame and adulation. Why do people go racing? Because it's a challenge. Because it's intellectually fascinating. But most of all, because it's fun.

People like to solve puzzles, and racing is the ultimate puzzle. You figure in all these different factors, and then something comes along, something that you never thought about, and invalidates all your ideas. That's frustrating, but also fascinating. Because tomorrow you get a new chance to start over again. Perhaps that's the ultimate appeal of racing...racing is a microcosm of life, but every weekend you get to start over again, fresh and new. If you don't find the answers next weekend, there's always next month or next year. No matter what happens, there's always another racing season.

Racers are constantly looking ahead and obsessed with detail, so they often can't see the longer perspective that assures them a place in history. Motor racing is an on-going process, a living, changing, growing organism with a life of its own. Over the ten decades during which men have competed in automobiles, they have repeatedly had to solve the same problems, only in less time, at higher speeds, as the years go by. There are lessons to be learned from the experiences of those racers in the past, for history does in fact travel in a direction, in cycles, like a ray of light.

This book started out as a simple history of the Indianapolis Motor Speedway

(above) Just before the start of the first postwar 500 in 1919. Winner Howdy Wilcox is in the #3 Peugeot on the front row. Eight of the thirty-three starting cars were French Grand Prix machines, two more were American-built copies of European Grand Prix cars and four more were built by recent emigres. Ten of the drivers were from another country. The point? Even in the early days, the Indianapolis 500 was a Big Deal that attracted attention from all over the world.

and the races that have been held there since 1911. But it grew into more than that. The Indianapolis 500 has consistently been the most important motor race in the world each year, with the biggest purses, the most famous drivers, the most advanced cars. But nothing exists in a vacuum. A history of Indy, of necessity, becomes a history of motor racing in general. And that history is international, not provincial. For seventy-five years, men have gathered from all over the civilized world at Indianapolis in May. Naturally, their ideas have come from all over, too. During many eras, the connection between Indy and Formula One racing, for example, has been surprisingly strong. Without understanding these global connections, it is impossible to understand the history of the Indy 500 and just how important it really is.

Racing history is a smooth upward curve punctuated by sudden spikes of innovation. Those spikes of innovation are usually the result of one man's inspired idea. Since 1911, there have been only a handful of these revolutionaries in racing. Men like Louis Chevrolet, Harry Miller, Frank Kurtis, A.J. Watson, Colin Chapman, Gordon Coppuck and Nigel Bennett come along only once a generation, and they define that era as their own. Racing drivers get all the glory, but these quiet engineers working behind the scenes are as much heroes as anyone, because they are the ones who advance racing, who take the lessons learned and start their own revolution. This book is their story, too.

What's the attraction of the Indianapolis Motor Speedway? Al Unser, Jr., the 1990 PPG Indy Car World Series Champion sums it all up perfectly. "The fascination of racing," he says, "is that it's constantly different. It's never the same, so it never becomes dull. Every lap I learn something new. I don't even know Indianapolis the way I should. There are only four turns, and I've been around them a million times. But I learn something new every lap I go around the Speedway.

"Every time I get in a race car, it gets my blood going. The speed, the horsepower, the control. Do it all perfectly, without any mistakes, and that's the best day a man could have."

(below) Brazilian Emerson Fittipaldi wins the 1989 Indianapolis 500 in Pat Patrick's British-built Penske/Chevrolet Indy V-8, a perfect example of the international flavor of Indy car racing.

THE EARLY DAYS 1909-1922

Imagine you're behind the wheel of a brand-new, high-tech race car in the Indianapolis 500...of 1911. Sitting high off the ground, squeezed into a leather-lined bucket, the steel edge of the seat painfully cutting into your ribs when you reach outside to the shift lever, you're forced to let the gigantic wooden steering wheel vibrate madly through your numb fingers. Your jockey-size riding mechanic pumps a handle to pressurize gasoline to the engine with one hand, wrapping his other arm around your shoulders to give you room to steer in the cramped cockpit. He stinks of an explosive combination of oil, rubber, bad gasoline and fear, and blinks owlishly out at you from behind rainbow-streaked goggles. His face, like yours, is sealed in a black goo thrown up by the cars ahead.

Your race car, a primitive buckboard overpowered even by the 100 hp its gigantic engine grudgingly pumps out, chatters over the unyielding bricks. There

(below) The first turn of the first Indianapolis 500, Tuesday, May 30, 1911: shark-toothed Cases of Will Jones #9 and Joe Jagersberger #8 chase Louis Disbrow's Pope-Hartford #5.

are no brakes to speak of, turning would benefit more from prayers than muscle, you can barely see through the haze of oil smoke that hangs over the track. And yet, you're roaring down the straights at over 90 mph, scrubbing off speed to hit 70 through the corners. Every few laps, you have to stop and replace a primitive

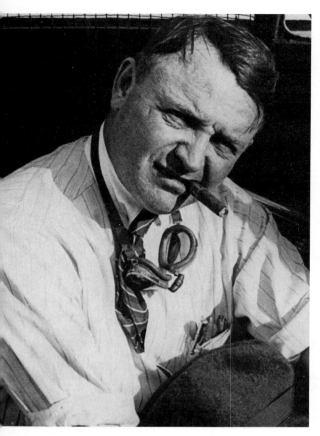

tire that's been worn down to the cord, a knuckle-busting job that has to be done, according to the rules, by you and your mechanic without help. Dangerous, difficult and often painful, this motor racing business, but one you wouldn't trade for anything in the world.

Why? Because there is nothing more intoxicating than this new sport of motor racing, nothing you can do that is so much *fun*. So challenging, but so rewarding. You and your buddies—the newspapers call you "daredevils of speed"—you who race, crash and sometimes die in these frighteningly dangerous leviathans, are easily the best-paid athletes in the country. First prize in this one 500 mile race pays $10,000, not bad compared to the five dollars a day you made last year working as a rich businessman's chauffeur.

But none of your buddies is out here because of the money. They love it, they love racing. You all do. As one wise guy told a reporter, "I race because when the race is finished, the sky is bluer, the women are prettier and the steaks taste better." What more could a man want? And so you peer hopefully into that hanging cloud of blue oil smoke and press the throttle down.

THE FIRST MOTOR RACE

The first organized motor race was sponsored by the Paris newspaper *Petit Journal* and run over public roads from Paris to Rouen on July 22, 1894. This was barely eight years after Gottlieb Daimler and Wilhelm Maybach had built the very first motorcar. In other words, motor racing is nearly as old as the automobile itself. There were a hundred and two entries for that seminal French event, but only nineteen actually made it to the starting line under their own power. The fastest, a two-ton steam tractor conducted by the Comte de Dion, wheezed the 79 miles from Paris to Rouen at the astonishingly high average speed of 11.6 mph.

Inspired by the publicity surrounding the race from Paris to Rouen—it was our great-grandparents' equivalent of putting a man on the moon, after all—H.H. Kohlsatt, publisher of the *Chicago Times-Herald*, sponsored the first motor race in America on Thanksgiving Day, 1894. Six intrepid starters slithered through 8 inches of snow from downtown Chicago to Evanston and back. Frank Duryea won the $2000 first prize by racing 54 miles in 8 hours and 23 minutes, a heady average of 6.5 mph. Among the obstacles he had to overcome were finding a blacksmith's shop that would open on a holiday to repair his broken steering gear and collecting his brother Charles—who was the pit crew—from a leisurely lunch at the local pub.

Duryea's motor car, with its tall wooden wheels driven by a 4 hp, one-cylinder engine mounted under the seat, looked exactly like a buggy without the horse. And that's what it was...a horseless carriage, not a racing car. On the other hand, the Duryea machine was the first gasoline-engined vehicle to win a race anywhere in the world, and thus the humble progenitor of every internal combustion race car that's taken to the track in the past century.

(above) As great a showman as he was a driver, Barney Oldfield started his career in 1902 in Henry Ford's 999, set the world Land Speed Record at 131.275 mph in 1910 with his incredible Blitzen Benz and retired with the equally famous Golden Submarine in 1918. He set hundreds of speed records and ran the first unofficial 100 mph lap at the Indianapolis Speedway, but never won the race. He was fifth in both 1914 and '16, the only two 500s he entered. His trademark cigar was actually a shock absorber to keep his teeth from chattering together on the bumpy dirt tracks of those days.

There were hundreds of motorized competitions in many countries over the next ten years, often organized by a local newspaper hoping to garner publicity and give its reporters something exciting to write about. There were enough races so that by 1900, it was possible for probably two dozen brave pioneers to make a living as professional racing drivers. Of course, many of those early heroes were independently wealthy, and raced *pour le sport* rather than for something as crass as a purse full of money or a silver cup. Sometimes, there were only two or three machines in a race, but even that was novel enough to draw spectators by the hundreds of thousands to witness a "grudge match." Those two or three primitive automobiles were likely the first self-propelled vehicles most of the spectators had ever seen.

There were straight-line land-speed records, reliability runs, races on the private

(below) The original tar and crushed stone surface of the Speedway broke up badly during the first event in August, 1909, and was immediately replaced. Lewis Strang stays in the groove and out of the slippery gravel as he passes the old timing and scoring towers in his 200 hp Fiat.

roads of rich men's estates, but the most important were the mammoth long-distance races in Europe. Starting with Paris-Bordeaux-Paris, they soon grew into incredible country-to-country events...Paris to Amsterdam, Paris to Berlin, Paris to Vienna, Paris to Madrid. As you can see, Paris was, quite literally, the center of the world automobile industry in those days.

The immense spectacle of these early races is almost impossible for us to imagine today, sort of the Superbowl, Wimbledon, the Olympics and the world soccer championship all rolled into one. Some 3 million people turned out to cheer during the 15-hour, 615 mile Paris to Vienna race of 1902, for example. The winner of that event, Marcel Renault, was one of those killed in the tragic Paris-Madrid race of 1903, which was stopped by the French government at Bordeaux because of the bloody carnage. Paris-Madrid was the last

1911

Winner: Ray Harroun,
Marmon Wasp, 74.602 mph
Winner's Purse: $14,250
Total Purse: $27,550
Pace Car: Carl Fisher,
Stoddard-Dayton

David Bruce-Brown's huge red Fiat led much of the first half, but Ray Harroun was in front when it counted. Harroun designed the Marmon's wasp-tailed body, installed the first rearview mirror on a racing car and came out of retirement to drive. He ran without a mechanic and re-retired after his win.

Number	Driver	Sponsor/Team	Engine Type/Displacement	Chassis	Qualifying	Start/Finish	Laps
32	Ray Harroun	Nordyke & Marmon	Marmon I-6/477 cu.in.	Marmon	Starting	28/1	200
33	Ralph Mulford	Lozier Motor	Lozier I-4/544 cu.in.	Lozier	position	29/2	200
28	David Bruce-Brown	Fiat/E.E. Hewlett	Fiat I-4/589 cu.in.	Fiat	assigned by	25/3	200
11	Spencer Wishart	Mercedes/Spencer Wishart	Mercedes I-4/583 cu.in.	Mercedes	order of	11/4	200
31	Joe Dawson	Nordyke & Marmon	Marmon I-4/495 cu.in.	Marmon	entry date.	27/5	200
2	Ralph DePalma	Simplex Automobile	Simplex I-4/597 cu.in.	Simplex	Starters had	2/6	200
20	Charlie Merz	National Motor Vehicle	National I-4/447 cu.in.	National	to average	18/7	200
12	W.H. "Jack" Turner	Amplex/Simplex Automobile	Amplex I-4/443 cu.in.	Amplex	75 mph for	12/8	200
15	Fred Belcher	Knox Automobile	Knox I-6/432 cu.in.	Knox	a quarter-	13/9	200
25	Harry Cobe	Jackson Automobile	Jackson I-4/559 cu.in.	Jackson	mile to	22/10	200
10	Gil Anderson	Stutz/Ideal Motor Vehicle	Wisconsin I-4/390 cu.in.	Stutz	qualify for	10/11	200
36	Hughie Hughes	Mercer Motors	Mercer I-4/300 cu.in.	Mercer	the race.	32/12	200
30	Lee Frayer	Firestone/Columbus Buggy	Firestone I-4/432 cu.in.	Firestone		26/13	N/A
21	Howdy Wilcox	National Motor Vehicle	National I-4/589 cu.in.	National		19/14	N/A
37	Charles Bigelow	Mercer Motors	Mercer I-4/300 cu.in.	Mercer		33/15	N/A
3	Harry Endicott	Inter-State Automobile	Inter-State I-4/390 cu.in.	Inter-State		3/16	N/A
41	Howard Hall	Velie Motors	Velie I-4/334 cu.in.	Velie		36/17	N/A
46	Billy Knipper	Benz/E.A. Moross	Benz I-4/444 cu.in.	Benz		40/18	N/A
45	Bob Burman	Benz/E.A. Moross	Benz I-4/520 cu.in.	Benz		39/19	N/A
38	Ralph Beardsley	Simplex Automobile	Simplex I-4/597 cu.in.	Simplex		34/20	N/A
18	Eddie Hearne	Fiat/Edward A. Hearne	Fiat I-4/487 cu.in.	Fiat		16/21	N/A
6	Frank Fox	Pope Manufacturing	Pope-Hartford I-4/390 cu.in.	Pope		6/22	N/A
27	Ernest Delaney	Cutting/Clark-Carter Auto	Cutting I-4/390 cu.in.	Cutting		24/23	N/A
26	Jack Tower	Jackson Automobile	Jackson I-4/432 cu.in.	Jackson		23/24	N/A
23	Mel Marquette	McFarlan/Speed Motors	McFarlan I-6/377 cu.in.	McFarlan		20/25	N/A
42	Bill Endicott	Cole Motor Car	Cole I-4/471 cu.in.	Cole		37/26	N/A
4	Johnny Aitken	National Motor Vehicle	National I-4/589 cu.in.	National		4/27	125
9	Will Jones	J.I. Case T.M.	Wisconsin I-4/284 cu.in.	Case		9/28	122
1	Lewis Strang	J.I. Case T.M.	Wisconsin I-4/284 cu.in.	Case		1/29	109
7	Harry Knight	Westcott Motor Car	Westcott I-6/421 cu.in.	Westcott		7/30	90
8	Joe Jagersberger	J.I. Case T.M.	Wisconsin I-4/284 cu.in.	Case		8/31	87
35	Herbert Lytle	Apperson Brothers	Apperson I-4/546 cu.in.	Apperson		31/32	82
19	Harry Grant	Alco/American Locomotive	Alco I-6/580 cu.in.	Alco		17/33	51
17	Charles Basle	Buick Motor	Buick I-4/594 cu.in.	Buick		15/34	46
5	Louis Disbrow	Pope Manufacturing	Pope-Hartford I-4/390 cu.in.	Pope		5/35	45
16	Arthur Chevrolet	Buick Motor	Buick I-4/594 cu.in.	Buick		14/36	30
39	Caleb Bragg	Fiat/Caleb S. Bragg	Fiat I-4/487 cu.in.	Fiat		35/37	24
24	Fred Ellis	Jackson Automobile	Jackson I-4/355 cu.in.	Jackson		21/38	22
34	Teddy Tetzlaff	Lozier Motor	Lozier I-4/544 cu.in.	Lozier		30/39	20
44	Arthur Greiner	Amplex/Simplex Motor	Amplex I-4/443 cu.in.	Amplex		38/40	12

of the great country-to-country races. They were a mixed blessing, at best. Millions of people were exposed to motorcars; but dozens were killed and in many countries, automobiles were either banned or restricted to a top speed of 20 mph. In parts of Europe, it took decades to undo the damage done to the reputation of motor racing by these legendary, but bloody, gladiatorial combats.

The basic problem was the unbelievably rapid advance of technology, which

moved too quickly for the race organizers to handle. In 1895, Emile Levassor blasted from Paris to Bordeaux and back at an average of 14.9 mph. His state-of-the-art Panhard had a 2.4-liter two-cylinder engine that produced 4 hp. By 1902, the Panhard factory racing car had a four-cylinder engine displacing 13.7-liters, rated at 70 hp and capable of driving the lightweight, wood-framed machine to almost 90 mph. Just about every component was drilled to save weight, while the driver and mechanic balanced on a wooden board bolted across the frame rails. Driving such over-powered contraptions for hundreds of miles of potholes and blinding dust was not so much dangerous as downright suicidal.

JAMES GORDON BENNETT

Starting in 1899, James Gordon Bennett—publisher of the *New York Herald*, but an expatriate resident of Paris—sponsored the famous series of races that bear his name. Gordon Bennett was determined to *organize* motor racing, the first, but certainly not the last, man to chase that elusive goal. In cooperation with l'Automobile Club de France, he drew up the first rules for motor racing, many of them identical to the rules which still govern racing today.

(above) "Death-Defying Daredevils of Speed" roar into Turn Two during the 1912 500. Spencer Wishart's Mercedes #7 leads winner Joe Dawson's National #8, Bill Endicott's Schacht #18 and Bob Burman's Cutting #15. Behind the wooden pedestrian bridge is a vehicle bridge to get cars into the "field," as the infield was called back then.

(left) A great moment in sports: Ralph DePalma gamely pushes his Mercedes to the finish line after blowing up the engine 3.5 miles short of winning the 1912 Indy 500. The best driver of his era, DePalma won over 2000 races in a twenty-five year career—plus the world land speed record at 149 mph in 1919. He won only one Indy 500, in 1915, but his pluck and gallantry made him a hero to fans and competitors alike.

(above) The first start/finish "pagoda" burned the morning after the 1925 race. It was replaced by this even more pictur-esque version which survived until 1956 when it was deliberately razed.

THE BRICKYARD

Carl Fisher was the co-owner of Prest-O-Lite, which made carbide headlamps for automobiles. In those days before World War I, much of the auto industry was headquartered around Indianapolis, not Detroit, and Fisher thought they needed a combination race track/test track. He and three Indiana auto business buddies—Arthur Newby of National Motors, Frank Wheeler of Wheeler-Schebler Carburetor and Fisher's Prest-O-Lite partner Jim Allison—bought 320 acres northwest of Indianapolis and started building a 2.5-mile rectangular track in February, 1909. Each turn was a quarter-mile long, joining two 5/8-mile straights and two 1/8-mile straights. The whole thing fit into an area 1 mile by 1/2 mile and was soon flanked by wooden fences, huge wooden stands and three wooden timing towers on the infield side near the start/finish line.

The original course was paved in a mix of tar and crushed stone, 50 feet wide on the straights and 60 feet wide in the corners. The corners were banked with earth to an angle of 9 degrees 12 minutes, then paved. During the first race on August 19, 1909, the track surface deteriorated drastically, causing at least five deaths. Fisher immediately had the whole track repaved with 3,200,000 bricks. It took the work crew only two months to hand-lay the 10 lb. bricks.

Lewis Strang won the first exhibition race at the new "brickyard" on December 17, 1909, driving his 200 hp Fiat. Starting on May 27, 1910, there was a series of 42 separate races over three days. This elaborate program was repeated over Fourth of July weekend and Labor Day. But Carl Fisher decided that for 1911, there would be just one race, a 500-miler on Memorial Day, with a stupendous purse of $27,550, counting contingency money. Thus is immortality born. ■

(above) Racer Lewis Strang examines a model of the Speedway in February, 1909. He's standing where the Speedway Motel is now. Note the four wooden pegs in the infield which provided pivots for string and nails used to draw the constant-radius corners of the model.

(left) Indianapolis Motor Speedway founders Arthur Newby, Frank Wheeler, Carl Fisher and James Allison.

1912

Winner: Joe Dawson, National, 78.72 mph
Winner's Purse: $20,000
Total Purse: $52,225
Pace Car: Carl Fisher, Stutz Roadster

Ralph DePalma led from lap 3 through 198, when his Mercedes put a rod through the crankcase. DePalma and his mechanic Rupert Jeffkins pushed the car over a mile to the pits to become an enduring symbol of true grit. Joe Dawson was as surprised as anyone when he received the checkered flag.

Number	Driver	Sponsor/Team	Engine Type/Displacement	Chassis	Qualifying	Start/Finish	Laps
8	Joe Dawson	National Motor Vehicle	National I-4/491 cu.in.	National	86.13	7/1	200
3	Teddy Tetzlaff	Fiat/E.E. Hewlett	Fiat I-4/589 cu.in.	Fiat	84.24	3/2	200
21	Hughie Hughes	Mercer Motors	Mercer I-4/301 cu.in.	Mercer	81.81	17/3	200
28	Charlie Merz	Stutz/Ideal Motor Car	Wisconsin I-4/390 cu.in.	Stutz	78.88	22/4	200
18	Bill Endicott	Schacht Motor Car	Wisconsin I-4/390 cu.in.	Schacht	80.57	15/5	200
2	Len Zengel	Stutz/Ideal Motor Car	Wisconsin I-4/390 cu.in.	Stutz	78.85	2/6	200
14	Johnny Jenkins	White Indianapolis	White I-6/490 cu.in.	White	80.82	11/7	200
22	Joe Horan	Lozier/Dr. W.H. Chambers	Lozier I-4/545 cu.in.	Lozier	80.48	18/8	200
9	Howdy Wilcox	National Motor Vehicle	National I-4/590 cu.in.	National	87.20	8/9	200
19	Ralph Mulford	Knox/Ralph Mulford	Knox I-6/597 cu.in.	Knox	87.88	16/10	200
4	Ralph DePalma	Mercedes/E.J. Schroeder	Mercedes I-4/583 cu.in.	Mercedes	86.02	4/11	198
15	Bob Burman	Cutting/Clark-Carter Auto	Cutting I-4/598 cu.in.	Cutting	84.11	12/12	157
12	Bert Dingley	Simplex/Bert Dingley	Simplex I-4/597 cu.in.	Simplex	80.77	10/13	116
25	Joe Matson	Lozier/O. Applegate	Lozier I-4/545 cu.in.	Lozier	79.90	21/14	110
7	Spencer Wishart	Mercedes/Spencer Wishart	Mercedes I-4/583 cu.in.	Mercedes	83.95	6/15	82
1	Gil Anderson	Stutz/Ideal Motor Car	Wisconsin I-4/390 cu.in.	Stutz	80.93	1/16	80
17	Billy Liesaw	Marquette-Buick/Thomson	Buick I-4/594 cu.in.	Marquette	77.51	14/17	72
5	Louis Disbrow	J.I. Case T.M.	Case I-6/450 cu.in.	Case	76.54	24/18	67
23	Mel Marquette	McFarlan/Speed Motors	McFarlan I-6/425 cu.in.	McFarlan	78.08	19/19	63
6	Eddie Hearne	J.I. Case T.M.	Case I-6/450 cu.in.	Case	81.85	5/20	55
16	Eddie Rickenbacker	Firestone/Columbus Buggy	Firestone I-4/345 cu.in.	Firestone	77.30	13/21	43
29	David Bruce-Brown	National Motor Vehicle	National I-4/590 cu.in.	National	88.45	23/22	25
10	Harry Knight	Lexington Motor Car	Lexington I-6/422 cu.in.	Lexington	75.92	9/23	6
24	Len Ormsby	Opel/I.C. Stern & B.C. Noble	Opel I-4/450 cu.in.	Opel	84.09	20/24	5

The Gordon Bennett Cup was for national teams of three cars each. Each car had to weigh between 400 kg and 1000 kg, carry a driver and mechanic and have all its components manufactured in the country it represented. To control the race, a system of colored flags was invented, essentially the same system we use today. Each Gordon Bennett race had to cover between 341 and 404 miles.

To differentiate between the cars of different nationalities, the teams were assigned national colors—blue for France, red for Italy, green for Britain, white or silver for Germany, white and blue for America—just as a jockey wears the racing colors of his horse's owner. This system of national colors has lasted right up until the present day—Ferrari Formula One cars are still Italian Racing Red, Mercedes-Benz Group C racers are still silver—to the point where Jaguars and Lotuses seem to be designed in British Racing Green, Porsches in German Silver, Alfas in Racing Red. The anonymous genius who assigned those national colors so long ago seems to have had not only an instinctive understanding of psychological color theory, but also a firm grasp of national character.

The first Gordon Bennett race was held in France; then the whole event moved to the previous winner's home country, similar to the way the America's Cup is still run. Gordon Bennett Cup races were held on a closed course made from public roads, just as temporary road courses are created today. Indeed, there are very few differences between the way Formula One or CART Indy Car races are organized now and the way James Gordon Bennett ran his races ninety years ago. As much as anyone else, Gordon Bennett is responsible for the incredibly rapid advance of Edwardian racing cars...and motorcars in general.

WILLIE K. AND EARLY RACING IN AMERICA

Wealthy American automobile enthusiast William K. Vanderbilt, Jr., sponsored the initial Vanderbilt Cup race on October 8, 1904. Patterned after the Gordon Bennett races, the Vanderbilt Cup was contested over a 284 mile course made up from public roads starting and ending in Westbury, Long Island. American George Heath won with a 90 hp Panhard. The next year, American spectators were treated to the sight of the top European drivers with their factory team racers from Renault, Mercedes, Fiat and Darracq. By 1906, the Vanderbilt Cup was *the* sporting event of the year, at least around the New York area. Half-a-million spectators jammed Long Island streets, and for 1907 Willie K. had to cancel the race because nobody could figure out how to keep the spectators out of the road.

Vanderbilt had a solution, however: build a private road. His Long Island Motor Parkway from Queens to Lake Ronkonkoma was the first toll road exclusively for motorcars. The 1908-1910 Vanderbilt Cup races logically incorporated long portions of Mr. Vanderbilt's private highway, closed off for the occasion. That makes the Vanderbilt Cup the first American road race run on a private, closed course.

Spectators in 1912 could munch on a ham and cheese sandwich for 10 cents, chicken sandwich for 25 cents or a chicken box lunch for $1.00. A cushion to soften the hard wooden bleachers rented for 15 cents.

(below) Sometimes the driver even had to do his own tire changes. If mechanic Harry Goetz had done the hard work during this 1909 Marmon pit stop, maybe engineer/driver Ray Harroun wouldn't have designed a single-seater and left Goetz at home for the 1911 500.

1913

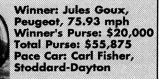

Winner: Jules Goux, Peugeot, 75.93 mph
Winner's Purse: $20,000
Total Purse: $55,875
Pace Car: Carl Fisher, Stoddard-Dayton

Frenchman Jules Goux cruised to victory in his revolutionary DOHC Peugeot while his rivals shredded their primitive tires in a futile attempt to catch him. Goux and his riding mechanic kept themselves hydrated by downing a pint of champagne at each of his six pit stops, plus more in victory circle.

Number	Driver	Sponsor/Team	Engine Type/Displacement	Chassis	Qualifying	Start/Finish	Laps
16	Jules Goux	Peugeot	Peugeot I-4/448 cu.in.	Peugeot	86.03	7/1	200
22	Spencer Wishart	Mercer Motors	Mercer I-4/300 cu.in.	Mercer	81.99	19/2	200
2	Charlie Merz	Stutz/Ideal Motor Car	Wisconsin I-4/400 cu.in.	Stutz	84.46	16/3	200
9	Albert Guyot	Sunbeam Motor Car	Sunbeam I-6/368 cu.in.	Sunbeam	80.75	2/4	200
23	Theodore Pilette	Mercedes-Knight/Patterson	Knight I-4/251 cu.in.	Mercedes	75.52	13/5	200
12	Howdy Wilcox	Gray Fox/Frank Fox	Pope-Hartford I-4/390 cu.in.	Pope	81.46	20/6	200
29	Ralph Mulford	Mercedes/E.J. Schroeder	Mercedes I-4/449 cu.in.	Mercedes	80.79	22/7	200
31	Louis Disbrow	J.I. Case T.M.	Case I-4/449 cu.in.	Case	82.76	23/8	200
35	Willie Haupt	Mason Motor	Duesenberg I-4/350 cu.in.	Duesenberg	80.76	15/9	200
25	George Clark	Tulsa Auto Manufacturing	Wisconsin I-4/340 cu.in.	Tulsa	75.91	27/10	200
4	Bob Burman	Keeton Motor	Wisconsin I-4/449 cu.in.	Keeton	84.17	21/11	188
3	Gil Anderson	Stutz/Ideal Motor Car	Wisconsin I-4/400 cu.in.	Stutz	82.63	14/12	187
5	Robert Evans	Mason Motor	Duesenberg I-4/350 cu.in.	Duesenberg	82.01	4/13	158
17	Billy Liesaw	Anel/Will Tompson	Buick I-4/318 cu.in.	Buick	78.02	3/14	148
19	Caleb Bragg	Mercer Motors	Mercer I-4/424 cu.in.	Mercer	87.34	1/15	128
10	Billy Knipper	Henderson Motor Car	Duesenberg I-4/350 cu.in.	Knipper	80.26	11/16	125
27	Teddy Tetzlaff	Isotta-Fraschini	Isotta I-4/444 cu.in.	Isotta	81.30	8/17	118
32	Joe Nikrent	J.I. Case T.M.	Case I-4/449 cu.in.	Case	78.89	24/18	67
6	Jack Tower	Mason Motor	Duesenberg I-4/350 cu.in.	Duesenberg	88.23	25/19	51
28	Vincenzo Trucco	Isotta	Isotta I-4/444 cu.in.	Isotta	81.94	18/20	39
1	Harry Endicott	Nyberg Auto	Nyberg I-6/377 cu.in.	Nyberg	76.35	10/21	23
15	Paul Zuccarelli	Peugeot	Peugeot I-4/448 cu.in.	Peugeot	85.83	26/22	18
21	Ralph DePalma	Mercer Motors	Mercer I-4/340 cu.in.	Mercer	76.30	12/23	15
26	Harry Grant	Isotta	Isotta I-4/444 cu.in.	Isotta	75.96	6/24	14
18	Johnny Jenkins	Schacht Motor Car	Schacht I-4/299 cu.in.	Schacht	82.84	17/25	13
8	Don Herr	Stutz/Ideal Motor Car	Wisconsin I-4/400 cu.in.	Stutz	82.84	5/26	7
33	Bill Endicott	J.I. Case T.M.	Case I-6/448 cu.in.	Case	85.70	9/27	1

GRAND PRIX

After the debacle of Paris-Madrid in 1903, European racing was in the doldrums for a couple of years. James Gordon Bennett switched his allegiance to airplanes rather than motorcars, while other sponsors were content to hold less dangerous "reliability trials" rather than real races. This is at least partially why the French, German and Italian teams were perfectly happy to make the long ocean voyage to Long Island for the Vanderbilt Cup. Finally, in 1906, l'Automobile Club de France stepped in and organized a race—obviously inspired by the Gordon Bennett Cup and Vanderbilt Cup events—run for 12 laps over 64 miles of closed-off public roads near LeMans, France. The ACF continued with most of the Gordon Bennett rules—the car could weigh a maximum of 1000 kg (2204 lbs.), had to carry a riding mechanic and be painted in its national racing colors.

These first Grand Prix rules merely encouraged building absurdly lightweight machines fitted with huge engines. The most powerful of the thirty-two starters in 1906 was a four-cylinder Panhard with a displacement of 18,279cc and pistons the diameter of pie plates. Hungarian Ferenc Szisz' winning 13-liter Renault covered 768 miles of rural French dirt roads at an average of 63 mph to win *Le Grand Prix*. The leading cars were easily hitting 100 mph...and were virtually unmanageable thanks to nose-heavy weight distribution, flimsy chassis and tires that were little more than rubber-coated canvas tubes. Racing primitive cars with unlimited horsepower on rutted dirt roads was almost absurdly dangerous, and the first steps to make motor racing safer were belatedly taken in 1906.

For the 1907 Kaiserpreise—the German equivalent of the French Grand Prix—engine displacement was restricted to a maximum of 8.0-liters. For the second French Grand Prix, minimum allowable fuel consumption was 9.4 miles-per-gallon, which favored smaller, and hopefully slower, cars. In 1908, the ACF came out with the first truly international racing rules. Contestants in the French Grand Prix at Dieppe had to drive cars with a minimum weight of 2425 lbs. and a maximum engine displacement of 13-liters. This guaranteed that the cars would have at least some structural integrity and a limit of about 150 hp from the engines of that time. Despite the restrictions, the Dieppe grid was filled with out and out racing cars with top speeds of about 105 mph, running on dirt and gravel roads with insufficient tires, two-wheel brakes and no safety equipment at all. The cars were so fast, it was beyond the ability of the organizers to control the crowds and prepare the roads. Grand Prix races were effectively banned between 1908 and 1912 because they were simply too dangerous.

SPEEDWAYS AND HORSE TRACKS

Obviously, what was needed was a place where automobiles could be raced under controlled conditions. In other words, a race track. Englishman H.F. Locke King built the world's first automobile race track in the autumn of 1906, on the grounds of the Brooklands estate in Weybridge, Surrey. Locke King's track was a mammoth pear-shaped banked oval of cast concrete, 2.75 miles around, plus a half-mile "fin-

Qualifying between 1912 and 1919 consisted of the best out of three timed laps. The grid was determined by order of entry in 1912, as it had been the first year, and by a blind drawing in '13 and '14. A grid determined by qualifying speed was used for the first time in 1915.

(below) Early auto races used a dangerous standing start with dozens of smoking cars lined up wheel-to-wheel as in this 1910 Indy grid. Speedway president Carl Fisher invented the now universal rolling start behind a pace car for the 1911 500. The racers followed in rows of five.

1914

Winner: Rene Thomas, Delage, 82.47 mph
Winner's Purse: $20,000
Total Purse: $51,675
Pace Car: Carl Fisher, Stoddard-Dayton

Rene Thomas's Delage made only 105 hp, but also weighed only 2300 lbs. and could top 100 mph with ease. The top four finishers were all Europeans, in French machines. Hapless Ray Gilhooley flipped his Isotta and gave the world a new slang expression, "to pull a real Gilhooley."

Number	Driver	Sponsor/Team	Engine Type/Displacement	Chassis	Qualifying	Start/Finish	Laps
16	Rene Thomas	L. Delage	Delage I-4/380 cu.in.	Delage	94.54	15/1	200
14	Arthur Duray	Peugeot/Jacques Munier	Peugeot I-4/183 cu.in.	Peugeot	90.00	10/2	200
10	Albert Guyot	Delage/Albert Guyot	Delage I-4/380 cu.in.	Delage	89.15	11/3	200
6	Jules Goux	Peugeot/Jules Goux	Peugeot I-4/345 cu.in.	Peugeot	98.13	19/4	200
3	Barney Oldfield	Stutz Motor Car	Stutz I-4/434 cu.in.	Stutz	87.25	30/5	200
9	Josef Christiaens	Excelsior/Josef Christiaens	Excelsior I-6/446 cu.in.	Excelsior	91.21	7/6	200
27	Harry Grant	Sunbeam Motor Car	Sunbeam I-6/273 cu.in.	Sunbeam	86.46	26/7	200
5	Charles Keene	Beaver Bullet/Charles Keene	Wisconsin I-4/449 cu.in.	Keene	86.87	27/8	200
25	Billy Carlson	Maxwell/US Motor	Maxwell I-4/445 cu.in.	Maxwell	93.36	5/9	200
42	E. Rickenbacker	Duesenberg	Duesenberg I-4/361 cu.in.	Duesenberg	88.14	23/10	200
23	Ralph Mulford	Mercedes/E.J. Schroeder	Peugeot I-4/448 cu.in.	Mercedes	88.21	6/11	200
43	Willie Haupt	Duesenberg	Duesenberg I-4/361 cu.in.	Duesenberg	89.39	28/12	200
31	Billy Knipper	Keeton Motor	Wisconsin I-4/449 cu.in.	Keeton	89.57	12/13	200
7	Georges Boillot	Peugeot/Georges Boillot	Peugeot I-4/345 cu.in.	Peugeot	99.86	29/14	141
34	Ernst Friedrich	Ettore Bugatti	Bugatti I-4/390 cu.in.	Bugatti	87.73	18/15	134
1	Louis Disbrow	Bob Burman	Wisconsin I-4/449 cu.in.	Burman	86.79	24/16	128
19	Spencer Wishart	Mercer Motors	Mercer I-4/445 cu.in.	Mercer	92.69	25/17	122
2	Earl Cooper	Stutz Motor Car	Stutz I-4/343 cu.in.	Stutz	88.02	14/18	118
21	Caleb Bragg	Mercer Motors	Mercer I-4/445 cu.in.	Mercer	92.97	9/19	117
15	Art Klein	King/Arthur H. Klein	Wisconsin I-4/449 cu.in.	King	86.87	8/20	87
38	William Chandler	Braender Bulldog	Duesenberg I-4/449 cu.in.	Mulford	87.54	4/21	69
4	Howdy Wilcox	Gray Fox/Frank Fox	Pope-Hartford I-4/432 cu.in.	Fox	90.76	3/22	67
13	George Mason	Mason Motor	Duesenberg I-4/361 cu.in.	Duesenberg	87.10	13/23	66
17	Bob Burman	Bob Burman	Wisconsin I-4/449 cu.in.	Burman	90.41	22/24	47
26	Joe Dawson	Marmon/Charles E. Erbstein	Marmon I-4/445 cu.in.	Marmon	93.55	17/25	45
24	Gil Anderson	Stutz Motor Car	Stutz I-4/416 cu.in.	Stutz	90.49	16/26	42
49	Ray Gilhooley	Isotta/G.M. Heckschew	Isotta I-4/375 cu.in.	Isotta	84.20	20/27	41
8	Teddy Tetzlaff	Maxwell/US Motor	Maxwell I-4/445 cu.in.	Maxwell	96.36	2/28	33
12	Jean Chassagne	Sunbeam Motor Car	Sunbeam I-6/273 cu.in.	Sunbeam	88.31	1/29	20
48	S.F. Brock	Ray	Wisconsin I-4/449 cu.in.	Mercer	87.83	21/30	5

ishing straight" such as you'd have at a horse track. The roadway was 100 feet wide, nearly twice the width of most modern race tracks. There were covered garages, a clubhouse with bars and restaurant, even a billiard room and changing rooms for the jockeys, er, ah...drivers.

The first race at Brooklands was July 6, 1907, and like every subsequent race, it was a handicap event in which the slower cars started first and the faster cars caught them up, all theoretically finishing in a dead heat. Like much else at Brooklands, this was a rather quaint concept borrowed from horse racing, very unlike wheel-to-wheel American racing. The big track survived until Vickers Armstrong destroyed part of the banking in order to build a huge aircraft factory in 1939. Brooklands was the cradle of British motor racing, but it was never very important internationally. It was always very exclusive and upper-class. The

Brooklands advertising slogan, "The right crowd and no crowding," says it all.

With the exception of Monza in Italy and Montlhery in France—both built in the early-Twenties—Brooklands was the only "Indy style" oval in Europe. But in America, there were dozens, if not hundreds, of oval race tracks. Every county fair had at least one. True, they were dirt and designed for racing horses, but that didn't stop early-day promoters.

Put a dozen bellowing racers on a half-mile oval and you had a spectacle that yokels from all over the county would flock to see.

Promoters like Carl Fisher—yes, *that* Carl Fisher—Alex Sloan and especially, Barney Oldfield created lucrative careers by staging "races" on county fair horse tracks.

Oldfield was the King of Speed. He would start out the event by setting a "track record"—he paid the timers, but who knew—then lead the race. He'd have "mechanical trouble," then dramatically sweep from behind—often making some bogus "repair" on the fly—and clinch his "victory" in the last corner. Of course, Oldfield and his buddy, promoter Bill Pickens, owned all the cars and paid all the drivers. Another racer might occasionally win, but unless he had a goldarn good excuse for passing Oldfield, he'd probably be on the milk train home to Iowa before morning.

Think what you please, but those county fair promoters whipped up enthusiasm

(left) 1915 500: Ralph DePalma's winning Mercedes, the Grey Ghost, was one of the all-conquering 1914 Grand Prix cars. It had a 4.5-liter, 115 hp, single-overhead camshaft four-cylinder engine derived from Mercedes aircraft engines. Even back then, Mercedes enjoyed a reputation for building fast and rugged cars. Top speed: 112 mph.

"LES CHARLATANS" AND THE FIRST MODERN MOTORCAR

The first modern automobile engine appeared in a Peugeot racing car which won the Dieppe Grand Prix in 1912 and the Indianapolis 500 in 1913. How this innovative design came about is still a great mystery, and the team that created it has come down the decades to us with the derogatory label *Les Charlatans*. Some historians claim that engineer Marc Birkigt of Hispano-Suiza, generally acknowledged as one of the most brilliant automotive designers of all time, created the first engine of this type in 1911, and that his test driver, Italian Paolo Zuccarelli, stole Birkigt's ideas and sold them to Peugeot. Other historians, equally expert, claim that Birkigt had nothing to do with it, and that *Les Charlatans* revolutionized the automobile all by themselves.

What we do know is that racing drivers Jules Goux, Paolo Zuccarelli and Georges Boillot went to Robert Peugeot in 1911 and convinced him to bankroll the construction of a trio of new and radical Grand Prix racing cars. Monsieur Peugeot set up a separate small workshop for this group, whom his regular Peugeot engineers immediately labelled *Les Charlatans*. The three, who were primarily racing drivers, after all, hired Swiss engineer Ernest Henry—who, like Marc Birkigt, was from Geneva—to draw the blueprints that would eventually turn their grandiose ideas into hard steel, iron and aluminum.

Most engines in those days used two camshafts mounted down in the crankcase, one to operate intake valves and one to operate exhaust valves. The combustion chamber was broad, flat and inefficient. *Les Charlatans'* landmark Peugeot engine had the combustion chamber of each cylinder efficiently shaped like a dome, with the sparkplug screwed right in the center. Instead of long vertical valve stems operated by distant cams, they put the gear-driven camshafts *over* the head so that the valve gear could be very lightweight. They used cams to close the valves as well as open them. This type of precise mechanical valve closing is called "desmodromic," and it is still incredibly rare even on racing engines. The dome-shaped combustion chamber encouraged them to use two small intake valves and two small exhaust valves for each cylinder, rather than one big valve on each side the way conventional engines were arranged.

For 1913, the team refined their already successful design. They eliminated the complicated desmodromic valve gear in favor of conventional valve springs, invented the cup-type cam follower, added spur-gears for the cam drives and produced the first dry-sump oil system with a remote oil container to hold the oil away from the barrel-shaped crankcase. The Peugeot chassis was quite conventional compared to the engine, but it still used some of the first knock-off wire

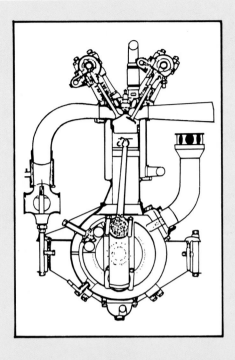

wheels instead of demountable "clincher" rims on wooden spoke wheels and adjustable friction shock absorbers. It was decades ahead of the competition in 1913.

Of course, *Les Charlatans* won everywhere they went. Boillot ran away with the 1912 French Grand Prix at Dieppe, the most prestigious race in the world in those days. His Peugeot was a 7.6-liter monster. These big cars were outlawed, so the team built virtually the same car in 5.6, 4.5 and 3.0-liter versions that were, if anything, even more successful. At the 500, they won in 1913, 1916 and 1919; second in 1914 and '15.

More importantly, virtually every racing car engine since 1913 has been a copy of *Les Charlatans'* design. From the Ballot—also drawn by Ernest Henry—which showed up at Indy in 1919 to today's Ilmor and Cosworth V-8s, all have been derived from the 1913 Peugeot. The famous Millers of the Twenties, the venerable Meyer-Drake Offenhauser of the Thirties...nobody has been too proud to copy from *Les Charlatans*.

Very expensive, limited-production passenger cars like Jaguar, Ferrari and Alfa Romeo have used such an engine since the Forties. But only in the past few years has an engine with double-overhead cams, four-valves-per-cylinder and hemispherical combustion chambers appeared under the hood of mass-produced automobiles that anyone can buy. Of course, there have been a few changes in eight decades. But they have been changes of execution, not concept. In 1913, if *Les Charlatans* had had today's high-strength alloys, high-octane fuel and computerized controls, their engine would have looked much like the one in your Chevrolet. ■

(left) Engineering cross-section of the Peugeot engine shows the dual overhead camshafts, four-valves-per-cylinder, cup-type cam followers, hemispherical combustion chambers, crossflow head, central sparkplugs and barrel crankcase with external oil sump. All this in 1913—an engine with these features is still considered "state-of-the-art" today!

(below) Because of the war in France, Peugeot stopped building race cars in 1914. To fill out the wartime grid, the Speedway itself entered these three Premiers in 1916. They were literally copies of the all-conquering 4.5-liter Peugeots, though ironically, never as fast.

(far left) Fashion-plate Fred Wagner enjoyed a checkered career as starter for the 500 in 1911 and 1912.
(upper left) Track maintenance crews in 1912.
(above) The most dangerous hazard in early day racing was a blow-out from tires crudely made from cotton cord under a thin coating of rubber.
(left) Ray Harroun's famous Marmon Wasp, winner of the first Indy 500 and now on display at the Indianapolis Motor Speedway Hall of Fame Museum.

1915

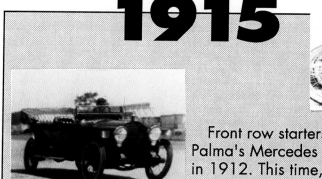

Winner: Ralph DePalma, Mercedes, 89.84 mph
Winner's Purse: $20,000
Total Purse: $51,200
Pace Car: Carl Fisher, Packard

Front row starters DePalma and Resta dueled for the entire 500 miles. De-Palma's Mercedes put a rod through the crankcase on lap 197, just as it had in 1912. This time, however, DePalma was able to crawl around on three cylinders and finish less than 4 minutes ahead of the charging Resta.

Number	Driver	Sponsor/Team	Engine Type/Displacement	Chassis	Qualifying	Start/ Finish	Laps
2	Ralph DePalma	Mercedes/E.C. Patterson	Mercedes I-4/274 cu.in.	Mercedes	98.58	2/1	200
3	Dario Resta	Peugeot Auto Import	Peugeot I-4/274 cu.in.	Peugeot	98.47	3/2	200
5	Gil Anderson	Stutz Motor Car	Stutz I-4/296 cu.in.	Stutz	95.14	5/3	200
4	Earl Cooper	Stutz Motor Car	Stutz I-4/296 cu.in.	Stutz	96.77	4/4	200
15	Eddie O'Donnell	Duesenberg	Duesenberg I-4/299 cu.in.	Duesenberg	88.93	11/5	200
8	Bob Burman	Peugeot/Bob Burman	Peugeot I-4/296 cu.in.	Peugeot	92.40	7/6	200
1	Howdy Wilcox	Stutz Motor Car	Stutz I-4/296 cu.in.	Stutz	98.90	1/7	200
10	Tom Alley	Duesenberg	Duesenberg I-4/299 cu.in.	Duesenberg	90.00	9/8	200
19	Billy Carlson	Maxwell/US Motor	Maxwell I-4/298 cu.in.	Maxwell	84.11	16/9	200
7	Noel Van Raalte	Sunbeam Motor Car	Sunbeam I-4/271 cu.in.	Sunbeam	86.87	14/10	200
28	Willie Haupt	Emden/R.E. Donaldson	Emden I-4/298 cu.in.	Emden	80.36	24/11	200
14	Harry Grant	Sunbeam/Fortuna Racing	Sunbeam I-6/278 cu.in.	Sunbeam	89.29	10/12	184
21	Tom Orr	Maxwell/US Motor	Maxwell I-4/298 cu.in.	Maxwell	83.55	17/13	168
6	Jean Porporato	Sunbeam Motor Car	Sunbeam I-4/271 cu.in.	Sunbeam	94.74	6/14	164
18	Joe Cooper	Sebring/Miles & Gwin	Duesenberg I-4/299 cu.in.	Duesenberg	85.55	15/15	154
22	Ralph Mulford	Duesenberg	Duesenberg I-4/299 cu.in.	Duesenberg	82.72	18/16	124
12	George C. Babcock	Peugeot Auto Import	Peugeot I-4/188 cu.in.	Peugeot	89.46	12/17	117
9	Art Klein	Kleinart/Art Klein	Duesenberg I-4/299 cu.in.	Duesenberg	90.45	8/18	111
23	E. Rickenbacker	Maxwell/US Motors	Maxwell I-4/298 cu.in.	Maxwell	81.97	19/19	103
27	Louis Chevrolet	Cornelian/Louis Chevrolet	Sterling I-4/103 cu.in.	Cornelian	81.01	23/20	76
17	John DePalma	Delage/James E. Wilson	Delage I-4/299 cu.in.	Delage	87.04	13/21	41
24	John A. Mais	John A. Mais	Mercer I-4/298 cu.in.	Mais	81.97	20/22	23
26	George Hill	Bugatti/C.W. Fuller	Bugatti I-4/300 cu.in.	Bugatti	81.52	22/23	20
25	G.C. Cox	Cino-Purcell/Edward McNay	Mercer I-4/299 cu.in.	Cino	81.52	21/24	12

for motor racing and motorcars in general...and trained most of the drivers who went on to find fame and fortune in legitimate racing. By 1920 or so, the staged county fair "races" were done for. It was hard to fool the rubes with bogus racing after they'd seen the world from a troop train during World War I.

THE BOARDS

Back around World War I, there was another type of oval track peculiar to America, the notorious high-speed "boards." In the Gay Nineties, before there were cars, the big craze was for bicycles. And, more particularly, for bicycle racing. Enterprising promoters built severely-banked saucers—usually an eighth-mile or quarter-mile long—for bicycle races. Called "velodromes," they were built entirely of wood and paved with 2x4s. Compared to any other material available in 1900, 2x4s were durable, smooth, inexpensive and easy to repair...just what was needed for bicycles ripping along at 35 mph, handlebar to handlebar, pedal to pedal.

In 1909, using the proven velodrome construction methods, engineers Fred

Moscovics and Jack Prince built the first all-wood banked automobile speedway at Playa del Rey outside Los Angeles. Officially called a "motordrome" though everyone referred to it as simply the "boards," it was a smashing success. By 1915, there were a half-dozen wooden saucers across the country; by 1931, there were twenty-four, including Beverly Hills, Sheepshead Bay in Brooklyn and Atlantic City. Like the earlier bicycle tracks, the boards were paved with 2x4s and severely banked at up to 45 degrees—the turns at the Indianapolis Speedway are banked to less than 10 degrees—so that daredevils could race around them at over 100 mph with their hands off the steering wheel. For sheer speed, no race tracks have ever approached the boards.

In their day, the boards offered the fastest, safest, most exciting, most popular racing in the world. For example, in 1915 Ralph DePalma won the Indianapolis 500 before 60,000 spectators at an average speed of 89.84 mph. Three weeks later, Dario Resta averaged 97.58 mph for 500 miles on the Maywood Speedway in Chicago, a 2-mile board track. There were 80,000 spectators to witness Resta's world's record, the fastest 500 miles ever run up to that time.

What happened to the boards? Well, for one thing, the service life of a million board feet of 2x4s exposed to the weather turned out to be between five and seven years. Then the tracks developed lethal splinters that could take out a driver's eye, not to mention potholes; neighborhood kids would sneak in and watch the races by poking their heads up through the track. Imagine that hallucinatory sight as you came steaming down the straight at 120 mph. This deterioration turned the boards from smooth, safe saucers into dangerous traps, and races into games of "dodge the hole." It became routine to have carpenters replacing boards from underneath, during the race itself.

With the Depression, there was no money for maintenance, and the board tracks—those that hadn't already been torn down to make way for housing developments—just rotted away. The Beverly Hills board track, for example, was built just about where the fancy shops along exclusive Rodeo Drive are now located.

REAL RACE CARS FOR REAL RACES

The boards are mostly forgotten today, but they were incredibly important to the development of American racing. In the very early dirt track days, say from 1900 to 1910, virtually all American racing cars were stripped-down passenger cars. The Europeans, on the other hand, were already build-

Jack Benny Special is what they should have called it. The most penny-pinching racer in 500 history was a Maxwell that finished ninth in 1914. Ray Harroun designed a special carburetor that allowed the Maxwell to cover 500 miles on 30 gallons of kerosene, which at 6 cents a gallon ran up a total fuel bill of $1.80. "Rochester. Oh, Rochester..."

(below) Louis Chevrolet and his Frontenac led laps 66 through 74 of the 1919 Indianapolis 500.

ing true racing cars, designed from the wheels up for competition. Once the boards and the Indianapolis Motor Speedway came along, stripped passenger cars simply didn't cut it anymore; "stock" cars were neither fast enough nor durable enough to compete with Grand Prix machines. American racing engineers like Louis Chevrolet, Fred and Augie Duesenberg and Harry Miller were virtually forced to create purpose-built race cars, and that drastically changed the shape of motor racing in America.

It took the American engineers a decade to get their act together, however. From 1911 till 1919, the Indy 500 was dominated by European cars and drivers. It's easy to see why. With only a few exceptions—most importantly, the French Grand Prix—over-the-road racing in Europe was effectively banned in most countries. There were few private race courses. So while the Europeans had these neat Grand Prix race cars, they had no place to race them. In 1911, when Carl Fisher announced his $27,550 purse for the first Indianapolis 500, Indianapolis became the most important race in the world. Drivers and cars from all over Europe soon made the trek to Indiana to run for that astronomical purse.

Interestingly, while the Europeans had these wonderful cars, and many of them were experienced drivers, they weren't at all used to the close, wheel-to-wheel racing that Americans raised on dirt ovals and the boards took for granted. In a pre-war European Grand Prix, you might have two or three dozen contestants, but they'd be strung out over miles of roadway. A fast car might zip up through the dust and pass a slower car now and then, but most of the time, the car you passed was either in the pits being repaired or parked by the side of the road, getting new tires. Wheel-to-wheel racing for the lead, constant lapping of slower cars in traffic, aerodynamic drafting, "nerfing" and "banging wheels" to get ahead were all concepts virtually unknown to the Europeans.

Foreign drivers weren't even familiar with the concept of a "groove," something American dirt track drivers had already figured out by 1905 or so. When you went blatting down a string-straight Route Nationale at 100 mph, sheer bravery was more important than any geometric "line" that was theoretically the fastest way through a corner. In Grand Prix racing in those days, when you came to a corner, you slowed down and went around, then accelerated up to speed again on the straight. There was no special trick to it at all.

In 1913, Ralph DePalma reportedly had to show Jules Goux the proper way through the corners at the Indianapolis Motor Speedway by having Goux tuck in behind him for a few laps. Goux, one of the first Europeans to race at Indianapolis, of course went on to win in the earliest of the DOHC Peugeots that came to dominate racing, worldwide. It wasn't that DePalma was such a good teacher; the Peugeot was so much faster on the straights Goux could coast through the corners and still handily out-run the American cars by miles.

A TRULY INTERNATIONAL FORMULA

As early as 1908, it was accepted that l'Automobile Club de France was the regulator of worldwide racing. The ACF eventually evolved into the Federation Internationale de l'Automobile, which still controls most interna-

tional racing today. From the very beginning, the ACF sanctioned different classes of cars designed to a "formula." *Grand Prix* cars were the fastest, Formula One. From 1908 until 1920, Grand Prix cars had to weigh a minimum of 1100 kg (2425 lbs.). From 1908 until 1911, maximum allowable engine displacement was 13.0-liters. The cars were too fast. So for 1912 Formula One was reduced to 8.0-liters.

This formula was instantly turned to a shambles by the revolutionary 7.6-liter DOHC Peugeot, capable of nearly 120 mph. So for 1913 Formula One was reduced to 5.6-liters, then in 1914 to only 4.5-liters. The winning cars—Peugeots and SOHC Mercedes— were *still* going 120 mph down the straights, too fast for most race courses of the day except for the American boards and the Indianapolis Motor Speedway.

World War I intervened before the ACF could reduce the Formula even further. That left the American Automobile Association Contest Board and Carl Fisher of Indianapolis as the most important arbiters of international racing. For 1915 Fisher reduced the displacement limit for Indianapolis cars to 300 cubic inches. This allowed both the pre-war 4.5-liter (274.5 cubic inch) European Grand Prix cars and American dirt track "mid-size" cars, which were built around modified passenger car engines of up to 300 cubic inches. It also had the effect of giving the American "stock blocks" an extra 25 cubic inches of displacement to partially offset the superior efficiency of the Peugeots and Mercedes. Indianapolis stayed with the successful 300 cubic inch formula through 1919. The aging European cars still won, but the American cars were now at least somewhat competitive.

As a young man, Carl Fisher had competed in the Gordon Bennett Cup races, and he was a firm believer that racing should be as international as possible. After World War I, the French reorganized Grand Prix racing under the direction of the newly-formed International Sporting Commission of the *Association Internationale de l'Automobile Clubs Reconnus.* One of the AIACR's first decrees was to reduce the International Formula to a maximum engine size of 3.0-liters in an 800 kg (1763 lb.) car. Conveniently, this was already the formula which Carl Fisher, his track manager T.E. "Pop" Myers and the AAA Contest Board had suggested for their 1920 season. It was a breakthrough. Not only were the Indianapolis 500 and Grand Prix formulas the same, but the French had followed the Americans, rather than vice-versa. If you want first-hand evidence of how important the Indianapolis 500 had grown in less than a decade, here's your answer. The French racing bureaucracy following the lead of the Americans? *Sacre bleu!*

For the first time, American race car builders were forced to compete on an equal footing with European Grand Prix machines.

(below) Italian-born, British-raised Dario Resta had impeccable manners, a wealthy and beautiful wife who understood racing—she was driver Spencer Wishart's sister—and an almost uncanny ability behind the steering wheel. He came to America in 1915 and won just about every race he entered except the Indianapolis 500, where he was second. In 1916, he won both the 500 and the AAA Championship. Resta later retired in deference to his wife's wishes. He ran a few races in the Twenties, and was killed at Brooklands, England in 1924, when his Sunbeam blew a tire. Despite his abbreviated career, Resta was considered one of the best drivers of his day.

1916

Winner: Dario Resta,
Peugeot, 84.00 mph
Winner's Purse: $12,000
Total Purse: $31,350
Pace Car: Frank
E. Smith, Premier

Shortened to 300 miles (500 kilometers) out of respect for the war in Europe, this year's race had the smallest starting field and fewest spectators of any 500. Dario Resta dominated the race in the Peugeot with which he had finished second in 1915. This was the last event at Indianapolis until 1919.

Number	Driver	Sponsor/Team	Engine Type/Displacement	Chassis	Qualifying	Start/Finish	Laps
17	Dario Resta	Peugeot Auto Racing	Peugeot I-4/274 cu.in.	Peugeot	94.40	4/1	120
1	Wilbur D'Alene	Duesenberg	Duesenberg I-4/299 cu.in.	Duesenberg	90.87	10/2	120
10	Ralph Mulford	Peugeot/Ralph Mulford	Peugeot I-4/274 cu.in.	Peugeot	91.09	20/3	120
14	Josef Christiaens	Sunbeam Motor Car	Sunbeam I-6/299 cu.in.	Sunbeam	86.08	14/4	120
15	Barney Oldfield	Delage/Barney Oldfield	Delage I-4/275 cu.in.	Delage	94.33	5/5	120
4	Pete Henderson	Maxwell/Prest-O-Lite Racing	Maxwell I-4/298 cu.in.	Maxwell	91.33	9/6	120
29	Howdy Wilcox	Premier/Indy Speedway	Premier I-4/274 cu.in.	Premier	93.81	6/7	120
26	Art Johnson	Crawford/William Chandler	Duesenberg I-4/298 cu.in.	Crawford	83.69	17/8	120
24	William Chandler	Crawford/William Chandler	Duesenberg I-4/298 cu.in.	Crawford	84.84	15/9	120
9	Ora Haibe	S. Osteweg	Wisconsin I-4/296 cu.in.	Osteweg	87.08	13/10	120
12	Tom Alley	Ogren Motor Car	Duesenberg I-4/299 cu.in.	Duesenberg	82.04	19/11	120
8	Louis Chevrolet	Frontenac/Chevrolet	Frontenac I-4/300 cu.in.	Frontenac	87.69	21/12	82
28	Gil Anderson	Premier/Indy Speedway	Premier I-4/274 cu.in.	Premier	95.94	3/13	75
25	Dave Lewis	Crawford/William Chandler	Duesenberg I-4/298 cu.in.	Crawford	83.12	18/14	71
18	Johnny Aitken	Peugeot/Indy Speedway	Peugeot I-4/274 cu.in.	Peugeot	96.69	1/15	69
21	Jules DeVigne	Delage/Harry Harkness	Delage I-4/274 cu.in.	Delage	87.17	12/16	61
27	Tom Rooney	Premier/Indy Speedway	Premier I-4/274 cu.in.	Premier	93.39	7/17	48
7	Arthur Chevrolet	Frontenac/Chevrolet	Frontenac I-4/300 cu.in.	Frontenac	87.74	11/18	35
19	Charles Merz	Peugeot/Indy Speedway	Peugeot I-4/274 cu.in.	Peugeot	93.33	8/19	25
5	E. Rickenbacker	Maxwell/Prest-O-Lite Racing	Maxwell I-4/298 cu.in.	Maxwell	96.44	2/20	9
23	Aldo Franchi	Peusun/Aldo Franchi	Sunbeam I-4/299 cu.in.	Peugeot	84.12	16/21	9

This had the unexpected result of enticing German-American Fred Duesenberg to enter four cars in the 1921 French Grand Prix, the first race held in France after World War I. The Duesenberg team was sponsored by Franco-American sparkplug manufacturer Albert Champion. Irish-American driver Jimmy Murphy and his 3.0-liter Duesenberg handily won, thanks mostly to superior hydraulic brakes that allowed Murphy to dive deeper into the corners and to a virtually indestructible Duesenberg that finished the race with a hole in the radiator, no water in the block and no tire on one rim.

Typical of European racing in those days, Murphy finished 15 minutes ahead of second-place Ralph DePalma's Ballot. The French Grand Prix was simply not as competitive as the Indianapolis 500. Murphy and his Duesenberg went into the record books as the first American driver and the first American car to win a major European motor race. Of course, he also won the Indianapolis 500 mile race in 1922 in this same car. This was also the last victory for an American car in a Grand Prix until Dan Gurney won with his All-American Racers Eagle at the Belgian Grand Prix in 1967.

Murphy's Grand Prix victory in a Duesenberg is important because it proved that American racers were finally competitive against the best European cars and drivers, something that a lot of people found hard to believe after the almost complete European domination of American racing from 1913 till 1919. That Murphy's Duesenberg was essentially a copy of a pre-war Mercedes Grand Prix car is beside the point. Murphy and the Duesenberg brothers had waved the stars and stripes in France as effectively as any doughboy.

For 1922, the Grand Prix Formula was reduced to 2.0-liter engines in cars which weighed at least 650 kg (1433 lbs.). And for the first time since the Gordon Bennett rules of 1899, the cars were single-seaters, devoid of a riding mechanic. The Speedway waited a year before switching the Indianapolis 500 over to these tiny monopostos, allowing the teams to get another year out of their 3.0-liter cars.

It was that kind of businesslike thinking that made Indianapolis so popular with drivers and car owners. In 1920, most of the teams were ready to replace their old cars—some of them dating back to 1914—with new machinery. It was the

(left) Shy and quiet dandy Jules Goux was twenty-two when he started seriously racing in 1907, and nearing thirty when he won the Indianapolis 500 in 1913. He was also one of "Les Charlatans" who created the revolutionary DOHC Peugeot. World War I didn't slow him down; like many racing drivers, he became a chauffeur. He was just as successful after the war; this photo shows him drinking champagne after finishing third at Indianapolis in 1919. His last wins came in European Grands Prix in 1926, when he was almost forty— a very advanced age for a racing driver in those dangerous days. Goux lived another forty years, and died in bed.

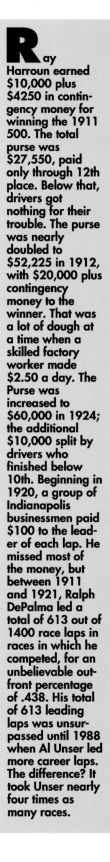

perfect time to switch formulas without incurring too much financial hardship. But to throw those cars away after only two years; that was silly and wasteful. The Speedway management stretched another year out of the 3-liter two-seaters to give "the boys" a chance to recoup their investment before they made them fall back in line with the European Grand Prix cars. One of the unforeseen effects of that decision was that in 1922, neither Duesenberg nor any other American racing car manufacturer had cars that were suitable to race in European Grands Prix.

Jimmy Murphy did race at Monza in 1923 with a 2-liter Miller, finishing third. But already, the "International Formula" that was meant to tie Grand Prix and AAA racing together was coming apart at the seams. For the decade of the Twenties, specialized American cars would win on American oval tracks, specialized European cars would win Grand Prix road races. And rarely would the two cross paths.

THE GREATEST SPECTACLE IN RACING

When it was first built in 1909, the Indianapolis Motor Speedway was just another fledgling race track, albeit larger and more ambitious than most. It was a pretty good ride by Model T Ford from downtown Indianapolis, and Indianapolis was a pretty good ride by train from anywhere else. There was nothing to lure paying spectators to this unimposing oval bulldozed out of an Indiana farm except the expectation of superior motor racing. Unfortunately, the first race at the hurriedly-completed Speedway on August 19, 1909, was an unmitigated disaster. Not only were there several fatal accidents caused by the track itself, but the tar/crushed stone track surface was a potholed mess by the time the racing stopped. Carl Fisher and his partners had already spent a fortune and had nothing positive to show for it.

This was a major turning point in American racing, right there in the ruins of Carl Fisher's dream, August of 1909. Fisher could have walked away and cut his losses, but instead he characteristically dug in his heels and rushed to have the track repaved. Reinforced concrete as used at Brooklands was considered, but rejected as too expensive and too prone to winter frost damage. Brick was the most durable substitute available in 1909, and the moment Carl Fisher had his Speedway paved with brick, it became the most sophisticated motor racing facility in America. Originally, Fisher had planned a road course wandering through the infield as banked ovals like Pocono or Michigan International Speedway have today, but that was never laid down. The Speedway partners simply couldn't afford it. And so Indy survived as a paved, banked oval...and changed the face of American racing forever.

Brooklands in England was a larger, faster and more expensively-built oval track than the Indianapolis Motor Speedway, and the upper-class owners and drivers looked down their stiff upper lips at spectators who worked for a living or drivers who expected to be paid to risk their necks. And so Brooklands remained a backwater of international racing for three decades. Carl Fisher was a lot better businessman, and a genius of a promoter. In 1910, he made two basic decisions that

Ray Harroun earned $10,000 plus $4250 in contingency money for winning the 1911 500. The total purse was $27,550, paid only through 12th place. Below that, drivers got nothing for their trouble. The purse was nearly doubled to $52,225 in 1912, with $20,000 plus contingency money to the winner. That was a lot of dough at a time when a skilled factory worker made $2.50 a day. The Purse was increased to $60,000 in 1924; the additional $10,000 split by drivers who finished below 10th. Beginning in 1920, a group of Indianapolis businessmen paid $100 to the leader of each lap. He missed most of the money, but between 1911 and 1921, Ralph DePalma led a total of 613 out of 1400 race laps in races in which he competed, for an unbelievable out-front percentage of .438. His total of 613 leading laps was unsurpassed until 1988 when Al Unser led more career laps. The difference? It took Unser nearly four times as many races.

1919

Winner: Howdy Wilcox,
Peugeot, 88.05 mph
Winner's Purse: $20,000
Total Purse: $55,275
Pace Car: Jesse Vincent,
Packard V-12

Qualifying speeds broke 100 mph for the first time, with Rene Thomas averaging almost 105 mph. Howdy Wilcox cruised to a win in a prewar Peugeot owned by the Speedway, while most of his competition either crashed or broke down. Three men were killed, two more critically injured.

Number	Driver	Sponsor/Team	Engine Type/Displacement	Chassis	Qualifying	Start/ Finish	Laps
3	Howdy Wilcox	Peugeot/Indy Speedway	Peugeot I-4/275 cu.in.	Peugeot	100.01	2/1	200
14	Eddie Hearne	Durant/R. Cliff Durant	Stutz I-4/299 cu.in.	Stutz	94.50	8/2	200
6	Jules Goux	Peugeot/Indy Speedway	Premier I-4/275 cu.in.	Peugeot	95.00	22/3	200
32	Albert Guyot	Ernest Ballot	Ballot I-8/296 cu.in.	Ballot	98.30	3/4	200
26	Tom Alley	Bender/Ahlberg Bearing	Bender I-4/289 cu.in.	Bender	92.20	28/5	200
4	Ralph DePalma	Packard Motor Car	Packard I-12/299 cu.in.	Packard	98.20	4/6	200
7	Louis Chevrolet	Frontenac Motors	Frontenac I-4/300 cu.in.	Frontenac	103.10	12/7	200
27	Ira Vail	Hudson Motor Car	Hudson I-6/289 cu.in.	Hudson	94.10	10/8	200
21	Denny Hickey	A.C. Stickle	Hudson I-6/289 cu.in.	Hoskins	92.50	27/9	200
41	Gaston Chevrolet	Frontenac Motors	Frontenac I-4/300 cu.in.	Frontenac	100.40	16/10	200
31	Rene Thomas	Ernest Ballot	Ballot I-8/296 cu.in.	Ballot	104.70	1/11	200
8	Earl Cooper	Stutz/Earl Cooper	Stutz I-4/299 cu.in.	Stutz	94.25	9/12	200
23	Elmer T. Shannon	Mesaba/Elmer T. Shannon	Duesenberg I-4/299 cu.in.	Shannon	91.70	29/13	200
17	Ora Haibe	Hudson Motor Car	Hudson I-6/289 cu.in.	Hudson	92.80	26/14	200
37	Andre Boillot	Baby Peugeot/Jules Goux	Peugeot I-4/275 cu.in.	Peugeot	89.50	32/15	195
48	Ray Howard	Peugeot/A.G. Kaufman	Peugeot I-4/275 cu.in.	Peugeot	95.00	21/16	130
22	Wilbur D'Alene	Duesenberg	Duesenberg I-4/299 cu.in.	Duesenberg	94.20	23/17	120
15	Louis LeCocq	Roamer/Roscoe Sarles	Duesenberg I-4/299 cu.in.	Duesenberg	92.90	25/18	96
29	Art Klein	Peugeot/Arthur H. Klein	Peugeot I-4/275 cu.in.	Peugeot	94.90	7/19	70
19	Charles Kirkpatrick	Detroit/Frank P. Book	Mercedes copy I-4/274 cu.in.	Mercedes	90.00	11/20	69
33	Paul Bablot	Ernest Ballot	Ballot I-8/296 cu.in.	Ballot	94.90	6/21	63
10	Eddie O'Donnell	Duesenberg	Duesenberg I-4/299 cu.in.	Duesenberg	97.30	5/22	60
12	Kurt Hitke	Roamer/Roscoe Sarles	Duesenberg I-4/299 cu.in.	Duesenberg	93.50	24/23	56
1	Cliff Durant	Chevrolet/R. Cliff Durant	Stutz I-4/299 cu.in.	Stutz	96.50	20/24	54
9	Tommy Milton	Duesenberg	Duesenberg I-4/299 cu.in.	Duesenberg	89.90	31/25	50
34	Louis Wagner	Ernest Ballot	Ballot I-8/296 cu.in.	Ballot	101.70	13/26	44
18	Arthur Thurman	Arthur Thurman	Duesenberg I-4/299 cu.in.	Duesenberg	98.00	18/27	44
43	Omar Toft	Darco/Omar Toft	Miller I-4/289 cu.in.	Miller	91.50	30/28	44
2	Ralph Mulford	Frontenac/Ralph Mulford	Frontenac I-4/300 cu.in.	Frontenac	100.50	15/29	37
36	J.J. McCoy	J.J. McCoy	N/A I-4/293 cu.in.	McCoy	86.50	33/30	36
39	Joe Boyer	Frontenac Motors	Frontenac I-4/300 cu.in.	Frontenac	100.90	14/31	30
5	W.W. Brown	C.L. Richards	Hudson-Brett I-6/288 cu.in.	Brown	99.80	17/32	14
28	Roscoe Sarles	Barney Oldfield	Miller I-4/289 cu.in.	Miller	97.70	19/33	8

guaranteed that the Indianapolis Motor Speedway would be the most important race track in the world, and the Indianapolis 500 the most important single race.

First, he made the unprecedented move of holding just one race each yeear, and that a grueling 500-miler. And then he made sure that he offered the richest purse in racing. In 1912, when he increased the total purse to $50,000 and first prize to $20,000, the Indianapolis 500 became the highest paying sporting event in the the world. His competitors thought he was crazy, but Fisher knew what he was doing.

The huge purse and resulting media attention meant that the 500 took on a life of its own, over and above being one of the races that counted towards the AAA

National Championship. Even before World War I, many American drivers and engineers thought of the rest of the AAA season as merely a warm-up for the 500. Others chose to skip the remaining races to concentrate solely on the Indianapolis 500 International Sweepstakes. Among other things, this meant that many teams headquartered in Indianapolis year-round, which increased both the importance of the race and of the Speedway as a test track.

Indianapolis immediately attracted the best cars, the best drivers and the newest innovations. Witness Ray Harroun's unusual Marmon in the inaugural 1911 race. Car builders knew that their latest technological advances would get the most attention if introduced amidst all the hoopla that surrounded the 500, drivers knew that a reputation could be made overnight and passenger car manufacturers knew that having their name painted on the side of the winning car was worth millions in free publicity. Racing in the Indianapolis 500 International Sweepstakes became not only the pinnacle of a driver's career, but a legitimate year-round business. And that was good for the drivers and teams, the fledgling American automobile industry, the paying spectators who now flocked to see the best racing in the country, and, of course, Carl Fisher and his partners, who made a tidy profit on their original investment.

(above) Even in 1920, there were hordes of "International Motoring Journalists" ready to record the minute-by-minute news from Speedway, Indiana, and whisk it by wire and newsreel to the waiting world. Chicago station WGN started the first Indianapolis 500 radio broadcasts in 1921. The reports were sponsored by Prest-O-Lite, which had been owned by Speedway President Carl Fisher until 1917.

1920

Winner: Gaston Chevrolet,
Monroe, 88.62 mph
Winner's Purse: $21,400
Total Purse: $93,550
Pace Car: Barney Oldfield,
Marmon 34

Ralph DePalma dominated the race for yet another time, until his Ballot caught fire on lap 187. DePalma stopped so his riding mechanic and nephew, Pete DePaolo, could beat out the fire. Now running on only four cylinders, the Ballot slowed, and the field swept by.

Number	Driver	Sponsor/Team	Engine Type/Displacement	Chassis	Qualifying	Start/ Finish	Laps
4	Gaston Chevrolet	Monroe/William Small	Frontenac I-4/183 cu.in.	Frontenac	91.55	6/1	200
25	Rene Thomas	Ernest Ballot	Ballot I-8/181 cu.in.	Ballot	93.95	18/2	200
10	Tommy Milton	Duesenberg	Duesenberg I-8/181 cu.in.	Duesenberg	90.20	11/3	200
12	Jimmy Murphy	Duesenberg	Duesenberg I-8/181 cu.in.	Duesenberg	88.70	15/4	200
2	Ralph DePalma	Ballot/Ralph DePalma	Ballot I-8/181 cu.in.	Ballot	99.15	1/5	200
31	Eddie Hearne	Duesenberg	Duesenberg I-8/182 cu.in.	Duesenberg	88.05	9/6	200
26	Jean Chassagne	Ernest Ballot	Ballot I-8/181 cu.in.	Ballot	95.45	4/7	200
28	Joe Thomas	Monroe/William Small	Frontenac I-4/181 cu.in.	Frontenac	92.80	19/8	200
33	Ralph Mulford	Ralph Mulford	Duesenberg I-8/182 cu.in.	Mulford	N/A	23/9	200
15	Pete Henderson	Revere Motor Car	Duesenberg I-4/181 cu.in.	Duesenberg	81.15	17/10	200
32	John Boling	C.L. Richards	Brett I-6/179 cu.in.	Brett	81.85	14/11	199
6	Joe Boyer	Frontenac Motor	Frontenac I-4/183 cu.in.	Frontenac	96.90	2/12	192
9	Ray Howard	Peugeot Auto Racing	Peugeot I-4/182 cu.in.	Peugeot	84.60	10/13	150
29	Eddie O'Donnell	Duesenberg	Duesenberg I-8/182 cu.in.	Duesenberg	88.20	12/14	149
16	Jules Goux	Peugeot/Jules Goux	Peugeot I-4/182 cu.in.	Peugeot	84.30	21/15	148
34	Willie Haupt	Meteor Motors	Duesenberg I-8/182 cu.in.	Duesenberg	85.48	13/16	146
7	Bennett Hill	Frontenac Motor	Frontenac I-4/183 cu.in.	Frontenac	90.55	8/17	115
3	Louis Chevrolet	Monroe/William Small	Frontenac I-4/183 cu.in.	Frontenac	96.30	3/18	94
18	Howdy Wilcox	Peugeot/Jules Goux	Peugeot I-4/182 cu.in.	Peugeot	88.82	20/19	65
5	Roscoe Sarles	Monroe/William Small	Frontenac I-4/182 cu.in.	Frontenac	90.75	7/20	58
8	Art Klein	Frontenac Motor	Frontenac I-4/183 cu.in.	Frontenac	92.70	5/21	40
19	Jean Porporato	Gregoire/Jean Porporato	Gregoire I-4/182 cu.in.	Gregoire	79.98	22/22	23
17	Andre Boillot	Peugeot/Jules Goux	Peugeot I-4/182 cu.in.	Peugeot	85.40	16/23	16

A DECADE OF PROGRESS

The typical race car of 1911 was built off the chassis of a big luxury car. Most of them had huge four-cylinder T-head engines; a few were powered by an Inline-6. The wheels were made of ash wood, there were simple drum brakes on the rear wheels only. Instead of a heavy limousine body, it would be fitted with a simple "doghouse" hood that covered the engine, floorboards and dashboard literally made from wooden boards, a skimpy pair of bucket seats bolted directly to the frame rails and a pair of "bolster" tanks—they looked like tubular sofa bolsters that were popular back then—to hold gasoline and oil. The quality of workmanship was good, but the materials were impossibly crude by modern standards.

For example, because of poor gaskets and ill-fitting piston rings and valves, even the most advanced racers deposited immense amounts of oil on the track in addition to the oil they burned in blue clouds. The best cars dropped around a dozen gallons of oil on the brick track during a 500 mile race—that's *gallons*, not quarts—while the average was over 20 gallons. There is a record of one leaky machine that consumed an unbelievable 104 gallons of oil during one Indianapo-

(left) The whole point of the 1915 Cornelian was efficiency, as designer/team leader Louis Chevrolet demonstrates by hefting its lightweight, 112 cubic inch, 35 hp engine. The Cornelian's monocoque chassis, all-independent suspension and streamlined body were extremely advanced for the time and led to Chevrolet's equally-advanced Frontenac (above). Among its features were a single overhead cam and extensive use of aluminum...a rare and expensive material in 1916. The 300 cubic inch, four-cylinder Frontenac weighed some 500 lbs. less than its competition in 1916, and in later, 183 cubic inch, double-overhead cam form won the 500 in 1920. An eight-cylinder version won again in 1921.

POWER TO SPARE

In a very real sense, early day racing was as much a battle between engine designers as between drivers. Peugeot's double-overhead cam design was not yet recognized as the most efficient answer, and so engineers kept trying new configurations. Their biggest problem was in translating advanced ideas into working machines, given the inaccurate machining, poor metallurgy, crude lubricants and terrible gasoline with which they had to work.

Nineteenth-century steam engines used cast iron cylinders and pistons, soft

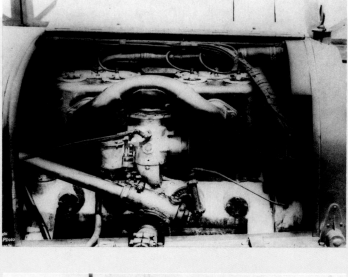

De Lage Motor 3865

(top right) The engine in Spencer Wishart's 1914 Mercer was from a stock Mercer passenger car and typical of crude T-head engines of the period. It produced only 58 hp from 300 cubic inches, with a safe redline of just 1800 rpm. Top speed at Indy? About 90 mph in a 2300 lb. car.

(right) The engine in Rene Thomas's Indianapolis-winning 1914 Delage Grand Prix car produced 130 hp from 380 cubic inches. It would safely rev to 3100 rpm, thanks to a curious horizontal valve arrangement with four valves and two sparkplugs per cylinder. Top speed, about 115 mph.

(below) Barney Oldfield works on the aero engine of his Blitzen Benz, a 21.5-liter, four-cylinder monster that created 200 hp at 1600 rpm. It had overhead valves and two plugs per cylinder. This Benz design was very influential on engines which ran in the Indianapolis 500.

lead "babbitt" bearings and "splash" lubrication in which oil is haphazardly splashed into the bearings. Up until about 1915, most internal combustion engines used this same primitive technology. Crankshaft speeds were limited to only 2000 rpm; above that, early engines with unbalanced crankshafts would pound their lead bearings to bits...just before the rods came through the block.

Because of low-octane gas, compression ratios were limited to about 4:1, which gave a "brake mean effective pressure" on the piston tops of about 115 psi. This translates to about 15 hp for every liter (61 cubic inches) of displacement. Compare that meager output to the 100 hp per liter that modern passenger car engines produce or the 300 hp per liter of today's Indy racing engines.

There are three basic ways to increase output in any internal combustion engine...spin the crankshaft faster, cram more mixture into the cylinders under pressure or burn more mixture in larger cylinders with larger piston tops. Since higher crankshaft speeds were unattainable and supercharging was just being invented, early engines were *big*.

The largest engines in the 1911 Indianapolis 500 were four-cylinder Simplexes which displaced 597 cubic inches; each cylinder was nearly as big as the entire engine in a modern Indy car. But as specific power output rapidly increased thanks to better gas, better metallurgy and better engineering—30 hp per liter was common by 1920—engine size was limited year by year until by 1920 the maximum was only 183 cubic inches.

Power output dropped as the engines became smaller—the winning 1913 Peugeot developed 162 hp; the winning 1920 Ballot developed 107

hp—but laps speeds increased thanks to better tires, stiffer chassis, better brakes and lighter, more aerodynamic cars that were more reliable and easier to drive. You can't really tell from the results, but the cars that contested the Indianapolis 500 in 1922 were dramatically better than even the best machines of a decade earlier.

The standard engine design for American Indy cars up until 1915 was the four-cylinder T-head. This used a camshaft mounted low in the block on each side of the cylinders to operate long, long vertical valve stems. The valves were mounted "upside down" and opened shallow inlet and exhaust passages which led into the flat-topped combustion chamber. In an engineering drawing, the cylinder and inlet/exhaust passages described the letter "T", hence T-head. T-head engines are inherently slow-revving and inefficient because of their heavy valve gear and restricted gas passages.

The revolutionary double-overhead camshafts of the 1913 Peugeot were copied by nearly every European designer, but American engineers in the 1914-1922 period were much more taken with the single-overhead camshaft, four-valves-per-cylinder engine that powered Ralph DePalma's Indy-winning Mercedes in 1915. Based on a Mercedes aero engine designed by Daimler's chief engineer, Wilhelm Maybach, this featured fabricated block/head construction, a tower-driven camshaft and a sparkplug in each side of the combustion chamber. Thanks to its efficient layout and reduced internal friction, the Mercedes—and its American copies—could produce 25 hp per liter, quite good for that era.

The best American cars of the period were conceived, built and driven by the Chevrolet brothers, Louis, Gaston and Arthur. Louis was the leader. Beginning in 1916, his Frontenac racers were the first race cars to benefit from a generous amount of aluminum, which made them 500 lbs. lighter than the competition. Engines were SOHC copies of the Mercedes with dry sump and pressure lubrication. These four-cylinder Frontenacs were the fastest cars on American race tracks circa 1916-1919.

For 1920, Louis and his young engineer, Cornelius Van Ranst, switched to

(left) The 183 cubic inch Duesenberg of 1920 was essentially a scaled-down version of the 300 cubic inch Inline-8 of the previous year. It had a single-overhead camshaft, three valves per cylinder and thanks to meticulous construction and full-pressure lubrication, a redline of 4200 rpm. It produced only about 92 hp. (below) In 1921, young engineer Cornelius Van Ranst designed this Inline-8, 183 cubic inch Frontenac for Louis Chevrolet. This featured double-overhead cams with a narrow included angle between the valves of 38 degrees rather than the 60 degrees that was more common. It made 100 hp at 3200 rpm.

DOHC heads and Gaston won the 500. The next year, they produced a DOHC Inline-8 and won again. That marked the end of the SOHC engine in American racing and the complete domination of cars with double-overhead camshafts. It was also the turning point between the wild and crazy early days and the remarkably mature engine designs of the Twenties. ■

1921

Winner: Tommy Milton, Frontenac, 89.62 mph
Winner's Purse: $26,400
Total Purse: $86,650
Pace Car: Harry Stutz, H.C.S. Series 6

Once again, Ralph DePalma led until putting a rod through the block on lap 112. Surprise winner Tommy Milton was a substitute for Gaston Chevrolet, brother of Frontenac designer and builder Louis Chevrolet. Gaston had been killed during a race at the famous board track in Beverly Hills.

Number	Driver	Sponsor/Team	Engine Type/Displacement	Chassis	Qualifying	Start/Finish	Laps
2	Tommy Milton	Frontenac/Louis Chevrolet	Frontenac I-8/178 cu.in.	Frontenac	93.05	20/1	200
6	Roscoe Sarles	Duesenberg Straight 8	Duesenberg I-8/184 cu.in.	Duesenberg	98.35	2/2	200
23	Percy Ford	Frontenac/Stanley Kandul	Frontenac I-4/182 cu.in.	Frontenac	87.00	8/3	200
5	Eddie Miller	Duesenberg Straight 8	Duesenberg I-8/182 cu.in.	Duesenberg	83.85	9/4	200
16	Ora Haibe	Sunbeam Motor Car	Sunbeam I-8/182 cu.in.	Sunbeam	93.50	13/5	200
9	Albert Guyot	Duesenberg Straight 8	Duesenberg I-8/183 cu.in.	Duesenberg	87.78	14/6	200
3	Ira Vail	Leach/Ira Vail	Miller I-8/181 cu.in.	Leach	82.35	10/7	200
21	Bennett Hill	Duesenberg/John Thiele	Duesenberg I-8/183 cu.in.	Duesenberg	87.75	15/8	200
8	Ralph Mulford	Frontenac/Louis Chevrolet	Frontenac I-8/183 cu.in.	Frontenac	91.70	21/9	177
15	Rene Thomas	Sunbeam Motor Car	Sunbeam I-8/181 cu.in.	Sunbeam	83.75	17/10	144
27	Tom Alley	Frontenac/L.L. Corum	Frontenac I-4/182 cu.in.	Frontenac	80.50	18/11	133
4	Ralph DePalma	Ballot/Ralph DePalma	Ballot I-8/176 cu.in.	Ballot	100.75	1/12	112
1	Eddie Hearne	Revere/E.A. Hearne	Duesenberg I-8/182 cu.in.	Duesenberg	96.18	4/13	111
24	Jimmy Murphy	Duesenberg Straight 8	Duesenberg I-8/184 cu.in.	Duesenberg	93.60	19/14	107
17	Riley J. Brett	Junior/George L. Wade	Brett I-6/179 cu.in.	Brett	87.70	16/15	91
28	C.W. Van Ranst	Frontenac/C.W. Van Ranst	Frontenac I-4/183 cu.in.	Frontenac	88.35	23/16	87
7	Joe Boyer	Duesenberg Straight 8	Duesenberg I-8/184 cu.in.	Duesenberg	96.65	3/17	74
19	Jean Chassagne	Peugeot/Jean Chassagne	Peugeot I-4/182 cu.in.	Peugeot	91.00	6/18	65
22	Jules Ellingboe	Frontenac/Jules Ellingboe	Frontenac I-4/182 cu.in.	Frontenac	95.40	5/19	49
14	Andre Boillot	Talbot-Darracq/Coatalen	Sunbeam I-8/181 cu.in.	Sunbeam	97.60	11/20	41
18	Louis Fontaine	Junior/George L. Wade	Brett I-6/179 cu.in.	Brett	88.30	7/21	33
25	Joe Thomas	Duesenberg Straight 8	Duesenberg I-8/184 cu.in.	Duesenberg	96.25	22/22	25
10	Howdy Wilcox	Peugeot/Jules Goux	Peugeot I-4/176 cu.in.	Peugeot	96.00	12/23	22

lis 500. That's an average of 5 miles per gallon of oil—this notorious junker actually used more oil than gasoline. By the end of the 500 miles in those primitive years, racing on the brick track was like skating on ice.

A decade later, the average Indy car wasn't going much faster—Ray Harroun's winning average of 74.602 mph in 1911 would have put him in fourteenth position in 1922, 20 mph behind winner Jimmy Murphy—but the cars were light years ahead. For starters, they were nearly all purpose-built racing cars, designed from the ground up for the Indianapolis 500. Every one carried an aerodynamic body with wind-splitting narrow grille, smooth sides and teardrop pointed tail. Knock-off wire wheels for quick tire changes were standard, and the new straight-sided tires wore like iron compared to the pneumatic clincher tires of 1911.

The leaders even had excellent four-wheel hydraulic brakes with metallic brake pads like we still use today. Even better, from the drivers' point of view, race car engines of the Twenties leaked much less oil than earlier engines, so they deposited only a modicum of oil on the track. That meant that even after 500 miles, it was possible to still be racing, not hanging on for dear life on an oiled skidpad.

The biggest changes were in size and weight. The cars were much smaller and by 1922, nearly every car featured a lot of lightweight aluminum in both the engine and bodywork. And of course the engine was now a comparatively tiny 3.0-liter, most usually an Inline-8 with at least one and more likely two overhead camshafts. Specific power output was just about double what it had been in 1911, per cubic inch of displacement.

All of this made the actual driving in races a lot easier than it had been a decade earlier. Racing had already become a game of skill, rather than sheer daring and endurance. It had also become a rich man's game. In 1911, it was perfectly possible to buy, beg or borrow a stock car chassis—most big cars in those days were sold without bodywork, anyway—and build a race car in your backyard shop for a few hundred dollars. Virtually nothing that you could do, or knew how to do, required anything more than simple hand tools.

By 1922, to have a chance at winning the Memorial Day Classic, you needed a Duesenberg, Miller or Frontenac that had been assembled in a state-of-the-art machine shop with parts sourced from all over the country. To buy one cost $10,000; even a little Frontenac-modified Model T Ford that had no hope of winning at the Indianapolis 500 International Sweepstakes cost $2500. Considering you could buy a stock Model T Runabout for $319, that was pretty pricey for a race car that could never be more than an also-ran.

In 1911, virtually every car at Indianapolis was sponsored by the car company that built the chassis. What that meant in some cases was that, like Ray Harroun's Marmon, the car was actually owned, built and entered by the factory and the driver was a hired employee. For many other drivers, however, "sponsorship" consisted of discount parts or technical advice. But there was still some very direct connection between the Indianapolis-based racing fraternity and the North American motorcar industry.

A decade later, most of the cars were entered by either the driver himself or a small and specialized racing car manufacturer like Duesenberg or Frontenac. Sponsorship might come from anywhere, Mom's grocery money to the flower shop down the street. Major automobile manufacturers were as conspicuously absent from the Indianapolis Motor Speedway after World War I as they had been ubiquitous on the entry lists before.

(above) Tommy Milton in victory lane after winning the 500 in 1921. With him are Frontenac owners Arthur and Louis Chevrolet. Milton twice won the Indianapolis 500 and also the AAA National Championship. He also finished among the top three in 82 out of the 104 championship races he entered, an incredible record that's never been beaten. Amazingly, Milton was blind in one eye—had been from birth—and memorized the eye charts in order to pass his physical.

1922

Winner: Jimmy Murphy, Duesenberg/Miller, 94.48 mph
Winner's Purse: $26,200
Total Purse: $70,575
Pace Car: Barney Oldfield, National

Jimmy Murphy put a new Miller engine in his old Duesenberg chassis—already famous for winning the 1921 French Grand Prix—and led three-quarters of the Indy 500. This was the first time the pole-sitter also won, the first win for a Miller engine and the first win for a Duesenberg chassis.

Number	Driver	Sponsor/Team	Engine Type/Displacement	Chassis	Qualifying	Start/Finish	Laps
35	Jimmy Murphy	Jimmy Murphy	Miller I-8/181 cu.in.	Duesenberg	100.50	1/1	200
12	Harry Hartz	Duesenberg Straight 8	Duesenberg I-8/182 cu.in.	Duesenberg	99.97	2/2	200
15	Eddie Hearne	Ballot/ Jules Goux	Ballot I-8/180 cu.in.	Ballot	95.60	23/3	200
17	Ralph DePalma	Duesenberg/DePalma	Duesenberg I-8/181 cu.in.	Duesenberg	99.55	3/4	200
31	Ora Haibe	Duesenberg Straight 8	Duesenberg I-8/177 cu.in.	Duesenberg	92.90	14/5	200
24	Jerry Wonderlich	Duesenberg Straight 8	Duesenberg I-8/182 cu.in.	Duesenberg	97.76	7/6	200
21	I.P. Fetterman	Duesenberg Straight 8	Duesenberg I-8/180 cu.in.	Duesenberg	93.28	13/7	200
1	Ira Vail	Disteel Duesenberg	Duesenberg I-8/183 cu.in.	Duesenberg	96.75	9/8	200
26	Tom Alley	Monroe/William Small	Frontenac I-4/182 cu.in.	Frontenac	94.05	12/9	200
10	Joe Thomas	Duesenberg Straight 8	Duesenberg I-8/181 cu.in.	Duesenberg	88.80	17/10	200
3	"Cannonball" Baker	Frontenac/Louis Chevrolet	Frontenac I-8/183 cu.in.	Frontenac	89.60	16/11	200
34	Cliff Durant	R. Cliff Durant	Miller I-8/181 cu.in.	Miller	95.85	11/12	200
22	W. Douglas Hawkes	Bentley	Bentley I-4/182 cu.in.	Bentley	81.90	19/13	200
18	Jack Curtner	Fronty-Ford/Jack Curtner	Fronty-Ford I-4/181 cu.in.	Ford T	N/A	21/14	160
25	Wilbur D'Alene	Monroe/ William Small	Frontenac I-4/182 cu.in.	Frontenac	87.80	18/15	160
9	Frank Elliott	Leach/Ira Vail	Miller I-8/181 cu.in.	Miller	97.75	8/16	195
27	L.L. Corum	Monroe/ William Small	Frontenac I-4/183 cu.in.	Frontenac	89.65	15/17	169
19	C. Glenn Howard	Fronty-Ford/Chevrolet	Fronty-Ford I-4/181 cu.in.	Ford T	83.90	27/18	165
5	Ralph Mulford	Frontenac/Louis Chevrolet	Frontenac I-4/182 cu.in.	Frontenac	99.20	5/19	161
7	Peter DePaolo	Frontenac/Louis Chevrolet	Frontenac I-8/183 cu.in.	Frontenac	96.20	10/20	110
6	Art Klein	Frontenac/Louis Chevrolet	Frontenac I-4/183 cu.in.	Frontenac	87.15	25/21	105
4	Leon Duray	Frontenac/Louis Chevrolet	Frontenac I-4/183 cu.in.	Frontenac	99.25	4/22	94
2	Roscoe Sarles	Frontenac/Louis Chevrolet	Frontenac I-4/183 cu.in.	Frontenac	98.00	6/23	88
8	Tommy Milton	Leach/Tommy Milton	Miller I-8/181 cu.in.	Milton	94.40	24/24	44
14	Jules Goux	Ballot/Jules Goux	Ballot I-8/180 cu.in.	Ballot	96.95	22/25	25
23	Jules Ellingboe	Duesenberg Straight 8	Duesenberg I-8/182 cu.in.	Duesenberg	95.50	20/26	25
16	Howdy Wilcox	Peugot/Howard Wilcox	Peugeot I-8/177 cu.in.	Peugeot	86.10	26/27	7

Times had changed. People were buying passenger cars as fast as the manufacturers could pump them out. The passenger automobile was already a proven quantity, and there was no reputation for reliability left to prove on the race track. Even the most casual racing fan knew that the Fronty-Ford that flashed past the stands at the Indianapolis Motor Speedway bore little relationship to the Model T Ford in his driveway and that Jimmy Murphy's Duesenberg bore even less. Motor racing in America had grown away from the passenger car business and become a self-sufficient business of its own. It was a very specialized business, a business of small businessmen working in dingy garages by themselves, mostly cut off from the rest of the car business and even from similar racers in Europe. But the American teams were going it alone, and though they didn't know it yet, they were about to enter the most exciting period in the history of American motor racing. And in those halcyon days, American racing was synonymous with the Indianapolis Motor Speedway.

THE ROARING TWENTIES 1923-1929

By 1923, the Indianapolis Motor Speedway was universally acknowledged as the center of American racing and the Indianapolis 500 as the most important race in the world. Many American race teams headquartered at the Speedway year-round, where they could test nine months of the year and travel conveniently by truck to other tracks around the Midwest or by railroad train to tracks on either coast.

One basic decision guaranteed that the Indianapolis 500 would always be the world's premier motor race; Carl Fisher was careful to make sure that the purse for the 500 was the highest payout in sports. Between prize money, lap money and endorsements, the winner each year could be pretty sure of being the highest-paid athlete not only in motor racing, but among all sports figures in the country.

For example, Babe Ruth's salary was $52,000 a year from 1922 through 1926, $70,000 a year from 1927 through 1929. This was simply astronomical at a time when the average baseball player made $7000 a year and the average working man around $1500. One of Ruth's most famous quips was delivered in 1930, when a reporter asked him if he thought it was proper that a mere baseball player should earn more than Herbert Hoover, the President of the United States. "Well," mused the Sultan of Swat, "I had a better year than he did."

Throughout the Twenties, the Indianapolis 500 winner usually had a better year than The Babe. The Memorial Day Classic paid $20,000 to win and $10,000 for second, plus $100 for each lap led and around $20,000 in contingency money. If he led most of the 200 laps, the 500 winner could conceivably earn more in one day than Babe Ruth earned all season.

(below) Part of the most colorful team ever to run at the Speedway...Polish Count Louis Zborowski in his streamlined Bugatti GP car. Ettore Bugatti sent a five-car team in 1923, all driven by European noblemen. Count Zborowski, of course, was more famous for his aero-engined monsters, all called Chitty-Chitty-Bang-Bang and immortalized in Ian Fleming's famous book for children.

1923

Winner: Tommy Milton, Miller, 90.95 mph
Winner's Purse: $28,500
Total Purse: $83,425
Pace Car: Fred Duesenberg, Duesenberg Model A

The first 500 for the new single-seaters, this was also the first win for the jewel-like Millers that would dominate American racing until the end of the decade. His relatively easy win—though too-small gloves badly blistered his hands—also made Tommy Milton the first two-time Indianapolis winner.

Number	Driver	Sponsor/Team	Engine Type/Displacement	Chassis	Qualifying	Start/ Finish	Laps
1	Tommy Milton	H.C.S. Motor	Miller I-8/121 cu.in.	Miller	108.17	1/1	200
7	Harry Hartz	R. Cliff Durant	Miller I-8/121 cu.in.	Miller	103.70	2/2	200
5	Jimmy Murphy	R. Cliff Durant	Miller I-8/121 cu.in.	Miller	104.05	9/3	200
6	Eddie Hearne	R. Cliff Durant	Miller I-8/121 cu.in.	Miller	97.30	14/4	200
23	L.L. Corum	Barber-Warnock Ford	Fronty-Ford I-4/122 cu.in.	Ford T	86.65	7/5	200
31	Frank Elliott	R. Cliff Durant	Miller I-8/121 cu.in.	Miller	93.25	16/6	200
8	Cliff Durant	R. Cliff Durant	Miller I-8/121 cu.in.	Miller	102.65	10/7	200
15	Max Sailer	Mercedes/Daimler Motoren	Mercedes I-4/121 cu.in.	Mercedes	90.55	20/8	200
19	Prince deCystria	Bugatti/Prince deCystria	Bugatti I-8/122 cu.in.	Bugatti	88.90	22/9	200
34	Wade Morton	Duesenberg	Duesenberg I-8/121 cu.in.	Duesenberg	88.00	24/10	200
16	Christian Werner	Mercedes/Daimler Motoren	Mercedes I-4/121 cu.in.	Mercedes	95.20	15/11	200
18	Pierre de Viscaya	Bugatti/Martin de Alzaga	Bugatti I-8/122 cu.in.	Bugatti	90.30	6/12	166
28	Leon Duray	R. Cliff Durant	Miller I-8/121 cu.in.	Miller	89.90	21/13	136
4	Dario Resta	Packard Motor Car	Packard I-6/122 cu.in.	Packard	98.02	3/14	88
2	Ralph DePalma	Packard Motor Car	Packard I-6/ 122 cu.in.	Packard	100.42	11/15	69
26	Harlan Fengler	R. Cliff Durant	Miller I-8/121 cu.in.	Miller	90.75	19/16	69
25	Howdy Wilcox	H.C.S. Motor	Miller I-8/121 cu.in.	Miller	81.00	8/17	60
3	Joe Boyer	Packard Motor Car	Packard I-6/122 cu.in.	Packard	98.80	13/18	59
35	Bennett Hill	Harry A. Miller	Miller I-8/120 cu.in.	Miller	91.20	18/19	44
27	Count L. Zborowski	Bugatti/Count L. Zborowski	Bugatti I-8/122 cu.in.	Bugatti	91.80	5/20	41
29	Earl Cooper	R. Cliff Durant	Miller I-8/121 cu.in.	Miller	99.40	12/21	21
22	Raoul Riganti	Bugatti/Martin de Alzaga	Bugatti I-8/122 cu.in.	Bugatti	95.30	23/22	19
14	C. Lautenschlager	Mercedes/Daimler Motoren	Mercedes I-4/121 cu.in.	Mercedes	93.20	17/23	14
21	Martin de Alzaga	Bugatti/Martin de Alzaga	Bugatti I-8/122 cu.in.	Bugatti	92.90	4/24	6

Both stars could easily double their earnings with endorsements, of course. In addition, most drivers also contested the rest of the races that made up the AAA National Championship.

Run at forgotten board or dirt ovals like Culver City, Charlotte, Atlantic City, Altoona, Langhorne, Salem and Cleveland, the remainder of the AAA season put together was worth about as much as an Indianapolis win—another dramatic indication of just how rich the Indianapolis purse really was in those free-spending days. Bottom line, the top half-dozen American racing drivers each year were in the same tax bracket as Babe Ruth...not to mention President Hoover.

THE 2.0-LITER INTERNATIONAL FORMULA

The International Formula for Grand Prix racing was reduced to 2.0-liter (122 cubic inch) engines for 1922, with a minimum weight of 650 kg (1433 lbs). Essentially, this was the same type of small car that had been legal for *voiturette* racing before the war. The idea was to make Grand Prix cars less expensive to

build and race, as well as slower and safer. The cars were still two-seaters; riding mechanics weren't decreed "optional" in Grand Prix racing until 1925. Partly this was because of the dreadful post-war economic situation in Europe. The same car that was a Grand Prix racer this weekend might be fitted with fenders and entered in a sports car race next weekend.

Virtually all European Grand Prix cars of the Twenties were designed to be versatile all-rounders. Many were even street-legal and could be driven to the races and hopefully back home again afterwards. There was little prize or appearance money in European racing; it was mostly *pour le sport*. Understandably, amateur drivers wanted to get the most track time with the least expense, so they demanded race cars that fit more than one narrow category.

Despite the inevitable compromises such versatility always entails, the Twenties are considered a "Golden Age" in Grand Prix racing design, thanks to a couple of classic machines: the famous Alfa Romeo P2 designed by Vittorio Jano and the lovely—if uncompetitive—Bugatti Type 35. Ernest Henry once again redrew *Les Charlatans* DOHC Peugeot to create a pretty GP car for Sunbeam, and there was an interesting Delage. For the most part, even these European factory teams were underfinanced, and Grands Prix were in decline throughout the Twenties. The Depression almost wiped them out for good.

SINGLE-SEATERS

The AAA agreed to follow the 2.0-liter International Formula beginning in 1923, except that they made optional two-seater cars with room for a riding mechanic in favor of single-seaters. Racing cars were reliable enough by 1923 that an onboard mechanic had become a superfluous anachronism. Unlike the contemporary Type 35 Bugatti, the cars that resulted from the Indy rule were not versatile at all. They had no purpose but to race as quickly as possible around an oval track. Indeed, by 1923 the cars that Duesenberg or Miller brought to Indianapolis were as far removed from contemporary passenger cars as today's Lolas or Penskes are different from your Lumina sedan.

The 1923 rule changes meant that American and European racing cars were theoretically identical, except that the Europeans had two narrow seats crammed into the bodywork, the Americans just one. Of course, it was easy enough to put a tonneau cover over the second seat and turn any of the European cars into a *monoposto*. Witness the extra body panels on the factory Bugattis which appeared at Indianapolis in 1923.

Despite all this, there was surprisingly little crossover between American racing and European Grands Prix during the Twenties. The cars were superficially similar on the specifications page, but in truth they were very different. Mostly this was because of the tracks. The Europeans still raced on temporarily closed public roads or permanent "road courses" that simulated the straights,

Driving 500 miles in an early-day racing car was so exhausting that even the best racers routinely let a relief driver put in an hour or so in mid-race. Curiously, very few winning cars were handled by two drivers...Cyrus Patschke subbed for Ray Harroun in 1911; Don Herr for Joe Dawson in 1912; Howdy Wilcox for Tommy Milton in 1923; Norm Batten for Pete DePaolo in 1925. L.L. Corum and Joe Boyer split the driving chores in 1924 as did Floyd Davis and Mauri Rose in 1941. Every other winner went the whole distance on his own.

1924

Winner: Lora L. Corum/
Joe Boyer, Duesenberg,
98.23 mph
Winner's Purse: $20,050
Total Purse: $66,550
Pace Car: Louis Pettijohn,
Cole Master Model V-8

A classic battle between Duesenberg and Miller, it was decided only in the last twenty laps when hard-driving Joe Boyer replaced conservative L.L. Corum in the fastest Duesenberg and swept around the Millers of Earl Cooper and Jimmy Murphy to take the lead. Murphy was killed at Syracuse in September.

Number	Driver	Sponsor/Team	Engine Type/Displacement	Chassis	Qualifying	Start/ Finish	Laps
15	L.L. Corum-J. Boyer	Duesenberg	Duesenberg I-8/121 cu.in.	Duesenberg	93.333	21/1	200
8	Earl Cooper	Studebaker/Earl Cooper	Miller I-8/121 cu.in.	Miller	103.900	6/2	200
2	Jimmy Murphy	Miller/Jimmy Murphy	Miller I-8/121 cu.in.	Miller	108.037	1/3	200
4	Harry Hartz	R. Cliff Durant	Miller I-8/121 cu.in.	Miller	107.130	2/4	200
3	Bennett Hill	Harry A. Miller	Miller I-8/121 cu.in.	Miller	104.840	5/5	200
12	Peter DePaolo	Duesenberg	Duesenberg I-8/121 cu.in.	Duesenberg	99.280	13/6	200
14	Fred Comer	R. Cliff Durant	Miller I-8/121 cu.in.	Miller	92.880	16/7	200
6	Ira Vail	Ira Vail	Miller I-8/121 cu.in.	Miller	96.400	15/8	200
32	Antoine Mourre	Antoine Mourre	Miller I-8/121 cu.in.	Miller	99.490	9/9	200
19	Bob McDonough	Harry A. Miller	Miller I-8/121 cu.in.	Miller	91.550	18/10	200
18	Jules Ellingboe	Harry A. Miller	Miller I-8/121 cu.in.	Miller	102.600	7/11	200
7	Jerry Wonderlich	R. Cliff Durant	Miller I-8/121 cu.in.	Miller	99.360	11/12	200
16	Cliff Durant	R. Cliff Durant	Miller I-8/121 cu.in.	Miller	101.610	8/13	199
26	Bill Hunt	Barber-Warnock Ford	Fronty-Ford I-4/122 cu.in.	Ford T	85.040	19/14	191
31	Ora Haibe	Albert Schmidt	Mercedes I-4/120 cu.in.	Mercedes	92.810	17/15	182
28	Alfred E. Moss	Barber-Warnock Ford	Fronty-Ford I-4/122 cu.in.	Ford T	85.270	20/16	177
27	Fred Harder	Barber-Warnock Ford	Fronty-Ford I-4/122 cu.in.	Ford T	82.770	22/17	177
9	Joe Boyer	Duesenberg	Duesenberg I-8/121 cu.in.	Duesenberg	104.840	4/18	176
1	Eddie Hearne	R. Cliff Durant	Miller I-8/121 cu.in.	Miller	99.230	14/19	151
21	Frank Elliott	Miller/Frank. R. Elliott	Miller I-8/121 cu.in.	Miller	99.310	12/20	149
5	Tommy Milton	Miller/Tommy Milton	Miller I-8/121 cu.in.	Miller	105.200	3/21	110
10	Ernie Ansterberg	Duesenberg	Duesenberg I-8/121 cu.in.	Duesenberg	99.400	10/22	2

corners, dips and hills of the open road. Americans raced on oval tracks...bricks, boards or dirt. The Europeans needed handling, braking and mid-range torque. The Americans needed flat-out horsepower. Teams from Mercedes, Bugatti and other European manufacturers showed up once in a while at the Indianapolis 500—you could earn not only a fortune but a priceless reputation, all in one day—but unlike the previous decade when European makes ruled American racing, in the Twenties there were only two names that won. And both were 100 percent American.

DUESENBERG VERSUS MILLER

Duesenberg ruled the early-Twenties; Miller ruled the late-Twenties. Among other things, brothers Fred and Augie Duesenberg perfected shell bearings that allowed higher engine speeds, the centrifugal supercharger and four-wheel hydraulic brakes. The Duesenbergs' real goal was building high-performance passenger cars; racing was simply a way to publicize their name and attract financial backers. Fred and Augie weren't really interested in building racing cars for sale; Duesenberg ran a team of cars owned by the factory, with hired drivers behind the wheel. This meant there were never more than a handful of Duesenbergs in any one race. On the other hand, those four or five were as impeccable as Augie could make them.

Harry Miller built only racing cars—the most perfect, jewel-like racing cars ever constructed by anybody, anywhere. They were made with the precision of a fine watch, and cost the earth. Miller pioneered all sorts of advances, from aluminum pistons and engine blocks to off-beat carburetors to intercooled superchargers to practical front-wheel drive. Unlike Duesenberg, Miller made racing cars for sale to anyone who could afford his steep pricetag. Ultimately, this meant that Miller not only out-ran and out-engineered Duesenberg, but his cars out-numbered his rivals. By the late Twenties, Miller cars literally filled the grid at Indy.

Ironically, the great rivals Miller and Duesenberg worked together during World War I building an aero/marine engine designed by Ettore Bugatti (curiously enough, Ernest Henry of DOHC Peugeot fame also worked on this engine, in France). Bugatti's engine was a U-16, made by placing two Inline-8s side by side and gearing their crankshafts together. It also had single-overhead camshafts and three valves for each cylinder. For the first postwar Indianapolis 500 in 1919, both Ernest Henry and Fred Duesenberg designed Inline-8s based on this Bugatti design, and even when their engines became tiny in the late-Twenties, they were still designed with eight cylinders in a row thanks to Bugatti's example.

When Harry Miller built his first postwar Indy engine for 1921, he essentially combined the best features of the Duesenberg with the best features of the Henry-designed Ballot to create a double-overhead cam, four-valves-per-cylinder Inline-8 that was better than either of the other two. It still harked back to that seminal Bugatti aero engine, of course.

(below) During the 1927 race, Norm Batten heroically steered his burning Miller safely away from the pits and over to the track edge before bailing out. Ironically, he and racer Earl DeVore were lost at sea when the *S.S. Vestris* sank just a year later. The two were on their way to a race in Argentina.

CAPTAIN EDDIE

(below) Fearless young racing driver "Rick" Rickenbacher—he later changed the spelling of his name to make it sound less German—carried the stars and stripes on his red-white-blue Duesenberg into 10th place in the 500 of 1914. In 1915 and '16, his Maxwell Special dropped out early.

Edward V. Rickenbacker literally grew up with the automobile and aviation industries. When his father was killed in 1903, 13-year-old Eddie left school to support his family. After two years of odd jobs and a mail-order degree in mechanical engineering, he ended up as a mechanic at 75 cents a day. Soon he was working for Lee Frayer in an early motorcar factory, and when Frayer got involved in racing Eddie went along as his riding mechanic. Rickenbacker started racing himself in 1910, as a way of generating publicity for the Firestone-Columbus cars he was now distributing in the Upper Midwest.

Eddie and Lee Frayer co-drove a light car called the Red Wing into thirteenth place in the inaugural Indianapolis 500 of 1911, then Eddie got it up as high

as sixth in 1912 before burning a valve. Rickenbacker then drove for Mason, Duesenberg, Peugeot and Maxwell, eventually running his own four-car team of Maxwell Specials that made him as well known as Dario Resta or Barney Oldfield in the barn-storming days of motor racing prior to World War I.

As soon as the Americans got into World War I, Eddie was in uniform. He started out as Billy Mitchell's chauffeur, but at age 27 convinced Mitchell to send him to flight school and then assign him to the famous 94th Aero Pursuit "Hat in the Ring" Squadron. In less than seven months, Rickenbacker downed twenty-two German planes and four balloons to become America's "Ace of Aces," Captain and CO of the 94th and probably our most famous World War I hero. A subsequent nationwide War Bond drive made him a household name across America.

With a group of financial backers, he started the Rickenbacker Motor Company in 1921, to build "The Car Worthy Of Its Name." His mid-price, six-cylinder and eight-cylinder machines were the first mass-produced passenger cars with four-wheel brakes, but the marque never really caught on. Captain Eddie left the company in 1926, owing some $250,000 which he eventually repaid. Backed by a different group of Detroit investors, in late 1927 Rickenbacker bought the Indianapolis Motor Speedway for $700,000 from Carl Fisher and Jim Allison. Simultaneously, he became vice-president of LaSalle.

Two years later Captain Eddie got into the fledgling airline industry working for American Airways. In 1934, he switched to North American Aviation, which soon changed its name to Eastern Airlines. In 1938, Rickenbacker helped raise $3.5 million to buy Eastern. He became president in 1948 and chairman of the board in 1953.

During World War II, Rickenbacker helped organize the Military Air Transport Service, then served as a traveling fact-finder for Secretary of War Henry Stimson. On one of these trips, his plane crashed in the Pacific—he and six others survived 24 days on an open life raft.

(below) Indianapolis Motor Speedway president and LaSalle vice-president Captain Edward V. Rickenbacker cuts a pretty conservative figure in 1929—a long way from his days as a dirt track racer—but check the intensity in those "fighter pilot eyes."

In 1945, Rickenbacker sold the now run-down Indianapolis Motor Speedway to Terre Haute's Tony Hulman. Captain Eddie probably lost money on the Speedway over the years—he carried it through the Depression and made any number of improvements, then sold it for what he paid for it—but he eventually retired from Eastern Airlines a wealthy man. He died on July 23, 1973, while visiting Switzerland.

Captain Eddie packed his 82 years with an enviable variety, and through it all brought a rare combination of old-fashioned patriotism, honesty, intelligence and physical bravery to everything he did. His contributions to the Indianapolis Motor Speedway and the American automobile industry are immeasurable. He truly was a larger-than-life hero. ∎

1925

Winner: Peter DePaolo, Duesenberg, 101.13 mph
Winner's Purse: $28,800
Total Purse: $87,750
Pace Car: Eddie Rickenbacker, Rickenbacker 8

Pete DePaolo started on the front row and led most of the way, despite having to stop to have his blistered hands taped. For the second year in a row, the Duesenberg team out-raced the horde of Millers that dominated the grid. Dave Lewis' second-place car was the first front-drive Miller in the 500.

Number	Driver	Sponsor/Team	Engine Type/Displacement	Chassis	Qualifying	Start/Finish	Laps
12	Peter DePaolo	Duesenberg	Duesenberg I-8/122 cu.in.	Duesenberg	113.083	2/1	200
1	Dave Lewis	Junior 8/R. Cliff Durant	Miller I-8/121 cu.in.	Miller	109.061	5/2	200
9	Phil Shafer	Duesenberg	Duesenberg I-8/122 cu.in.	Duesenberg	103.523	22/3	200
6	Harry Hartz	Miller/Harry Hartz	Miller I-8/121 cu.in.	Miller	112.433	3/4	200
4	Tommy Milton	Miller/Tommy Milton	Miller I-8/121 cu.in.	Miller	104.366	11/5	200
28	Leon Duray	Miller/Harry Hartz	Miller I-8/121 cu.in.	Miller	113.196	1/6	200
8	Ralph DePalma	Miller/Ralph DePalma	Miller I-8/122 cu.in.	Miller	108.607	18/7	200
38	Peter Kreis	Duesenberg	Duesenberg I-8/122 cu.in.	Duesenberg	106.338	9/8	200
15	Dr. W.E. Shattuc	Miller/Dr. W.E. Shattuc	Miller I-8/121 cu.in.	Miller	102.070	14/9	200
22	Pietro Bordino	Fiat/Pietro Bordino	Fiat I-8/121 cu.in.	Fiat	107.661	8/10	200
5	Fred Comer	Miller/Harry Hartz	Miller I-8/121 cu.in.	Miller	104.296	12/11	200
27	Frank Elliott	Miller/Richard G. Doyle	Miller I-8/121 cu.in.	Miller	104.910	10/12	200
24	Earl DeVore	Miller/Bancroft & Pope	Miller I-8/121 cu.in.	Miller	97.799	15/13	198
14	Bob McDonough	Miller/Tommy Milton	Miller I-8/121 cu.in.	Miller	101.931	20/14	188
23	Wade Morton	Duesenberg	Duesenberg I-8/122 cu.in.	Duesenberg	95.821	16/15	156
17	Ralph Hepburn	Miller/Earl Cooper	Miller I-8/121 cu.in.	Miller	108.489	6/16	144
2	Earl Cooper	Miller/R. Cliff Durant	Miller I-8/121 cu.in.	Miller	110.487	4/17	127
3	Bennett Hill	Miller/Harry A. Miller	Miller I-8/121 cu.in.	Miller	104.167	13/18	69
29	Herbert Jones	Herbert Jones	Miller I-8/121 cu.in.	Miller	89.401	17/19	69
19	Ira Vail	R.J. Johnson	Miller I-8/121 cu.in.	Miller	104.785	19/20	63
7	M.C. Jones	H.J. Skelly	Fronty-Ford I-4/122 cu.in.	Ford T	88.478	21/21	33
10	Jules Ellingboe	Miller/Jerry Wonderlich	Miller I-8/121 cu.in.	Miller	107.832	7/22	24

The first postwar engines from both Duesenberg and Miller were for the 3.0-liter (183 cubic inch) formula. Then when the formula changed to 2.0-liters (122 cubic inches) for 1923, both designers essentially just reduced their designs to two-thirds scale. Miller made two important innovations; he increased the number of main bearings to five and he added hemispherical—rather than wedge-shaped—combustion chambers between his camshafts. The new Miller 122 ran away with the Memorial Day Classic.

Fred Duesenberg brought his own revolution to Indianapolis in 1924. He got together with Dr. Sanford Moss, the genius who developed the practical supercharger, and he added centrifugal superchargers to the Duesenberg racers. They simply overwhelmed the previously unbeatable Millers. Legend has it that the morning after the 1924 race, Harry Miller and his sidekick Leo Goossen were at the door of Allison Engineering in Indianapolis when it opened, begging all the information they could get about superchargers.

The next year, Miller showed up at the Speedway not only with a supercharger of his own, but the first practical front-wheel drive car and the first race car with a DeDion front suspension. This was the famous front-wheel drive Miller that radically

FRED AND AUGIE

Fred Duesenberg was the older, the engineering genius. Augie was the little brother, the master craftsman who could build what Fred designed. They started out as teen-agers with a bicycle shop in Rockford, Iowa, then got into the nascent automobile industry in 1902, working for Rambler and then Mason. In the 1913 Indianapolis 500, the brothers entered a trio of Mason racers; the cars finished mid-pack.

Buoyed by their modest success and hooked on motor racing, they left Mason and started building racing cars and high-performance boat engines as The Duesenberg Motor Company. During World War I, they crafted marvelous boat and aero engines and, after the war, moved to Indianapolis, "the nation's racing capitol," to do what they wanted to do most...build fast cars.

And so they did. Duesenbergs won the French Grand Prix in 1921, the Indianaplis 500 in 1922, '24, '25 and '27, and consistently placed near the top for nearly two decades. They held dozens of speed records—Tommy Milton's 156.04 mph Land Speed Record was most famous—and even some boat and aviation records. A pre-war Duesenberg-powered boat was the first to hit 60 mph; Horace Dodge's 1933 *Notre Dame* racer was propelled by a 622 cubic inch, DOHC W-24 (three banks of eight cylinders each). Indeed, some of Fred Duesenberg's boat engines are far more advanced than anything he did for cars.

The first Duesenberg passenger car was shown at the New York Auto Show in 1920. It was built like a Swiss watch, but cost nearly twice as much as a Cadillac. The money ran out in 1926, and Fred joined E.L. Cord's Auburn-Cord-Duesenberg empire. The total of 470 "cost no object" Duesenberg Models J and SJ were the result, arguably the finest passenger cars ever built in America.

Fred Duesenberg was killed driving one of his own passenger cars on July 26, 1932, and the Duesenberg passenger car company died soon after. Augie Duesenberg continued building race cars and marine engines for many years, all of them powerful, durable, beautifully built. And, understandably, *very* expensive. The great Ken Purdy once wrote, "Duesenberg is a legend that will live as long as men worship beauty and power on wheels." He might just have said what our grandparents said: "It's a Duesie." ■

(left) Augie and Fred Duesenberg (with jacket) flank Pete DePaolo, who wears the Leo Krauss crown presented to Indianapolis 500 winners. The year is 1925.
(below) The 91 cubic inch Duesenberg engine of 1926-1929 used eight tiny cylinders, double-overhead cams and a huge centrifugal supercharger to develop about 145 hp at 6500 rpm.
(bottom) Benny Shoaff's 1928 Duesenberg shows the elaborate supercharger intercooler, claimed to add about 30 hp for a total of 175 hp or so.

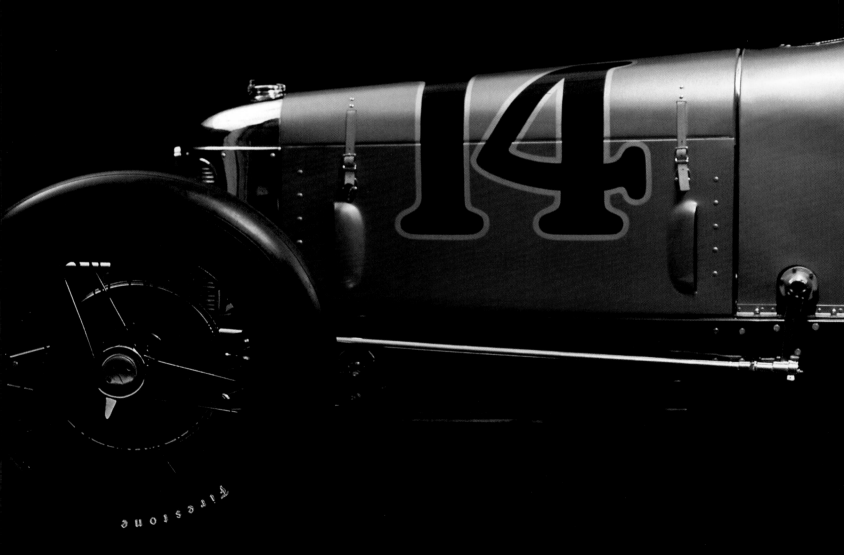

The Fronty Ford Racing Car Complete

WITH this powerful car you are bound to win. Your skill, plus Fronty-Ford performance, can get you in on the big money every time! The Fronty-Ford stands up under the most severe driving. Lightning get-away and great speed are characteristics of the Fronty-Ford. It is the most consistent and sensational performer on half-mile dirt tracks ever built. The best proof of its speed and reliability was demonstrated in its performance in the Indianapolis 500-mile race, May 30, 1923. In this race it placed fifth, defeating all foreign entries and many of the best American entries.

SPECIFICATIONS

Motor—(See Fronty-Ford Racing Motor on Page 6).

Body—Special all-steel, one-man body. (Two-man body for small additional sum.) Double tank in tail of body—capacity, 16 gallons gas; 3 gallons oil.

Wheel-Base—94 inches.

Frame—Standard Ford frame shortened for 94-in. wheel-base (longer if desired).

Front Axle—Standard Ford I-beam. Special radius rods, No. 250 Front underslung brackets.

Rear Axle—Standard Ford housings and gears. Special axle shafts, ball bearings and radius rods.

Wheels—Special 28x4 drop center wire wheels.

Springs—Standard Ford springs, lowered. Hartford shock absorbers.

Steering Gear—Special center control. Spring steel steering wheel. Special steering knuckles.

Radiator—Special Fronty model, made with Fedders high efficiency core.

Feed—Pressure, gas and oil.

Gear Ratio—Optional; 3-1 for straight-away, 3¾-1 for speedway, 3.63-1 for mile dirt track, 4-1 for half-mile dirt track.

Thread—Standard.

Weight—1,350 pounds.

Color—Optional.

Speed—Model R Head—96 miles per hour, straightaway. Model S-R Head—104 miles per hour, straightaway. Model D-O Head—110 miles per hour, straightaway.

No. 214—With Model R Head...**$1,850.00**
No. 214A—With Model S-R Head **2,000.00**
No. 214B—With Model D-O Head **2,300.00**

Fronty Fords Built to Order

FRONTY-FORDS are also built to special specifications for those who want features different from those incorporated in the regular models of Fronty-Ford racing cars. Write or call for prices and information.

To Remember When Ordering

WHEN ORDERING, to avoid error, state both number and name of parts desired. Specify method of shipment. Send 25 per cent of price with order, balance to be paid C. O. D. Our book, "How to Build a Fronty-Ford," gives complete instructions on how to build a Fronty-Ford racing car. Sent on receipt of $2.00, or free of charge with orders amounting to $50.00 or more. A handling charge of 10 per cent will be made on all merchandise returned for credit. Do not return any material without first receiving instructions from us. (This applies to any items listed in this catalog.)

(extreme left) The famous 500 crown for the "King of Speed."
(far left) The pagoda burns on June 1, 1925.
(left) 1923 advertisement for Louis Chevrolet's Frontenac conversion on the Model T Ford promised 110 mph in race trim. The price was right, but contemporary Duesenbergs and Millers could hit 120-130 mph.
(below) Louis Meyer won the 1928 500 in this jewel of a rear-drive Miller 91. At $10,000, it wasn't cheap, but then again it could hit 160 mph with a 91 cubic inch engine.

1926

Winner: Frank Lockhart, Miller, 95.904 mph
Winner's Purse: $35,600
Total Purse: $88,100
Pace Car: Louis Chevrolet, Chrysler Imperial Model 80

The first year of the 1.5-liter Formula, the race was stopped at 400 miles because of rain. Peter Kreis had caught the flu a few days before; unknown substitute driver Frank Lockhart—who had never raced on a paved track before—won in storybook fashion and became America's darling overnight.

Number	Driver	Sponsor/Team	Engine Type/Displacement	Chassis	Qualifying	Start/ Finish	Laps
15	Frank Lockhart	Miller/Peter Kreis	Miller I-8/90 cu.in.	Miller	95.780	20/1	160
3	Harry Hartz	Miller/Harry Hartz	Miller I-8/90 cu.in.	Miller	109.542	2/2	158
36	Cliff Woodbury	Boyle/Cliff R. Woodbury	Miller I-8/90 cu.in.	Miller	105.109	14/3	158
8	Fred Comer	Miller/Harry Hartz	Miller I-8/90 cu.in.	Miller	100.612	13/4	155
12	Peter DePaolo	Duesenberg	Duesenberg I-8/90 cu.in.	Duesenberg	96.709	27/5	153
6	Frank Elliott	Miller/Frank Elliott	Miller I-8/91 cu.in.	Miller	105.873	8/6	152
14	Norman Batten	Miller/Norman Batten	Miller I-8/91 cu.in.	Miller	101.428	16/7	151
19	Ralph Hepburn	Miller/Ralph Hepburn	Miller I-8/91 cu.in.	Miller	102.517	15/8	151
18	John Duff	Elcar/Al Cotey	Miller I-8/91 cu.in.	Miller	95.546	28/9	147
4	Phil Shafer	Miller/Phil Shafer	Miller I-8/90 cu.in.	Miller	106.647	5/10	146
31	Tony Gulotta	Miller/Harry Hartz	Miller I-8/91 cu.in.	Miller	102.789	12/11	142
16	Bennett Hill	Harry A. Miller	Miller I-8/90 cu.in.	Miller	105.876	7/12	136
33	Thane Houser	George G. Abell	Miller I-8/90 cu.in.	Miller	93.672	21/13	102
27	W. Douglas Hawkes	E.A.D. Eldridge	Anzani I-4/91 cu.in.	Eldridge	94.977	17/14	91
1	Dave Lewis	Front Drive Miller	Miller I-8/90 cu.in.	Miller	107.009	4/15	91
5	Earl Cooper	Front Drive Miller	Miller I-8/90 cu.in.	Miller	111.735	1/16	73
9	Cliff Durant	Locomobile Junior 8/Durant	Locomobile I-8/90 cu.in.	Fengler	104.855	11/17	60
29	Ben Jones	Duesenberg Two-Cycle	Duesenberg I-8/90 cu.in.	Duesenberg	92.142	18/18	54
26	E.A.D. Eldridge	E.A.D. Eldridge	Anzani I-4/91 cu.in.	Eldridge	89.777	23/19	45
23	L.L. Corum	Albert Schmidt	Argyle I-6/91 cu.in.	Schmidt	88.849	24/20	44
24	Steve Nemesh	Albert Schmidt	Argyle I-6/91 cu.in.	Schmidt	92.937	22/21	41
7	Jules Ellingboe	Miller/F.P. Cramer	Miller I-8/90 cu.in.	Miller	106.376	6/22	39
10	Leon Duray	Locomobile Junior 8/Durant	Locomobile I-8/90 cu.in.	Fengler	109.186	3/23	33
17	Fred Lecklider	Nickel Plate/Earl DeVore	Miller I-8/91 cu.in.	Miller	100.398	26/24	24
28	Jack McCarver	Hamlin Front Drive/Chevrolet	Fronty-Ford I-4/90 cu.in.	Ford T	86.418	25/25	23
34	Bon McDougall	Miller/R.G. McDougall	Miller I-8/91 cu.in.	Miller	105.180	9/26	19
22	Dr. W.E. Shattuc	Miller/Dr. W.E. Shattuc	Miller I-8/91 cu.in.	Miller	104.977	10/27	15
39	Albert Guyot	Albert Guyot	Argyle I-6/91 cu.in.	Schmidt	88.580	19/28	8

altered the shape of racing cars for a decade to come. The front-wheel drive Miller didn't win its first time out—Dave Lewis was a half-lap behind Pete DePaolo's Duesenberg in 1925—but it soon became the most successful racing car in the world. At the time, people thought the Miller 122 was the most incredible racing machine they'd ever seen.

THE MARCH OF PROGRESS

Almost everything was improved on race cars during the early-Twenties, not just the engines. Thomas Midgley, an engineer at GM Research, discovered the anti-knock properties of tetraethyl lead in 1922. Tommy Milton won the 500 in 1923 with leaded gas in his tank and a high-for-the-time 7.5:1 compression ratio. Firestone came out with the first fat "balloon" tires in 1925, which put more rubber in contact with the track surface and allowed a much lower inflation pressure than

THE PRODIGY

Frank Lockhart's life story is too improbable to be fiction; even the worst Hollywood hack screenwriter would dismiss it. Lockhart barely graduated from high school, yet he was admitted to Cal Tech thanks to his intuitive grasp of engineering and higher math. He didn't go, of course; his widowed mother was dirt poor. Instead, Frank built his first race car from borrowed parts; he put the engine together on his mother's kitchen table. He didn't win with that car, but with a borrowed Duesenberg—people were always lending Frank things—he was almost unbeatable in the hothouse of Southern California dirt tracks.

During Frank's first visit to Indianapolis, in 1926, Miller driver Pete Kreis became seriously ill and offered his car to Lockhart. This was a tremendous leap of faith for Kreis, because Frank was virtually unknown outside of Los Angeles at the time. Starting from the seventh row, Lockhart was second by lap 30, first by lap 60. He was never headed after that and ran away with the 500. It was his first big-time race, his first race on a paved track. He was 23 years old.

Harry Miller gave Frank a factory Miller for the rest of the season, and he won enough big races to almost clinch the AAA National Championship. He ended up second for the season, behind the famous Harry Hartz. Lockhart and Miller had a falling out, because Frank fitted the first supercharger intercooler to his Miller. Lockhart took some of his winnings and bought the car from Miller. He set track records everywhere he went. At Roberts Dry Lake in the Mojave Desert, he hit 171.02 mph...that from an engine of 1.5-liters. At the time, the absolute Land Speed Record was only 174.883 mph, held by Malcolm Campbell's aero-engined 22.3-liter *Bluebird*.

At the 1927 500, Frank easily led for the first 300 miles, then broke a connecting rod. He used the $11,000 he earned for leading so many laps to build a streamlined Land Speed Record car of his own using two Miller engines geared together. With $15,000 from Stutz, Lockhart went to Daytona Beach in February, 1928. The car flipped at 225 mph. Two months later, he was back at Daytona with the repaired Stutz Black Hawk. On April 25, 1928, Frank Lockhart was killed instantly when he crashed after a tire exploded. He had already prepared a Miller for the Indianapolis race just a month away. The car ran the 1928 event, then returned in '29. Ray Keech won the 1929 500 in Frank Lockhart's final car. Improbable? Sure. But not for the legend that is Frank Lockhart. ∎

(left) Smart, ambitious, devilishly handsome and almost supernaturally talented, young Frank Lockhart took Indianapolis by storm in 1926. In the 1927 500—which he led decisively until his engine blew up—he carried #2 in honor of having placed second in the AAA National Championship the previous year. (below) Lockhart's Stutz Black Hawk was really a Miller fitted with two 91 cubic inch engines. It was tiny and marvelously streamlined. Some experts claim the fully-covered front wheels acted as rudders and made the car impossible to steer at high speeds, leading to Lockhart's two crashes. This photo was taken at Daytona Beach in April, 1928, mere moments before Lockhart was killed.

1927

Winner: George Souders, Duesenberg, 97.545 mph
Winner's Purse: $30,625
Total Purse: $89,850
Pace Car: Willard "Big Boy" Rader, LaSalle 303

Speeds were way up, as the sensational Frank Lockhart qualified on the pole at 120 mph and ran away with the race until his Miller put a rod through the block on lap 121. Virtually all the other fast cars broke as well, while unknown George Souders soldiered along to inherit the win.

Number	Driver	Sponsor/Team	Engine Type/Displacement	Chassis	Qualifying	Start/ Finish	Laps
32	George Souders	Duesenberg/William White	Duesenberg I-8/90 cu.in.	Duesenberg	111.551	22/1	200
10	Earl DeVore	Miller/F.P. Cramer	Miller I-8/90 cu.in.	Miller	107.497	15/2	200
27	Tony Gulotta	Miller/Anthony Gulotta	Miller I-8/90 cu.in.	Miller	107.765	27/3	200
29	Wilbur Shaw	Jynx/Fred Clemons	Miller I-8/90 cu.in.	Miller	104.465	19/4	200
21	Dave Evans	Duesenberg/David E. Evans	Duesenberg I-8/91 cu.in.	Duesenberg	107.360	28/5	200
14	Bob McDonough	Cooper Engineering	Miller I-8/90 cu.in.	Cooper	113.175	7/6	200
16	Eddie Hearne	Miller/Harry Hartz	Miller I-8/90 cu.in.	Miller	105.115	18/7	200
6	Tommy Milton	Detroit/Tommy Milton	Miller I-8/90 cu.in.	Detroit	108.758	25/8	200
25	Cliff Bergere	Miller/Muller Brothers	Miller I-8/91 cu.in.	Miller	108.820	14/9	200
5	Frank Elliott	Junior 8/Frank Elliott	Miller I-8/91 cu.in.	Miller	109.682	13/10	200
31	Fred Frame	Miller/O.B. Dolfinger	Miller I-8/90 cu.in.	Miller	106.859	33/11	199
42	Jim Hill	Nickel Plate/Earl DeVore	Miller I-8/90 cu.in.	Miller	107.392	32/12	197
24	Benny Shoaff	Perfect Circle Duesenberg	Duesenberg I-8/91 cu.in.	Duesenberg	110.152	31/13	198
41	Wade Morton	Thompson Valve/Duesenberg	Duesenberg I-8/91 cu.in.	Duesenberg	108.075	26/14	152
44	Al Melcher	Miller/Charles Haase	Miller I-8/90 cu.in.	Miller	102.918	20/15	144
43	Louis Schneider	Miller/Fred Lecklider	Miller I-8/91 cu.in.	Miller	109.910	23/16	137
9	Peter Kreis	Cooper Engineering	Miller I-8/90 cu.in.	Cooper	109.900	12/17	123
2	Frank Lockhart	Perfect Circle Miller/Lockhart	Miller I-8/90 cu.in.	Miller	120.100	1/18	120
15	Cliff Woodbury	Boyle Valve/Cliff Woodbury	Miller I-8/90 cu.in.	Miller	113.200	6/19	108
26	"Dutch" Bauman	Harry S. Miller	Miller I-8/90 cu.in.	Miller	106.078	17/20	90
35	Al Cotey	Elcar/Al Cotey	Miller I-8/91 cu.in.	Miller	106.295	29/21	87
17	Dr. W.E. Shattuc	Miller/Dr. W.E. Shattuc	Miller I-8/91 cu.in.	Miller	107.060	16/22	83
23	Fred Lecklider	Elgin Piston Pin/Henry Kohlert	Miller I-8/91 cu.in.	Miller	105.729	30/23	49
19	Ralph Hepburn	Boyle Valve/Cliff Woodbury	Miller I-8/91 cu.in.	Miller	114.209	5/24	39
1	Harry Hartz	Erskine Miller/Harry Hartz	Miller I-8/90 cu.in.	Miller	116.739	4/25	38
3	Peter DePaolo	Perfect Circle Miller/DePaolo	Miller I-8/90 cu.in.	Miller	119.510	2/26	31
12	Leon Duray	Miller Front Drive/Leon Duray	Miller I-8/90 cu.in.	Miller	118.788	3/27	26
4	Bennett Hill	Cooper Engineering	Miller I-8/90 cu.in.	Miller	112.013	9/28	26
18	Jules Ellingboe	Earl Cooper	Miller I-8/90 cu.in.	Miller	113.239	21/29	25
8	Norman Batten	Miller/Norman K. Batten	Miller I-8/90 cu.in.	Fengler	111.940	10/30	24
38	Babe Stapp	Duesenberg	Duesenberg I-8/91 cu.in.	Duesenberg	109.555	24/31	24
22	Jack Petticord	Boyle Valve/Cliff Woodbury	Miller I-8/91 cu.in.	Miller	109.920	11/32	22
7	Dave Lewis	Miller Front Drive/Dave Lewis	Miller I-8/90 cu.in.	Miller	112.275	8/33	21

the previous "straight side" tires. With only 30 psi in the tires, Indy cars became much more stable, softer riding and better handling. By the mid-Twenties, every Indy car had quite effective four-wheel hydraulic drum brakes, quick-change wire wheels and a surprisingly stiff ladder frame with leaf spring suspension and friction shock absorber at each corner. The front-wheel drive Millers even had inboard front brakes that reduced unsprung weight and improved aerodynamics.

A JEWEL NAMED 91

For the 1926 season, the International Grand Prix Formula was reduced even further, to 1.5-liter (91 cubic inch) engines in 600 kg (1322 lb.) cars. They could

be either single-seaters or two-seaters, though since the two-seaters were also eligible for sports car racing, most of the Grand Prix cars were two-seaters with a tonneau over the unoccupied passenger seat. In Europe, this formula—while not exactly the death of Grand Prix racing—was not popular. Alfa Romeo, Fiat and Sunbeam all withdrew their factory teams, leaving the field to Bugatti, Delage and Talbot. The most sophisticated of these machines was the little Delage. It used an Inline-8 with DOHC and two superchargers each with its own carburetor to develop about 165 hp at 6500 rpm. Considering that's nearly 2 hp per cubic inch—over sixty years ago—it seems pretty impressive.

It is to laugh. Harry Miller's masterpiece, the Miller 91, produced a minimum of 230 hp at 7000 rpm and could be boosted to 300 hp at 8500 rpm for short periods. That's over 3.3 hp per cubic inch! By comparison, today's turbocharged Indy V-8s produce about 4.5 hp per cubic inch, and they're the most powerful engines for their size available. The highest-performance passenger car engines currently available produce only about 1.5 hp per cubic inch. Even by modern standards, the performance of a Miller 91 is simply incredible.

But think what Miller had to work with. In 1926, there were no computers and no fuel-injection. Aluminum and chrome-moly steel were exotic materials. Gaskets and lubricants were still so primitive that Miller designed his engines with a one-piece head and block, so there was no head gasket to leak. He also used as few welds as possible; early gas welding was too primitive to be trusted at 160 mph. Even high-octane racing fuel—a mix of gasoline, benzol and alcohol—was so poor that compression ratios of higher than about 8:1 were impossible.

If you could build a Miller 91 to run on today's fuels and lubricants, with nearly double the compression ratio and today's advanced metallurgy, surely you'd see well over 4 hp per cubic inch. Miller's engineering was so fine it would still be advanced. If you doubt this, remember that the Miller-designed 1926 engine that became the immortal Offy ultimately produced three times the horsepower it made when it was first created, thanks to improvements in fuels, turbocharging and

(below) Leon Duray put this exquisite front-wheel drive Miller 91 on the 500 pole in 1928 at a record-setting 122.391 mph. One of the best drivers of his era, the French-sounding Duray was actually named George Stewart. He was turned into the "foreign ace" Leon Duray by promoter Alex Sloan. There was even an account of Duray's exploits as a World War I fighter pilot. Stewart/Duray was not a fake behind the wheel, though. He competed in eight Indianapolis 500s, usually starting from the front row, but his cars often broke before the end. His best finish was sixth in 1925. He usually ran up front for the AAA National Championship, too, but his "win, blow or put a hole in the fence" style wasn't conducive to winning championships. But it sure made him popular with racing fans.

THE VISIONARY

Harry Armenius Miller was clairvoyant. "I don't do these things," he confessed, "I get help. Somebody is telling me what to do." Whoever he was, that Somebody was some intuitive engineer. In 1896, Miller was working in a bicycle shop in San Francisco. He was 21 years old, a self-taught mechanic. He looked at a bicycle; he looked at a small stationary engine. And he invented the motorcycle. It does not diminish his achievement that Gottlieb Daimler and Wilhelm Maybach had already invented it ten years earlier.

The next year, Miller and his new bride took the train back to Menomonie, Wisconsin, so she could meet his family. While he was there, Miller built a four-cylinder engine with an attached propeller that was light enough to hang on the back of a row boat. After the Millers returned to California, a local Menomonie machinist named Olie Evenrude patented his version of Harry Miller's device. Evenrude called it an outboard motor.

The next year, Miller invented—and this time patented—a new design of sparkplug. Then he invented the Master carburetor. He sold the Master patents, then invented the superior Miller "jet bar" carburetor that was a critical component of American racing engines for three decades. Miller built his first complete racing engine in 1914, for Bob Burman. It was an improved copy of the DOHC Peugeot. In 1916, Miller built an even better four-cylinder for Barney Oldfield. Oldfield fitted it to his famous streamlined Golden Submarine coupe.

During World War I, Harry Miller and his assistant, Fred Offenhauser, worked on the Bugatti DOHC U-16 aero engine which Fred and Augie Duesenberg were building for the government. Miller did the carburetors. In 1920, Miller built a 183 cubic inch Inline-8 that Jimmy Murphy used to replace the Duesenberg engine in his race car. The resulting Duesenberg/Miller won the

(top) Harry Miller, circa 1927.
(above) Pete DePaolo wrecked his front-wheel drive Miller in qualifying for the 1928 500, but the car was repaired for Wilbur Shaw to drive while Pete watched from his stretcher. Notice how low he sits in the narrow machine.
(below) Leon Duray's famous Packard Cable team of 1929 Millers: one rear-drive, two front-drives.

Indianapolis 500 its first time out. More than anything else, this one hybrid car made the reputations of Murphy, Duesenberg and Miller. It also started the Duesenberg-Miller rivalry that fueled American racing throughout the Twenties.

As the formula shrank during the Twenties, The Team—Miller, Offenhauser and Leo Goossen—essentially just reduced the size of their brilliant DOHC Inline-8 until they produced their crown Jewel, the Miller 91. They also built complete cars, either rear-wheel drive or front-wheel drive. In the mid-Twenties, when you could buy a new Model T for $260, a 1400 lb. rear-drive Miller cost $10,000, a front-drive Miller cost $15,000. A replacement engine—330 lbs. of exquisitely-machined Unobtainium that produced 300 hp at 8500 rpm and could pull a Miller to 170 mph—cost $5000. The Miller 91s were bargains beyond measure, perhaps the finest racing cars that have ever been built.

In 1929, at the height of his success, Harry Miller sold his business and went east to design the front-wheel drive system of the Cord L-29. When he returned, "The Team" opened Rellimah—H.A. Miller, spelled backwards—and designed a new 183 cubic inch Inline-8. Fred Frame won the 1932 Memorial Day Classic with this engine. Cut in half to create a four-cylinder, this later became the all-conquering 90 cubic inch Offenhauser Midget engine. At about the same time, a racer named Bill White fitted his car with a four-cylinder Miller boat-racing engine originally designed in 1926. This achieved legendary status as the Offenhauser—later Meyer-Drake Offenhauser—engine that remained competitive in American racing for fifty years.

(below) Exquisitely-built, the 1926-'29 Miller 91 still looks modern. DOHC, four-valves-per-cylinder and centrifugal supercharger delivered about 250 hp from 1.5-liters...over sixty years ago! (bottom) Start of the 1929 Indianapolis 500. Millers filled 27 of 33 starting positions.

Rellimah went bankrupt in 1933. Expensive racing cars were not exactly in fashion at the time. Harry Miller went on to design the rush-job Miller-Ford two-seaters for Indianapolis and, later on, the unbelievably advanced four-wheel drive Gulf-Miller machines. In 1939, disfigured by cancer of the face, Miller moved to Detroit where he spent the last years of his life designing a transverse-engine, front-wheel drive economy sedan very similar to the Volkswagen Rabbit of the Seventies. That final project—like so much else in Miller's life—was a good three or four decades ahead of its time. Who knows? Maybe Harry Miller really could see into the future. And bring back what he saw. ■

1928

Winner: Louie Meyer, Miller, 99.482 mph
Winner's Purse: $28,250
Total Purse: $90,750
Pace Car: Joe Dawson, Marmon Model "78"

Leon Duray dominated the first 62 laps, until his Miller had some problems. Jimmy Gleason inherited the lead, but his excited mechanic poured water on the magneto instead of into the radiator during a pit stop at lap 195. Louie Meyer passed the stationary Gleason to take his first Indianapolis victory.

Number	Driver	Sponsor/Team	Engine Type/Displacement	Chassis	Qualifying	Start/Finish	Laps
14	Louie Meyer	Miller/Alden Sampson, II	Miller I-8/90 cu.in.	Miller	111.352	13/1	200
28	Lou Moore	Miller/Charles Haase	Miller I-8/90 cu.in.	Miller	113.826	8/2	200
3	George Souders	State Auto Insurance/White	Miller I-8/90 cu.in.	Miller	111.444	12/3	200
15	Ray Keech	Simplex Piston Ring/Yagle	Miller I-8/90 cu.in.	Miller	113.421	10/4	200
22	Norman Batten	Miller/Norman K. Batten	Miller I-8/90 cu.in.	Fengler	106.585	15/5	200
7	Babe Stapp	Miller/Phil Shafer	Miller I-8/90 cu.in.	Miller	116.887	5/6	200
43	Billy Arnold	Boyle Valve	Miller I-8/90 cu.in.	Miller	111.926	20/7	200
27	Fred Frame	State Auto Insurance/White	Duesenberg I-8/91 cu.in.	Duesenberg	107.501	14/8	200
25	Fred Comer	Boyle Valve	Miller I-8/90 cu.in.	Miller	113.690	9/9	200
8	Tony Gulotta	Stutz Blackhawk/Burgamy	Miller I-8/90 cu.in.	Miller	117.031	4/10	200
24	Louis Schneider	Armacost Miller/Schneider	Miller I-8/91 cu.in.	Miller	114.036	7/11	200
12	Dave Evans	Boyle Valve	Miller I-8/90 cu.in.	Miller	108.264	23/12	200
29	Henry Kohlert	Elgin Piston Pin	Miller I-8/91 cu.in.	Miller	93.545	28/13	180
23	Deacon Litz	Miller/A.B. Litz	Miller I-8/91 cu.in.	Miller	106.213	17/14	161
39	Jimmy Gleason	Duesenberg/H.C. Henning	Duesenberg I-8/91 cu.in.	Duesenberg	111.708	21/15	195
5	Cliff Durant	Detroit/Tommy Milton	Miller I-8/90 cu.in.	Detroit	99.990	18/16	175
33	Johnny Seymour	Marmon/Cooper Engineering	Miller I-8/90 cu.in.	Cooper	111.673	11/17	170
6	Earl DeVore	Chromolite/Metals Protection	Miller I-8/90 cu.in.	Miller	109.810	24/18	161
4	Leon Duray	Miller/Leon Duray	Miller I-8/90 cu.in.	Miller	122.391	1/19	133
38	Sam Ross	Aranem/Reed & Mulligan	Miller I-8/90 cu.in.	Miller	106.572	16/20	132
26	Ira Hall	Duesenberg/Henry Maley	Duesenberg I-8/91 cu.in.	Duesenberg	96.886	27/21	115
32	Peter Kreis	Marmon/Cooper Engineering	Miller I-8/90 cu.in.	Cooper	112.906	19/22	73
10	Cliff Woodbury	Boyle Valve	Miller I-8/90 cu.in.	Miller	120.418	2/23	55
16	Ralph Hepburn	Harry A. Miller	Miller I-8/90 cu.in.	Miller	116.354	6/24	48
1	Wilbur Shaw	Flying Cloud/Peter DePaolo	Miller I-8/90 cu.in.	Miller	100.956	29/25	42
18	Benny Shoaff	Duesenberg	Duesenberg I-8/91 cu.in.	Duesenberg	102.409	26/26	35
41	C.W. Belt	Green Engineering	Green V-8/91 cu.in.	Green	96.026	25/27	32
21	Cliff Bergere	Miller/Cliff Bergere	Miller I-8/90 cu.in.	Miller	119.956	3/28	7
34	Russ Snowberger	Cooper Engineering	Miller I-8/90 cu.in.	Cooper	111.618	22/29	4

materials. But the basic design remained the same—and competitive—for an astounding five decades.

THE GOLDEN AGE

The great Duesenberg-Miller rivalry spurred development at a breakneck pace. In the early Twenties, the 3.0-liter cars could hit about 120 mph down the straights at Indianapolis and about 80 mph through the banked turns. They were averaging about 100 mph for a lap. In the late Twenties, the little 1.5-liter cars had engines only half the size, but they also weighed about 500 lbs. less and, thanks to supercharging, developed about 100 hp more than the bigger cars. They could still get through the corners at only around 90 mph, but now they were averaging 120 mph per lap—Leon Duray actually cut one lap at 124.02 mph in 1928, a single-

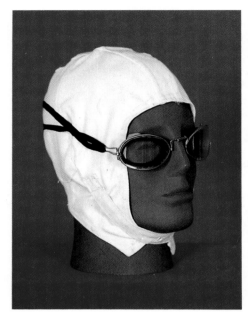

lap record that survived for a decade. The little Millers were hitting 160 mph down the straights at Indianapolis. Even more impressive, Harry Miller's cars were always considered to be overbuilt and overweight compared to Fred Duesenberg's. That made them safer and more durable, but also meant that the engine had to work even harder than necessary to tow that extra weight around a race track.

No problem. At the Packard Proving Grounds—a banked 2.5-mile concrete oval—on June 14, 1928, Leon Duray set a new World Closed Course Speed Record at 148.17 mph. By comparison, the lap record at the similar Brooklands track in England wasn't set until years later, and then by a 24-liter aero-engined monster that ran 143 mph (the "Ladies Lap Record" at Brooklands was held by Gwenda Hawkes in a Miller 91 at 135.95 mph; she later went 147.80 mph at Montlhery in her Miller, the absolute lap record at that French oval).

It is not hyperbole to point out that the Miller 91, with an engine smaller than

(left) White canvas "helmet" was standard issue for almost all motor racing up into the Thirties. As a safety device, it was good for keeping your hair out of your eyes. Helmets and glass goggles were adapted by fliers of open-cockpit biplanes who faced many of the same problems and dangers as racing drivers.
(below) Summation of the Golden Era: Ray Keech takes the flag at the 1929 Indianapolis 500. He's driving the Miller 91 that Frank Lockhart had built for himself.

1929

Winner: Ray Keech, Miller, 97.585 mph
Winner's Purse: $31,950
Total Purse: $95,150
Pace Car: George Hunt, Studebaker President

Louie Meyer led most of the way, but his Miller stalled during its very last pit stop and it was 7 minutes before the frantic crew could get him going again. By that time, Ray Keech had zipped by in the Miller originally built for Frank Lockhart, who'd been killed during a land speed record attempt at Daytona.

Number	Driver	Sponsor/Team	Engine Type/Displacement	Chassis	Qualifying	Start/Finish	Laps
2	Ray Keech	Simplex Piston Ring/Yagle	Miller I-8/90 cu.in.	Miller	114.905	6/1	200
1	Louie Meyer	Miller/Alden Sampson, II	Miller I-8/90 cu.in.	Miller	114.704	8/2	200
53	Jimmy Gleason	A.S. Duesenberg	Duesenberg I-8/91 cu.in.	Duesenberg	110.345	23/3	200
43	Carl Marchese	Marchese Brothers	Miller I-8/92 cu.in.	Miller	108.440	25/4	200
42	Freddy Winnai	A.S. Duesenberg	Duesenberg I-8/91 cu.in.	Duesenberg	113.892	21/5	200
48	"Speed" Gardner	Chromolite/F.P. Cramer	Miller I-8/90 cu.in.	Miller	105.985	28/6	200
6	Louis Chiron	Delage/Louis Chiron	Delage I-8/90 cu.in.	Delage	107.351	14/7	200
9	Billy Arnold	Boyle Valve/Cliff Woodbury	Miller I-8/90 cu.in.	Miller	114.752	7/8	200
25	Cliff Bergere	Armacost Miller/Cliff Bergere	Miller I-8/90 cu.in.	Miller	103.687	32/9	200
34	Fred Frame	Cooper Engineering	Miller I-8/90 cu.in.	Cooper	111.328	22/10	193
28	Frank Brisko	Burbach/Frank Brisko	Miller I-8/89 cu.in.	Miller	105.857	29/11	180
17	Phil Shafer	Miller/Phil Shafer	Miller I-8/90 cu.in.	Miller	111.628	18/12	150
3	Lou Moore	Majestic Miller/Charles Haase	Miller I-8/90 cu.in.	Miller	110.677	13/13	198
36	Frank Farmer	Miller/William Albertson	Miller I-8/91 cu.in.	Miller	107.979	26/14	140
49	Wes Crawford	Miller/Marian Batten	Miller I-8/90 cu.in.	Fengler	108.607	24/15	127
4	Peter Kreis	Detroit/Tommy Milton	Miller I-8/90 cu.in.	Detroit	112.528	17/16	91
23	Tony Gulotta	Packard Cable/Leon Duray	Miller I-8/90 cu.in.	Miller	112.146	11/17	91
5	Bob McDonough	Miller Front Drive/M.R. Dodds	Miller I-8/90 cu.in.	Miller	111.614	19/18	74
46	Bill Lindau	Miller/Painter & Hufnagle	Miller I-8/88 cu.in.	Miller	102.509	33/19	70
31	Herman Schurch	Armacost Miller/Schneider	Miller I-8/91 cu.in.	Miller	107.477	27/20	70
38	Johnny Seymour	Cooper Engineering	Miller I-8/90 cu.in.	Cooper	114.307	16/21	65
21	Leon Duray	Packard Cable/Leon Duray	Miller I-8/90 cu.in.	Miller	119.087	2/22	65
29	Rick Decker	Miller/Rickliffe Decker	Miller I-8/91 cu.in.	Miller	105.288	30/23	61
26	Deacon Litz	Rusco Durac/A.B. Litz	Miller I-8/90 cu.in.	Miller	114.526	9/24	56
27	Albert Karnatz	Richards/Reed & Mulligan	Miller I-8/91 cu.in.	Miller	104.749	31/25	50
47	Ernie Triplett	Buckeye Duesenberg/Cunard	Duesenberg I-8/91 cu.in.	Duesenberg	114.789	20/26	48
12	Russ Snowberger	Cooper Engineering	Miller I-8/90 cu.in.	Cooper	113.622	10/27	45
32	Babe Stapp	Spindler Miller/William White	Miller I-8/90 cu.in.	Duesenberg	115.618	4/28	40
35	Jules Moriceau	Thompson Products	Amilcar I-6/78 cu.in.	Amilcar	105.609	15/29	30
37	Peter DePaolo	Boyle Valve/Cliff Woodbury	Miller I-8/90 cu.in.	Miller	115.093	5/30	25
18	Ralph Hepburn	Packard Cable/Leon Duray	Miller I-8/90 cu.in.	Miller	116.543	3/31	14
10	Bill Spence	A.S. Duesenberg	Duesenberg I-8/91 cu.in.	Duesenberg	111.649	12/32	14
8	Cliff Woodbury	Boyle Valve/Cliff Woodbury	Miller I-8/90 cu.in.	Miller	120.599	1/33	3

that in a Honda Civic, was the fastest race car in the world in its day, regardless of size. There were only fifty Miller 91s built, and only a dozen were front-wheel drive. But even if there had been only one, it would have been the greatest race car of all time.

In concept and craftsmanship, these tiny Millers were superior to anything that appeared on American race tracks for at least the next decade. Thanks to generous sponsors with virtually unlimited budgets, The Team—Harry Miller, Leo Goossen and Fred Offenhauser—were able to dominate Indy with race cars that were more than mere machines, more than disposable means to an end. The Miller 91 was a priceless work of art. Supreme in its time, and for all time.

THE DEPRESSION ERA 1930-1936

In 1927, when he bought the Indianapolis Motor Speedway from Carl Fisher, Eddie Rickenbacker was already convinced that the costs of racing had gotten completely out of hand. Even at the height of the Golden Era, there were very few racers who could afford $15,000 for one of Harry Miller's masterpieces, plus $5000 each for a couple of spare engines and another $10,000 or so for miscellaneous hand-finished bits. By the time you added in mechanics and transportation and all the other hidden costs of racing, a top team could easily spend $50,000 in the month of May. That was just to run one race! Remember, Captain Eddie had just bought the entire Speedway for $2000 an acre, and the Average Joe who came to watch was driving a car that cost him less than $1000. Things were seriously out of whack.

The AAA Contest Board finally drew up a new set of rules for the 1930 season. These coincided with the Crash of '29 that brought on the Great Depression, but this was just happenstance. The new formula was already in the works before the economy fell apart. The new rules essentially outlawed the exquisite

(below) Despite the Depression, the crowds still filled the stands at Indianapolis in 1930. Louie Meyer's modified Stevens/Miller is in for a leisurely pit stop. Check out the crude "pits"— wooden enclosures with sawdust on the floor to absorb spilled oil.

Indianapolis Motor Speedway

1930

Winner: Billy Arnold, Miller, 100.448 mph
Winner's Purse: $50,300
Total Purse: $96,250
Pace Car: E.L. Cord, Cord L-29 Cabriolet

The first year of the Depression Era "Junk" Formula brought back riding mechanics and mixed stock passenger car chassis with "real" race cars. The real racers won, led by dirt tracker Billy Arnold—who talked himself into a ride, qualified on the pole and led every lap except the first two.

Number	Driver	Sponsor/Team	Engine Type/Displacement	Chassis	Qualifying	Start/Finish	Laps
4	Billy Arnold	Miller-Hartz	Miller I-8/152 cu.in.	Summers	113.263	1/1	200
16	Shorty Cantlon	Miller Schofield/White	Miller I-4/183 cu.in.	Stevens	109.810	3/2	200
23	Louis Schneider	Bowes Seal Fast/Schneider	Miller I-8/121 cu.in.	Stevens	106.107	4/3	200
1	Louie Meyer	Alden Sampson, II	Miller V-16/201 cu.in.	Stevens	111.290	2/4	200
6	Bill Cummings	Duesenberg/Peter DePaolo	Duesenberg I-8/244 cu.in.	Stevens	106.173	22/5	200
24	Dave Evans	Jones & Maley/David Evans	Miller I-8/138 cu.in.	Stevens	97.342	33/6	200
15	Phil Shafer	Coleman Front Drive	Miller I-4/183 cu.in.	Coleman	102.279	8/7	200
22	Russ Snowberger	Russell Snowberger	Studebaker I-8/336 cu.in.	Snowberger	104.577	7/8	200
25	Leslie Allen	Allen Miller Products	Miller I-4/183 cu.in.	Miller	101.919	9/9	200
27	L.L. Corum	Stutz/Milton Jones	Stutz I-8/322 cu.in.	Stutz	94.130	17/10	200
38	Claude Burton	V8/Ira Vail	Oakland I-8/251 cu.in.	Oakland	95.087	16/11	196
42	Letterio Cucinotta	Maserati/Letterio Cucinotta	Maserati I-8/122 cu.in.	Maserati	91.584	30/12	185
41	Chet Miller	Fronty/Thomas Mulligan	Fronty-Ford I-4/176 cu.in.	Ford T	97.360	15/13	161
46	Harry Butcher	Butcher Brothers	Buick I-6/332 cu.in.	Buick	87.003	38/14	127
17	Ernie Triplett	Allen Guiberson	Miller I-4/183 cu.in.	Whippet	105.618	6/15	125
21	Zeke Meyer	Miller/Zeke Meyer	Miller I-8/138 cu.in.	Miller	95.357	34/16	115
10	Mel Keneally	MAVV/J. Talbot	Miller I-4/150 cu.in.	Whippet	103.327	23/17	114
35	J.C. McDonald	Romthe/William Richards	Studebaker I-8/336 cu.in.	Studebaker	98.953	13/18	112
9	Tony Gulotta	MAVV/J. Talbot	Miller I-4/150 cu.in.	Whippet	100.033	20/19	79
28	Roland Free	Julius Slade	Chrysler I-6/268 cu.in.	Chrysler	89.639	37/20	69
33	Frank Farmer	Betholine Miller/M.A. Yagle	Miller I-8/101 cu.in.	Miller	100.615	11/21	69
3	Wilbur Shaw	Empire State Motors	Miller I-8/152 cu.in.	Smith	106.132	25/22	54
34	Joe Huff	Gauss Front Drive	Miller I-8/100 cu.in.	Cooper	101.178	26/23	48
29	Joe Caccia	William Alberti	Duesenberg I-8/260 cu.in.	Duesenberg	97.606	14/24	43
44	Bill Denver	Gabriel Nardi	Duesenberg I-8/260 cu.in.	Duesenberg	90.650	35/25	41
36	Cy Marshall	Duesenberg/George Henry	Duesenberg I-8/262 cu.in.	Duesenberg	100.846	10/26	29
32	Charles Moran	DuPont Motors	DuPont I-8/322 cu.in.	DuPont	89.733	19/27	22
7	Jimmy Gleason	Waverly Oil/Mulligan	Miller I-8/125 cu.in.	Miller	93.709	24/28	22
14	Lou Moore	Coleman Motors	Miller I-4/183 cu.in.	Coleman	99.867	12/29	22
12	Deacon Litz	Duesenberg/Henry Maley	Duesenberg I-8/150 cu.in.	Duesenberg	105.755	31/30	22
8	Babe Stapp	A.S. Duesenberg	Duesenberg I-8/143 cu.in.	Duesenberg	104.950	32/31	18
39	Johnny Seymour	Herman Gauss	Miller I-8/100 cu.in.	Cooper	93.376	18/32	21
5	Peter DePaolo	Duesenberg/Peter DePaolo	Duesenberg I-8/244 cu.in.	Stevens	99.956	21/33	19
45	Marion Trexler	Trexler/M.M. Lain	Lycoming I-8/298 cu.in.	Auburn	92.978	29/34	19
19	Speed Gardner	Miller Front Drive/Gardner	Miller I-8/151 cu.in.	Miller	95.585	27/35	14
48	Rick Decker	Hoosier Pete/Clemon Motors	Clemons I-4/197 cu.in.	Mercedes	92.293	36/37	8
26	Baconi Borzachini	Alfieri Maserati	Maserati V-16/244 cu.in.	Maserati	95.213	28/36	7
18	Chet Gardner	Buckeye/James Booth	Duesenberg I-8/150 cu.in.	Duesenberg	105.811	5/38	1

$15,000 Miller 91s in favor of modified passenger cars. The racers promptly labelled it the "Junk" Formula, but within a matter of months it was the only thing standing between them and the bread lines. Instead of having to find somebody like GM heir Cliff Durant to underwrite a new Miller 91, a privateer could build a competitive Speedway car for $1500. That was still a lot of money when nobody had two cents to rub together, but a lot less money than a Miller.

TWO FORMULAS AGAIN

The AAA's new rules demanded a maximum engine displacement of 366 cubic inches (6.0-liters), no more than two valves per cylinder (changed to four valves per cylinder starting with 1931), no superchargers (except on two-cycle engines), a minimum weight of 1750 lbs. (795 kg) and two seats. The riding mechanic was back! In most respects, this new Indianapolis formula wasn't much different from the International Formula of 1913.

Once again, the Indianapolis formula and the Grand Prix formula were different. Up through 1930, Europeans held to the 1.5-liter supercharged cars. Then in response to the Depression, the Grand Prix rules were changed to essentially an

(left) Shock-absorbing crash helmets replaced cloth and leather flying helmets in the mid-Thirties. In truth, these early laminated helmets offered no real protection in an accident, though they did ward off stones thrown up on the dirt tracks.

unlimited "Formula Libre" that allowed virtually any type and size of car. The minimum Grand Prix race length was 10 hours, with a mandatory driver change.

This European Formula Libre produced two of the most glorious racing cars ever built—Alfa Romeo's P3 and Bugatti's Type 59. But after only three years, the Grand Prix formula was adjusted yet again. Now the rules allowed a *maximum* weight of 750 kg (1650 lbs.) along with a minimum race length of 500 kilometers (310 miles). The Alfa and Bugatti were still eligible, but it didn't matter. Adolf Hitler had fixated on racing as yet another way to prove Aryan Supremacy, and all the other teams in Europe—most of them woefully underfinanced—were swept away between

(above) Drivers were tough back then: young Wilbur Shaw drove relief for Phil Pardee in the 1931 500, and sailed over the Northeast wall in Pardee's Duesenberg. Unhurt, Shaw walked back to the pits and did a second relief stint in Jimmy Gleason's Duesenberg, which finished sixth.

1931

Winner: Lou Schneider,
Bowes Seal Fast Special,
96.629 mph
Winner's Purse: $29,500
Total Purse: $81,800
Pace Car: Willard "Big
Boy" Rader, Cadillac 370

Billy Arnold led every lap from lap 7 on, only to crash just 37 laps from the end when his rear axle broke. Both he and his mechanic, Spider Matlock, were injured and a wheel from the car flew clear out of the Speedway. Lucky Lou Schneider inherited the lead.

Number	Driver	Sponsor/Team	Engine Type/Displacement	Chassis	Qualifying	Start/Finish	Laps
23	Lou Schneider	Bowes Seal Fast/Schneider	Miller I-8/151 cu.in.	Stevens	107.210	13/1	200
34	Fred Frame	Duesenberg/Harry Hartz	Duesenberg I-8/150 cu.in.	Duesenberg	109.273	8/2	200
19	Ralph Hepburn	Harry Miller/Ralph Hepburn	Miller I-8/230 cu.in.	Miller	107.933	10/3	200
21	Myron Stevens	Jadson/Louis Meyer	Miller I-8/230 cu.in.	Stevens	107.463	35/4	200
4	Russ Snowberger	Russell Snowberger	Studebaker I-8/336 cu.in.	Snowberger	112.796	1/5	200
33	Jimmy Gleason	Denny Duesenberg	Duesenberg I-8/243 cu.in.	Duesenberg	111.400	20/6	200
25	Ernie Triplett	Buckeye/James Booth	Duesenberg I-8/151 cu.in.	Duesenberg	111.034	5/7	200
36	Stubby Stubblefield	Jones-Miller/Milton Jones	Miller I-4/183 cu.in.	Willys-Knight	108.797	9/8	200
28	Cliff Bergere	Elco Royale/Elco Grease	Reo I-8/358 cu.in.	Reo	106.781	14/9	200
27	Chet Miller	R.G. "Buddy" Marr	Hudson I-8/234 cu.in.	Hudson	106.185	15/10	200
44	George Howie	George N. Howie	Chrysler I-8/356 cu.in.	Dodge	102.844	30/11	200
12	Phil Shafer	Phil Shafer	Buick I-8/270 cu.in.	Rigling	105.103	23/12	200
8	Dave Evans	Cummins Engine Company	Cummins I-4/361 cu.in.	Duesenberg	96.871	17/13	200
72	Al Aspen	William Alberti	Duesenberg I-8/266 cu.in.	Duesenberg	102.509	31/14	200
59	Sam Ross	Miller/William Yahr	Miller I-4/158 cu.in.	Rigling	104.642	37/15	200
69	Joe Huff	Goldberg Brothers	Miller I-8/100 cu.in.	Cooper	102.386	40/16	180
5	Deacon Litz	Henry Maley	Duesenberg I-8/151 cu.in.	Duesenberg	111.531	4/17	177
37	Tony Gulotta	Hunt/D.A. "Ab" Jenkins	Studebaker I-8/337 cu.in.	Rigling	111.725	19/18	167
1	Billy Arnold	Miller-Hartz	Miller I-8/151 cu.in.	Summers	116.080	18/19	162
57	Luther Johnson	Bill Richards	Studebaker I-8/336 cu.in.	Studebaker	107.652	12/20	156
55	Billy Winn	Hoosier Pete/F.E. Clemons	Clemons I-8/226 cu.in.	Rigling	105.405	36/21	138
16	Frank Brisko	Brisko-Atkinson	Miller I-8/151 cu.in.	Stevens	106.286	27/22	138
26	Gene Haustein	Fronty-Ford	Fronty-Ford I-4/219 cu.in.	Ford T	108.395	34/23	117
41	Joe Russo	Russo/George Henry	Duesenberg I-8/260 cu.in.	Rigling	104.822	16/24	109
17	Speed Gardner	Nutmeg State/C.E. Ricketts	Miller I-8/151 cu.in.	Miller	109.820	7/25	107
14	Lou Moore	Boyle Valve	Miller I-8/230 cu.in.	Miller	103.725	38/26	103
2	Shorty Cantlon	Harry Miller/William White	Miller V-16/301 cu.in.	Miller	110.372	26/27	88
3	Bill Cummings	Empire State Gas Motors	Miller I-8/215 cu.in.	Cooper	112.563	2/28	70
24	Freddy Winnai	Bowes Seal Fast/Schneider	Miller I-8/122 cu.in.	Stevens	105.899	28/29	60
32	Phil Pardee	Duesenberg/Phil Pardee	Duesenberg I-8/243 cu.in.	Duesenberg	107.772	11/30	60
31	Paul Bost	Empire State Gas Motors	Miller I-8/215 cu.in.	Rigling	112.125	3/31	35
35	Frank Farmer	Jones-Miller/Milton Jones	Miller I-4/183 cu.in.	Willys-Knight	108.303	22/32	32
58	George Wingerter	George Wingerter	Duesenberg I-8/266 cu.in.	Duesenberg	100.139	32/33	29
7	Louie Meyer	Alden Sampson	Miller V-16/200 cu.in.	Stevens	113.953	25/24	28
39	Babe Stapp	Rigling & Henning	Duesenberg I-8/260 cu.in.	Rigling	110.125	6/35	9
48	John Boling	Morton & Brett/Grapho Metal	M&B I-8/226 cu.in.	M&B	102.860	24/36	7
54	Leon Duray	Leon Duray	Duray V-16/230 cu.in.	Stevens	103.134	29/37	6
49	Harry Butcher	Harry Butcher	Buick I-8/273 cu.in.	Buick	99.343	33/38	6
10	Herman Schurch	Hoosier Pete/F.E. Clemons	Clemons I-8/226 cu.in.	Rigling	102.845	39/39	5
67	Francis Quinn	Tucker Tappett/James Wade	Ford I-4/221 cu.in.	Miller	111.321	21/40	3

1934 and 1940 by the "Silver Arrows" of Auto Union and Mercedes-Benz. While the Americans struggled to turn flathead Hudsons and Studebakers into 130 mph racers, the Germans were blitzkreiging Grands Prix with supercharged, 650 hp, V-16 aerodynamic wunderkars that could hit 250 mph in a straight line and were so exotic they might just as well have come from Mars instead of Stuttgart. Never

The Studebaker Fleet

STUDEBAKER?

One of the purposes of the stock-block formula was to lure passenger car manufacturers back to Indy racing. And one of the Speedway's first catches was Studebaker, in 1932. Starting with the top-line President sedan, Studebaker built five of the prettiest cars ever to run at Indianapolis. The frames and bodies were farmed out to the Rigling and Henning race shop in Indianapolis. R&H did a magnificant job, crafting superbly finished cars that still look stylish today. The running gear was mostly stock President. But Studebaker's engineers spent hours with their dynamometer, hot-rodding their engines.

The side-valve Studebaker Inline-8 was given a milled head for higher compression—a heady 7.5:1—aluminum Bohnalite pistons, a different camshaft, exhaust headers and a Bosch magneto. Four Stromberg carburetors replaced the stock single carburetor and manifold. Running on a 50/50 mix of leaded gasoline and benzol, these 336 cubic inch (5.5-liter) engines developed 196 hp at a low 4400 rpm.

(left) Best of the stock-blocks were these five Studebaker factory entries that appeared in 1932. The fastest qualified at 115.6 mph...not bad at all for a 2600 lb. racer built out of a Studebaker President. Cliff Bergere finished third in the race. These Studebakers produced nearly 200 hp and were dead reliable and beautifully finished.
(below) At least three of the original five sturdy Studebakers are still around, and two of them still compete in vintage races.

The five team cars used 2.92 or 3.07:1 differential ratios, to keep the revs below 4000 rpm at a top speed of about 130 mph. Cliff Bergere brought one Stude home in third. For 1933, Stude added another five, more streamlined cars. This time, Studebakers were sixth through twelfth. And after that they vanished from racing almost as quickly as they had come. Still, the ten Studebakers of 1932 and '33 were by far the most successful of the Indianapolis stock-blocks. ■

PRESTON TUCKER

(far left) 1932: Leon Duray's riding mechanic, Charlie Lyon, uses a radio to talk to his crew. (left) 1933: Before the start of the pre-race children's pushmobile event. (above) 1936: Master promoter Preston Tucker arrives by Harley. (below) 1935: Ted Horn's Miller/Ford was the highest placed of that ill-fated team.

1932

Winner: Fred Frame, Miller, 104.144 mph
Winner's Purse: $31,050
Total Purse: $93,900
Pace Car: Edsel Ford, Lincoln KB Sports Roadster

Once again, Billy Arnold and Spider Matlock were injured when they crashed while leading. Teammate Fred Frame, driving a similar Miller-Hartz Special, went on to win ahead of rookie Howdy Wilcox II and the gorgeous Studebaker Special of Cliff Bergere.

Number	Driver	Sponsor/Team	Engine Type/Displacement	Chassis	Qualifying	Start/Finish	Laps
34	Fred Frame	Miller-Harry Hartz	Miller I-8/182 cu.in.	Wetteroth	113.856	27/1	200
6	Howdy Wilcox II	Lion Head/William Cantlon	Miller I-4/220 cu.in.	Stevens	113.468	6/2	200
22	Cliff Bergere	Studebaker	Studebaker I-8/337 cu.in.	Rigling	111.503	10/3	200
61	Bob Carey	Louis Meyer	Miller I-8/249 cu.in.	Stevens	111.070	14/4	200
4	Russ Snowberger	Hupp Comet/Snowberger	Hupmobile I-8/361 cu.in.	Snowberger	114.326	4/5	200
37	Zeke Meyer	Studebaker	Studebaker I-8/337 cu.in.	Rigling	110.745	38/6	200
35	Ira Hall	Duesenberg/G.B. Hall	Duesenberg I-8/243 cu.in.	Stevens	114.206	5/7	200
65	Freddy Winnai	Foreman Axle Shaft/Maley	Duesenberg I-8/151 cu.in.	Duesenberg	108.755	35/8	200
2	Billy Winn	Duesenberg/Fred Frame	Duesenberg I-8/151 cu.in.	Duesenberg	111.801	9/9	200
55	Joe Huff	Highway Parts/S.C. Goldberg	Cooper V-16/183 cu.in.	Cooper	110.402	15/10	200
33	Phil Shafer	Shafer "8"	Buick I-8/272 cu.in.	Rigling	110.708	26/11	197
36	Kelly Petillo	Jones-Miller	Miller I-4/190 cu.in.	Miller	104.465	40/12	189
25	Tony Gulotta	Studebaker	Studebaker I-8/337 cu.in.	Rigling	108.896	20/13	184
15	Stubby Stubblefield	Gilmore/Sparks & Weirick	Miller I-4/220 cu.in.	Adams	112.899	25/14	178
18	Peter Kreis	Studebaker	Studebaker I-8/337 cu.in.	Rigling	110.270	17/15	178
46	Luther Johnson	Studebaker	Studebaker I-8/337 cu.in.	Rigling	111.218	11/16	164
3	Wilbur Shaw	Miller/Ralph Hepburn	Miller I-8/230 cu.in.	Miller	114.326	22/17	157
24	Deacon Litz	Bowes Seal Fast/John Rutner	Duesenberg I-8/151 cu.in.	Duesenberg	109.546	19/18	152
10	Bill Cummings	Bowes Seal Fast/Schneider	Miller I-8/151 cu.in.	Stevens	111.204	12/19	151
57	Malcolm Fox	William Richards	Studebaker I-8/336 cu.in.	Studebaker	111.149	32/20	132
9	Chet Miller	Hudson/R.G. "Buddy" Marr	Hudson I-8/255 cu.in.	Hudson	111.053	29/21	125
7	Ernie Triplett	Floating Power/William White	Miller I-4/220 cu.in.	Miller	114.935	31/22	125
1	Louis Schneider	Bowes Seal Fast/Schneider	Miller I-8/151 cu.in.	Stevens	110.681	30/23	125
41	Joe Russo	Art Rose/George Henry	Duesenberg I-8/261 cu.in.	Rigling	108.791	21/24	107
8	Lou Moore	Boyle Valve	Miller I-8/268 cu.in.	Miller	117.363	1/25	79
14	Juan Gaudino	Golden Seal/Juan Gaudino	Chrysler I-8/358 cu.in.	Chrysler	107.466	36/26	71
29	Al Miller	Hudson/R.G. "Buddy" Marr	Hudson I-8/255 cu.in.	Hudson	110.129	18/27	66
42	Doc MacKenzie	Ray Brady	Studebaker I-8/337 cu.in.	Studebaker	108.154	39/28	65
32	Frank Brisko	Brisko-Atkinson	Miller I-8/151 cu.in.	Stevens	111.149	13/29	61
72	Ray Campbell	Folly Farm/E.D. Stairs	Graham I-8/245 cu.in.	Graham	108.969	34/30	60
5	Billy Arnold	Miller-Hartz	Miller I-8/151 cu.in.	Summers	116.290	2/31	59
27	Bryan Saulpaugh	Harry Miller/William White	Miller V-16/303 cu.in.	Miller	114.369	3/32	55
16	Louie Meyer	Alden Sampson II	Miller V-16/220 cu.in.	Stevens	112.471	7/33	50
21	Al Aspen	Brady & Nardi	Studebaker I-8/340 cu.in.	Duesenberg	108.008	23/34	31
49	Johnny Kreiger	Consumers/Duesenberg	Duesenberg I-8/138 cu.in.	Duesenberg	109.276	33/35	30
48	Wes Crawford	Boyle Valve/M.J. Boyle	Duesenberg I-8/137 cu.in.	Miller	110.396	16/36	28
17	Paul Bost	Empire State/Paul Bost	Miller I-8/215 cu.in.	Cooper	111.885	8/37	18
58	Bob McDonough	Miller Four Wheel Drive	Miller I-8/308 cu.in.	Miller	113.276	24/38	17
45	Gus Schrader	Harry Miller/William Burden	Miller I-8/308 cu.in.	Miller	112.003	28/39	7
26	Al Gordon	Lion Tamer/G.D. Harrison	Miller I-4/220 cu.in.	Miller	111.290	37/40	3

in this entire Century of the Automobile has the gulf between European and American motor racing been so great. The Indianapolis 500 and AAA National Championship were very much entities unto themselves in those years of the Great Depression. There was no cross-pollination of ideas across the Atlantic as there had been in the early years, and as there would be in the future.

WONDROUS VARIETY

There were any number of ways to build a race car for the new Speedway formula. Back before 1922, the cars had weighed 1763 lbs., carried a riding mechanic and used a 3.0-liter engine. In other words, they fit the new rules perfectly though with engines only half the allowable size. Many long-established race teams still had one of these cars sitting in the back of the shop. It could be dragged out of retirement and refurbished for almost nothing.

Another alternative for an established team was to keep the 91 cubic inch or 122 cubic inch Duesenberg or Miller they already had, widen the body to fit two people and add a little weight to make the minimum. They would be giving away a lot of displacement, but nobody figured a stock-block car, even with 366 cubic inches, would be faster than a Miller 91.

Many tuners tried to get more displacement by using two small racing engines together. Remember, both the Duesenberg and Miller Inline-8 racing engines had been inspired by a Bugatti U-16 that was two Inline-8s placed side by side, with their crankshafts geared together. Frank Lockhart had reversed the process by putting two Miller 91s side by side to power his 1928 Land Speed Record car. A couple of other teams did the same thing in the Thirties using Miller 91, 122 and 183 Inline-8s placed next to each other to form a U-16. Because Miller's engines had a one-piece block and head but detachable crankcase, they could also be fairly easily mounted on a common crankcase to make a V-16.

Yet other backyard mechanics replaced the engine in their old race car with a larger passenger car powerplant. Particularly popular was the Inline-8 from the mid-Twenties Duesenberg Model A. This was very similar in design to Duesenberg's racing engines, and one of the few American passenger car powerplants with an overhead camshaft. It displaced 260 cubic inches, and could be easily hopped-up to reliably make over 150 hp.

THE HOT-RODDERS

Studebaker, Hudson, Buick, Stutz, Chrysler, Lycoming and Ford were among the other passenger car engines tried in low-slung racers. With the exception of the little Fords, most of these engines were near the 366 cubic inch limit. Virtually all of them were very straightforward, flathead designs with either four, six or eight cylinders. They could be cheaply hot-rodded by milling the head for more compression, using better pistons and valves, more carburetors, a cam with more overlap, exhaust headers, a lightened flywheel...all the stuff that hot-rodders have been

Louie Meyer was there at the start of two beloved 500 traditions. In 1933, he was the first winner to receive a bottle of milk in Victory Lane. In 1936, he was the first winner to receive the sterling silver Borg-Warner Trophy, which today carries a likeness of every 500 winner since Harroun in 1911.

(below) Classic Miller/Ford cockpit from 1935— brushed aluminum dash, three-spoke "banjo" wheel, white-on-black gauges and, surprisingly, a big 160 mph speedometer but no tachometer. It wouldn't look out of place in a sports car today.

MILLER/FORD

It was another of Preston Tucker's bright ideas. In 1934, his friend Harry Miller—who even then was recognized as the greatest racing car designer in the world—was out of work. It was the height of the Depression, and there was no market for the cost-no-object race cars Miller liked to build. Operating on the two sound business principles of "If you need money, go where the money is" and "You don't ask, you don't get," Preston Tucker got together with another friend, Edsel Ford. Edsel, of course, was second-in-command and heir apparent at Ford Motor Company.

Tucker's proposal was that Ford finance the construction of ten cars for the Indianapolis 500. Harry Miller would design and build them, Ford would supply the engines and running gear. Of course they would win, and then Ford dealers coast to coast would sell the dickens out of the new Ford V-8, which already had something of a reputation as a hot performer.

Edsel liked the idea; his father Henry thought it was another of Preston Tucker's preposterous schemes. In the end, Edsel finally sprang a paltry $25,000 budget that was paid to Tucker through Ford's advertising agency, N.W. Ayer. By the time the deal was done, Miller had just 79 days to build ten cars.

Miller had always built every part of his cars from scratch in his own shop. He used the 221 cubic inch (3.6-liter) Ford V-8 block, heads, crankshaft, rods and valves. Everything else was either a proprietary racing part or built by Miller.

What he created in an incredibly short

period of time were ten of the prettiest cars you've ever seen, the quintessential Indy racers of the stock-block era. As usual, Miller's machines were at least a decade ahead of his competition and his engineering ideas are still valid.

The Miller/Fords had deep, 6 inch frame rails connected by tubular crossmembers. A modified version of the tried-and-true Miller front-wheel drive transaxle sat at the front, with twin transverse quarter-elliptic leaf springs. The rear axle was also independently sprung on quarter-elliptics, making this the first Indy car with all-independent suspension.

The Ford V-8 sat backwards from its usual position, driving the front wheels. Since there was no driveshaft to the rear axle, the driver and mechanic could sit on the floor. A simple aluminum body incorporating a cut-down 1935 Ford grille made this one of the most graceful race cars of all time. Aluminum fairings over the axles were an early attempt at streamlining.

Harry Miller was used to doing the impossible, but building and sorting out ten cars in eleven weeks was too much, even for him. Most of the Miller/Fords were ready in time, but only four qualified for the 500. The fastest was Ted Horn, at 113.213 mph (7 mph off the pace), but he only completed 145 laps to finish sixteenth. By then, all three other Miller/Fords had already dropped out with the same problem. The culprit was a needle-bearing universal joint that connected the steering shaft to the steering gear. In the cramped engine compartment, Miller had mounted the support for this steering over the hot exhaust manifold. As the race went on, the bearing heated up, the grease leaked out, the bearing seized and the driver couldn't turn the steering wheel. Not fun.

Preston Tucker's total bill was $75,000, not $25,000. Henry Ford was so furious, he took all ten Miller/Fords and locked them in a warehouse for two years. Finally, Ford suppliers Lou Fageol and Lewis Welch were allowed to buy nine of the ten. They appeared at Indy sporadically until 1948, never finishing higher than mid-pack. The Miller/Fords were neat cars which pioneered new ideas, but with too much of Preston Tucker, too little of Harry Miller. ∎

(Left) Harry Miller and driver George Bailey pose with a Miller/Ford and two of the V-8 sedans Ford supplied as official cars at the Speedway in 1935. (below) Ted Horn's flathead V-8 used two Stromberg carburetors, made about 150 hp at 4400 rpm. Most of the technology was the same as that used by hot-rodders in the Fifties.

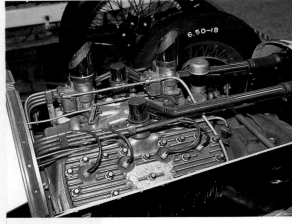

(left) Most of the Miller/Fords had four Stromberg carburetors, aluminum Bohnalite heads—reversed because the radiator was now "behind" the backwards engine—and typical hop-up parts including 9.5:1 aluminum pistons. The overbuilt chassis and transaxle later handled up to 500 hp when a Novi V-8 was fitted, more than three times the Ford's modest output.

1933

Winner: Louie Meyer, Miller, 104.162 mph
Winner's Purse: $18,000
Total Purse: $54,450
Pace Car: Byron Foy, Chrysler Imperial Custom-8

Not the best year at the Memorial Day Classic...there was a driver's strike before the race, the purse was reduced because of the Depression, five men were killed and the race itself was more like a demolition derby. Lou Meyer won his second 500 ahead of Wilbur Shaw, both in Millers.

Number	Driver	Sponsor/Team	Engine Type/Displacement	Chassis	Qualifying	Start/ Finish	Laps
36	Louie Meyer	Tydol/Louie Meyer	Miller I-8/258 cu.in.	Miller	116.977	6/1	200
17	Wilbur Shaw	Mallory/Leon Duray	Miller I-4/220 cu.in.	Stevens	115.497	23/2	200
37	Lou Moore	Foreman Axle/Maley & Scully	Miller I-4/255 cu.in.	Duesenberg	117.843	4/3	200
21	Chet Gardner	Sampson Radio	Miller V-16/201 cu.in.	Stevens	112.319	15/4	200
8	Stubby Stubblefield	Shafer "8"/Phil Shafer	Buick I-8/284 cu.in.	Rigling	114.784	10/5	200
38	Dave Evans	Arthur Rose	Studebaker I-8/260 cu.in.	Rigling	109.448	36/6	200
34	Tony Gulotta	Studebaker	Studebaker I-8/336 cu.in.	Rigling	113.578	12/7	200
4	Russ Snowberger	Russell Snowberger	Studebaker I-8/336 cu.in.	Snowberger	110.769	17/8	200
9	Zeke Meyer	Studebaker	Studebaker I-8/336 cu.in.	Rigling	111.099	16/9	200
46	Luther Johnson	Studebaker	Studebaker I-8/336 cu.in.	Rigling	110.097	20/10	200
6	Cliff Bergere	Studebaker	Studebaker I-8/336 cu.in.	Rigling	115.643	9/11	200
47	L.L. Corum	Studebaker	Studebaker I-8/336 cu.in.	Rigling	110.465	18/12	200
49	Willard Prentiss	Jack C. Carr/Kleinschmidt	Duesenberg I-8/365 cu.in.	Rigling	107.776	40/13	200
14	Raoul Riganti	Golden Seal/Raoul Riganti	Chrysler I-8/305 cu.in.	Chrysler	108.081	27/14	200
29	Gene Haustein	Lawrence Martz	Hudson I-8/235 cu.in.	Hudson	107.603	28/15	197
26	Deacon Litz	Bowes Seal Fast/A.B. Litz	Miller I-4/220 cu.in.	Miller	113.138	14/16	197
18	Joe Russo	Wonder Bread/Duesenberg	Duesenberg I-8/275 cu.in.	Duesenberg	112.531	31/17	192
51	Doc MacKenzie	Ray Brady	Studebaker I-8/340 cu.in.	Duesenberg	108.073	39/18	192
27	Kelly Petillo	Yahr-Miller	Miller I-4/213 cu.in.	Smith	113.037	25/19	168
28	Chet Miller	R.G. "Buddy" Marr	Hudson I-8/255 cu.in.	Hudson	112.025	32/20	163
19	Al Miller	R.G. "Buddy" Marr	Hudson I-8/255 cu.in.	Hudson	109.799	24/21	161
68	Bennet Hill	S.C. Goldberg	Cooper V-16/190 cu.in.	Cooper	110.264	19/22	158
45	Babe Stapp	Boyle Products	Miller I-4/221 cu.in.	Miller	116.626	29/23	156
32	Wesley Crawford	Boyle Products/Frank Brisko	Miller I-8/151 cu.in.	Stevens	109.862	26/24	147
5	Bill Cummings	Boyle Products	Miller I-8/270 cu.in.	Miller	118.521	1/25	136
15	Lester Spangler	Miller/Harry Hartz	Miller I-4/255 cu.in.	Miller	116.903	7/26	132
65	Freddy Winnai	James Kemp	Duesenberg I-8/154 cu.in.	Duesenberg	110.018	35/27	125
57	Malcolm Fox	Universal Service/Richards	Studebaker I-8/337 cu.in.	Studebaker	112.922	30/28	121
12	Fred Frame	Miller-Hartz	Miller I-8/182 cu.in.	Wetteroth	117.864	3/29	85
64	Mark Billman	Kemp-Mannix	Duesenberg I-8/265 cu.in.	Duesenberg	112.410	22/30	79
53	Johnny Sawyer	Lencki-Madis/Lencki & Unger	Miller I-4/220 cu.in.	Miller	110.590	34/31	77
2	Peter Kreis	Frame-Miller	Miller I-8/151 cu.in.	Summers	114.370	11/32	63
16	Ernie Triplett	Floating Power/White	Miller I-4/220 cu.in.	Weil	117.685	5/33	61
25	Shorty Cantlon	Sullivan & O'Brien/Cantlon	Miller I-4/220 cu.in.	Stevens	113.384	13/34	50
3	Mauri Rose	Gilmore/Joe Marks	Miller I-8/248 cu.in.	Stevens	117.649	42/35	48
58	Frank Brisko	F.W.D. Auto	Miller I-8/308 cu.in.	Miller	118.388	2/36	47
10	Ira Hall	Denny Duesenberg	Duesenberg I-8/249 cu.in.	Stevens	115.739	8/37	37
23	Ralph Hepburn	Highway Truck/Goldberg	Cooper V-16/330 cu.in.	Cooper	110.001	41/38	33
59	Ray Campbell	G&D/Tulio Gulotta	Hudson I-8/244 cu.in.	Hudson	108.650	37/39	24
24	Paul Bost	Frame-Miller Duesenberg	Miller I-4/220 cu.in.	Duesenberg	111.330	33/40	13
61	Rick Decker	Miller/Bessie Decker	Miller I-8/167 cu.in.	Miller	108.280	38/41	13
22	Lou Schneider	Edelweiss/W.R. Blackburn	Miller I-8/151 cu.in.	Stevens	109.850	21/42	1

doing ever since and routinely do even today. There were no "secrets." Most of these stock-blocks produced between 150 and 200 hp, enough to zip the fastest cars up to 140 mph on the straights at Indianapolis. Thanks to new hydraulic shock absorbers and Firestone Speedway Special tires, they were averaging 95

mph through the corners. That was faster than the little Miller 91s of the Twenties. The Millers had been faster on the straights thanks to more horsepower and better aerodynamics, but lap speeds were remarkably similar for the thoroughbred Millers and the mongrel stock-blocks.

There was tremendous variety in the chassis used to hold these different stock-block engines. People put them into old race car chassis, they built racing bodies onto the stock passenger car frame or they built a new body/chassis to accept the stock-block engine. Almost overnight, a whole new industry sprang up to supply this demand. Small shops, building only a handful of cars each year, would create a car into which you could fit whatever engine you happened to have. Modest car builders like Myron Stevens, Phil Somers, Emil Diedt, Curly Wetteroth, Cotton Henning and Herman Rigling supplanted the legendary stars Harry Miller and Fred Duesenberg.

In the best sense of the word, these new guys were glorified hot-rodders. They would build a frame either from scratch or from passenger car frame rails held together with narrowed crossmembers. They'd adapt left-over Miller or production car hardware to fit. They'd craft a lightweight aluminum body, fit aftermarket knock-off wheels, a Ford transmission, racing hydraulic shock absorbers and a rear axle from almost anything. A famous Fred Frame Duesenberg-powered car had a Bugatti axle, Ford gearbox and Miller brakes. It was pretty typical of the stock-block racers, and remarkably successful.

The buyer could choose his own engine builder, who was usually another hot-rodder with a different specialty. No matter what components were used, the cars were built to last. Not only did they have to run at Indianapolis, they had to survive the rough and tumble of AAA dirt tracks for the season—hopefully for many seasons—with a minimum of maintenance on a shoestring budget. From a professional builder, such a "rolling chassis"—everything but the engine and gearbox—could be had for $2500 in the mid-Thirties. That wouldn't have bought a front-wheel drive transaxle for a Miller 91.

"THE TEAM" IN THE THIRTIES

Harry Miller, Leo Goossen and Fred Offenhauser went their separate ways after Rellimah went bankrupt in 1933. Before that, Harry Miller had designed a new series of Inline-8s, a modular design that could be ordered in your choice of bore and stroke sizes. Displacements ranged from 180 to 270 cubic inches with double-overhead cams and four valves per cylinder. While most of the stock-block engines were doing well to produce 0.5 hp per cubic inch and were limited to about 4000 rpm, these Miller racing engines could

Between 1933 and 1938, the Speedway changed the qualifying rules. Instead of 4 laps (10 miles), you had to run for 10 laps (25 miles). The slowest qualifier to make the race during this era was Dave Evans in 1934, who ran 102.414 mph in his Cummins diesel. The fastest qualifier was Ronney Householder, who finally broke Leon Duray's decade-old Miller 91 record with a 125.769 mph average in 1938. He was driving a supercharged Adams/Sparks.

(below) How stock is stock? Chet Miller's stock-block Hudson Special is dwarfed by a Hudson sedan with which it shares the engine, trans, rear axle...and not much else. These race cars could hit 130 mph, at a time when a stock sedan was considered "hot" if it could top 80 mph.

1934

Winner: "Wild Bill" Cummings, Miller, 104.863 mph
Winner's Purse: $29,725
Total Purse: $83,775
Pace Car: Willard "Big Boy" Rader, LaSalle Series 350

For the first time, Indianapolis cars were restricted as to the amount of oil and gas they could use. Winner Wild Bill Cummings averaged 12.9 mpg of gas, better than many passenger cars. Mauri Rose was just 27 seconds behind after 500 miles, making this by far the closest Indianapolis finish so far.

Number	Driver	Sponsor/Team	Engine Type/Displacement	Chassis	Qualifying	Start/Finish	Laps
7	Bill Cummings	Boyle Products/Henning	Miller I-4/220 cu.in.	Miller	116.116	10/1	200
9	Mauri Rose	Leon Duray	Miller I-4/220 cu.in.	Stevens	116.044	4/2	200
2	Lou Moore	Foreman Axle/CA Racers	Miller I-4/255 cu.in.	Miller	113.442	20/3	200
12	Deacon Litz	Stokely Foods/A.B. Litz	Miller I-4/220 cu.in.	Miller	113.731	19/4	200
16	Joe Russo	Duesenberg/Joe Russo	Duesenberg I-8/275 cu.in.	Duesenberg	113.115	24/5	200
36	Al Miller	Shafer "8"/Phil Shafer	Buick I-8/286 cu.in.	Rigling	113.307	8/6	200
22	Cliff Bergere	Floating Power/White	Miller I-4/220 cu.in	Weil	115.243	18/7	200
10	Russ Snowberger	Russell Snowberger	Studebaker I-8/336 cu.in.	Snowberger	111.428	9/8	200
32	Frank Brisko	F.W.D. Auto	Miller I-4/255 cu.in.	Miller	116.894	3/9	200
24	Herb Ardinger	Angelo Lucenti	Graham I-8/265 cu.in.	Graham	111.722	14/10	200
17	Kelly Petillo	Red Lion/Joe Marks	Miller I-4/255 cu.in.	Adams	119.329	1/11	200
5	Stubby Stubblefield	Cummins Engine Company	Cummins I-4/364 cu.in.	Duesenberg	105.921	29/12	200
31	Ralph Hepburn	Miller/Ralph Hepburn	Miller I-8/254 cu.in.	Miller	114.321	11/13	164
18	George Barringer	Boyle Products/H.C. Henning	Miller I-4/270 cu.in.	Miller	113.859	12/14	161
26	Phil Shafer	Shafer "8"/Phil Shafer	Buick I-8/292 cu.in.	Rigling	113.816	6/15	130
49	Charles Crawford	Detroit Gasket	Ford V-8/221 cu.in.	Ford	108.784	28/16	110
8	Tony Gulotta	Schroeder/Floyd Smith	Studebaker I-8/250 cu.in.	Cooper	113.733	7/17	94
1	Louie Meyer	Ring Free/Lou Meyer	Miller I-4/255 cu.in.	Stevens	112.332	13/18	92
6	Dave Evans	Cummins Engine Company	Cummins I-4/364 cu.in.	Duesenberg	102.414	22/19	81
15	Shorty Cantlon	Sullivan & O'Brien/Cantlon	Miller I-4/220 cu.in.	Stevens	117.875	15/20	76
4	Chet Gardner	Sampson Radio	Miller V-16/201 cu.in.	Stevens	114.786	5/21	72
51	Al Gordon	Abels & Fink/Paul Weirick	Miller I-4/239 cu.in.	Adams	116.273	17/22	66
35	Rex Mays	Frame Miller-Duesenberg	Miller I-4/220 cu.in.	Duesenberg	113.639	23/23	53
42	Dusty Fahrnow	Superior Trailer/Goldberg	Cooper V-16/330 cu.in.	Cooper	113.070	25/24	28
41	Johnny Sawyer	Burd Piston/Lencki & Unger	Lencki I-4/183 cu.in.	Miller	109.808	21/25	27
33	Johnny Seymour	Streamline Miller/Fred Frame	Miller I-4/200 cu.in.	Adams	108.591	33/26	22
45	Rick Decker	Carter Carburetor/Decker	Miller I-8/171 cu.in.	Miller	110.895	27/27	17
3	Wilbur Shaw	Lion Head/Joe Marks	Miller I-8/249 cu.in.	Stevens	117.647	2/28	15
73	Doc MacKenzie	Cresco/Mikan & Carson	Studebaker I-8/337 cu.in.	Mikan-Carson	111.933	26/29	15
29	Gene Haustein	Lawrence Martz	Hudson I-8/257 cu.in.	Hudson	109.426	31/30	13
63	Harry McQuinn	Michel DeBaets	Miller I-4/220 cu.in.	Rigling	111.067	30/31	13
58	George Bailey	Roy Scott	Studebaker I-8/360 cu.in.	Snowberger	111.063	16/32	12
46	Chet Miller	Bohnalite Ford/Bohn Brass	Ford V-8/221 cu.in.	Ford	109.252	32/33	11

easily churn out 1.0 hp per cubic inch at 5500 rpm. They were very successful not only at Indianapolis, but also in the AAA National Championship right up until World War II.

Another Miller engine led to what we now call the Offy. This was a compact four-cylinder, originally designed for powerboat racing in 1926. It had all of the recognizable Miller trademarks: a one-piece block and head, aluminum barrel crankcase, double-overhead camshafts, four valves per cylinder, pentroof combustion chambers and tubular connecting rods. The whole engine only weighed 350 lbs., about the same as the eight-cylinder 91, yet this one displaced either 151 or 183 cubic inches (2.5 or 3.0-liters).

THREE-TIME WINNER

The first three-time winner of the Indianapolis 500 also won the AAA National Championship three times. Plus he was a heck of a mechanic, a savvy businessman...and one of the nicest men you'd ever want to meet. Louie Meyer started out in racing as a mechanic, working for his brother Eddie Meyer, Jr. Their father had been a racer in his day, and the two brothers were raised into racing. After years as a mechanic, Louie was standing in Wilbur Shaw's pit at the 1927 500. Shaw needed a relief driver; Louie did 41 laps and decided that what he really wanted to do was drive a race car, not turn wrenches.

In 1928, team owner Alden Sampson bought Meyer a Miller 91 for the AAA season. Now you have to remember that Meyer's total experience of Indianapolis racing was 41 laps the previous year. After letting the hot-shoes lead, he eased into first with only 18 laps to go and won his first 500...the first race he'd ever completed. Meyer then went on to win the AAA National Championship.

It was no fluke. In 1929, he was leading at Indianapolis after 390 miles, but stalled in the pits for 7 minutes. He still finished second and won the AAA Championship again. After a couple of frustrating years trying to sort out the U-16 Sampson, Meyer came back in 1933 with a Miller to win both the 500 and the AAA Championship yet again. He won again at Indianapolis in 1936, this time in a car he'd built himself, and came within a blink of winning his fourth 500 in 1939 before crashing.

In 1933, Fred Offenhauser and Meyer started building Harry Miller-designed engines, and in 1946, Dale Drake and Meyer bought the Offy business. Meyer-Drake came to dominate American racing for decades with the famous Offy engine. In the Sixties, Louie sold out to Dale Drake, then developed the Ford four-cam engine which eventually supplanted the Offy as the powerplant to have. In a very real sense, then, Louie Meyer held mastery over American racing as mechanic, driver and engine-builder for over fifty years. A truly remarkable man. ∎

(top) Louie Meyer in 1939.
(above) He had his four top AAA Championship awards made into a necklace and bracelet for his wife.
(left) The winner in 1928, 1933 and 1936.

1935

Winner: Kelly Petillo, Wetteroth/Offy, 106.240 mph
Winner's Purse: $30,600
Total Purse: $78,575
Pace Car: Harry Mack, Ford 48 Convertible

The new Offenhauser engine—derived from a Harry Miller boat racing powerplant—beat the Millers its first time out, starting a dynasty that would last for over four decades. Wilbur Shaw was second for the second time in three years, thanks to a rain storm that prevented him from catching Petillo.

Number	Driver	Sponsor/Team	Engine Type/Displacement	Chassis	Qualifying	Start/Finish	Laps
5	Kelly Petillo	Gilmore Speedway/Petillo	Offy I-4/260 cu.in.	Wetteroth	115.095	22/1	200
14	Wilbur Shaw	Gil Pirrung	Offy I-4/220 cu.in.	Shaw	116.854	20/2	200
1	Bill Cummings	Boyle Products/H.C.Henning	Miller I-4/221 cu.in.	Miller	116.901	5/3	200
22	Floyd Roberts	Abels & Fink/Earl Haskell	Miller I-4/255 cu.in.	Miler	118.671	3/4	200
21	Ralph Hepburn	Veedol/Ralph Hepburn	Miller I-8/258 cu.in.	Miller	115.156	7/5	200
9	Shorty Cantlon	Sullivan & O'Brien/Cantlon	Miller I-4/220 cu.in.	Stevens	118.205	19/6	200
18	Chet Gardner	Sampson Radio/Sampson	Miller I-4/220 cu.in.	Stevens	114.556	9/7	200
16	Deacon Litz	Sha-Litz	Miller I-4/220 cu.in.	Miller	114.488	13/8	200
8	Doc MacKenzie	Gil Pirrung	Miller I-4/220 cu.in.	Rigling	114.294	15/9	200
34	Chet Miller	Milac Front Drive/Fred Frame	Miller I-8/151 cu.in.	Summers	113.552	17/10	200
19	Fred Frame	Miller-Hartz	Miller I-8/183 cu.in.	Wetteroth	114.701	8/11	200
36	Louie Meyer	Ring Free/Lou Meyer	Miller I-4/255 cu.in.	Stevens	117.938	4/12	200
15	Cliff Bergere	Victor Gasket/Phil Shafer	Buick I-8/284 cu.in.	Rigling	114.162	16/13	196
62	Harris Insinger	Cresco/Mikan & Carson	Studebaker I-8/336 cu.in.	Mikan-Carson	117.729	31/14	185
4	Al Miller	Boyle Products/H.C. Henning	Miller I-4/260 cu.in.	Rigling	115.303	21/15	178
43	Ted Horn	Ford V-8/Harry Miller	Ford V-8/220 cu.in.	Miller-Ford	113.213	26/16	145
33	Rex Mays	Gilmore/Paul Weirick	Miller I-4/269 cu.in.	Adams	120.736	1/17	123
7	Lou Moore	Foreman Axle/Lou Moore	Miller I-4/255 cu.in.	Miller	114.180	23/18	116
37	George Connor	Marks-Miller	Miller I-8/248 cu.in.	Stevens	114.321	14/19	112
2	Mauri Rose	Front Wheel Drive Auto	Miller I-4/255 cu.in.	Miller	116.470	10/20	103
44	Tony Gulotta	Bowes Seal Fast/Leon Duray	Miller I-4/220 cu.in.	Stevens	115.459	6/21	102
39	Jimmy Snyder	Blue Prelude/Joel Thorne	Studebaker I-8/336 cu.in.	Snowberger	112.249	30/22	97
41	Frank Brisko	Art Rose/Kenneth Schroeder	Studebaker I-8/250 cu.in.	Rigling	113.307	24/23	79
42	Johnny Seymour	Ford V-8/Harry Miller	Ford V-8/220 cu.in.	Miller-Ford	112.696	27/24	71
17	Babe Stapp	Marks-Miller	Miller I-4/255 cu.in.	Adams	116.736	12/25	70
35	George Bailey	Ford V-8/Harry Miller	Ford V-8/220 cu.in.	Miller-Ford	113.432	29/26	65
3	Russ Snowberger	Boyle Products/Henning	Miller I-8/270 cu.in.	Miller	114.209	11/27	59
26	Louis Tomei	Burd Piston Ring/Joe Lencki	Lencki I-8/220 cu.in.	Miller	110.794	32/28	47
46	Bob Sall	Ford V-8/Harry Miller	Ford V-8/220 cu.in.	Miller-Ford	110.519	33/29	47
6	Al Gordon	Cocktail Hour/White	Miller I-4/220 cu.in.	Weil	119.481	2/30	17
27	Freddy Winnai	Gyro-Duesenberg/Hartz	Miller I-4/234 cu.in.	Duesenberg	115.138	28/31	16
45	Clay Weatherly	Bowes Seal Fast/Leon Duray	Miller I-4/220 cu.in.	Stevens	115.902	25/32	9
66	Harry McQuinn	Michel DeBaets	Miller I-4/220 cu.in.	Rigling	111.111	18/33	4

A racer named Bill White adapted one of these 3.0-liter Miller marine engines to his dirt track car in the late-Twenties. He got Leo Goossen and Fred Offenhauser interested in the project, and they made a few design improvements. When the Indy rules were changed for 1930, here was a perfect engine, ready to race.

White and his driver Shorty Cantlon took a Miller marine engine to Indianapolis in 1930, qualified on the front row, finished second and then took second in the AAA National Championship, too. Obviously, the Miller marine engine was a great idea. All sorts of other racers rushed to pull engines out of boats and plug them into their cars. Bill Cummings won the 500 in 1934 with a Miller marine engine, even though it has often been mistakenly described as an Offy. It wasn't.

THE VENERABLE OFFY

Harry Miller was no dummy. He saw the success White and Cantlon were having with his marine engine, and in 1931 he decided to create an all-new engine, similar to the old marine powerplant, but incorporating everything he'd learned since 1926. The goal was to have a simple, reliable, easy-to-own racing engine that could be competitive at Indianapolis or dirt tracks and sold for $2000. What appeared from Leo Goossen's drawing board was a typical Miller engine, but beefed up and enlarged to fit the new rules. Miller went ahead and made the tooling to produce this new four-cylinder, but before he really got going, he ran out of money and declared bankruptcy.

Fred Offenhauser bought the rights to this new engine, hired Leo Goossen and, with the help of Louie Meyer, took it into production as the Offenhauser Engineering Company. The rest is history. The Offy was available as a 200 hp, 220 cubic inch (3.6-liter) or a 225 hp, 255 cubic inch (4.2-liter). It would spin to 5500 rpm, weighed only 385 lbs. and cost exactly $2000. The Offy was obviously so much better than any stock-block could possibly be that eleven of them showed up at Indy in 1934. One of the old Miller marine engines won. The next year, Kelly Petillo took the Offy 255 to the first of its dozens of wins at the Indianapolis 500. Overnight, it became the only powerplant to have.

HOTBED OF COMPETITION

The 1930-1936 formula may have been "junk," but ironically it produced some of the most interesting cars, largest fields and closest races in 500 history. It also gave birth to the Offy, an engine any formula could be proud of. Because of the connection—however tenuous—between the cars on the track and the cars on the street, the junk formula also lured passenger car manufacturers back to Indy for the first time since before World War I. Companies like Studebaker, Hudson, Stutz and Ford publicized their racing efforts, which in turn helped to publicize the Indianapolis Motor Speedway. Eddie Rickenbacker made a real effort to improve safety at the Speedway during these years, too. For the first

(below) Just before the start in 1935. Rex Mays, Al Gordon and Floyd Roberts are the front row, surrounded by crew members and officials in pith helmets. Infield spectators are standing on their cars or homebuilt scaffolding to get a better view; crude snow fences keep them out of the pits. Check out the trackside Norge at the right edge of the photo which held film for the photographers and refreshments for the officials.

1936

Winner: Louie Meyer, Stevens/Miller, 109.069 mph
Winner's Purse: $31,300
Total Purse: $82,525
Pace Car: Tommy Milton, Packard 120 Convertible

For the first third of the race, Wilbur Shaw and Babe Stapp dueled in Offy-powered cars—both built by Shaw. Both cars broke, however, and Lou Meyer inherited the lead and went on to win his third Indianapolis 500. He was the first three-time winner, and also the first to be presented with the pace car.

Number	Driver	Sponsor/Team	Engine Type/Displacement	Chassis	Qualifying	Start/Finish	Laps
8	Louie Meyer	Ring Free/Lou Meyer	Miller I-4/255 cu.in.	Stevens	114.171	28/1	200
22	Ted Horn	Miller-Hartz	Miller I-8/183 cu.in.	Wetteroth	116.564	11/2	200
10	Doc MacKenzie	Gilmore Speedway/Petillo	Offy I-4/262 cu.in.	Wetteroth	116.961	4/3	200
36	Mauri Rose	Four Wheel Drive Auto	Miller I-4/255 cu.in.	Miller	113.890	30/4	200
18	Chet Miller	Boyle Motor Products	Miller I-4/212 cu.in.	Summers	117.675	3/5	200
41	Ray Pixley	Fink Auto/Clarence Felker	Miller I-4/203 cu.in.	Miller	116.703	25/6	200
3	Wilbur Shaw	Gilmore/Wilbur Shaw	Offy I-4/255 cu.in.	Shaw	117.503	9/7	200
17	George Barringer	Kennedy Tank/Phil Shafer	Offy I-4/255 cu.in.	Rigling	112.700	14/8	200
53	Zeke Meyer	Boyle Motor Products	Studebaker I-8/251 cu.in.	Cooper	111.476	32/9	200
38	George Connor	Marks Miller/Joe Marks	Miller I-4/255 cu.in.	Adams	116.269	5/10	200
35	Freddy Winnai	Midwest Red Lion Racing Team	Offy I-4/255 cu.in.	Stevens	116.221	12/11	199
9	Ralph Hepburn	Art Rose/Ralph Hepburn	Offy I-4/255 cu.in.	Miller	112.673	24/12	196
28	Harry McQuinn	Sampson Radio	Miller I-4/247 cu.in.	Stevens	114.118	27/13	196
7	Shorty Cantlon	Hamilton-Harris/White	Miller I-4/247 cu.in.	Weil	116.912	10/14	194
33	Rex Mays	Gilmore/Paul Weirick	Sparks I-4/239 cu.in.	Adams	119.644	1/15	192
54	Doc Williams	Superior Trailer/Race Car	Miller I-4/246 cu.in.	Cooper	112.837	23/16	192
32	Lou Moore	Burd Piston Ring/Moore	Offy I-4/255 cu.in.	Miller	113.996	29/17	185
19	Emil Andres	J. Stewart Carew	Cragar I-4/212 cu.in.	Whippet	111.455	33/18	184
4	Floyd Roberts	Burd Piston Ring/Joe Lencki	Offy I-4/255 cu.in.	Stevens	112.403	15/19	183
14	Frank Brisko	Elgin-Piston Pin	Brisko I-4/255 cu.in.	Miller	114.213	20/20	180
12	Al Miller	Boyle Motor Products	Miller I-4/258 cu.in.	Smith	116.138	17/21	119
42	Cliff Bergere	Bowes Seal Fast	Miller I-4/220 cu.in.	Stevens	113.377	7/22	116
15	Deacon Litz	Deacon Litz/A.B. Litz	Miller I-4/220 cu.in.	Miller	115.997	26/23	108
21	Babe Stapp	Gil Pirrung	Offy I-4/255 cu.in.	Shaw	118.945	2/24	89
5	Billy Winn	Harry Miller/James Winn	Miller I-4/255 cu.in.	Miller	114.648	19/25	78
52	Frank McGurk	Abels Auto Ford/Charles Worley	Cragar I-4/214 cu.in.	Adams	113.102	22/26	51
27	Louis Tomei	Wheeler's/Babe Stapp	Miller I-4/214 cu.in.	Wetteroth	111.078	8/27	44
44	Herb Ardinger	Bowes Seal Fast	Miller I-4/220 cu.in.	Stevens	115.082	6/28	38
6	Chet Gardner	Chester Gardner	Offy I-4/255 cu.in.	Duesenberg	116.000	18/29	38
43	Jimmy Snyder	Belanger Miller	Miller I-8/249 cu.in.	Stevens	111.291	16/30	21
47	Johnny Seymour	Sullivan & O'Brien/Cantlon	Miller I-4/246 cu.in.	Stevens	113.169	21/31	13
46	Fred Frame	Burd Piston Ring/Moore & Fengler	Miller I-4/255 cu.in.	Miller	112.877	31/32	4
2	Bill Cummings	Boyle Motor Products	Offy I-4/255 cu.in.	Miller	115.939	13/33	0

time since 1909, substantial changes were made to the track itself. The four turns were widened and completely new retaining walls and catch fences were put up.

It was all a great success. By 1936, America was coming out of the worst of the Depression, the Speedway was in better shape than ever, the grids were fast and full. Everything was working perfectly. That meant, of course, that it was time to change! But for seven years, the most unrestricted formula in Indianapolis history had allowed the greatest variety of cars ever to mix it up together, all of them with a surprisingly good chance of winning. Ironically, a stock-block never did win the Indianapolis 500; Harry Miller's exquisite pure racing engines dominated just as completely as they had in the Twenties. But the junkers came *this* close.

THE WIDE-OPEN ERA 1937-1941

It was the Indianapolis Speedway that precipitated the new, more liberal rules that changed American racing after 1936. Not Eddie Rickenbacker's Speedway administration, but the track itself. By redesigning and widening the turns in 1936, the Indianapolis oval had been made a much safer place to race. Encouraged, Captain Eddie repaved the four turns and the short chutes with asphalt in 1937, then the approaches to the turns in 1938. The infield fences were moved back and a lot more run-out room provided on the inside of the corners. In 1940, Rickenbacker paved the whole back straight. Indeed, the only remaining brick at The Brickyard was now on the front straight, and that was deliberately left bare for sentimental reasons. From the dangerous, dilapidated track of the early-Thirties, the Speedway was transformed into a spiffy state-of-the-art paved oval that was probably the safest race track in the country.

THE 1937 FORMULA

The old "Junk" Formula had been a success, not the least because it had kept top speeds at Indianapolis in the 140 mph range and lap speeds under 120. That was about as fast as one dared to go on the deteriorating bricks. Now that the track seemed so much smoother and safer, Rickenbacker figured they could let the cars go a little faster. That would make both the racers and the spectators happy.

The tricky part was to preserve the competitiveness of cars that were already racing, while opening up the field to new ideas. So the AAA changed the rules in two stages. For 1937, the formula was essentially the same as it had been

(below) It may not look like much, but Lee Oldfield's 1937 homebuilt was the first mid-engine entry at the Indianapolis 500, twenty-four years before Jack Brabham's Cooper/ Climax started the "mid-engine revolution." Oldfield's car has a rare Marmon V-16 engine, four-wheel independent suspension, inboard drum brakes. It arrived too late to qualify though it did practice.

1937

Winner: Wilbur Shaw,
Shaw/Offy, 113.580 mph
Winner's Purse: $35,075
Total Purse: $92,135
Pace Car: Ralph DePalma,
LaSalle Series 37-50
Roadster

Slowed near the end by low oil pressure, Wilbur Shaw let Ralph Hepburn close to within 2.16 seconds at the finish line. After years of near misses, Shaw finally hung on to prove the worth of the sleekly-aerodynamic Gilmore Special he'd built himself.

Number	Driver	Sponsor/Team	Engine Type/Displacement	Chassis	Qualifying	Start/ Finish	Laps
6	Wilbur Shaw	Shaw-Gilmore	Offy I-4/255 cu.in.	Shaw	122.791	2/1	200
8	Ralph Hepburn	Hamilton-Harris/Meyer	Offy I-4/255 cu.in.	Stevens	118.809	6/2	200
3	Ted Horn	Miller-Harry Hartz	Miller I-8/182 cu.in.	Wetteroth	118.608	32/3	200
2	Louie Meyer	Boyle/H.C. Henning	Miller I-8/268 cu.in.	Miller	119.619	5/4	200
45	Cliff Bergere	Midwest Red Lion/George Lyons	Offy I-4/255 cu.in.	Stevens	117.546	16/5	200
16	Bill Cummings	Boyle/H.C. Henning	Offy I-4/255 cu.in.	Miller	123.455	1/6	200
28	Billy DeVore	Miller/H.E. Winn	Miller I-4/255 cu.in.	Stevens	120.192	14/7	200
38	Tony Gulotta	Burd Piston Ring/Joe Lencki	Offy I-4/255 cu.in.	Rigling	118.788	7/8	200
17	George Connor	Joe Marks/Miller	Miller I-4/265 cu.in.	Adams	120.240	12/9	200
53	Lou Tomei	Sobonite Plastics/S.S. Engineering	Studebaker I-8/336 cu.in.	Rigling	116.437	18/10	200
31	Chet Gardner	Burd Piston Ring/Chester Gardner	Offy I-4/255 cu.in.	Duesenberg	117.342	9/11	199
23	Ronney Householder	Henry J. Topping	Miller I-4/234 cu.in.	Viglioni	116.464	10/12	194
62	Floyd Roberts	Joel Thorne	Miller I-4/269 cu.in.	Miller	116.996	17/13	194
35	Deacon Litz	Motorola/A.B. Litz	Miller I-4/220 cu.in.	Miller	116.372	11/14	191
32	Floyd Davis	Joel Thorne	Miller I-4/255 cu.in.	Snowberger	118.942	24/15	190
34	Shorty Cantlon	Bowes Seal Fast/Bill White Cars	Miller I-4/228 cu.in.	Weil	118.555	25/16	182
42	Al Miller	Joel Thorne	Miller I-4/255 cu.in.	Snowberger	118.518	26/17	170
1	Mauri Rose	Burd Piston Ring/Lou Moore	Offy I-4/270 cu.in.	Miller	118.540	8/18	127
41	Ken Fowler	Lucky Teeter	McDowell I-4/233 cu.in.	Wetteroth	117.421	29/19	116
25	Kelly Petillo	Kelly Petillo	Offy I-4/318 cu.in.	Wetteroth	124.129	20/20	109
43	George Bailey	Duray-Sims	Miller I-4/220 cu.in.	Stevens	117.497	28/21	107
54	Herb Ardinger	Chicago Raw Hide Oil/Welch	Offy I-4/255 cu.in.	Welch	121.983	3/22	106
24	Frank Brisko	Elgin Piston Pin/Frank Brisko	Brisko I-6/350 cu.in.	Stevens	118.213	15/23	105
44	Frank Wearne	Leon Duray	Miller I-4/220 cu.in.	Stevens	118.220	33/24	99
26	Tony Willman	F.W.D./Peter DePaolo	Miller I-4/255 cu.in.	Miller	118.242	27/25	95
10	Billy Winn	Miller/James Winn	Miller I-4/255 cu.in.	Miller	119.922	4/26	85
12	Russ Snowberger	Russ Snowberger	Packard I-8/282 cu.in.	Snowberger	117.354	30/27	66
33	Bob Swanson	Fink/Paul Weirick	Sparks I-4/269 cu.in.	Adams	121.920	21/28	52
47	Harry McQuinn	Sullivan-O'Brien	Miller I-4/247 cu.in.	Stevens	121.822	22/29	47
7	Chet Miller	Boyle/H.C. Henning	Miller I-8/154 cu.in.	Summers	119.213	13/30	36
15	Babe Stapp	Henry J. Topping	Maserati I-8/305 cu.in.	Maserati	117.226	31/31	36
5	Jimmy Snyder	Sparks/Joel Thorne	Sparks I-4/337 cu.in.	Adams	125.287	19/32	27
14	Rex Mays	Bowes Seal Fast/Bill White Cars	Alfa Romeo I-8/232 cu.in.	Alfa Romeo	119.968	23/33	24

since 1930—maximum displacement of 366 cubic inches (6.0-liters), 1750 lb. minimum weight, two-man bodywork. The important differences were that superchargers would be allowed for the first time since 1929 and that the cars would have to run on gasoline rather than the "dope" made of alcohol, benzol, acetone and other volatile explosives that crew chiefs secretly brewed in the back of their Gasoline Alley garages.

The gasoline the AAA required wasn't low-octane pump gas, but rather high-octane aviation fuel. Even in the late-Thirties gasoline was pretty poor by modern standards. The leaded "Avgas" used at Indy was equivalent in potency to what we would call 87 octane Regular. Gasoline was a lot less explosive than dope, so it

was safer. It was easier to detect cheating in gasoline by using a specific gravity test, too. Gasoline also slowed the cars down a bit, but it was expected that the addition of superchargers would eventually counteract the loss of power and race speeds would go up. That's exactly what happened, though it took a few years.

The 1937 Formula actually had very little effect at Indianapolis. Offy and Miller 255s still dominated, though now there were some fitted with superchargers. There were also a couple of supercharged Maseratis and Alfas back in the pack. The only all-new engine built for this rule was the supercharged Sparks-Thorne. It was instantly 20 mph faster down the back straight at Indy than any car that had run there since 1929, which allowed Jimmy Snyder to break Leon Duray's long-standing Miller 91 lap record, albeit with a car that had almost four times the engine displacement of the incredible little Miller.

VANDERBILT CUP

In 1936, a small group of wealthy Eastern sports car enthusiasts—a rare breed in America in those days—organized a "Formula Libre" road race at Roosevelt Field on Long Island. This was the airport from which Charles Lindbergh had started for Paris, a symbolic connection between Europe and America which the organizers found appropriate. They joined the runways to form a 3.98-mile circuit. They called their event the Vanderbilt Cup, in honor of Willie K.'s great Long Island over-the-road races at the turn-of-the-century.

By promising a huge purse and scheduling the race on October 12, a month after the regular racing season was over in Europe, they managed to attract a surprisingly high-quality field of cars from both Europe and America. It was the first time Grand Prix cars had been seen in America in over a decade. The elite Mercedes and Auto Union teams couldn't be bothered to come, but the 300 mile race was won by Tazio Nuvolari in an Alfa Romeo, followed by Jean-Pierre Wimille in a Bugatti, two more Alfas, a Maserati...and AAA National Champion Mauri Rose in Lou Moore's Burd Piston Ring Special, an old Miller chassis fitted with a 255 cubic inch Offy that had finished seventeenth at Indy with Moore himself driving.

Packard presented 1936 winner Louie Meyer with the pace car, then used that fact in advertising. GM thought this was such a clever idea that in 1937 they gave their LaSalle pace car to Wilbur Shaw. It became a tradition...every winner since has received the keys to the pace car.

(left) Retired champion Pete DePaolo was the team chief for the FWD Truck Company. Their one-off Harry Miller racer had four-wheel drive, a two-man body and Miller 303 cubic inch (5.0-liter) V-8. In five years of trying, the car's best finish was in 1936, when Mauri Rose started thirtieth and finished fourth. (right) Tony Gulotta was eighth in this Burd Special in 1937. It's typical of the era—255 Offy engine in Rigling chassis, amateur streamlining and fancy paint job.

GOOSSEN AND OFFENHAUSER

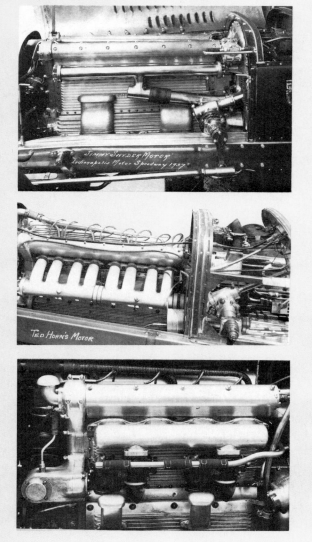

When Eddie Rickenbacker had the AAA rules rewritten for 1937 and then again for '38, he sparked an exciting round of pure-racing engine development. *Everybody* had a bright idea for a new engine. Significantly, most of those people went to see Harry Miller's proteges, Leo Goossen and Fred Offenhauser. Goossen was a master draftsman who could take even the wildest ideas and mold them into a workable design; Offenhauser was a master machinist who could take Goossen's drawings and build an engine that could win at Indianapolis. All it took was a little time and a lot of money.

Goossen/Offenhauser created many different engines for the new formula. The first was called Sparks-Thorne because the engine concept was by a young California engineer named Art Sparks, who got his money from flamboyant New York railroad/banking/real estate heir Joel Thorne. Sparks and Goossen came up with a 337 cubic inch (5.5-liter) Inline-6 that was essentially the small Miller-designed Offy 225 (3.7-liter) Inline-4 with an extra two cylinders.

Sparks made a few changes from the Miller "Bible." He used H-section connecting rods rather than tubular rods and a different style of main bearing. He also drove the supercharger with a long torsion shaft that ran down the outside of the crankcase. This first Sparks-Thorne Six was so powerful—450 hp, 550 lbs-ft of torque—that Jimmy Snyder immediately surpassed Leon Duray's nine-year-old Indy track record in 1937. He was hitting 160 mph on the straights.

When the rules were changed to 3.0-liter cars in 1938, Sparks shortened the stroke on his engine, ran it at higher rpm and still developed 400 hp. Sparks also built a 271 cubic inch (4.5-liter) version without a supercharger which Joel Thorne himself drove into seventh at Indy in 1939 and 5th in 1940. Thorne Engineering's supercharged cars did even better, leading in 1938, second in '39, third in 1941, then first in 1946. The Sparks-Thorne turned out to be one of the best engines of its era.

The second Goossen-Offenhauser engine was Louie Meyer's idea. He had California hot-rodders Ed and Bud Winfield use two 91 cubic inch Offy midget engines back to back as patterns to cast a new block, a 3.0-liter Inline-8. Almost all the parts were stock Offenhauser, except for the crankshaft and long shafts to drive the supercharger that ran through hollow camshafts. Running on pump gas, this inexpensive hybrid developed about 350 hp, enough to put Rex Mays on the front row and into second in the 500 two years in a row.

The third Goossen-Offenhauser engine was a 3.0-liter, DOHC V-8 that was also classic Harry Miller engineering,

conceptually a pair of Offy midget engines on a common 90 degree crankcase. Goossen drove the supercharger with a shaft that went forward from a gear-drive off the back of the crank and sat in the valley of the V where the camshaft lives on an overhead-valve V-8.

This engine was designed to fit into a Miller-Ford chassis owned by the ubiquitous Winfields, and was financed by Ford V-8 engine rebuilder Lou Welch. Welch was from Novi, Michigan. Yes, indeed. The famous Novi V-8 that competed for twenty-five years was actually designed as a way for a couple of L.A. hot-rodders to inexpensively add horsepower to an old race car that was already obsolete. The Novi wasn't particularly successful at first—the engine alone weighed 575 lbs. and the supercharger design was inefficient—but it was later developed into one of the most powerful engines ever to run at the Speedway. The Novi had great potential.

In addition to these new engines, Offenhauser Engineering continued to make parts for the Inline-8 engines that Harry Miller had designed for the 1930 formula, and which were still being used. They also did parts for the old Miller marine engines, and of course, their own Offenhauser. Despite all these fancy new supercharged engines, an unsupercharged 255 cubic inch Offy won at Indianapolis in 1937, an unsupercharged 270 cubic inch Miller marine engine won in 1938, an unsupercharged 270 cubic inch Offy in 1941. Offys were third in 1939 and '40, too, so they were definitely competitive. Offys also ruled the AAA dirt tracks and throughout this period the majority of the cars that contested the Indianapolis 500 were Offy or Miller-powered.

Finally, there was a real oddball that was surprisingly successful at Indianapolis. This was the Sampson Special, powered by the U-16 that Frank Lockhart had built for his 1928 Stutz Blackhawk Land Speed Record car, the car in which he was killed. Lockhart's engine was literally two Miller 91s placed side by side and geared together to make a twin-supercharged 3.0-liter that produced over 400 hp.

In a Riley Brett chassis, this ancient product of Lockhart, Miller, Goossen and Offenhauser finished sixth in 1940 with Bob Swanson at the wheel. It was like seeing the Ghost of Indy Past, right there among the living. It was more proof, as though more proof were needed, of how long a shadow Harry Miller cast—aided by Fred Offenhauser and Leo Goossen. ∎

(top) Sparks-Thorne 3.0-liter Six of 1938 developed 400 hp at 6500 rpm, enough to win the 500 in 1946. Note the shaft-driven supercharger and finned intercooler. (left) In 1938, Louie Meyer, with help from Leo Goossen, Fred Offenhauser, Ed and Bud Winfield, put together two 1.5-liter midget engines geared back to back to make a 3.0-liter Inline-8 with central power takeoff that delivered 350 hp at 6500 rpm on pump gas. Under the hood of the Bowes Seal Fast Special, this unique, low-cost Eight ran the 500 ten times, bringing Rex Mays to second in 1940 and '41. But sadly, it never won at Indianapolis.

1938

Winner: Floyd Roberts,
Wetteroth/Miller,
117.200 mph
Winner's Purse: $32,075
Total Purse: $91,075
Pace Car: Stuart Baits,
Hudson 112

California Sprint Car driver Floyd Roberts started on the pole, led most of the race and easily won from Chet Miller, who fell behind Wilbur Shaw at the very end. Shaw was a full three laps behind Roberts in his curious but successful Gilmore Special.

Number	Driver	Sponsor/Team	Engine Type/Displacement	Chassis	Qualifying	Start/ Finish	Laps
23	Floyd Roberts	Burd Piston Ring/Lou Moore	Miller I-4/270 cu.in.	Wetteroth	125.681	1/1	200
1	Wilbur Shaw	Wilbur Shaw	Offy I-4/256 cu.in.	Shaw	120.987	7/2	200
3	Chet Miller	I.B.E.W./Boyle Racing	Offy I-4/255 cu.in.	Summers	121.898	5/3	200
2	Ted Horn	Miller-Hartz	Miller I-8/182 cu.in.	Wetteroth	121.327	6/4	200
38	Chet Gardner	Burd Piston Ring/Joe Lencki	Offy I-4/257 cu.in.	Rigling	120.435	18/5	200
54	Herb Ardinger	Offenhauser/Lewis Welch	Offy I-4/255 cu.in.	Miller-Ford	119.022	14/6	199
45	Harry McQuinn	Carl Marchese	Miller I-8/151 cu.in.	Marchese	119.492	25/7	197
58	Billy DeVore	P.R.&W./Joel Thorne	Offy I-4/255 cu.in.	Stevens	116.339	30/8	185
22	Joel Thorne	Thorne Engineering	Offy I-4/256 cu.in.	Shaw	119.155	13/9	185
29	Frank Wearne	Indiana Fur/Paul Weirick	Offy I-4/270 cu.in.	Adams	121.405	17/10	181
43	Duke Nalon	Kohlert-Miller	Miller I-8/154 cu.in.	Fengler	113.828	33/11	178
12	George Bailey	Barbasol/Leon Duray	Duray I-4/182 cu.in.	Weil	116.393	29/12	166
27	Mauri Rose	I.B.E.W./Boyle Racing	Maserati I-6/91 cu.in.	Maserati	119.796	9/13	165
16	Ronney Householder	Thorne-Sparks/Joel Thorne	Sparks I-6/179 cu.in.	Adams	125.769	10/14	154
6	Jimmy Snyder	Sparks-Thorne/Joel Thorne	Sparks I-6/179 cu.in.	Adams	123.506	15/15	150
5	Louie Meyer	Bowes Seal Fast/Bowes Racing	Winfield I-8/179 cu.in.	Stevens	120.525	12/16	149
17	Tony Gulotta	Hamilton-Harris/Tony Gulotta	Offy I-4/255 cu.in.	Stevens	122.499	4/17	130
55	Al Miller	Domont's Pepsi-Cola/Jack Holly	Miller I-4/255 cu.in.	Miller	119.420	22/18	125
15	George Connor	Marks-Miller	Miller I-4/272 cu.in.	Adams	120.326	19/19	119
9	Cliff Bergere	Kraft's Real Rye/George Lyons	Miller I-8/151 cu.in.	Stevens	114.464	32/20	111
33	Henry Banks	Louis Kimmel	Voelker V-12/273 cu.in.	Mller	116.279	31/21	109
35	Kelly Petillo	Kelly Petillo	Offy I-4/271 cu.in.	Wetteroth	119.827	21/22	100
21	Louis Tomei	P.O.B. Perfect Seal/H.E. Winn	Miller I-4/255 cu.in.	Miller	121.599	24/23	88
7	Bill Cummings	I.B.E.W./Boyle Racing	Miller I-8/268 cu.in.	Miller	122.393	16/24	72
14	Russ Snowberger	D-X/Russell Snowberger	Miller I-4/255 cu.in.	Snowberger	124.027	2/25	56
34	Babe Stapp	McCoy Auto Service/Bill White	Miller I-4/228 cu.in.	Weil	120.595	8/26	54
10	Tony Willman	Murrell Belanger	Miller I-8/247 cu.in.	Stevens	118.458	26/27	47
8	Rex Mays	Alfa-Romeo/Bill White Cars	Alfa-Romeo I-8/182 cu.in.	A.R.-Weil	122.845	3/28	45
42	Emil Andres	Elgin Piston Pin	Brisko I-6/272 cu.in.	Adams	.117.126	28/29	45
37	Ira Hall	Greenfield/Nowiak & Magnee	Studebaker I-8/250 cu.in.	Nowiak	118.255	27/30	44
26	Frank Brisko	Shur-Stop Brake/Frank Brisko	Brisko I-6/271 cu.in.	Stevens	121.921	11/31	39
36	Al Putnam	Troy Tydol/Arthur M. Sims	Miller I-4/220 cu.in.	Stevens	116.791	23/32	15
47	Shorty Cantlon	Kamm's/Thomas O'Brien	Miller I-4/247 cu.in.	Stevens	120.906	20/33	13

This first Vanderbilt Cup race was such a success that the one for 1937 was scheduled for July, right in the midst of the racing season. The big European teams split their efforts, some drivers going to Long Island, some to the Belgian Grand Prix the following weekend. In those days, you couldn't get cars and drivers from continent to continent in less than a week. This time the Germans came.

As eyewitness Ralph Stein wrote, "The Alfas of the previous year had shocked us with their power...but the Germans of 1937 overwhelmed us, turned our knees to jelly, and stunned our brains with the earthshaking crash and scream of their exhausts, their unbelievable speed."

Bernd Rosemeyer won in his Auto Union, Dick Seaman was second in a Mer-

cedes. By far the most impressive driver was Rex Mays, the best American racer of his generation, who dragged a year-old Alfa Romeo into third place behind the flying Silver Arrows. Indy driver Joel Thorne was sixth, in another Alfa.

The Vanderbilt Cup races of 1936 and '37 did a couple of things. They made Grand Prix teams aware of racing in America, which for most of them was a lost continent. When Frenchman Rene Dreyfus was told he was going to Indianapolis a few years later, he couldn't find "Indiana, USA" on the maps available in France.

American racers were just as parochial. Most of them had heard rumors of the Mercedes and Auto Unions and knew names like Nuvolari and Caracciola, but that was all. A few enlightened racers, like Wilbur Shaw, went to Europe to race at the ovals of Brooklands, Montlhery and Monza. But that was rare. Seeing those incredible cars—and the equally incredible Nuvolari—opened up a lot of minds on this side of the Atlantic.

The Vanderbilt Cup allowed the Europeans and Americans to meet and appreciate each other's skills; the masterful Nuvolari had nothing but praise for Rex Mays, whom he considered "world class." But most importantly, it introduced the American racers to European equipment. When the Grand Prix rules were changed for 1938 and the Speedway decided to follow the new European formula, there was a rush to acquire Grand Prix cars which had been superior in the Vanderbilt Cup races. Surely they would have an advantage at Indy, too.

AN INTERNATIONAL FORMULA, AGAIN

In 1937, European Grands Prix were still being contested by 750 kg (1650 lb.) cars of unlimited displacement and over 600 hp. The Silver Arrows of Mercedes-Benz and Auto Union simply ran away and hid. For 1938, the French-headquartered AIACR which ran international racing appointed a *Commission Sportive Internationale.* The CSI was instructed to devise a new Grand Prix formula that would reduce speeds, reduce costs and end the German monopoly.

The American Automobile Association adopted the CSI's new International Formula simultaneously, starting with the 1938 season. Remember that the AAA formula and Grand Prix formula had been the same up until 1929, then different through 1937. The CSI's clever new formula allowed normally-aspirated engines up to 4.5-liters and supercharged engines up to 3.0-liters. This was the first time any regulatory group had tried to create an equitable

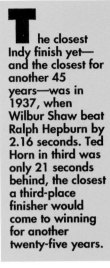

The closest Indy finish yet—and the closest for another 45 years—was in 1937, when Wilbur Shaw beat Ralph Hepburn by 2.16 seconds. Ted Horn in third was only 21 seconds behind, the closest a third-place finisher would come to winning for another twenty-five years.

(left) Pete DePaolo with the greatest racing driver of all time, Italian Tazio Nuvolari. The Flying Mantuan visited Indianapolis in 1938, but did not race. Notice his exotic-to-America Pirelli coveralls and the turtle pin he always wore for good luck.
(below) A Firestone "tire guy" checks Floyd Roberts' winning Wetteroth/Miller in 1938.

WILBUR SHAW

Dynamic Wilbur Shaw grew up in Shelbyville and Greensburg, Indiana, only 30 miles from the Speedway. Even as a kid, he rode the railroad train into Indianapolis, then made his way out to the Speedway on his bicycle. His hero was driver Tommy Milton, for whom he acted as a helper. Shaw left home in 1918 and got a job selling storage batteries in Indianapolis. He was sixteen.

In his spare time, he started building his own dirt track car out of cast-off bits and pieces. The local half-mile track wouldn't let him run it. He built another car, this one with the help of the track official who had turned down the first car. Called the RED for Shaw's new mentor Roscoe E. Dunning, this one proved to be almost unbeatable. Wilbur Shaw won races at dirt tracks all over the Midwest during the 1922 season. He was only 20 years old.

For the next five years, the naturally gifted Shaw earned a handsome living competing on dirt tracks and the infamous boards. He drove almost any car he was offered, and won more often than not. He earned a reputation as a "charger" who'd rather put a hole in the fence than finish second, but that was fine with car owners who wanted to win races, too. By 1927, Shaw had successfully raced from Ascot in California to Atlantic City in New Jersey.

For the 1927 Indianapolis 500, Wilbur Shaw drove Fred Clemon's famous Jynx Special, a rear-drive Miller. He finished fourth, only 7 seconds behind the third-place car. The next year, his Miller broke early, but Shaw co-drove Ray Keech's car into fourth. In 1929, Shaw didn't make it to Indianapolis; in 1930 he broke down while running in third; in 1931 he was a relief driver for the Duesenberg team.

During the 1931 race, Shaw took over for Phil Pardee but was unable to see clearly over the Duesenberg's high cowling. On lap 61, he slid up the banking in Turn Three and hit the outer wall with enough force to vault completely over the top. Unhurt, Shaw returned to the pits and drove relief in Jimmy Gleason's identically-painted car, much to the confusion of his friends who thought they saw Shaw steaming by in the same car that they'd watched clear the wall.

Shaw looked like a potential winner in 1932, but a rear axle failed while he was leading near the three-quarter mark in a Miller owned by his friend Ralph Hepburn. In 1933, retired Speedway lap-record holder Leon Duray put Shaw into one of his Millers. Shaw was second behind Louie Meyer and went on to finish third for the season in the AAA Championship. He broke early at Indian-

(top) Legendary mechanic and car builder Cotton Henning—crew chief on Mike Boyle's Maserati—confers with Wilbur Shaw during qualifying in 1939. (above) Later that May: Sweat-drenched Shaw talks to the NBC radio audience from Victory Lane. (right) After winning in 1937, Shaw was second in 1938. He's driving his famous streamlined "Pay Car" that ran well in nine 500s between 1936 and '48—one of the most successful Indianapolis race cars ever built.

apolis in 1934, but came back to finish second again in 1935, behind Kelly Petillo. He finished third in the AAA Championship again, too.

For 1936, Gilmore Oil bankrolled a radically-streamlined machine inspired by an earlier Gilmore Special Stubby Stubblefield had run in 1932, nicknamed the "Catfish." Shaw and Myron Stevens built the new car themselves. In the Memorial Day Classic, they went to the front with the new car until forced to make pit stops in order to secure loose bodywork. That lost them 17 minutes. They climbed back up the charts until they were only 13 minutes behind the winner, Louis Meyer, who won his third Indianapolis 500. Shaw finished seventh.

Finally, in 1937, Shaw came home the winner as his streamliner began to earn a nickname of its own, "The Pay Car." The Pay Car and Shaw were second at Indianapolis in 1938. Even after he turned it over to other drivers, the Pay Car continued to finish in the Top Ten at the Speedway for several more years. Indeed, it was one of the most successful cars ever to run the 500.

Shaw himself drove a new Maserati 8CTF Grand Prix car owned by Chicago industrialist Mike Boyle. The combination was unbeatable. Shaw ran away with the Memorial Day Classic two years in a row in 1939 and 1940. He might have been the first four-time Indianapolis 500 winner, but a wheel collapsed while he was leading on lap 152 in 1941, sending him into the Turn One wall.

Shaw worked for Firestone's aircraft division in Akron, Ohio, during World War II. Near the end of the war, Firestone sent him to conduct a 500 mile test of a new synthetic rubber tire at the Speedway. The track was in deplorable condition. As soon as the test was over, Shaw headed for New York to meet with Eddie Rickenbacker and confirm that the Speedway was up for sale. After weeks of searching for someone to purchase the Indianapolis Speedway and continue to operate it, Shaw thankfully found Tony Hulman in Terre Haute.

The most successful driver in the entire first half of the Speedway's existence, Shaw now retired to become President and General Manager under Tony Hulman. He continued to hold both positions until his death in a private aircraft crash on October 30, 1954. Wilbur Shaw's total contributions to the Indianapolis Motor Speedway are inestimable, first as a driver, then as a car builder who created one of the first successful streamlined race cars, and later for his role in saving the Speedway from extinction. ■

(below) The start in 1939: Louie Meyer #45 leads Wilbur Shaw #2. The two ran about this close for 197 laps, until Meyer crashed and was thrown from his car. Amazingly, he walked away, but retired from racing on the spot. Shaw went on to win his second 500, his first in the Boyle Maserati. He won again in this car in 1940 and was leading after 152 laps in 1941 when a defective wheel put him into the Turn One wall. After that, Shaw retired, too.

1939

Winner: Wilbur Shaw,
Maserati, 115.035 mph
Winner's Purse: $27,375
Total Purse: $87,050
Pace Car: Charles Chayne,
Buick Roadmaster

1938 winner Floyd Roberts was killed and Chet Miller seriously injured in a multi-car accident; Lou Meyer retired from racing after crashing on lap 198 while dueling for the lead with Wilbur Shaw; Shaw cruised to the finish in the first European car to win in two decades.

Number	Driver	Sponsor/Team	Engine Type/Displacement	Chassis	Qualifying	Start/ Finish	Laps
2	Wilbur Shaw	Boyle Racing Headquarters	Maserati I-8/183 cu.in.	Maserati	128.977	3/1	200
10	Jimmy Snyder	Thorne Engineering	Sparks I-6/182 cu.in.	Adams	130.138	1/2	200
54	Cliff Bergere	Offenhauser/Lewis Welch	Offy I-4/270 cu.in.	Miller-Ford	123.835	10/3	200
4	Ted Horn	Boyle Racing Headquarters	Miller I-8/268 cu.in.	Miller	127.723	4/4	200
31	Babe Stapp	Alfa Romeo/Bill White Cars	Alfa Romeo I-8/181 cu.in.	Weil	125.000	16/5	200
41	George Barringer	Bill White Race Cars	Offy I-4/228 cu.in.	Weil	120.935	15/6	200
8	Joel Thorne	Thorne Engineering	Sparks I-6/272 cu.in.	Adams	122.177	20/7	200
16	Mauri Rose	Wheeler's/W. Wilbur Shaw	Offy I-4/256 cu.in.	Shaw	124.896	8/8	200
14	Frank Wearne	Burd Piston/Moore & Roberts	Offy I-4/270 cu.in.	Wetteroth	125.074	17/9	200
26	Billy DeVore	Leon Duray-Barbasol	Duray I-4/182 cu.in.	Weil	116.527	33/10	200
62	Tony Gulotta	Burd Piston Ring/George Lyons	Offy I-4/259 cu.in.	Stevens	121.749	27/11	200
45	Louie Meyer	Bowes Seal Fast/Bowes Racing	Winfield I-8/179 cu.in.	Stevens	130.067	2/12	197
18	George Connor	Joseph Marks	Offy I-4/255 cu.in.	Adams	123.208	12/13	195
51	Tony Willman	Burd Piston Ring/Joe Lencki	Lencki I-6/270 cu.in.	Lencki	122.771	26/14	188
58	Louis Tomei	Alfa-Romeo/Frank Griswold	Alfa Romeo I-8/264 cu.in.	Alfa Romeo	118.426	30/15	186
15	Rex Mays	Thorne Engineering	Sparks I-6/182 cu.in.	Adams	126.413	19/16	145
9	Herb Ardinger	Miller-Hartz	Miller I-8/182 cu.in.	Wetteroth	124.125	9/17	141
35	Kelly Petillo	Kay Jewelers/Kelly Petillo	Offy I-4/270 cu.in.	Wetteroth	123.660	24/18	141
49	Mel Hansen	Joel Thorne	Offy I-4/270 cu.in.	Shaw	121.683	14/19	113
38	Harry McQuinn	Elgin Piston Pin/F. Burren	Brisko I-6/271 cu.in.	Blume	117.287	32/20	110
3	Chet Miller	Boyle Racing Headquarters	Miller I-4/255 cu.in.	Summers	126.318	5/21	109
25	Ralph Hepburn	Hamilton-Harris/Tony Gulotta	Offy I-4/270 cu.in.	Stevens	122.204	13/22	107
1	Floyd Roberts	Burd Piston Ring/Lou Moore	Offy I-4/270 cu.in.	Wetteroth	128.968	23/23	106
37	Ira Hall	Greenfield/Magnee & Nowiak	Studebaker I-8/271 cu.in.	Nowiak	121.188	18/24	89
21	Russ Snowberger	D-X/Russell Snowberger	Miller I-4/258 cu.in.	Snowberger	123.199	25/25	50
17	George Bailey	Harry A. Miller	Miller I-6/180 cu.in.	Miller	125.821	6/26	47
56	Floyd Davis	W.B.W./Ed Walsh	Offy I-4/255 cu.in.	Miller	119.375	29/27	43
42	Al Miller	Kennedy Tank/Paul Weirick	Offy I-4/270 cu.in.	Adams	123.233	28/28	41
29	Frank Brisko	National Seal/Frank Brisko	Brisko I-6/272 cu.in.	Stevens	123.351	11/29	38
44	Emil Andres	Chicago Flash/Jimmy Snyder	Offy I-4/255 cu.in.	Stevens	121.212	21/30	22
32	Bob Swanson	Sampson Motors	Sampson I-16/183 cu.in.	Stevens	129.431	22/31	19
47	Shorty Cantlon	Auto Services/Associated	Offy I-4/262 cu.in.	Stevens	125.567	7/32	15
53	Deacon Litz	Maserati/Richard T. Wharton	Maserati I-8/182 cu.in.	Maserati	117.979	31/33	7

displacement ratio between supercharged and unsupercharged cars, in this case a ratio of 1 to 1.5.

There was a sliding scale of minimum car weight relative to displacement that started at 400 kg (880 lbs.) for the smallest displacement cars and went up to 850 kg (1870 lbs.). Mechanics were once again optional, but most car builders were happy to save that extra weight. From now on, all "real" race cars would be *monoposto* with room for only the driver.

Grand Prix cars still ran on exotic fuels, and so from 1938 on the AAA rules were for "free fuel." Some teams went back to their exotic home brews, others stayed with Avgas or even 81 octane "pump" gas. Methanol-based "dope" was

worth about 50 hp over gasoline, but since alcohol also has about half the energy density of gasoline—56,500 BTU per gallon versus 120,000 BTU—it meant the cars either had to carry twice as much fuel or make twice as many pit stops. In the late-Thirties, it became pretty much standard at Indy to use dope during qualifying for that extra bit of speed, then gasoline in the race itself for fewer pit stops. The sacrifice in speed was usually worth the savings in time.

THE EUROPEAN CARS

The way the 1938 International Formula worked out in Europe, Delahaye and Talbot built normally-aspirated, 4.5-liter Grand Prix machines that were essentially sports cars without fenders. These produced between 225 and 250 hp at 5000 rpm and were hopelessly outclassed. Alfa Romeo, Bugatti and Maserati built supercharged 3.0-liter Inline-8s that made between 270 and 350 hp at 6500 rpm and were hopelessly outclassed, too. Mercedes and Auto Union built supercharged 3.0-liter V-12s that made between 470 and 490 hp at 7500 rpm and dominated the 3.0-liter Formula as thoroughly as their predecessors had dominated the 750 kg Formula.

Prewar European racing ended when Tazio Nuvolari in an Auto Union won the Yugoslavian Grand Prix at Belgrade on September 3, 1939. No one knew it at the time, but this would be the last Grand Prix race for six years, almost to the day. There were three minor events in Italy in 1940, including one called Targa Florio and one called Mille Miglia, but these were short voiturette races not worthy of those great names.

Grand Prix Auto Unions and Mercedes were owned and raced by their factories for the "Glory of the Fatherland." Nobody was allowed to buy one, not even their professional drivers. They were so high-strung that it required a legion of mechanics to keep them going, so complex that they cost a fortune to maintain, let alone to build. Letting one out of the hands of the factory was simply out of the question.

There's no doubt that the 200 mph Silver Arrows of Mercedes and Auto Union could have run away with the Indianapolis 500. Surprisingly, the powerful German teams chose not to compete. Indeed, in the late-Thirties, even though the 500 purse was still the highest payout in sports anywhere in the world, not one Euro-

(top) Handsome Harry Schell talks to driver Rene Dreyfus during Indy practice in 1940. Escaping from war in France, Harry's mother, wealthy American expatriate Lucy O'Reilly Schell, entered two 8CTF Maseratis at Indianapolis. Her team, *Ecurie Bleu,* had Luigi Chinetti as team manager, Rene Dreyfus and Rene LeBegue as drivers. Dreyfus blew his engine in practice, later joined the American Army and after the war opened a famous Manhattan restaurant, *Le Chanticlair.* LeBegue finished tenth at Indianapolis, returned to France and was killed during the war. Chinetti stayed in the U.S., became the Ferrari importer and made a fortune. He also won LeMans three times, as well as many other sports car races. Harry Schell opened his own bar in Paris called *L'Action Automobile* and became a well-known Grand Prix driver in the Fifties on the Maserati, Ferrari, Vanwall and BRM teams. He was killed in a Cooper at Silverstone in 1960.
(bottom) Yet another 8CTF Maserati, this one owned by an Argentinian syndicate and driven by Raoul Riganti, who crashed and flipped after only 24 laps of the 1940 500.

GULF-MILLER

It was a dream assignment. In the midst of The Great Depression, Gulf Oil Company decided that there was nothing for it, they just had to win the Indianapolis 500 with a car running on pump gas rather than the specially-brewed aviation fuel that racers used. So in June of 1937, they hired Harry Miller—who better?—to design and build a four-car team. He had the full facilities of Gulf Research & Development, any staff he wanted, a literally unlimited budget. And eleven months, which was four times longer than it had taken him to build ten Miller-Fords in 1935.

Miller could have improved one his dozens of existing engine and chassis designs, the ones that were still winning at Indy with clocklike regularity. Typically, he decided instead to give Gulf a technical *tour de force*, the most advanced and wonderful car that anybody had ever engineered from the ground up for the sole purpose of circling the Indianapolis Speedway. After all, he had all the time and money in the world.

In Europe, the mid-engine Auto-Union designed by Ferdinand Porsche seemed to have more potential than typical front-engine racers. So Miller determined to build a mid-engine car. But his would have four-wheel drive. A driveshaft brought the power forward from the engine to the front transaxle; a second shaft brought the power back again to the rear axle. At the cost of a lot of mechanical complexity, Miller achieved not only four-wheel drive, but almost perfect 50/50 weight distribution.

There were many other innovations. Four-wheel disc brakes—the first disc brakes on an Indy car. All-independent suspension. Aerodynamically-shaped outboard fuel tanks centered in the wheelbase to maintain weight distribution as the tanks emptied. Fabricated frame rails that also formed part of the bodywork—the first monocoque body/chassis at Indianapolis. The engine offset in the frame to improve weight distribution in the Speedway's left turns. Aerodynamic bodywork brought tight around the engine and driver, then widening at the bottom. Axles

(above) May 1937: Harry Miller and George Bailey on a cold Indiana day. Even from here you can see the incredible workmanship that characterized all Miller's cars. The 180 cubic inch, six-cylinder DOHC engine has a built-in 45 degree cant to the left, dual-entry centrifugal supercharger driven off the rear of the crankshaft, exhaust headers that face straight-up, huge finned intercooler that sticks out the left side. It produced about 250 hp at 6400 rpm on 81 octane gasoline. (left) George Barringer in the restyled Gulf-Miller practicing in 1941.

covered by aerodynamic fairings. Inboard-mounted shock absorbers operated by remote levers. These are all things we take for granted now...because Harry Miller thought of them first fifty years ago.

Miller outdid himself with the engine. The 1938 rule was for 3.0-liter engines, supercharged. Miller created a short-stroke six-cylinder with double-overhead cams, designed from scratch to be both offset in the chassis and canted to one side. The crankshaft-driven supercharger had vanes on both sides of a single rotor, with a carburetor for each entry. It ran at five times engine speed, or 32,000 rpm.

Harry Miller was a mystic. A creative genius. But he was not a pragmatic development engineer. In the glory days, actually building Miller's cars and getting his ideas to work had been done by Fred Offenhauser and Leo Goossen. Without The Team to keep him in check, Miller spent 7000 hours on each of the Gulf-Millers and exceeded his generous budget. Every piece had to be specially made, and each car was artistically finished inside and out. But they also weren't finished in time. Nor did they work very well.

One Gulf-Miller was assembled for the 500 in 1938, but it didn't arrive in time to qualify. Miller and his crew of Gulf engineers worked all year, and managed to have three cars ready for 1939. Johnny Seymour crashed and his car burned to the ground. In 1940, George Bailey crashed and was killed. His car burned, too. George Barringer's new car was withdrawn at the "suggestion" of the AAA. In June he took it to Bonneville and ran 158 mph to set a dozen Class D speed records. That was the Gulf-Miller's best performance. Barringer's second car burned at Indianapolis in 1941 during the famous Gasoline Alley fire on race day morning. Gulf sold him the remaining car in 1946, and he got Preston Tucker to sponsor it on the premise that both the Gulf-Miller and new Tucker Torpedo were "rear-engine." Barringer was killed racing at Atlanta in the summer of 1946, so Al Miller ran the car for Tucker in 1947. They might just as well have stayed home.

The Gulf-Miller was one of the most advanced designs ever to run at Indianapolis, forty years ahead of its time in many ways. It was also the most expensive flop in racing history and Harry Miller's only failure. Seemed like a good idea at the time. ■

(top) 1941 version of the Gulf-Miller unclothed. How modern it looks with mid-engine, monocoque-style deep frame rails, perfect weight distribution.
(above) George Bailey lost his life in the accident that precipitated this blaze in 1940. Three out of the four Gulf-Millers were destroyed by fire. The cars were restyled for 1941 to protect the side gas tanks.
(left) The one remaining Gulf-Miller sitting in the old Gasoline Alley. It's in the Indianapolis Speedway Museum today.

1940

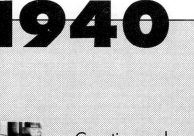

Winner: Wilbur Shaw,
Maserati, 114.277 mph
Winner's Purse: $30,725
Total Purse: $85,525
Pace Car: Harry Hartz,
Studebaker Champion

Coasting under yellow for the last 50 laps because of rain, Wilbur Shaw led a frustrated Rex Mays, Mauri Rose and Ted Horn to win his third Indianapolis 500. His car was the same Maserati in which he'd won in 1939, making Shaw and his mount the first back-to-back winners.

Number	Driver	Sponsor/Team	Engine Type/Displacement	Chassis	Qualifying	Start/ Finish	Laps
1	Wilbur Shaw	Boyle Racing Headquarters	Maserati I-8/179 cu.in.	Maserati	127.065	2/1	200
33	Rex Mays	Bowes Seal Fast	Winfield I-8/180 cu.in.	Stevens	127.850	1/2	200
7	Mauri Rose	Elgin Piston Pin/Lou Moore	Offy I-4/270 cu.in.	Wetteroth	125.624	3/3	200
3	Ted Horn	Boyle Racing Headquarters	Miller I-8/268 cu.in.	Miller	125.545	4/4	199
8	Joel Thorne	Thorne Donnelly/Joel Thorne	Sparks I-6/271 cu.in.	Adams	122.434	10/5	197
32	Bob Swanson	Sampson Motors	Sampson V-16/183 cu.in.	Stevens	124.882	20/6	196
9	Frank Wearne	Boyle Racing Headquarters	Offy I-4/257 cu.in.	Stevens	123.216	7/7	195
31	Mel Hansen	Harry Hartz	Miller I-8/182 cu.in.	Wetteroth	124.753	5/8	194
16	Frank Brisko	Elgin Piston Pin/Frank Brisko	Brisko I-6/271 cu.in.	Stevens	122.716	8/9	193
49	Rene LeBegue	Lucy O'Reilly Schell	Maserati I-8/183 cu.in.	Maserati	118.981	31/10	192
41	Harry McQuinn	Hollywood/Bill White Cars	Alfa Romeo I-8/181 cu.in.	Weil	122.486	15/11	192
25	Emil Andres	Belanger-Folz	Offy I-4/255 cu.in.	Stevens	122.963	22/12	192
28	Sam Hanks	Leon Duray	Duray I-4/182 cu.in.	Weil	123.064	14/13	192
6	George Barringer	Hollywood/Bill White Cars	Offy I-4/255 cu.in.	Weil	121.889	16/14	191
42	Joie Chitwood	Kennedy Tank/Paul Weirick	Offy I-4/270 cu.in.	Adams	121.757	26/15	190
26	Louis Tomei	Falstaff/Ed Walsh	Offy I-4/270 cu.in.	Miller	119.980	18/16	190
34	Chet Miller	Alfa Romeo/Wharton-Dewart	Alfa Romeo I-8/183 cu.in.	Alfa Romeo	121.392	27/17	189
14	Billy DeVore	Bill Holabird/W. Wilbur Shaw	Offy I-4/256 cu.in.	Shaw	122.197	32/18	181
44	Al Putnam	Refinoil/Anthony Gulotta	Offy I-4/255 cu.in.	Adams	120.818	28/19	179
61	Floyd Davis	Joseph Lencki	Lencki I-4/260 cu.in.	Lencki	120.797	33/20	157
35	Kelly Petillo	Indiana Fur/Kelly Petillo	Offy I-4/270 cu.in.	Wetteroth	125.331	13/21	128
21	Duke Nalon	Joseph Marks	Offy I-4/255 cu.in.	Silnes	121.790	25/22	120
17	George Robson	Marty Keller	Offy I-4/255 cu.in.	Miller-Ford	122.562	23/23	67
24	Babe Stapp	Frederick K. Surber	Offy I-4/262 cu.in.	Stevens	123.367	12/24	64
36	Doc Williams	Quillen/Doc Williams	Miller I-4/255 cu.in.	Cooper	122.963	19/25	61
10	George Connor	Joseph Lencki	Lencki I-6/265 cu.in.	Lencki	124.585	17/26	52
5	Cliff Bergere	Noc-Out Hose Clamp/Moore	Offy I-4/270 cu.in.	Wetteroth	123.673	6/27	51
38	Paul Russo	Elgin Piston Pin	Brisko I-6/271 culin.	Blume	120.809	29/28	48
54	Ralph Hepburn	Bowes Seal Fast/Winfield	Offy I-4/270 cu.in.	Miller-Ford	123.860	21/29	47
58	Al Miller	Alfa Romeo/Frank Griswold	Alfa Romeo I-8/177 cu.in.	Alfa Romeo	120.288	30/30	41
19	Russ Snowberger	Russell Snowberger	Miller I-4/255 cu.in.	Snowberger	121.564	11/31	38
27	Tommy Hinnershitz	Marks Offenhauser	Offy I-4/270 cu.in.	Adams	122.614	9/32	32
29	Raoul Riganti	Maserati/Raoul Riganti	Maserati I-8/183 cu.in.	Maserati	121.827	24/33	24

pean factory team ever arrived to try their luck. They would have been welcomed by Eddie Rickenbacker—imagine the publicity that would have surrounded the Auto Unions at Indianapolis—but none ever came.

A private team could buy a Delahaye, Talbot or Bugatti, but there was little point unless you wanted to bolt fenders over the wheels and go sports car racing. The French cars simply weren't competitive in Grands Prix or at Indy.

Alfa Romeo was supported by the Italian government; the cars were raced by the factory team of Scuderia Ferrari, owned by Enzo Ferrari. Alfa Grand Prix cars were disposed of at the end of each season, so it was possible to buy an Alfa GP car, albeit a well-used one, a year old. A few were tried—Rex Mays put one on

the front row in 1938—but they weren't reliable enough for a grueling 500 miles flat-out.

Then there was Maserati. A small family firm, Maserati was the Italian equivalent of Offenhauser Engineering. They would build anything that anybody was willing to pay for, but their standard products in 1938 were a 1.5-liter car for *voiturette* racing and 3.0-liter GP machine. Maserati's 3.0-liter 8CTF was powered by a long-stroke Inline-8 with double-overhead cams, four-valves-per-cylinder and two superchargers. It made 350 hp at 6500 rpm.

The Maserati design was actually very similar to that of the American Millers and Offenhausers. Indeed, it might have come right off Leo Goossen's drawing board except for the horizontally-split crankcase and the Roots rather than centrifugal superchargers. The Maserati wasn't competitive in Grands Prix. But it made about 100 horsepower more than the best unsupercharged Offys—though 50 hp less than the supercharged Sparks-Thorne—handled well, had superior brakes and was aerodynamically clean. Its weak point was a stroke 5 inches long that created an unacceptably high piston speed.

Any number of teams tried to win the 500 with a Maserati 8CTF; only one succeeded. Why? Because not only did they have a Maserati, they had experienced Indy car builder Cotton Henning as crew chief, brilliant Indianapolis winner and development driver Wilbur Shaw as driver and wealthy Mike Boyle as financier. Boyle didn't just buy a Maserati. He had Maserati build him a special 8CTF just for the Speedway, along with a container of spare parts. The team did have one speed secret, though. Other Maserati racers used the 6500 rpm redline specified by Maserati, and the pounding of the long connecting rods quickly destroyed the crankshaft bearings. The engines blew up with depressing regularity.

Henning's secret was that he geared Shaw's Maserati for 6000 rpm, tops. At that speed, the engine would run all day. It gave Shaw a little less acceleration off the corners, but the Maserati was still fast enough to win back-to-back 500s and come *this* close to winning three in a row. Boyle-Henning-Shaw-Maserati was by far the most successful team of 1939-1941.

(below) Rex Mays was a "racer's racer." He won the AAA National Championship in 1940 and '41 and finished second at Indianapolis both years, too. He was a demon on the dirt tracks and usually led the 500 (four times from the pole) before his over-extended car inevitably broke. He died in a racing accident at Del Mar in 1949, just two years after he had saved the life of racer Duke Dinsmore at Milwaukee by deliberately crashing his own car to avoid Dinsmore who'd been thrown out on the track.

THE CALIFORNIANS

Most observers, then and now, concentrate on the Boyle Maserati as the most important car in this era. But it was only one car. The rest of the Indianapolis field—and the rest of AAA racing—was dominated by the classic dirt track cars. These were simple, lightweight, robust racers with a rigid axle on leaf springs front and rear, narrow aluminum bodywork, knock-off wire wheels, Firestone tires, hydraulic drum brakes...and a 270 cubic inch Offy four-cylinder under the hood. You could buy an Offy for only $2500 and build a car for another $2500. That was a fraction of what Boyle's Maserati had cost. Plus—and it was a big plus—anybody could fix an Offy.

Faces Behind the Scenes, 1939: (above) Nurses from local hospitals staffed the Speedway Infirmary. (right) Bear alignment crew had to check every car before it was allowed on the track.

More Faces Behind the Scenes: (above left) Brinks guards deliver the valuable Borg-Warner Trophy, 1937. (above) Fan from Kentucky with early model RV was first-in-line spectator for the 1940 Memorial Day Classic. (below) Rainy day checkers in Harry McQuinn's Gasoline Alley garage, 1941. They're using the checker flag, oranges and a packing crate. (left) Lou Moore's Noc-Out Special won the 500 in 1941.

1941

Winner: Floyd Davis-Mauri Rose, Wetteroth/Offy, 115.117 mph
Winner's Purse: $29,200
Total Purse: $90,925
Pace Car: A.B. Couture, Chrysler Newport

Wilbur Shaw's Maserati once again dominated the race until a defective wheel put him into the wall on lap 152. Back in the pack, car owner Lou Moore replaced Floyd Davis with Mauri Rose—whose Maserati had also broken—and Rose carried the Noc-Out Hose Clamp Special to victory.

Number	Driver	Sponsor/Team	Engine Type/Displacement	Chassis	Qualifying	Start/Finish	Laps
16	F. Davis-M. Rose	Noc-Out Hose Clamp/Moore	Offy I-4/270 cu.in.	Wetteroth	121.106	17/1	200
1	Rex Mays	Bowes Seal Fast	Winfield I-8/180 cu.in.	Stevens	128.301	2/2	200
4	Ted Horn	T.E.C./Art Sparks	Sparks I-6/181 cu.in.	Adams	124.297	28/3	200
54	Ralph Hepburn	Bowes Seal Fast	Novi V-8/180 cu.in.	Miller-Ford	120.653	10/4	200
34	Cliff Bergere	Noc-Out Hose Clamp/Bergere	Offy I-4/270 cu.in.	Wetteroth	123.890	7/5	200
41	Chet Miller	Boyle Racing Headquarters	Miller I-8/268 cu.in.	Miller	121.540	9/6	200
15	Harry McQuinn	Ziffrin/Bill White	Alfa Romeo I-8/181 cu.in.	A.R.-Weil	125.449	4/7	200
7	Frank Wearne	Bill Holabird/Arthur M. Sims	Offy I-4/255 cu.in.	Shaw	123.890	6/8	200
45	Paul Russo	Leader Card/Carl Marchese	Miller I-8/137 cu.in.	Marchese	125.217	18/9	200
27	Tommy Hinnershitz	Joe Marks	Offy I-4/270 cu.in.	Adams	121.021	20/10	200
53	Louis Tomei	H-3/Hughes Brothers	Offy I-4/255 cu.in.	Miller-Ford	121.074	24/11	200
55	Al Putnam	Schoof/Val Johnson	Offy I-4/255 cu.in.	Wetteroth	121.951	31/12	200
26	Overton Phillips	Overton A. Phillips	Miller I-8/269 cu.in.	Bugatti	116.298	26/13	187
25	Joie Chitwood	Blue Crown/Joe Lencki	Lencki I-6/265 cu.in.	Lencki	120.329	27/14	177
17	Duke Nalon	Elgin Piston Pin	Maserati V-8/183 cu.in.	Maserati	122.951	30/15	173
14	George Connor	Boyle Racing Headquarters	Offy I-4/257 cu.in.	Stevens	123.984	13/16	167
47	Everett Saylor	Mark E. Bowles	Offy I-4/255 cu.in.	Weil	119.860	12/17	155
2	Wilbur Shaw	Boyle Racing Headquarters	Maserati V-8/179 cu.in.	Maserati	127.836	3/18	151
23	Billy DeVore	Hollywood Candy/Fred Surber	Offy I-4/272 cu.in.	Stevens	121.770	8/19	121
62	Tony Willman	George Lyons	Offy I-4/260 cu.in.	Stevens	123.920	25/20	117
42	Russ Snowberger	Hussey's Sportsman/Snowberger	Offy I-4/255 cu.in.	Snowberger	120.104	11/21	107
32	Deacon Litz	Sampson Motors	Sampson V-16/183 cu.in.	Stevens	123.440	29/22	89
8	Frank Brisko	Zollner Piston/Frank Brisko	Brisko I-6/271 cu.in.	Stevens	123.381	22/23	70
36	Doc Williams	Indiana Fur/Aero Marine	Offy I-4/255 cu.in.	Cooper	124.014	5/24	68
10	George Robson	Gilmore Red Lion/Leon Duray	Duray I-4/182 cu.in.	Weil	121.576	16/25	66
3	Mauri Rose	Elgin Piston Pin/Lou Moore	Maserati I-8/183 cu.in.	Maserati	128.691	1/26	60
22	Kelly Petillo	Air Lines Sandwich Shop/Petillo	Offy I-4/270 cu.in.	Wetteroth	124.417	19/27	48
12	Al Miller	Miller/Eddie Offutt	Miller I-6/180 cu.in.	Miller	123.478	14/28	22
9	Mel Hansen	Lou Fageol	Offy I-4/270 cu.in.	Miller-Ford	124.599	21/29	11
19	Emil Andres	Kennedy Tank/Joe Lencki	Lencki I-6/265 cu.in.	Lencki	122.266	15/30	5
5	Joel Thorne	Thorne Engineering/Joel Thorne	Sparks I-6/271 cu.in.	Adams	121.163	23/31	5
35	George Barringer	Miller/Eddie Offutt	Miller I-6/180 cu.in.	Miller	122.299	DNS	DNS
28	Sam Hanks	Tom Joyce 7-Up/Ed Walsh	Offy I-4/270 cu.in.	Kurtis	118.211	DNS	DNS

Despite the opening up of the AAA to foreign competitors and Wilbur Shaw's success with the Maserati, Indianapolis racing remained the property of Americans, specifically the ones from Southern California. All of the engines and many of the chassis came from the L.A. area. And the hottest drivers in the country were ones who'd honed their skills on West Coast dirt tracks, battling wheel-to-wheel sideways in the dirt, every Wednesday and Friday night. They brought their overheated aggression and their tough little cars to Indiana, and simply drove away from everyone else. There's nothing fancy about the Noc-Out Special that won the last 500 before the war, but it is the quintessential Offy-powered car of its time. It may not be very sophisticated, but it sure does get the job done.

THE ODDBALL ERA 1946-1952

The urge to go racing seems to be unquenchable. Sometimes, unbelievably so. World War II ended in Europe in May of 1945. The continent was a shambles, the very fabric of society was ripped asunder. Yet the first organized motor race was held only four months later, September 9, 1945, over the park roads of the Bois de Boulogne in Paris. A huge crowd watched a mixed bag of prewar racing and sports cars boom around the closed-off streets. The Bois de Boulogne race was a symbol, an important symbol of normalcy to a world in which the unthinkable had become all too real. It was not so much a race as a celebration that World War II was truly over.

By the spring of 1946, there were races all over Europe, including Grands Prix. These were conducted on improvised street circuits in *centre ville* Nice, Marseilles, Geneva, Milan, Torino, Paris. Because of the tight courses, lack of fuel, lack of new cars and other postwar shortages, races were run to the prewar *voiturette* formula for 1.5-liter cars, super-

(below) The Speedway was totally neglected during World War II. This is what the front straight looked like when Tony Hulman bought the sad old place in 1945. (bottom) Mel Hansen's Kurtis/Miller finished eleventh in 1946. It's typical of the cars of the immediate postwar period.

1946

Winner: George Robson, Adams/Sparks, 114.820 mph
Winner's Purse: $42,350
Total Purse: $115,450
Pace Car: Henry Ford II, Lincoln Continental Cabriolet

Only nine tired cars were still running after 500 miles, mostly due to the postwar shortage of parts to get them properly prepared. George Robson outlasted rookie Jimmy Jackson to finally give wealthy car owner/driver Joel Thorne an Indianapolis victory after a decade of trying.

Number	Driver	Sponsor/Team	Engine Type/Displacement	Chassis	Qualifying	Start/Finish	Laps
16	George Robson	Thorne Engineering	Sparks I-6/183 cu.in.	Adams	125.541	15/1	200
61	Jimmy Jackson	Jimmy Jackson	Offy I-4/255 cu.in.	Miller	120.257	5/2	200
29	Ted Horn	Boyle Maserati/Boyle Racing	Maserati I-8/179 cu.in.	Maserati	123.980	7/3	200
18	Emil Andres	Elgin Piston Pin/Frank Brisko	Maserati I-8/183 cu.in.	Maserati	121.139	11/4	200
24	Joie Chitwood	Noc-Out Hose Clamp/Peters	Offy I-4/270 cu.in.	Wetteroth	119.816	12/5	200
33	Louis Durant	Alfa Romeo/Milt Marion	Alfa Romeo I-8/182 cu.in.	Alfa Romeo	118.973	6/6	200
52	Gigi Villoresi	Maserati/Corvorado Filippini	Maserati I-8/181 cu.in.	Maserati	121.249	28/7	200
7	Frank Wearne	Wolfe Motors/Ervin Wolfe	Offy I-4/271 cu.in.	Shaw	121.233	29/8	197
39	Bill Sheffler	Jack Maurer/Bill Sheffler	Offy I-4/255 cu.in.	Bromme	120.611	25/9	139
17	Billy DeVore	William Schoof	Offy I-4/255 cu.in.	Wetteroth	119.876	31/10	167
41	Mel Hansen	Offenhauser/Ross Page	Duray I-4/183 cu.in.	Kurtis	121.431	27/11	143
25	Russ Snowberger	Jim Hussey's/R.A. Cott	Maserati I-8/183 cu.in.	Maserati	121.593	10/12	134
14	Harry McQuinn	Mobilgas/Robert Flavell	Sparks I-6/183 cu.in.	Adams	124.499	18/13	124
2	Ralph Hepburn	Novi Governor/W.C. Winfield	Novi V-8/180 cu.in.	Kurtis	133.944	19/14	121
12	Al Putnam	L.G.S. Spring Clutch/Kuehn	Offy I-4/255 cu.in.	Stevens	116.283	13/15	120
3	Cliff Bergere	Noc-Out Clamp/S. Bergere	Offy I-4/270 cu.in.	Wetteroth	126.471	1/16	82
45	Duke Dinsmore	Fred W. Johnston	Offy I-4/255 cu.in.	Adams	123.279	8/17	82
5	Chet Miller	Chet Miller	Offy I-4/255 cu.in.	Cooper	124.649	17/18	64
63	Jimmy Wilburn	Mobiloil/Bill White	Alfa Romeo I-8/181 cu.in.	A.R.-Weil	125.113	16/19	52
42	Tony Bettenhausen	Bristow-McManus	Miller I-8/183 cu.in.	Wetteroth	123.094	26/20	47
59	Danny Kladis	Grancor V8	Ford V-8/274 cu.in.	Miller-Ford	118.890	33/21	46
54	Duke Nalon	Maserati/Corvorado Filippini	Maserati I-4/91 cu.in.	Maserati	119.682	32/22	45
8	Mauri Rose	Blue Crown/Joe Lencki	Lencki I-6/265 cu.in.	Lencki	124.065	9/23	40
38	George Connor	Walsh Offenhauser/Ed Walsh	Offy I-4/270 cu.in.	Kurtis	120.006	30/24	38
48	Hal Robson	Phillips Miller/Overton Phillips	Miller I-8/269 cu.in.	Bugatti	121.466	23/25	37
15	Louis Tomei	Boxar Tool/Joseph Hosso	Brisko I-6/271 cu.in.	Stevens	119.193	22/26	34
31	Henry Banks	Automobile Shippers/Rassey	Offy I-4/255 cu.in.	Snowberger	120.220	21/27	32
64	Shorty Cantlon	H-3/Charles Hughes	Offy I-4/255 cu.in.	Miller-Ford	122.432	20/28	28
26	George Barringer	Tucker Torpedo/Barringer	Miller I-6/180 cu.in.	Miller	120.628	24/29	27
1	Rex Mays	Bowes Seal Fast	Winfield I-8/180 cu.in.	Stevens	128.861	14/30	26
32	Sam Hanks	Spike Jones/Schroeder	Sampson V-16/183 cu.in.	Stevens	124.762	3/31	18
47	Hal Cole	Don Lee	Alfa Romeo I-8/177 cu.in.	Alfa Romeo	120.728	4/32	16
10	Paul Russo	Fageol Twin Coach	Two Offy I-4/180 cu.in.	Fageol	126.183	2/33	16

charged. There were many more of these machines available, and, to be honest, few citizens of Europe wanted to be reminded of the prewar domination of Grands Prix by the Nazi-backed Silver Arrows. *Voiturette* racing was much safer all around.

FORMULA ONE

During 1946, the French reorganized the AIACR as the *Federation Internationale de l'Automobile*. The FIA remains the governing body of international racing, even today. The FIA promptly rewrote new rules for Grand Prix racing. Not surprisingly, they outlawed supercharged 3.0-liter cars in favor of supercharged 1.5-liter

voiturettes, or unsupercharged 4.5-liter machines with a minimum weight of 700 kg (1540 lbs.). For the first time, the premier series was officially named Formula One. There was also a Formula Two for 2.0-liter unsupercharged cars and a Formula Three for 500cc machines.

Surely by coincidence, Maserati, Alfa and Ferrari made the only supercharged 1.5-liter cars available, Talbot the only 4.5-liter Formula One machine. The German Silver Arrows were effectively cut out of Grand Prix racing. Most of the others might just as well have stayed home, too. Under the new Formula One, every car except the famous supercharged 1.5-liter Alfa Romeo 158/159 was outclassed. In Grands Prix between 1947 and 1951, the 158/159—nicknamed *Alfetta* or "little Alfa"—was hardly ever beaten.

OPENING UP AMERICAN RACING

In America, the AAA ran its first postwar race at a hastily prepared Indianapolis Motor Speedway in May, 1946. The competitors were a bunch of prewar cars dragged out of barns from New York to California. The AAA Contest Board had very different problems from Grand Prix organizers. Instead of relatively well-financed or even government-backed factory teams, the AAA was dealing with small private teams, most of whom were dependent on racing for their livelihood and were living from purse to purse. Instead of racing on closed-off city streets, American promoters still clung to their dirt ovals. And, thanks to Wilbur Shaw and Tony Hulman, we still had the Indianapolis Motor Speedway, too.

But the whole structure of American racing was unlike racing in Europe. Among other things, it was much more competitive, in the sense that literally dozens of drivers were running similar cars and engines. Theoretically, everyone had the same chance to win. In Europe, unless you were one of the Alfa Romeo factory drivers, there was no way you could win a Grand Prix.

So in 1947, when the FIA changed to the new Formula One, the AAA kept to the prewar rules for 3.0-liter supercharged or 4.5-liter unsupercharged cars. The only change the AAA made was to drop the prewar minimum weight of 1850 lbs. in favor of no

Ted Horn has the best finishing record of any driver who ever raced at Indianapolis. In nine races between 1936 and '48, he completed 1799 out of 1800 possible laps (he was a lap behind winner Wilbur Shaw in 1940) and finished second once, third four times and fourth four times.

(left) Just before the start of the first postwar 500 in 1946. The tired Gulf-Miller is already blowing oil smoke.
(below) George Robson's old Thorne takes the checker flag in 1946, just 34 seconds ahead of Jimmy Jackson's even older Miller/ Offy.

TONY

In 1945, when Wilbur Shaw went looking for someone with sufficient financial depth to buy the Indianapolis Motor Speedway from Eddie Rickenbacker, he didn't have much time, and he didn't have much to show. Shaw himself was a racing driver, not a track manager, and the Speedway itself, after four years of total neglect, was a mess. What Shaw needed was a buyer who was not only wealthy but astute enough to look beyond the weeds, the broken asphalt and the peeling paint to imagine what the Speedway could be.

The man Shaw found was Anton Hulman, Jr., the grandson of Herman Hulman, who'd started a wholesale distribution company in nearby Terre Haute, Indiana, back in the nineteenth century. With Hulman and Company as his nucleus, Tony Hulman had diversified into breweries, refineries and real estate, among many other holdings. He had become the owner of a highly successful conglomerate by 1945. Young Tony had been an outstanding athlete in both prep school and at Yale. He was a star in half-a-dozen track events—he had seven varsity letters—as well as a member of the undefeated 1923 Yale football team. But he had no more than a normal interest in motor racing, and only the average Hoosier's once-a-year interest in the 500.

Nevertheless, Tony Hulman paid Eddie Rickenbacker $700,000—a lot of money in 1945—to buy a weed-choked oval on the west side of Indianapolis. He had two good reasons. Reason One, he was from Indiana, his family was from Indiana, they had made their fortune in Indiana, and he felt that the world-renowned Indianapolis 500 should continue.

Reason Two, Hulman could see that properly fixed up and promoted, the Indianapolis Motor Speedway could be a highly profitable business. Both Carl Fisher and Eddie Rickenbacker had run the Speedway as more of a hobby than a livelihood. Tony got hooked on racing, but he was also a businessman.

From 1945 to 1954, Wilbur Shaw was president of the Speedway, spending millions of dollars of the Hulman family's money to resurrect it. When Shaw was killed in a plane crash, Tony Hulman took over as President—with Sam Hanks as his director of racing—and brought the Speedway to unexpected heights. Not only did he completely rebuild and modernize the old Brickyard, but he gave the 500 the highest-paying purse in sports. The Indianapolis 500 remained the most important motor race in the world.

When the AAA decided to retire from racing in 1955 to concentrate on its auto club functions, it was Tony Hulman who got the major American racing people together and founded the United States Auto Club to sanction not only the Indianapolis 500, but the annual National Championship and racing on all levels. In the Fifties and Sixties, USAC ran sprint cars, midgets, stock cars...even sports car road races. But it was the Indianapolis 500 that was always the jewel in USAC's crown. And Tony Hulman who was responsible for the success of both for over thirty years, until his death in October, 1977.

When he bought the Speedway in 1945—no doubt figuring that he could always sell the real estate for development if the racing thing didn't work out—American racing was still moribund from the war. When he said, "Gentlemen, start your engines!" for the last time in 1977, motor racing was the most popular spectator sport in the country, not to mention a multi-billion dollar business. Anton Hulman, Jr., had a lot to do with that. ■

(left above) Anton Hulman, Jr., in 1960 with his grandson Tony Hulman George, now president of the IMS Corporation.
(above) Speedway paperweights were given as mementos by Tony Hulman to special friends and VIPs.
(left) Tony Hulman, on the left, and Wilbur Shaw, on the right, help Loretta Young leave her hand and foot prints in cement before the 500 of 1951.

1947

Winner: Mauri Rose, Deidt/Offy, 116.338 mph
Winner's Purse: $33,425
Total Purse: $137,425
Pace Car: George W. Mason, Nash Ambassador

Lou Moore's famous Blue Crown Specials started their years of domination, with Mauri Rose beating Bill Holland. Rookie Holland had led most of the way, then obediently slowed when Moore held out the "EZ" sign. Instead of slowing, Rose speeded up to zip past Holland.

Number	Driver	Sponsor/Team	Engine Type/Displacement	Chassis	Qualifying	Start/ Finish	Laps
27	Mauri Rose	Blue Crown Spark Plug/Moore	Offy I-4/270 cu.in.	Deidt	120.040	3/1	200
16	Bill Holland	Blue Crown Spark Plug/Moore	Offy I-4/270 cu.in.	Deidt	128.756	8/2	200
1	Ted Horn	Bennett/H.C. Henning	Maserati I-8/179 cu.in.	Maserati	126.564	1/3	200
54	Herb Ardinger	Novi Governor Mobil/Winfield	Novi V-8/180 cu.in.	Kurtis	120.733	4/4	200
7	Jimmy Jackson	Jim Hussey/H.C. Henning	Offy I-4/258 cu.in.	Miller	122.266	10/5	200
9	Rex Mays	Bowes Seal Fast/Bowes Racing	Winfield I-8/180 cu.in.	Kurtis	124.412	20/6	200
33	Walt Brown	Permafuse/Milt Marion	Alfa Romeo I-8/182 cu.in.	Alfa Romeo	118.355	14/7	200
34	Cy Marshall	Tattersfield/Bill White	Alfa Romeo I-8/183 cu.in.	Weil	115.644	28/8	197
41	Fred Agabashian	Ross Page Offenhauser/Page	Duray I-8/183 cu.in.	Kurtis	121.478	23/9	191
10	Duke Dinsmore	Bill Schoof	Offy I-4/270 cu.in.	Wetteroth	119.840	27/10	167
58	Les Anderson	Kennedy Tank/Les Anderson	Offy I-4/270 cu.in.	Maserati	118.425	7/11	131
59	Pete Romcevich	Camco Motors Ford/Granatelli	Ford V-8/256 cu.in.	Miller-Ford	117.218	17/12	168
3	Emil Andres	Preston Tucker Parner/Lencki	Lencki I-6/265 cu.in.	Lencki	116.781	30/13	150
31	Frank Wearne	Superior Industries/Rassey	Offy I-4/263 cu.in.	Miller	117.716	15/14	128
47	Ken Fowler	Don Lee Alfa Romeo	Alfa Romeo I-8/177 cu.in.	Alfa Romeo	123.423	9/15	121
46	Duke Nalon	Don Lee Mercedes	Mercedes V-12/183 cu.in.	Mercedes	128.082	18/16	119
28	Roland Free	Bristow-McManus	Miller I-8/183 cu.in.	Wetteroth	119.526	12/17	87
29	Tony Bettenhausen	Murrell Belanger	Offy I-4/255 cu.in.	Stevens	120.980	25/18	79
25	Russ Snowberger	Federal Engineering/R.A. Cott	Maserati I-8/183 cu.in.	Maserati	121.331	6/19	74
52	Hal Robson	Richard Palmer	Offy I-4/255 cu.in.	Adams	122.096	16/20	67
18	Cliff Bergere	Novi Governor Mobil/Winfield	Novi V-8/180 cu.in.	Kurtis	124.957	2/21	62
8	Joie Chitwood	Fred Peters	Offy I-4/270 cu.in.	Wetteroth	123.157	22/22	51
24	Shorty Cantlon	Automobile Shippers/Rassey	Miller V-16/272 cu.in.	Snowberger	121.462	5/23	40
43	Henry Banks	Federal Engineering/Henning	Offy I-4/255 cu.in.	Miller-Ford	120.923	26/24	36
66	Al Miller	Preston Tucker/Clay Ballinger	Miller I-6/180 cu.in.	Miller	124.848	19/25	33
14	George Connor	Ed Walsh	Offy I-4/255 cu.in.	Kurtis	124.874	13/26	32
38	Mel Hansen	Flavell-Duffy	Sparks I-6/183 cu.in.	Adams	117.298	29/27	32
15	Paul Russo	Wolfe Motors, Tulsa	Offy I-4/271 cu.in.	Shaw	123.967	21/28	24
44	Charles Van Acker	Preston Tucker/Lencki	Lencki I-4/265 cu.in.	Stevens	121.049	24/29	24
53	Milt Fankhouser	Jack Maurer's Club/Fankhouser	Offy I-4/272 cu.in.	Stevens	119.932	11/30	16

weight restriction at all. The idea was to let inexpensive and abundant dirt track cars—most of which weighed less than 1700 lbs.—compete at Indianapolis.

The new rules worked a treat. They allowed bucks-down racers to run their old cars while encouraging bucks-up racers to explore the limits of technology, common sense and their wallets. No other era in Speedway history produced so many wild and crazy ideas.

THE INFLUENCE OF WORLD WAR II

Most of these crazy ideas were because of World War II. Some historians credit the U.S. automobile industry with winning the war...they were the ones who churned out Jeeps, tanks, guns, planes and ships faster than any other factories in

history. But the big passenger car companies relied on small outside suppliers for many of their designs, tools, patterns and machine work. Familiar racing names like Offenhauser Engineering and Thorne Engineering were major government contractors, just as the Duesenbergs and Harry Miller had been a generation earlier. Many of the new machine tools that built race cars for the Indianapolis 500 had originally been purchased in order to create tail skids for fighter planes or cooling jackets for machine guns.

The war spurred development in many areas, particularly in aviation. And a surprising number of aircraft innovations were applicable to racing cars. Things that modern motorists take for granted—high-octane gasoline, fuel-injection, disc brakes, hydraulic shock absorbers, cast alloy wheels, radial tires, tubular space frames, monocoque construction, turbochargers, intercoolers, the use of exotic metals like titanium—were either invented or proven on World War II aircraft. The war was a hot-bed of technological development that brought specific improvements, many of which were immediately adapted to Indianapolis cars.

But, more than hardware, the war gave a lot of Americans the feeling that anything was possible. All you had to do was work hard, be brave and not give up, and you would eventually win against overwhelming odds. In the Thirties, many people in this country still felt an inferiority complex when faced with the apparent sophistication of Europeans. The war made us the equals, if not the superiors, of any other country on earth. World War II gave Americans self-confidence.

The war had another curious effect on racing, too. Compared to night bombing runs over Berlin or carrier-based attacks in the Battle of Midway, civilian life could

(above) The 500, 1947: Ted Horn's pole-sitting Maserati #1 is the same car that took Wilbur Shaw to victory in 1939 and '40, Horn to third in 1946. He's being out-dragged by Mauri Rose's Blue Crown Special #27 and second-place starter Cliff Bergere's Novi #18. Five hours later, Horn finished third, with Bergere back in the pack. Rose won.
(below) The 500, 1946: Mauri Rose crashed the Lencki #8 next to where Paul Russo had already crashed his Fageol #10. Ralph Hepburn cruises past in the Novi #2.

BLUE CROWN SPECIAL

Lou Moore was the son of an Oklahoma builder who moved to Pomona, California, and bought an orange grove. A freeze the first winter busted him, and the family was left with nothing. Lou was out working as a machinist's helper when he was sixteen; he was a full-time racing driver when he was twenty. He never forgot the two bitter lessons he'd learned as a kid, he said. "Stick to what you know, and work like hell at it."

Moore worked so hard at racing he got a ride in the Indianapolis 500 in 1928. He was second behind Louie Meyer. He later collected a pair of thirds at there, as well, and started from the pole in 1932.

In 1937, he retired as a driver and started building his own racing cars. Floyd Roberts won in Moore's car in 1938, Mauri Rose and Floyd Davis shared Moore's winning car in 1941. These were both very straightforward Wetteroth chassis with Offy engines upon which Moore lavished time—he had no money—and meticulous attention to detail.

In August of 1946, Moore cut a sponsorship deal with the Blue Crown Spark Plug Company. It was enough so that by mortgaging his house as well, Moore could assemble the funds to build two completely new cars for the Indianapolis 500. Each one cost over $30,000, at a time when even the best race car could be bought for less than $10,000 (a new Ford sedan cost only $1185 in 1946; you could buy a Cadillac for $1920).

Remember Moore's motto: "Stick to what you know, work like hell." He started planning his new car in 1942. He hired Leo Goossen to design the front-wheel drive transaxle in 1943. By 1946, Moore had the whole thing planned out, right down to knowing he wanted a two-car team, what speeds they would each run and who would win. He even knew what kind of gasoline he'd buy.

Gas was the key to Moore's plan. World War II brought 115/145 aviation gas, with an octane rating of 110. This was equivalent to alcohol-based dope, and allowed Moore to use an Offy engine with a super-high 13.2:1 compression ratio. A 270 cubic inch Offy would reliably produce 270 hp at 5000 rpm on this Avgas. At Indianapolis, Moore's cars returned 12 mpg at racing speed, and could go 500 miles with only one pit stop. Racers using dope had to carry more fuel on board—which slowed them down—plus make two or three pit stops instead of one.

The rest of Moore's car was planned to be as lightweight and simple as possible. Like the Miller 91 of the Twenties, the front-drive Blue Crown allowed the driver to sit on the floor,

(above) The 500 grid, 1948: Lou Moore watches with folded arms while last-minute checks are made to Mauri Rose's car, which will eventually win. Rose's young teammate, Bill Holland, is the fellow with goggles around his neck. He'll be second. You can see that the cigar-shaped Blue Crown Special is literally knee-high to a mechanic and beautifully finished. With about 270 hp from a normally-aspirated 4.5-liter Offy, the cars could lap Indy at 130 mph and hit 160 mph on the back straight, 120 mph through the corners.

since there was no driveshaft. That was good for both weight distribution and aerodynamics. The chassis was stiff for good handling, the brakes were inboard to reduce unsprung weight, the bodywork was extremely low and smooth—only the driver's headrest was taller than the tires. Best of all, the Blue Crown weighed only 1650 lbs. dry, less than most dirt cars that weren't nearly as fast, durable or sophisticated. The Blue Crown looked *right*, both in blueprints and in real life, and that's usually a good test of a racing car. If it *looks* right, it *is* right.

Moore's drivers, Mauri Rose and Bill Holland, started third and eighth in 1947, drove conservatively according to plan and finished first and second. Holland led most of the way, but Rose passed him near the end for the win. Holland was mad, but Moore was happy he'd kept them from racing each other. In 1948, they started on the front row, and finished one-two again.

For 1949, Moore added a third car for George Connor, a conventional rear-drive Lesovsky/Offy. Holland and Connor drove to team orders and finished first and third, Rose was running in second, but disobeyed Moore and tried to challenge for the lead. His overstressed car broke, and he retired with only eight laps to go. Moore fired him on the spot.

In 1950, Moore added a fourth car, another rear-drive racer for Lee Wallard. Tony Bettenhausen's original Blue Crown broke early, but Holland, Connor and Wallard were moving cautiously through the field according to plan when the race was stopped at 138 laps because of rain. They were in second, sixth and eighth with no chance to move up. The one thing Moore hadn't calculated was that the Indianapolis 500 might be the Indianapolis 345.

He sold his team after that. With Mobil sponsorship, Duane Carter and Tony Bettenhausen finished eighth and ninth in the Blue Crown Specials in 1951, then Bettenhausen brought the last one to race into twenty-fourth in 1952. By then, Lou Moore had literally retired on his Indianapolis winnings. His idea of retirement was to become a NASCAR car owner and spend all his time at the races. He died of a heart attack while attending a NASCAR event. Right up to the end, Lou Moore stuck with what he knew. ■

(opposite page, bottom) Mauri Rose was a short, pipe-smoking engineer who'd be the last person at a party you'd pick as a racing driver. Appearances are deceiving. During his twenty-four-year career, he won the AAA National Championship in 1936 and Indy three times. He also invented the first prosthetic to allow an amputee to drive a car. (above) The 500 front row in 1947; Mauri Rose and his Blue Crown, Cliff Bergere and his Novi, Ted Horn and his Maserati. (left) 1949 winner Bill Holland receiving tires and gas during his single pit stop. Note the total absence of safety gear for the driver—he's wearing a T-shirt with the sleeves rolled up—or the fuel man—he's not even wearing gloves. (bottom) It's not as though safety gear wasn't needed. Minutes before that pit stop, Holland had driven his Blue Crown past the burning Novi of Duke Nalon, who was seriously injured.

1948

Winner Mauri Rose,
Deidt/Offy, 119.814 mph
Winner's Purse: $42,800
Total Purse: $171,075
Pace Car: Wilbur Shaw,
Chevrolet Stylemaster

Duke Nalon gave the Novi V-8 its best drive ever, dueling for the lead with Mauri Rose until a refueling mishap forced an extra pit stop. Rose and team-mate Bill Holland then finished 1-2 for the second straight year in Lou Moore's blue metallic front-wheel drive cars, with the Novi right behind.

Number	Driver	Sponsor/Team	Engine Type/Displacement	Chassis	Qualifying	Start/ Finish	Laps
3	Mauri Rose	Blue Crown Spark Plug/Moore	Offy I-4/270 cu.in.	Deidt	129.129	3/1	200
2	Bill Holland	Blue Crown Spark Plug/Moore	Offy I-4/270 cu.in.	Deidt	129.515	2/2	200
54	Duke Nalon	Novi Grooved Piston/Winfield	Novi V-8/180 cu.in.	Kurtis	131.603	11/3	200
1	Ted Horn	Bennett/H.C. Henning	Maserati I-8/179 cu.in.	Maserati	126.565	5/4	200
35	Mack Hellings	Don Lee Division	Offy I-4/270 cu.in.	KK2000	127.968	21/5	200
63	Hal Cole	City of Tacoma/Hal Cole	Offy I-4/247 cu.in.	KK2000	124.391	14/6	200
91	Lee Wallard	John Iddings	Offy I-4/233 cu.in.	Meyer	128.420	28/7	200
33	Johnny Mauro	Mauro/Alfa Romeo	Alfa Romeo I-8/182 cu.in.	Alfa Romeo	121.790	27/8	198
7	Tommy Hinnershitz	Kurtis-Kraft	Offy I-4/270 cu.in.	Kurtis	125.122	23/9	198
61	Jimmy Jackson	Howard Keck	Offy I-4/270 cu.in.	Deidt	127.510	4/10	193
4	Charles Van Acker	South Bend/Walter Redmer	Offy I-4/270 cu.in.	Stevens	125.440	12/11	192
19	Billy DeVore	Pat Clancy	Offy I-4/270 cu.in.	Kurtis	123.967	20/12	190
98	Johnny Mantz	Agajanian/Smith & Jones	Offy I-4/270 cu.in.	KK2000	122.791	8/13	185
6	Tony Bettenhausen	Belanger Motors	Offy I-4/270 cu.in.	Stevens	126.396	22/14	167
64	Hal Robson	Palmer Construction Racing	Offy I-4/247 cu.in.	Adams	122.796	18/15	164
36	Bill Cantrell	Fageol Twin Coach	Fageol I-6/273 cu.in.	Stevens	123.733	7/16	161
55	Joie Chitwood	Ted Nyquist	Offy I-4/268 cu.in.	Shaw	124.619	10/17	138
53	Bill Sheffler	Sheffler Offy	Offy I-4/270 cu.in.	Bromme	124.529	24/18	132
5	Rex Mays	Bowes Seal Fast Racing	Winfield I-8/180 cu.in.	Kurtis	130.577	1/19	129
31	Chet Miller	Don Lee/Mercedes	Mercedes V-12/183 cu.in.	Mercedes	127.249	19/20	108
52	Jack McGrath	Sheffler/Offenhauser	Offy I-4/255 cu.in.	Bromme	124.580	13/21	70
16	Duane Carter	Belanger Motors	Offy I-4/270 cu.in.	Wetteroth	126.015	29/22	59
26	Fred Agabashian	Ross Page/Offenhauser	Duray I-4/183 cu.in.	Kurtis	122.737	32/23	58
34	Les Anderson	Kennedy Tank/Les Anderson	Offy I-4/270 cu.in.	Kurtis	122.337	9/24	58
17	Mel Hansen	Schafer Gear Works/Weirick	Sparks I-4/177 cu.in.	Adams	122.117	33/25	42
76	Sam Hanks	Robert Flavell	Sparks I-6/181 cu.in.	Adams	124.266	15/26	34
51	Spider Webb	Fowle Brothers/Louis Bromme	Offy I-4/270 cu.in.	Bromme	125.545	30/27	27
9	George Connor	Bennett Brothers/H.C. Henning	Miller I-8/268 cu.in.	Stevens	123.018	17/28	24
74	Doc Williams	Clarke Motors/Ford Moyer	Offy I-4/255 cu.in.	Cooper	124.151	6/29	19
86	Mike Salay	Terman Marine Supply/Lorenz	Offy I-4/255 cu.in.	Wetteroth	123.393	31/30	13
8	Emil Andres	Tuffy's Offy/George Tuffanelli	Offy I-4/270 cu.in.	KK2000	123.550	16/31	11
25	Paul Russo	Federal Engineering/R.A. Cott	Maserati I-8/179 cu.in.	Maserati	122.595	25/32	7
65	Harry McQuinn	Frank Lynch Motors/Brisko	Maserati I-8/183 cu.in.	Maserati	122.154	26/33	1

seem pretty prosaic. A significantly large number of racing drivers in this postwar period were combat veterans of World War II. Not only were racers the personality type who'd naturally want to be where the action was, but when the war was over, the adrenalin rush of motor racing was the nearest they could get to the thrills of battle and still be socially acceptable.

Add it all together—pent-up demand, technological advancement, new blood looking for excitement, lots of discretionary money floating around thanks to lucrative defense contracts—and you have a prescription for an absolute boom in Indianapolis car racing. And that, of course, is exactly what happened in the immediate postwar period.

DIFFERENT FOLKS, DIFFERENT STROKES

Five broad categories of cars ran at Indianapolis in the late-Forties. There were old American prewar cars updated in a variety of ways, like the Miller-Ford that the Granatelli Brothers fooled around with, the Thorne cars and even some old Millers that were a decade old or more. None of them were particularly successful, aside from George Robson's Thorne, which outlasted the spotty competition to win in 1946. Most of these cars were capable of about 140 mph on the Speedway straights and 115 mph in the corners, for lap speeds around 125 mph. That was competitive in 1946 and '47, even marginally in 1948. After that, the newer cars simply went too fast for the old-timers to catch.

Then there were European Grand Prix cars, both leftover prewar cars and new postwar cars. The old Boyle Maserati with which Wilbur Shaw had ruled Indy just before the war was third in 1946 and '47, fourth in 1948. That's still pretty competive for a car that was now ten years old. Maserati brought a factory team of supercharged 1.5-liter 4CLs in 1946, and there were still some prewar Alfas available. None of them did much. In 1952, the Ferrari factory sent over a 4.5-liter V-12 Formula One car for Alberto Ascari, but neither looked much like the World Champions they were. The early Maseratis could lap at around 125 mph; the late Ferrari went 134 mph. Neither was competitive in its day.

The most exotic European machine to appear at Indianapolis was a fabulous Mercedes-Benz W-154 Grand Prix car that wealthy Californian Don Lee bought in England in 1947. The W-154 had a Roots-supercharged, double-overhead cam V-12 that produced 485 hp at 7600 rpm, a DeDion independent rear suspension and all sorts of exotic hardware. Duke Nalon qualified second fastest at Indy in 1947, averaging 128.082 mph. Unfortunately, there was never any chance of maintaining such a monster without factory assistance and parts. Lee's expensive Mercedes ran twice at Indianapolis, but didn't finish either time.

There were also all-new, highly-refined front-wheel drive cars during this period. The most successful were the Blue Crown Specials; the most famous were the Novis. These front-wheel drive cars ran away with the Memorial Day Classic for years, yet they left no lasting impression. By 1952, they were obsolete. Still, the supercharged Novi not only made a hell of a racket, it would zoom 170 mph on the straights and about 115 mph through the corners, for an average of 139 mph...the fastest car at Indianapolis during this period. Chet Miller's 139.034 mph in qualifying in 1952 set a benchmark that lasted until 1954 when the Kurtis roadsters took over.

Even more off-beat than the Novis were the various oddball cars that showed up at the Speedway: cars with six wheels, with a rear engine, with *two* engines, with a diesel. The variety was endless. Paul Russo did put the twin-engine Fageol on the 1946 Indianapolis front row before crashing and Freddie Agabashian put the Cummins diesel on the pole in 1952, but those were by far the best performances of any of the one-off oddballs that rolled out of Gasoline Alley garages carrying their builder's hopes and dreams.

Beginning in 1947, Borg-Warner's public relations department arranged for a Hollywood actress to be part of the Victory Lane ceremony. Carole Landis, Barbara Britton, Linda Darnell, Barbara Stanwyck, Loretta Young, Arlene Dahl, Jane Greer, Marie Wilson, Dinah Shore, Virginia Mayo, Cyd Charisse, Shirley MacLaine and Erin O'Brien kissed the winner until in 1959, Rodger Ward accidentally backed Erin O'Brien into a hot exhaust pipe while smooching and spoiled the fun.

Why did the Blue Crowns beat the faster, more powerful Novi in 1948? Well, the Novi only got 4 mpg; the Blue Crown got 12 mpg. To compensate, the Novi carried 110 gallons of exotic fuel. That added weight wore out the tires, so the Novi had to stop one more time. The Blue Crowns carried only 40 gallons of gas. If they'd carried 50 gallons, they could have gone all the way, but they still would have had to stop for tires, which lasted 300 miles.

ODDIES

Many cars were considered "odd" when they first appeared at Indianapolis: the DOHC Peugeot, the supercharged Duesenberg, the front-wheel drive Miller. But once these cars had proven successful, they were copied by everyone else and pretty soon these "revolutionary" oddities were considered normal. These are *not* the cars we're talking about here.

Our topic is the true oddball, the car so weird that even the most free-thinking observer wanders away shaking his head at the extent of human folly. For some reason, more of these cars appeared at Indianapolis between 1946 and 1952 than at any time before or since. It must have been something in the air.

FAGEOL TWIN COACH SPECIAL

Bus manufacturer Lou Fageol had a thing for lost causes. In the Thirties, he bought a couple of Miller-Fords from Ford Motor Company; in the Fifties he built Crosley engines and the Dual-Ghia, as well as a Porsche racing car with two engines, one under the hood to drive the front wheels, one under the trunk to drive the rear wheels.

That Fageol Porsche was just another rethink of the famous Fageol Twin Coach Special that Paul Russo put on the front row of the 1946 500. The Twin Coach had a conventional chassis, but two Offy 91 cubic inch Midget four-cylinders. The one in front drove the front wheels, the one in back drove the back wheels. Four-wheel drive! Each Offy had a Roots-type supercharger for a total of 320 hp. The engines were connected only by the throttle linkage, which could be unclipped so that the car could be driven from either end or both. Russo said it handled fine, no matter, but he crashed heavily after only 16 laps during the race itself, breaking his leg and destroying the car.

In 1948, Fageol returned to Indianapolis with a conventional rear-drive car built by Ed Winfield and powered by a six-cylinder bus engine. This qualified on the third row thanks to 260 hp at 5000 rpm. The SOHC design had three-valves-per-cylinder—one intake, two exhaust—with a separate header pipe for each exhaust valve. From the exhaust side, it looked like an Inline-12.

ROUNDS ROCKET

Frank Kurtis built this immaculate one-off for Nat Rounds. It reportedly cost $40,000 in 1949. The big innovation was putting the Offy 270 behind the driver where it drove the rear wheels through a Novi front-wheel drive transaxle. Suspension was independent all-around, with torsion bars and a DeDion rear axle. In most ways, this was the direct forerunner of the Offy-powered mid-engine cars of the mid-Seventies. Unfortunately, the Rounds Rocket weighed 2100 lbs., some 400 lbs. more than the Offy-powered competition. It failed to qualify in either 1949 or '50.

PAT CLANCY SPECIAL

Memphis trucking magnate Pat Clancy was used to vehicles with lots of wheels, so he saw nothing unusual in having car-builder A.J. Bowen scratch-build a car for the 500 that had three axles and six wheels. The idea was to get more rubber on the road for better traction in the corners. Bowen used two midget axles connected in tandem, for four-wheel drive... all at the back.

The rest of the car looked like a conventional dirt car, with an Offy under the hood. All six knock-off wheels were cast of magnesium, the first "mags" ever to appear at the Indianapolis 500. Driver Billy DeVore had no problems and finished twelfth in 1948. Jackie Holmes dropped out in 1949 with a broken halfshaft. Pat Clancy was right; his six-wheeler *was* faster through the corners. But because of the drag of the extra tires, it was also slower down the straights. Net gain: Zero.

CUMMINS DIESEL SPECIAL

Way back in 1931, the Cummins Engine Company of nearby Columbus, Indiana, put a diesel-powered car into thirteenth in the 500, mostly because it was so economical it never stopped for fuel. They tried again in 1934 and 1950, too, with disappointing results. So for 1952, Cummins had Frank Kurtis build the first "lay-down" roadster with the engine on its side and the driveshaft running next to, rather than under, the driver's seat. The supercharged, 401 cubic inch (6.6-liter) diesel set a track record of 138.010 mph in the hands of Freddie Agabashian. Starting from the pole, Agabashian had to stop early for tires, but had come back up to fifth place when his turbocharger inlet clogged from debris on the track and he coasted to a stop. Nowadays, Cummins' "$500,000 racing laboratory" appears occasionally on loan at the Indianapolis Speedway Museum. ■

Faces Behind the Scenes, 1946: (above) Nattily attired 500 starter Seth Klein. (right) George Connor drives the Firestone Tire Test Car while Harry Bennett rides the sulky and looks for unusual tire wear.

Faces Behind the Scenes, 1950: (left, above) Firemen from the C-O-Two Company douse a pit fire. They're wearing cotton trench coats soaked in alum that was supposed to make them fireproof. (right, above) The Brickyard was still brick in those days, at least on the front straight. (left) Johnnie Parsons won the 1950 500 in this eye-popping Kurtis/Offy.

1949

Winner: Bill Holland,
Deidt/Offy, 121.327 mph
Winner's Purse: $51,575
Total Purse: $179,050
Pace Car: Wilbur Shaw,
Oldsmobile "88"

For the third year in a row, Bill Holland and Mauri Rose dueled for nearly 500 miles. After 192 laps, the magneto strap on Rose's Blue Crown Special came loose, and the car coasted to a stop. Holland went on to win from rookie Johnnie Parsons driving a car built by Frank Kurtis.

Number	Driver	Sponsor/Team	Engine Type/Displacement	Chassis	Qualifying	Start/Finish	Laps
7	Bill Holland	Blue Crown Spark Plug/Moore	Offy I-4/270 cu.in.	Deidt	128.673	4/1	200
12	Johnnie Parsons	Kurtis-Kraft	Offy I-4/270 cu.in.	Kurtis	132.900	12/2	200
22	George Connor	Blue Crown Spark Plug/Moore	Offy I-4/270 cu.in.	Lesovsky	128.228	6/3	200
2	Myron Fohr	Carl Marchese	Offy I-4/270 cu.in.	Marchese	129.776	13/4	200
77	Joie Chitwood	Ervin Wolfe	Offy I-4/270 cu.in.	KK2000	126.863	16/5	200
61	Jimmy Jackson	Howard Keck	Offy I-4/268 cu.in.	Deidt	128.023	7/6	200
98	Johnny Mantz	J.C. Agajanian	Offy I-4/270 cu.in.	KK2000	127.786	9/7	200
19	Paul Russo	Tuffy's Offy/Charles Pritchard	Offy I-4/270 cu.in.	KK2000	129.487	19/8	200
9	Emil Andres	Tuffy's Offy/Charles Pritchard	Offy I-4/270 cu.in.	KK2000	126.042	32/9	197
71	Norm Houser	Troy Oil/Joe Langley	Offy I-4/243 cu.in.	Langley	127.756	24/10	181
68	Jim Rathmann	Pioneer Auto/John Lorenz	Offy I-4/270 cu.in.	Wetteroth	126.516	21/11	175
64	Troy Ruttman	Ray W. Carter	Offy I-4/270 cu.in.	Wetteroth	125.945	18/12	151
3	Mauri Rose	Blue Crown Spark Plug/Moore	Offy I-4/270 cu.in.	Deidt	127.759	10/13	192
17	Duane Carter	Murrell Belanger	Offy I-4/270 cu.in.	Stevens	128.233	5/14	182
29	Duke Dinsmore	Norm Olson	Offy I-4/270 cu.in.	Olson	127.750	15/15	174
8	Mack Hellings	Don Lee Motors	Offy I-4/270 cu.in.	KK2000	128.260	14/16	172
4	Bill Sheffler	Sheffler Offy	Offy I-4/270 cu.in.	Bromme	128.521	22/17	160
32	Johnny McDowell	Iddings/Henry Meyer	Offy I-4/233 cu.in.	Meyer	126.139	28/18	142
14	Hal Cole	Grancor Auto Specialists	Offy I-4/220 cu.in.	KK2000	127.168	11/19	117
38	George Fonder	Ray Brady	Sparks I-6/183 cu.in.	Adams	127.289	25/20	116
74	Bill Cantrell	Kennedy Tank/Leslie Anderson	Offy I-4/274 cu.in.	Kurtis	127.191	30/21	95
57	Jackie Holmes	Pat Clancy	Offy I-4/270 cu.in.	Kurtis	128.087	17/22	65
6	Lee Wallard	Maserati/Indianapolis Cars	Maserati I-8/181 cu.in.	Maserati	128.912	20/23	55
69	Bayliss Levrett	Wynn's Oil/Bayliss Levrett	Offy I-4/270 cu.in.	KK2000	129.236	29/24	52
5	Rex Mays	Novi Mobil/W.C. Winfield	Novi V-8/180 cu.in.	Kurtis	129.552	2/25	48
33	Jack McGrath	City of Tacoma/Leo Dobry	Offy I-4/247 cu.in.	KK2000	128.884	3/26	39
15	Fred Agabashian	Maserati/Indianapolis Cars	Maserati I-8/179 cu.in.	Maserati	127.007	31/27	38
52	Manuel Ayulo	Sheffler Offy	Offy I-4/255 cu.in.	Bromme	125.799	33/28	24
54	Duke Nalon	Novi Mobil/W.C. Winfield	Novi V-8/180 cu.in.	Kurtis	123.939	1/29	23
18	Sam Hanks	Love Machine & Tool/Marion	Offy I-4/270 cu.in.	KK2000	127.809	23/30	20
10	Charley Van Acker	Redmer/Geneva Van Acker	Offy I-4/270 cu.in.	Stevens	126.524	27/31	10
26	George Lynch	Automobile Shippers/Rassey	Offy I-4/270 cu.in.	Snowberger	127.823	8/32	1
37	Spider Webb	Grancor/Lou & Bruce Bromme	Offy I-4/270 cu.in.	Bromme	127.002	26/33	DNS

By far the vast majority of cars at Indianapolis during this era were conventional front-engine/rear-drive, Offy-powered upright "dirt cars." Dirt cars were impressively straightforward, simple, fast and inexpensive. And they worked as well as they had for decades. The driver still sat tall in the saddle, straddling the driveshaft, with the engine in front of him and the fuel tank behind. Both front and rear axles were usually solid, though now normally hung on torsion bars rather than transverse leaf springs.

Invariably, these dirt cars used a 270 cubic inch Offy, unsupercharged. With 350 hp hauling 1700 lbs., a good dirt car could hit 150 mph down the straights, 120 mph in the corners and average about 135 mph per lap. Cliff Griffith drove

his Offy-powered dirt car to a lap at 141.80 mph in 1956. That was the fastest any upright dirt car ever went in the Fifties, though Griffith did come back in 1964 and hit 144.323 mph in another Offy dirt car.

MEYER-DRAKE

One of the most important things to happen to postwar

American racing was such a little thing, really. In 1946, Louie Meyer and his former riding mechanic/crew chief Dale Drake started a new machine shop in Los Angeles. From Fred Offenhauser, they bought the rights to build and sell all the Miller and Offy engines. And they hired Leo Goossen full-time as their design chief. The Offy engine was pretty long-in-tooth by this time; it was virtually unchanged since Harry Miller had designed it fifteen years earlier. Meyer-Drake decided to update the Offy.

Starting in 1946, by 1952 Leo Goossen had gradually changed just about every detail of the Offy. He added Clevite main and rod bearings—the old Offy still used poured babbit bearings that had gone out of fashion on passenger cars a decade before—changed the cam profiles for better breathing, switched to stronger forged aluminum pistons, redrew the complicated gear-drive for the camshafts, strengthened the block and added Hilborn fuel-injection.

Invented by young Los Angeles hot-rodder Stu Hilborn, this injection system was dead simple. It didn't have the dynamic range of a good carburetor—in the late-Forties, most racers were using the Riley sidedraft that was pretty similar to the Winfield their fathers had used and the Miller their grandfathers ran—but Indianapolis cars spend most of their life running at or near top speed. And at a constant speed, fuel-injection is much more efficient than any carburetor.

Simply bolting Hilborn's injection onto an Offy was good for just about a 10 percent increase in horsepower and 2 mph in lap speeds. The new Meyer-Drake Offy with Hilborn injection typically produced 350 hp at 5400 rpm running on methanol or about 300 hp on Avgas. That was enough to win every 500 between 1947 and 1952 (the old Thorne won in 1946, an Offy was second). Indeed, the Offy's domination was so complete that by 1950 there was

Faces Behind the Scenes, 1949: (above) Imagine if you could get your hands on the contents of this souvenir stand today. The model race cars alone would send your kids to college. (below) Early Memorial Day morning at Gasoline Alley. The similar Offy-powered dirt cars are about to be driven by Myron Fohr #2, Norm Houser #71, Manny Ayulo #52 and Duke Dinsmore #29. The only decent finish in the group was Fohr, who came fourth.

1950

Winner: Johnnie Parsons, Kurtis/Offy, 124.002 mph
Winner's Purse: $57,458
Total Purse: $201,035
Pace Car: Benson Ford, Mercury Convertible

Johnnie Parsons, Bill Holland and Mauri Rose battled for the second straight year, but this time the new Kurtis was decisively faster than the Deidt front-wheel drive cars. The race was stopped after 345 miles because of rain, before Holland and Rose could make their planned moves toward the front.

Number	Driver	Sponsor/Team	Engine Type/Displacement	Chassis	Qualifying	Start/ Finish	Laps
1	Johnnie Parsons	Wynn's Friction/Kurtis-Kraft	Offy I-4/270 cu.in.	Kurtis	132.044	5/1	138
3	Bill Holland	Blue Crown Spark Plug/Moore	Offy I-4/270 cu.in.	Deidt	130.482	10/2	137
31	Mauri Rose	Offenhauser/Howard Keck	Offy I-4/270 cu.in.	Deidt	132.319	3/3	137
54	Cecil Green	John Zink/M.A. Walker	Offy I-4/270 cu.in.	KK3000	132.910	12/4	137
17	Joie Chitwood	Ervin Wolfe	Offy I-4/270 cu.in.	KK2000	130.757	9/5	136
8	Lee Wallard	Blue Crown Spark Plug/Moore	Offy I-4/270 cu.in.	Moore	132.436	23/6	136
98	Walt Faulkner	Grant Piston Ring/Agajanian	Offy I-4/270 cu.in.	KK2000	134.343	1/7	135
5	George Connor	Blue Crown Spark Plug/Moore	Offy I-4/270 cu.in.	Lesovsky	132.163	4/8	135
7	Paul Russo	Paul Russo & Ray Nichels	Offy I-4/270 cu.in.	Nichels	130.790	19/9	135
59	Pat Flaherty	Granatelli-Sabourin/Grancor	Offy I-4/270 cu.in.	KK3000	129.608	11/10	135
2	Myron Fohr	Bardahl/Carl Marchese	Offy I-4/270 cu.in.	Marchese	131.714	16/11	133
18	Duane Carter	Murrell Belanger	Offy I-4/176 cu.in.	Stevens	131.666	13/12	133
15	Mack Hellings	Tuffy's Offy/Charles Pritchard	Offy I-4/270 cu.in.	KK2000	130.687	26/13	132
49	Jack McGrath	Jack Hinkle	Offy I-4/270 cu.in.	KK3000	131.868	6/14	131
55	Troy Ruttman	Bowes Seal Fast Racing	Offy I-4/270 cu.in.	Lesovsky	131.912	24/15	130
75	Gene Hartley	Troy Oil/Joe Langley	Offy I-4/240 cu.in.	Langley	129.213	31/16	128
22	Jim Davies	Pat Clancy	Offy I-4/270 cu.in.	Ewing	130.402	27/17	128
62	Johnny McDowell	Pete Wales	Offy I-4/235 cu.in.	KK2000	129.692	33/18	128
4	Walt Brown	Tuffy's Offy/Charles Pritchard	Offy I-4/270 cu.in.	KK2000	130.454	20/19	127
21	Spider Webb	Fadely-Anderson/R.A. Cott	Offy I-4/270 cu.in.	Maserati	129.748	14/20	126
81	Jerry Hoyt	Ludson Morris	Offy I-4/270 cu.in.	KK2000	129.520	15/21	125
27	Walt Ader	Sampson Manufacturing	Offy I-4/177 cu.in.	Rae	129.940	29/22	123
77	Jackie Holmes	Norm Olson	Offy I-4/270 cu.in.	Olson	129.697	30/23	123
76	Jim Rathmann	Pioneer Auto Repair/Lorenz	Offy I-4/270 cu.in.	Wetteroth	129.959	28/24	122
12	Henry Banks	Indianapolis Race Cars	Offy I-4/180 cu.in.	Maserati	129.646	21/25	112
67	Bill Schindler	Automobile Shippers/Rassey	Offy I-4/270 cu.in.	Snowberger	132.690	22/26	111
24	Bayliss Levrett	Richard Palmer	Offy I-4/270 cu.in.	Adams	131.181	17/27	108
28	Fred Agabashian	Wynn's Friction/Kurtis-Kraft	Offy I-4/177 cu.in.	KK3000	132.792	2/28	64
61	Jimmy Jackson	Cummins Diesel	Cummins I-6/401 cu.in.	Kurtis	129.208	32/29	52
23	Sam Hanks	Merz Engineering/Milt Marion	Offy I-4/270 cu.in.	KK2000	131.593	25/30	42
14	Tony Bettenhausen	Blue Crown Spark Plug/Moore	Offy I-4/270 cu.in.	Deidt	130.947	8/31	30
45	Dick Rathmann	City of Glendale/A.J. Watson	Offy I-4/264 cu.in.	Watson	130.928	18/32	25
69	Duke Dinsmore	Brown Motor	Offy I-4/270 cu.in.	KK2000	131.066	7/33	10

only one engine in the Indianapolis 500 that was *not* an Offy, and that was a Cummins diesel that started in the last row. Just as they had since 1921, engines designed by Harry Miller continued to dominate American racing.

THE CAR BUILDERS

The standard engine for Indy cars was the Offy. And to build a car that could carry that Offy to Indy's Victory Lane, you had your choice of only a handful of car builders. These were all small shops with no more than a dozen employees, hand-crafting standardized midget, sprint and Indy car chassis from a stack of mild-steel or chrome-moly tubing, sheets of aluminum and unbelievable skill.

There were exactly five Indianapolis 500 car builders active in the late-Forties. Emil Deidt was still around, and he constructed the all-conquering Blue Crown Specials for Lou Moore. Deidt also built several copies of the Blue Crowns using blueprints he "borrowed" from Moore. The most successful was the Howard Keck Special, which finished sixth at Indianapolis in 1949. If you wanted an upright dirt-type car, Lujie Lesovsky and Gordon Schroeder built very tough—if very conventional—rear-wheel drive chassis suitable both for Indianapolis and dirt ovals.

But the up-and-comers were a pair of young engineers from Los Angeles. Eddie Kuzma started out as a Midget driver in the Thirties, then began building the most beautiful Offy Midgets, sprint cars and eventually Speedway cars. He was not a brilliant innovator, but he was probably the best fabricator and body man in the United States at the time. In 1948, he built the first sprint car with a tubular frame for J.C. Agajanian. Agajanian's drivers Duane Carter and Troy Ruttman won two championships in the famous "Old 98." In 1952, Ruttman put a similar Kuzma owned by Agajanian into Victory Lane.

By far the most successful of the five postwar car builders was Frank Kurtis. His first Speedway car ran in 1939, and later on he revolutionized Indianapolis with the first "roadster." But in the late-Forties he built a whole run of standardized race cars that were straightforward, robust and wonderful values. Kurtis was brimming with oddball ideas, but the conservative "Indianapolis Establishment" didn't want to know about them. Kurtis supplied what they wanted, sticking in his new ideas when they weren't looking.

His typical product of this era was the KK3000, which Johnnie Parsons qualified at 132.90 mph. The next year Parsons came back and won the 500 with this same car. By then, fourteen out of thirty-three Indianapolis starters were driving similar Kurtis cars. The KK3000 featured a lightweight tubular space frame like that in an airplane, welded up from chrome-moly steel. Unlike most dirt cars of the time which still used solid front axles, Kurtis' car had independent front suspension and torsion bars instead of springs. Compared to the competition, Kurtis machines were softer riding, better cornering and easier to drive. That makes a big difference in a 500 mile race.

NOVI
In 1946, Frank Kurtis built a new chassis for the prewar Novi V-8. Leo Goossen drew up a new front-wheel drive gearbox, similar to the one he had already designed for the Blue Crown Special except for a special low-mounted input shaft to lower the heavy Novi engine in the chassis. Kurtis used his typical independent front suspension on torsion bars, with a solid rear axle on leaf springs. Over this went an aluminum body similar to the one Emil Deidt was hammering out for the Blue Crown Specials. Indeed, the Novi and Blue Crowns

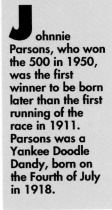

Johnnie Parsons, who won the 500 in 1950, was the first winner to be born later than the first running of the race in 1911. Parsons was a Yankee Doodle Dandy, born on the Fourth of July in 1918.

(below) 1951 winner Lee Wallard proudly sits in his upright Kurtis/Offy, the Belanger Special. Behind him (left to right) are Indianapolis 500 winners Bill Holland, Johnnie Parsons, Troy Ruttman and Bill Vukovich.

1951

Winner: Lee Wallard,
Kurtis/Offy, 126.244 mph
Winner's Purse: $63,612
Total Purse: $207,650
Pace Car: Dave Wallace,
Chrysler New Yorker

Mauri Rose flipped and retired from racing, Mike Nazaruk was second in the car with which Johnnie Parsons had won in 1950, and East Coast Sprint racer Lee Wallard ran away with the 500 driving a tiny Kurtis that wasn't much more than a scaled-up Sprint car. Offy dominated the field.

Number	Driver	Sponsor/Team	Engine Type/Displacement	Chassis	Qualifying	Start/ Finish	Laps
99	Lee Wallard	Murrell Belanger	Offy I-4/241 cu.in.	Kurtis	135.039	2/1	200
83	Mike Nazaruk	Jim Robbins	Offy I-4/270 cu.in.	Kurtis	132.183	7/2	200
9	Jack McGrath	Jack Hinkle	Offy I-4/270 cu.in.	KK3000	134.303	3/3	200
57	Andy Linden	George Leitenberger	Offy I-4/270 cu.in.	Sherman	132.226	31/4	200
52	Bobby Ball	Blakely/John McDaniel	Offy I-4/270 cu.in.	Schroeder	134.098	29/5	200
1	Henry Banks	Blue Crown Spark Plug/Hopkins	Offy I-4/270 cu.in.	Moore	133.899	17/6	200
68	Carl Forberg	Automobile Shippers/Rassey	Offy I-4/270 cu.in.	KK3000	132.890	24/7	193
27	Duane Carter	Mobilgas/Rotary Engineering	Offy I-4/272 cu.in.	Deidt	133.749	4/8	180
5	Tony Bettenhausen	Mobiloil/Rotary Engineering	Offy I-4/270 cu.in.	Deidt	131.950	9/9	178
18	Duke Nalon	Novi Purelube/Jean Marcenac	Novi V-8/181 cu.in.	Kurtis	136.498	1/10	151
69	Gene Force	Brown Motor	Offy I-4/270 cu.in.	KK2000	133.102	22/11	142
25	Sam Hanks	Peter Schmidt	Offy I-4/270 cu.in.	KK3000	132.998	12/12	135
10	Bill Schindler	H.A. Chapman	Offy I-4/270 cu.in.	KK2000	134.033	16/13	129
16	Mauri Rose	Pennzoil/Howard Keck	Offy I-4/270 cu.in.	Deidt	133.422	5/14	126
2	Walt Faulkner	Agajanian Grant Piston Ring	Offy I-4/270 cu.in.	Kuzma	136.872	14/15	123
76	Jim Davies	Parks Offenhauser/L.E. Parks	Offy I-4/270 cu.in.	Pawl	133.516	27/16	110
59	Fred Agabashian	Granatelli-Bardahl/Grancor	Offy I-4/270 cu.in.	KK3000	135.029	11/17	109
73	Carl Scarborough	McNamara/Lee Elkins	Offy I-4/270 cu.in.	KK2000	135.614	15/18	100
71	Bill Mackey	Karl Hall	Offy I-4/270 cu.in.	Hall	131.473	33/19	97
8	Chuck Stevenson	Bardahl/Carl Marchese	Offy I-4/270 cu.in.	Marchese	133.764	19/20	93
3	Johnnie Parsons	Wynn's Friction Proofing/Walsh	Offy I-4/270 cu.in.	KK3000	132.154	8/21	87
4	Cecil Green	John Zink/M.A. Walker	Offy I-4/270 cu.in.	KK3000	131.892	10/22	80
98	Troy Ruttman	Agajanian Featherweight	Offy I-4/270 cu.in.	KK2000	132.314	6/23	78
6	Duke Dinsmore	Brown Motors	Offy I-4/270 cu.in.	Schroeder	131.974	32/24	73
32	Chet Miller	Novi Purelube/Jean Marcenac	Novi V-8/181 cu.in.	Kurtis	135.798	28/25	56
44	Walt Brown	Federal Engineering	Offy I-4/270 cu.in.	KK3000	131.907	13/26	55
48	Rodger Ward	Deck Manufacturing/Bromme	Offy I-4/270 cu.in.	Bromme	134.867	25/27	34
23	Cliff Griffith	Ludson D. Morris	Offy I-4/270 cu.in.	KK2000	133.839	18/28	30
81	Bill Vukovich	Central Excavating/Pete Salemi	Offy I-4/270 cu.in.	Trevis	133.725	20/29	29
22	George Connor	Blue Crown Spark Plug/Moore	Offy I-4/270 cu.in.	Lesovsky	133.353	21/30	29
19	Mack Hellings	Tuffanelli-Derrico	Offy I-4/270 cu.in.	Deidt	123.925	23/31	18
12	Johnny McDowell	W.J./Maserati Race Cars	Offy I-4/180 cu.in.	Maserati	132.475	26/32	15
26	Joe James	Bob Estes Lincoln-Mercury	Offy I-4/270 cu.in.	Watson	134.098	30/33	8

are so similar that in fuzzy old photos, it's sometimes hard to tell which is which.

The Novi was fast, faster than the Blue Crowns. Ralph Hepburn hit 170 mph on the straights and immediately broke the Indianapolis 500 record with a 134.45 mph lap. At Muroc Dry Lake, the Novi topped 220 mph in a straight line. The Novi was also heavy. At 1920 lbs. it was 300 lbs. heavier than the superficially similar Blue Crown Special. The supercharged 3.0-liter V-8 made 500 hp at 7500 rpm, but it consumed a gallon of methanol per lap!

Unfortunately, the radical Novi design required the extra cooling power of alcohol, so they couldn't run gasoline. And all that extra weight—the already overweight Novi needed a 110 gallon fuel tank—simply wore out the tires. If the driv-

ers ran as fast as the Novi wanted to go, the tires vaporized. The fabled Novi was a beautifully-engineered, beautifully-constructed...*bad idea*. Its best-ever finish was Duke Nalon's third at Indianapolis in 1948 behind the far more successful Blue Crown Specials.

THE TRIUMPH OF CONSERVATISM

More oddball cars showed up in the Indianapolis 500 International Sweepstakes during the immediate postwar period than at any time before or since. And, by and large, they made no imprint at all. The real progress was made by a small group of Southern California car builders and racing equipment suppliers who slowly and carefully refined the traditional front-engine/rear-drive Offy-powered dirt car and ultimately made it faster than even the brilliantly-conceived front-wheel drive Blue Crown Specials. Without making any major changes, these dedicated craftsmen improved the basic upright dirt car from Speedway lap speeds of around 120 mph in 1946 to around 140 mph by 1951. How'd they find that extra speed?

Well, they got more horsepower and better durability out of the old Offy through a combination of improved components and Stu Hilborn's injection system. The Conze Brothers introduced aircraft-style disc brakes in 1951. These allowed the cars to go deeper into the corners and still have plenty of braking left at the end of the race. Ted Halibrand built the first magnesium wheels that reduced unsprung weight, and the first "pin drive" hubs to hold them. He also made the first quick-change differential that allowed mechanics to change rear axle ratios right there in the pits. Monroe built the first tubular shock absorbers for team owner Gene Cassaroll in 1950. Within two years, every Indy car used superior, direct-acting tubular shocks.

At the same time, chassis builders like Frank Kurtis were making tubular space frames out of strong and lightweight chrome-moly tubing—essentially a triangulated bridge girder—that had many times the torsional stiffness of old-fashioned ladder frames. These stiff new frames allowed all the other suspension and handling improve-

(below) The 500 start in 1951. Duke Nalon's Novi #18 on the pole, Lee Wallard's Kurtis dirt car #99 in front row center, Jack McGrath's Kurtis #9 on the outside. Wallard will win, McGrath will start and finish third. Things were more casual then...look at all the VIPs standing around the pit lane, directly in harm's way.

1952

Winner: Troy Ruttman, Kuzma/Offy, 128.922 mph
Winner's Purse: $61,743
Total Purse: $230,100
Pace Car: P.O. Peterson, Studebaker Commander

Freddie Agabashian put the diesel-powered Cummins on the pole, but "Mad Russian" Bill Vukovich—his family was originally from Yugoslavia—dominated the race until a steering pin broke only 8 laps from the end and he crashed. Another California Sprint car driver, 22-year-old Troy Ruttman, won.

Number	Driver	Sponsor/Team	Engine Type/Displacement	Chassis	Qualifying	Start/Finish	Laps
98	Troy Ruttman	J.C. Agajanian	Offy I-4/263 cu.in.	Kuzma	135.364	7/1	200
59	Jim Rathmann	Grancor-Wynn's Oil	Offy I-4/270 cu.in.	KK3000	136.343	10/2	200
18	Sam Hanks	Bardahl/Ed Walsh	Offy I-4/263 cu.in.	KK3000	135.736	5/3	200
1	Duane Carter	Belanger Motors	Offy I-4/262 cu.in.	Lesovsky	135.522	6/4	200
33	Art Cross	Bowes Seal Fast/Ray Brady	Offy I-4/270 cu.in.	KK4000	134.288	20/5	200
77	Jimmy Bryan	Peter Schmidt	Offy I-4/270 cu.in.	KK3000	134.142	21/6	200
37	Jimmy Reece	John Zink	Offy I-4/270 cu.in.	KK4000	133.993	23/7	200
54	George Connor	Federal Engineering	Offy I-4/270 cu.in.	KK3000	135.609	14/8	200
22	Cliff Griffith	Tom Sarafoff	Offy I-4/263 cu.in.	KK2000	136.617	9/9	200
5	Johnnie Parsons	Jim Robbins	Offy I-4/270 cu.in.	Kurtis	135.328	31/10	200
4	Jack McGrath	Jack Hinkle	Offy I-4/270 cu.in.	KK3000	136.664	3/11	200
29	Jim Rigsby	Bob Estes	Offy I-4/270 cu.in.	Watson	133.904	26/12	200
14	Joe James	Bardahl/Ed Walsh	Offy I-4/263 cu.in.	KK4000	134.953	16/13	200
7	Bill Schindler	H.A. Chapman	Offy I-4/270 cu.in.	Stevens	134.988	15/14	200
65	George Fonder	George Leitenberger	Offy I-4/270 cu.in.	Sherman	135.947	13/15	197
81	Eddie Johnson	Central Excavating/Salemi	Offy I-4/270 cu.in.	Trevis	133.973	24/16	193
26	Bill Vukovich	Fuel Injection/Howard Keck	Offy I-4/270 cu.in.	KK500A	138.212	8/17	191
16	Chuck Stevenson	Springfield Welding/Paoli	Offy I-4/263 cu.in.	KK4000	136.142	11/18	187
2	Henry Banks	Blue Crown Spark Plug/Hopkins	Offy I-4/263 cu.in.	Lesovsky	135.962	12/19	184
8	Manuel Ayulo	Coast Grain	Offy I-4/270 cu.in.	Lesovsky	135.982	28/20	184
31	Johnny McDowell	McDowell/Roger Wolcott	Offy I-4/263 cu.in.	Kurtis	133.939	33/21	182
48	Spider Webb	Granatelli Racing	Offy I-4/270 cu.in.	Bromme	135.962	29/22	162
34	Rodger Ward	Federal Engineering	Offy I-4/270 cu.in.	KK4000	134.139	22/23	130
27	Tony Bettenhausen	Blue Crown Spark Plug/Earl Slick	Offy I-4/270 cu.in.	Deidt	135.384	30/24	93
36	Duke Nalon	Novi Pure Oil/Lewis Welch	Novi V-8/181 cu.in.	Kurtis	136.188	4/25	84
73	Bob Sweikert	McNamara/Lee Elkins	Offy I-4/263 cu.in.	KK2000	134.983	32/26	77
28	Fred Agabashian	Cummins Diesel	Cummins I-6/401 cu.in.	Kurtis	138.010	1/27	71
67	Gene Hartley	Mel-Rae/Mel Wiggers	Offy I-4/270 cu.in.	KK4000	134.343	18/28	65
93	Bob Scott	Ludson Morris	Offy I-4/270 cu.in.	KK2000	133.953	25/29	49
21	Chet Miller	Novi Pure Oil/Lewis Welch	Novi V-8/181 cu.in.	Kurtis	139.034	27/30	41
12	Alberto Ascari	Enzo Ferrari	Ferrari V-12/271 cu.in.	Ferrari	134.308	19/31	40
55	Bobby Ball	Ansted/Rotary Engineering	Offy I-4/270 cu.in.	Stevens	134.725	17/32	34
9	Andy Linden	Miracle Power/Hart Fullerton	Offy I-4/183 cu.in.	KK4000	137.002	2/33	20

ments to do their job. It's interesting to see that while lap speeds at Indianapolis increased nearly 20 mph for the dirt-type cars in less than five years, top speed increased only about 10 mph. Most of the improvement was in cornering speeds.

Despite all the oddball new postwar ideas, the Indianapolis Establishment eventually won out. Basic designs laid down by Harry Miller in the early-Twenties were still being refined in the Fifties. In concept, there is little difference between Troy Ruttman's winning 1952 Kuzma/Offy and Tommy Milton's winning 1923 Miller. The increase in Indianapolis qualifying speeds is only 27 mph over three decades. That's an improvement of less than 1 mph per year, which is not exactly earth-shaking progress. But the groundwork had been laid for radical changes.

THE ROADSTERS 1953-1960

Changes. Radical changes. Changes everywhere. Just about everything to do with motor racing changed during the Fifties...the cars, the engines, the heroes, the villains, the tracks, the sponsors, the rules, even the organizers and the driver's crash helmets. Yet somehow, the overall racing machine kept roaring along at top speed, enjoying a decade of prosperity unmatched since the Twenties.

Immediately after World War II, there had been a period of inflation followed

(below) 1954 500 start: Jack McGrath #2 leads; winner Bill Vukovich #14 is back in nineteenth. It's a real mix of new, low-slung roadsters and upright dirt cars.

1953

Winner: Bill Vukovich, Kurtis/Offy, 128.740 mph
Winner's Purse: $89,496
Total Purse: $246,300
Pace Car: William C. Ford, Ford Sunliner

On a 130 degree track, Bill Vukovich started from the pole and led all but five laps of a race that saw other drivers crashing or asking for relief drivers. A Midget driver from Hades-hot Fresno, California, Vukovich was perfectly comfortable. Kurtis chassis and Offenhauser engines overwhelmed the field.

Number	Driver	Sponsor/Team	Engine Type/Displacement	Chassis	Qualifying	Start/ Finish	Laps
14	Bill Vukovich	Fuel Injection/Howard Keck	Offy I-4/270 cu.in.	KK500A	138.392	1/1	200
16	Art Cross	Springfield Welding/Paoli	Offy I-4/263 cu.in.	KK4000	137.310	12/2	200
3	Sam Hanks	Bardahl/Ed Walsh	Offy I-4/270 cu.in.	KK4000	137.531	9/3	200
59	Fred Agabashian	Grancor-Elgin Piston Pin	Offy I-4/270 cu.in.	KK500B	137.546	2/4	200
5	Jack McGrath	Jack Hinkle	Offy i-4/270 cu.in.	KK4000	136.602	3/5	200
48	Jimmy Daywalt	Sumar/Chapman Root	Offy I-4/270 cu.in.	KK3000	135.742	21/6	200
2	Jim Rathmann	Travelon Trailer/Ernest Ruiz	Offy I-4/270 cu.in.	KK500B	135.666	25/7	200
12	Ernie McCoy	H.A. Chapman	Offy I-4/270 cu.in.	Stevens	135.926	20/8	200
98	Tony Bettenhausen	J.C. Agajanian	Offy I-4/263 cu.in.	Kuzma	136.024	6/9	196
53	Jim Davies	Pat Clancy	Offy I-4/263 cu.in.	KK500B	135.262	32/10	193
9	Duke Nalon	Novi Governor/Jean Marcenac	Novi V-8/181 cu.in.	Kurtis	135.461	26/11	191
73	Carl Scarborough	McNamara/Lee Elkins	Offy I-4/270 cu.in.	KK2000	135.936	19/12	190
88	Manuel Ayulo	Peter Schmidt	Offy I-4/270 cu.in.	Kuzma	136.384	4/13	184
8	Jimmy Bryan	Blakely Oil/John McDaniel	Offy I-4/270 cu.in.	Schroeder	135.506	31/14	183
49	Bill Holland	Ray Crawford	Offy I-4/270 cu.in.	KK500B	137.868	28/15	177
92	Rodger Ward	M.A. Walker Electric	Offy I-4/270 cu.in.	Kurtis	137.468	10/16	177
23	Walt Faulkner	Automobile Shippers/Casaroll	Offy I-4/270 cu.in.	KK500A	137.117	14/17	176
22	Marshall Teague	Pure Oil/Hart Fullerton	Offy I-4/270 cu.in.	KK4000	135.721	22/18	169
62	Spider Webb	Lubri-Loy/3-L Racing Team	Offy I-4/270 cu.in.	KK3000	136.168	18/19	166
51	Bob Sweikert	Dean Van Lines	Offy I-4/270 cu.in.	Kuzma	136.872	29/20	151
83	Mike Nazaruk	Kalamazoo/Lee Elkins	Offy I-4/270 cu.in.	Turner	135.706	23/21	146
77	Pat Flaherty	Peter Schmidt	Offy I-4/270 cu.in.	KK3000	135.668	24/22	115
55	Jerry Hoyt	John Zink	Offy I-4/270 cu.in.	KK4000	135.731	7/23	107
4	Duane Carter	Miracle Power/Belanger	Offy I-4/270 cu.in.	Lesovsky	135.267	27/24	94
7	Paul Russo	Federal Engineering	Offy I-4/270 cu.in.	KK3000	136.219	17/25	89
21	Johnnie Parsons	Belond Equa-Flow	Offy I-4/270 cu.in.	KK500B	137.667	8/26	86
38	Don Freeland	Bob Estes	Offy I-4/270 cu.in.	Watson	136.867	15/27	76
41	Gene Hartley	Federal Engineering	Offy I-4/270 cu.in.	KK4000	137.263	13/28	53
97	Chuck Stevenson	J.C. Agajanian	Offy I-4/270 cu.in.	Kuzma	136.560	16/29	42
99	Cal Niday	Miracle Power/Belanger	Offy I-4/263 cu.in.	Kurtis	136.096	30/30	30
29	Bob Scott	Belond Equa-Flow/Bromme	Offy I-4/270 cu.in.	Bromme	137.431	11/31	14
56	Johnny Thomson	Dr. R.N. Sabourin	Offy I-4/270 cu.in.	Del Roy	135.262	33/32	6
32	Andy Linden	Cop-Sil-Loy/Rotary Engineering	Offy I-4/270 cu.in.	Stevens	136.060	5/33	3

by a recession, the standard up-and-down cycle that seems to have followed every war in history. But by 1953, Americans were sitting fat and happy, with lots of discretionary income, a deep-rooted interest in technology and a desire to get out and *go somewhere*. The expensive, high-speed, high-tech racing car was actually a perfect symbol for the era of Eisenhower, the H-bomb and Sputnik, Jack Kerouac and James Dean.

THE AGE OF SPECIALIZATION

Even in the early-Fifties, it was possible for a professional racing driver in America to build and maintain his car himself, perhaps with one or two friends. He

50¢ PAY NO MORE

OFFICIAL

Program

SPEEDWAY

37th 500-MILE RACE ... MAY 30, 1953

INDIANAPOLIS ☆ MOTOR ☆ SPEEDWAY ☆ CORPORATION

1954

Winner: Bill Vukovich,
Kurtis/Offy, 130.840 mph
Winner's Purse: $74,934
Total Purse: $269,375
Pace Car: W.C. Newberg,
Dodge Royal 500
Convertible

Because of mechanical troubles in qualifying, Bill Vukovich started way back in the seventh row. He worked his way steadily to the front, took the lead halfway through the 500 miles and easily won for the second year in Howard Keck's gray Kurtis roadster.

Number	Driver	Sponsor/Team	Engine Type/Displacement	Chassis	Qualifying	Start/ Finish	Laps
14	Bill Vukovich	Fuel Injection/Howard Keck	Offy I-4/270 cu.in.	KK500A	138.478	19/1	200
9	Jimmy Bryan	Dean Van Lines	Offy I-4/274 cu.in.	Kuzma	139.665	3/2	200
2	Jack McGrath	Jack B. Hinkle	Offy I-4/270 cu.in.	KK500C	141.033	1/3	200
34	Troy Ruttman	Automobile Shippers/Casaroll	Offy I-4/270 cu.in.	KK500A	137.736	11/4	200
73	Mike Nazaruk	McNamara/Lee Elkins	Offy I-4/270 cu.in.	KK500C	139.589	14/5	200
77	Fred Agabashian	Merz Engineering/Sperling	Offy I-4/271 cu.in.	KK500C	137.746	24/6	200
7	Don Freeland	Bob Estes	Offy I-4/270 cu.in.	Phillips	138.339	6/7	200
5	Paul Russo	Ansted Rotary/Hoosier Racing	Offy I-4/270 cu.in.	KK500A	137.678	32/8	200
28	Larry Crockett	Federal Engineering	Offy I-4/270 cu.in.	KK3000	139.557	25/9	200
24	Cal Niday	Jim Robbins	Offy I-4/270 cu.in.	Stevens	139.828	13/10	200
45	Art Cross	Berdahl/Ed Walsh	Offy I-4/270 cu.in.	KK4000	138.675	27/11	200
98	Chuck Stevenson	J.C. Agajanian	Offy I-4/270 cu.in.	Kuzma	138.776	5/12	199
88	Manuel Ayulo	Peter Schmidt	Offy I-4/270 cu.in.	Kuzma	138.164	22/13	197
17	Bob Sweikert	Lutes/Francis Bardazon	Offy I-4/270 cu.in.	KK4000	138.206	9/14	197
16	Duane Carter	Automobile Shippers/Casaroll	Offy I-4/270 cu.in.	KK4000	138.238	8/15	196
32	Ernie McCoy	Ray Crawford	Offy I-4/270 cu.in.	KK500B	138.419	20/16	194
25	Jimmy Reece	Emmett Malloy	Offy I-4/263 cu.in.	Pankratz	138.312	7/17	194
27	Ed Elisian	H.A. Chapman	Offy I-4/270 cu.in.	Stevens	137.794	31/18	193
71	Frank Armi	T.W. & W.T. Martin	Offy I-4/270 cu.in.	Curtis	137.673	33/19	193
1	Sam Hanks	Bardahl/Ed Walsh	Offy I-4/270 cu.in.	KK4000	137.994	10/20	191
35	Pat O'Connor	Hopkins/Motor Racers	Offy I-4/270 cu.in.	KK500C	138.084	12/21	181
12	Rodger Ward	Dr. R.N. Sabourin, D.C.	Offy I-4/270 cu.in.	Pawl	139.927	16/22	172
31	Gene Hartley	John Zink	Offy I-4/270 cu.in.	KK4000	139.061	17/23	168
43	Johnny Thomson	H.A. Chapman	Offy I-4/270 cu.in.	Nichels	138.787	4/24	165
74	Andy Linden	Brown Motor	Offy I-4/270 cu.in.	Schroeder	137.820	23/25	165
99	Jerry Hoyt	Murrell Belanger	Offy I-4/270 cu.in.	Kurtis	137.825	30/26	130
19	Jimmy Daywalt	Sumar/Chapman Root	Offy I-4/270 cu.in.	KK500C	139.789	2/27	111
38	Jim Rathmann	Burdahl/Ed Walsh	Offy I-4/270 cu.in.	KK500C	138.228	28/28	110
10	Tony Bettenhausen	Mel Wiggers	Offy I-4/270 cu.in.	KK500C	138.275	21/29	105
65	Spider Webb	Advance Muffler/Bruce Bromme	Offy I-4/270 cu.in.	Bromme	137.979	29/30	104
33	Len Duncan	Ray Brady	Offy I-4/270 cu.in.	Schroeder	139.217	26/31	101
15	Johnnie Parsons	Belond Equa-Flow/Calif. Muffler	Offy I-4/270 cu.in.	KK500C	139.578	15/32	79
51	Bill Homeier	Jones & Maley/Cars	Offy I-4/270 cu.in.	KK500C	138.948	18/33	74

could race this axe-simple upright car on dirt ovals, on the few paved ovals and at Indianapolis. All you had to change from one type of race to another were the tires and some suspensions settings. You could make a living racing once a year at Indianapolis, but most drivers trailered from town to town, following the AAA Championship Trail. In the winter time, you either worked on the car, took another job to help make ends meet or ran Midgets in Southern California. Life was simple.

By the mid-Fifties, no drivers built their own cars. Few even tuned their own cars. California supermarket heir Ray Crawford was about the only driver who could even *afford* his own car. To have any chance at all, you had to drive for a team. A team required a sponsor who was willing to spend $75,000 or more to see his

company's name painted on the side of your cars. Cars, plural.

Things had gotten so specialized that you needed a car designed just for Indianapolis Speedway, called, logically enough, a *Speedway car*; a car for shorter races on paved oval tracks, called a *Champ car* (because these races made up the National Championship Trail); and a smaller *Sprint car* for even shorter sprint races on dirt oval tracks. You could still run Midgets in the off-season, too.

To take care of this stable, it was necessary to have a full-time crew chief. It helped if he was a genius on the order of Clay Smith, Smokey Yunick, A.J. Watson or George Bignotti. Since every team's cars and engines were all essentially the same, a brilliant crew chief could come up with those little changes that make the difference between a winner and an also-ran. If you were really serious, you needed back-up cars for when you crashed, spare engines, mechanics, etc. In the mid-Fifties, when the dollar was still a dollar and Dinah Shore would sell you a Chevy V-8 convertible for $2300, a team gunning for the National Championship could easily have $75,000 just in hardware.

THE ROADSTER REVOLUTION

Partly, this was Frank Kurtis' fault. In 1952 the Cummins Diesel people came to him with a proposition. They wanted to run at Indianapolis using a huge 401 cubic inch (6.57-liter) Inline-6 designed for heavy trucks. Fitted with a turbocharger—the first turbo to run at the Speedway—this monster would make 400 hp at 4000 rpm, which was 50 hp more than an Offy. And the diesel just sipped fuel.

Kurtis' problem was how to package this beast. In a burst of inspiration, he laid the Cummins engine flat on its side, with the crankshaft on the left. Then he brought the driveshaft straight back to a quick-change differential offset in the rear axle. The driver sat on the floor next to the driveshaft. The whole thing was held together with a tubular space frame.

Around this Kurtis wrapped the lowest, tightest aluminum skin possible. Nothing stuck out at all. Freddie Agabashian put the Cummins Diesel on the pole and could have won the 500 with a little luck, but that's incidental to our story.

Because as soon as Frank Kurtis started building the Cummins

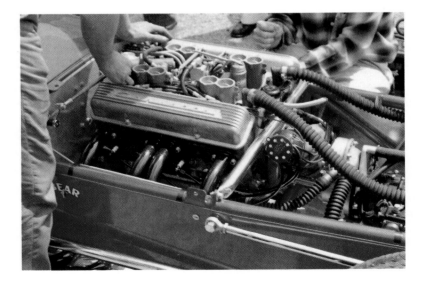

In 1952, the AAA Contest Board considered allowing "stock blocks" to run the 500 with 335 cubic inch displacement versus 270 cubic inches for the Offy. Chrysler Corporation blew the deal by having Joe James do a 500 mile demonstration run there, with a 400 hp Chrysler Hemi in his Kurtis. James averaged 134.35 mph, fast enough to have won the race that year. The AAA changed its mind about giving stock-blocks a break.

(top left) Tony Capanna of Los Angeles assaulted Indianapolis for years with a series of Dodge and DeSoto Hemi V-8s reduced in displacement to fit the 270 and later 256 cubic inch limits. Capanna's hand-built stock-blocks were as fast as the Offys, but never as reliable. None qualified for the 500 despite making 335 hp at 5500 rpm on alcohol.
(left) After the introduction of the lightweight, 265 cubic inch Chevrolet smallblock in 1955, any number of teams tried to run one. This example is in the San Diego Steel Products Special. It failed to qualify in 1960 despite fuel-injection and other hot-rod changes that raised output to 375 hp at 7500 rpm.

1955

Winner: Bob Sweikert, Kurtis/Offy, 128.209 mph
Winner's Purse: $76,138
Total Purse: $270,400
Pace Car: Thomas H. Keating, Chevrolet Bel Air

Bill Vukovich dominated his fourth Indy 500 in a row, until he crashed fatally on lap 57 in a multi-car accident precipitated when Rodger Ward went into the fence and flipped back onto the track. Art Cross and Don Freeland swapped the lead until both cars broke. Bob Sweikert won.

Number	Driver	Sponsor/Team	Engine Type/Displacement	Chassis	Qualifying	Start/ Finish	Laps
6	Bob Sweikert	John Zink	Offy I-4/270 cu.in.	KK500C	139.996	14/1	200
10	Tony Bettenhausen	H.A. Chapman	Offy I-4/270 cu.in.	KK500C	139.985	2/2	200
15	Jim Davies	Bardahl/Pat Clancy	Offy I-4/270 cu.in.	KK500B	140.274	10/3	200
44	Johnny Thomson	Peter Schmidt	Offy I-4/270 cu.in.	Kuzma	134.113	33/4	200
77	Walt Faulkner	Merz Engineerng	Offy I-4/270 cu.in.	KK500C	139.762	7/5	200
19	Andy Linden	Joseph Massaglia	Offy I-4/270 cu.in.	KK4000	139.098	8/6	200
71	Al Herman	T.W. & W.T. Martin	Offy I-4/270 cu.in.	Curtis	139.811	16/7	200
29	Pat O'Connor	Ansted Rotary	Offy I-4/270 cu.in.	KK500D	139.195	19/8	200
48	Jimmy Daywalt	Sumar/Chapman Root	Offy I-4/270 cu.in.	Kurtis	139.416	17/9	200
89	Pat Flaherty	Dunn Engineering	Offy I-4/272 cu.in.	KK500B	140.149	12/10	200
98	Duane Carter	J.C. Agajanian	Offy I-4/270 cu.in.	Kuzma	139.330	18/11	197
41	Chuck Weyant	Federal Engineering	Offy I-4/270 cu.in.	KK3000	138.063	25/12	196
83	Eddie Johnson	McNamara/Kalamazoo Sports	Offy I-4/270 cu.in.	Trevis	134.449	32/13	196
33	Jim Rathmann	Belond Miracle/Calif. Muffler	Offy I-4/270 cu.in.	Epperly	138.707	20/14	191
12	Don Freeland	Bob Estes	Offy I-4/270 cu.in.	Phillips	139.866	21/15	178
22	Cal Niday	D-A Lubricants/Racing Assoc.	Offy I-4/270 cu.in.	KK500B	140.302	9/16	170
99	Art Cross	Belanger Motors	Offy I-4/270 cu.in.	KK500C	138.750	24/17	168
81	Shorty Templeman	Central Excavating/Pete Salemi	Offy I-4/270 cu.in.	Trevis	135.014	31/18	142
8	Sam Hanks	Jones & Maley/Cars	Offy I-4/270 cu.in.	KK500C	140.187	6/19	134
31	Keith Andrews	John McDaniel	Offy I-4/270 cu.in.	Schroeder	136.049	28/20	120
16	Johnnie Parsons	Trio Brass/Carl Anderson	Offy I-4/270 cu.in.	KK500C	136.809	27/21	119
37	Eddie Russo	Dr. R.N. Sabourin, D.C.	Offy I-4/270 cu.in.	Pawl	140.116	13/22	112
49	Ray Crawford	Ray Crawford	Offy I-4/270 cu.in.	KK500B	139.206	23/23	111
1	Jimmy Bryan	Dean Van Lines	Offy I-4/270 cu.in.	Kuzma	140.160	11/24	90
4	Bill Vukovich	Lindsey Hopkins	Offy I-4/269 cu.in.	KK500C	141.071	5/25	56
3	Jack McGrath	Jack Hinkle	Offy I-4/270 cu.in.	KK500C	142.580	3/26	54
42	Al Keller	Sam Traylor Offy	Offy I-4/270 cu.in.	KK2000	139.551	22/27	54
27	Rodger Ward	Aristo Blue/E.R. Casale	Offy I-4/270 cu.in.	Kuzma	135.049	30/28	53
39	Johnny Boyd	Sumar/Chapman Root	Offy I-4/270 cu.in.	KK500D	136.981	26/29	53
68	Ed Elisian	Westwood Gauge/Wales	Offy I-4/270 cu.in.	KK4000	135.333	29/30	53
23	Jerry Hoyt	Jim Robbins	Offy I-4/270 cu.in.	Stevens	140.045	1/31	40
14	Fred Agabashian	Federal Engineering	Offy I-4/270 cu.in.	KK500C	141.933	4/32	39
5	Jimmy Reece	Emmett Malloy	Offy I-4/269 cu.in.	Pankratz	139.991	15/33	10

car, he saw that it was good and true and right. So he built another one for oil millionaire Howard Keck, which he called the KK500A.

The KK500A was designed around a conventional Offy engine, but with the engine tipped 36 degrees to the right—the Offy oil system wouldn't tolerate being laid flat on its side like the Cummins—the crankshaft/driveline offset 9 inches to the left, the driver offset to the right and sitting on the floor. Kurtis brought the bodywork right up around the driver's shoulders, leaving only his head sticking out. The first person to see the KK500A joked that it looked sort of like the modified Model T hot-rods used for amateur dirt-track racing in the Southwest. These were called "track roadsters." The name stuck.

The Kurtis roadster turned Indianapolis upside down. Tilting the engine and off-setting the drivetrain lowered the center of gravity and the lower body had less frontal area. But the real advantage of the roadster was that it put more than half of the car's weight on the left. In a high-speed left-hand corner at the Indianapolis Speedway, centrifugal force transferred about 400 lbs. of weight to the right side. But since the roadster was already biased to the left, in a Speedway corner the weight came out nearly equal left and right. The result? Better traction in the corners and more equal tire wear. It may not sound like much today, but the roadster of Frank Kurtis was the biggest innovation since the front-drive Miller 91.

GOING TO EXTREMES

Everyone agreed that Kurtis' concept of pre-loading the left side of an Indianapolis 500 car was a good one. But not everyone agreed as to how that should be done or how much. George Salih talked Leo Goossen into modifying the Offy so it could be laid down on its side, like the diesel in Kurtis' original Cummins. Why Kurtis didn't do this himself is curious. Anyway, because of the right-side camshaft and exhaust header sticking down, it made no sense to put the Offy literally on its side. Where would the exhaust go? So Goossen tipped the Offy 72 degrees instead of 90 degrees. Salih and car builder Quinn Epperly ruled the Speedway for two years with their "laydown" roadster.

Eddie Kuzma, who used to work for Kurtis before striking out on his own, reversed the head/block—you could do that on an Offy—so that the laydown en-

The best-running field in 500 history was in 1954. Only two cars failed to reach at least the 250 mile mark, and even Bill Homeier's last-place Kurtis/Offy completed 74 laps. During the race, Art Cross, Johnnie Parsons, Sam Hanks, Andy Linden and Jimmy Davies all took a turn in the Bardahl Special, setting a record for most drivers in a single car in a 500. They finished eleventh...probably because of all those pit stops to change drivers.

(left) In 1955, these three wives of drivers have nothing to do on Memorial Day except make a fashion statement and bask in attention from the photographers. Hats, skirts, shoes and pocketbooks—especially pocketbooks—sure have changed in thirty-five years. But Indianapolis photogs will still walk past the cars to take pictures of a pretty girl. That hasn't changed.

POPS VS THE KID

Frank Kurtis was no hot-eyed kid when he came up with the first Indy roadster in 1952. He'd built his first car in 1922, his first race car in 1930. In the Thirties, he was one of the small band of independent car builders who took over after Duesenberg and Miller faded from the scene. He was the first one to build a race car frame from lightweight chrome-moly tubing and simply *owned* West Coast Midget racing in the Thirties. He also built the front-wheel drive Novis for Ed Winfield, as well as the later rear-drive Novis in the mid-Fifties.

The Kurtis Era started with the KK3000 with which Johnnie Parsons finished second at Indianapolis in 1949, first in 1950. Among other innovations, the KK3000 had a chrome-moly tubular space frame and independent front suspension on torsion bars. It was both easier to drive and quicker out of the corners than the traditional upright dirt cars with their solid axles. Then there was the KK500A, the first roadster with the engine tilted over and the drivetrain run down the left side of the chassis. Bill Vukovich was literally unbeatable in that car in 1952, '53 and '54 thanks to its superior handling and reduced tire wear.

Typical of Frank Kurtis, this first car carried the front wheels on dual parallel trailing arms, the rear on single trailing arms. Almost immediately, there was a new model with dual parallel trailing arms front and rear. This gave way to a KK500 with a single leading arm and a single trailing arm on each side of the rear suspension. It was probably the most positively-located rigid rear axle on any race car in history. In this era, Ferrari sports/racing cars were viewed with goggle-eyed amazement by enthusiasts. But Ferrari was still using a rigid rear axle on longitudinal leaf springs. Frank Kurtis was two or three steps ahead.

Compared to small shops like Eddie Kuzma's or Quin Epperly's, Kurtis Kraft was a huge operation. In addition to the Indy cars and sprint cars, Kurtis produced over eight hundred Kurtis Midgets, a few dozen Kurtis sports cars and Kurtis house trailers, Jeep-like military vehicles and even Colonel Stapp's Mach 3 rocket sled.

In 1948 there were ten Kurtis cars in the 500; by 1953 twenty-four of the

(below) The first KK500A set a fashion in Speedway cars that lasted for over a decade. This specific car was one of the most successful. Bill Vukovich led most of the 1952 500 until his steering broke and he crashed with eight laps to go. In 1953 and '54 he won easily. In 1955, Vuky was killed while leading yet another 500 when his new KK500C slammed into the four-car wreck begun by Rodger Ward.

(below right) The 1952 Kurtis 500S sports car was essentially a two-seater KK500A with fenders and a big American V-8... usually a Chrysler Hemi. This one's in a modern vintage race, being driven by Carl Horton, of the famous Horton Safety Team.

thirty-three starters carried the Kurtis Kraft badge on the hood. Cars built by Frank Kurtis won the 500 five times between 1950 and 1955 and finished in the Top Five dozens of times. In his day, Kurtis ruled the Speedway as surely as Harry Miller did in the Twenties.

There was a great rivalry between old Frank Kurtis and young prodigy A.J. Watson, but the competition was actually pretty one-sided. Watson grew up working in his father's machine shop. He saw his first car race at Los Angeles' Bonelli Stadium in 1947; he built his first Indianapolis starter in 1950. In 1955, Watson prepared the Kurtis KK500C with which Bob Sweikert won the 500 and also the car with which he won the AAA National Championship. Sweikert was the first driver to win both since Wilbur Shaw in 1939. Ironically, the last Kurtis to win at Indianapolis was A.J. Watson's.

The Watson Era began in 1956, when A.J. built a new car for heating and cooling contractor John Zink of Tulsa. Pat Flaherty ran away with the 500. Compared to the Kurtis roadsters, Watson's cars were taller, but also longer, narrower, lighter and more aerodynamic. By mounting the Offy vertically on the left side and offsetting the body on the suspension, he concentrated even more weight to the inside. He also incorporated cockpit-adjustable "weight jackers" so that the driver could adjust the suspension as he raced along. Watson's cars didn't *look* fast like the low-slung Salih-Epperly laydowns, but they *went* fast.

Troy Ruttman put Zink's car on the outside of the front row in 1957; Watson roadsters occupied the entire front row in 1958. Both years, the Salih laydown won. After that, Indianapolis *belonged* to A.J. Watson. One of his cars won every 500 from 1959 through 1964. Even in '64, after the mid-engine revolution was well underway, Watson cars placed first through fourth, six out of the top ten. Rodger Ward's second-place 1964 car was a new mid-engine Watson, but A.J. never really followed up that initial success.

A.J. Watson continued as the crew chief for Bob Wilke's successful Leader Card team for decades. But he never recaptured the glory days, that stretch from 1956 till 1964 when a third of the starters came from his immaculate Burbank shop and one was sure to win. To Frank Kurtis belong the early-Fifties; to A.J. Watson belong the late-Fifties/early-Sixties. A rivalry? There's really no contest. ■

(above) A.J. Watson stands behind Pat Flaherty who drove Watson's first "ground up" roadster to victory in the 1956 500—the car's first time out—as well as a new lap record of 146.056 mph and four-lap qualifying average of 145.596 mph. They won two weeks later at Milwaukee, too. Right from the beginning, Watson located his Offy vertically on the left to concentrate as much weight as possible to the inside of the turns, then narrowed the bodywork to cut frontal area. Among many other innovations, Watson was the first 500 builder to make bodywork out of fiberglass and magnesium instead of aluminum.

1956

Winner: Pat Flaherty,
Watson/Offy, 128.490 mph
Winner's Purse: $93,819
Total Purse: $282,052
Pace Car: Irvin Woolson,
DeSoto Fireflite/Adventurer

Tulsa's John Zink saw his pink and white colors in the winner's circle for the second year in a row, on the first of A.J. Watson's machines to break the domination of Frank Kurtis. The race was almost flooded out and marred by accidents, including Dick Rathmann who spun *after* taking the checkered flag.

Number	Driver	Sponsor/Team	Engine Type/Displacement	Chassis	Qualifying	Start/ Finish	Laps
8	Pat Flaherty	John Zink	Offy I-4/270 cu.in.	Watson	145.596	1/1	200
4	Sam Hanks	Jones & Maley/Cars Inc.	Offy I-4/270 cu.in.	KK500C	142.051	13/2	200
16	Don Freeland	Bob Estes	Offy I-4/270 cu.in.	Phillips	141.699	26/3	200
98	Johnnie Parsons	J.C. Agajanian	Offy I-4/270 cu.in.	Kuzma	144.144	6/4	200
73	Dick Rathmann	McNamara/Kalamazoo Sports	Offy I-4/270 cu.in.	KK500C	144.471	4/5	200
1	Bob Sweikert	D-A Lubricants Racing	Offy I-4/270 cu.in.	Kuzma	143.033	10/6	200
14	Bob Veith	Federal Engineering	Offy I-4/270 cu.in.	KK500C	142.535	23/7	200
19	Rodger Ward	Filter Queen/Ed Walsh	Offy I-4/270 cu.in.	KK500C	141.171	15/8	200
26	Jimmy Reece	Massaglia Hotels	Offy I-4/270 cu.in.	Lesovsky	142.885	21/9	200
27	Cliff Griffith	Jim Robbins	Offy I-4/270 cu.in.	Stevens	141.471	30/10	199
82	Gene Hartley	Central Excavating/Pete Salemi	Offy I-4/270 cu.in.	Kuzma	142.846	22/11	196
42	Fred Agabashian	Federal Engineering	Offy I-4/270 cu.in.	KK500C	144.069	7/12	196
57	Bob Christie	Helse/H.H. Johnson	Offy I-4/270 cu.in.	KK500D	142.236	25/13	196
55	Al Keller	Sam Traylor	Offy I-4/270 cu.in.	KK4000	141.193	28/14	195
81	Eddie Johnson	Central Excavating/Pete Salemi	Offy I-4/270 cu.in.	Kuzma	139.093	32/15	195
41	Billy Garrett	Greenman-Casale	Offy I-4/263 cu.in.	Kuzma	140.559	29/16	194
64	Duke Dinsmore	Shannon's	Offy I-4/270 cu.in.	KK500A	138.530	33/17	191
7	Pat O'Connor	Ansted Rotary	Offy I-4/270 cu.in.	KK500D	144.980	3/18	187
2	Jimmy Bryan	Dean Van Lines	Offy I-4/270 cu.in.	Kuzma	143.741	19/19	185
24	Jim Rathmann	Lindsey Hopkins	Offy I-4/270 cu.in.	KK500C	145.120	2/20	175
34	Johnnie Tolan	Trio Brass Foundry/Anderson	Offy I-4/270 cu.in.	KK500C	140.061	31/21	173
99	Tony Bettenhausen	Belanger Motors	Offy I-4/270 cu.in.	KK500C	144.602	5/22	160
10	Ed Elisian	Hoyt Machine/Fred Sommer	Offy I-4/270 cu.in.	KK500C	141.382	14/23	160
48	Jimmy Daywalt	Sumar/Chapman Root	Offy I-4/270 cu.in.	KK500D	140.977	16/24	134
54	Jack Turner	Travelon Trailer/Ernest Ruiz	Offy I-4/270 cu.in.	KK500B	142.394	24/25	131
89	Keith Andrews	Dunn Engineering	Offy I-4/270 cu.in.	KK500B	142.976	20/26	94
5	Andy Linden	H.A. Chapman	Offy I-4/270 cu.in.	KK500C	143.056	9/27	90
12	Al Herman	Bardahl/Pat Clancy	Offy I-4/270 cu.in.	KK500B	141.610	27/28	74
49	Ray Crawford	Ray Crawford	Offy I-4/270 cu.in.	KK500B	140.884	17/29	49
15	Johnny Boyd	Bowes Seal Fast/Bignotti	Offy I-4/270 cu.in.	KK500E	142.337	12/30	35
53	Troy Ruttman	John Zink	Offy I-4/270 cu.in.	KK500C	142.484	11/31	22
88	Johnny Thomson	Peter Schmidt	Offy I-4/270 cu.in.	Kuzma	145.549	18/32	22
29	Paul Russo	Novi Vespa/Novi Racing	Novi V-8/183 cu.in.	Kurtis	143.546	8/33	21

gine canted out to the left. The cam covers and exhaust were 9 inches outside the bodywork, behind the left front wheel. Quin Epperly built a couple of cars like this, too. His looked as though the whole body had somehow shifted on the chassis.

Lujie Lesovsky tried a different tack. He put the driver on the left, with the left-leaning Offy's crankshaft and driveline to the right. Johnny Thomson put this car on the pole at Indianapolis in 1959, and finished third that year, fifth in 1960. Eddie Johnson was right behind him, with a similar car. Quin Epperly tried a similar arrangement in a car for Jimmy Bryan. As it turned out, none of these laydown designs were as effective as A.J. Watson's seemingly more conventional cars.

Watson kept the old Offy standing tall, the way God and Harry Miller meant it

OFFY

The venerable Offy DOHC four-cylinder remained essentially unchanged for four decades. At the same time, Leo Goossen reworked virtually every part of it over the years until it was reliably producing nearly twice the horsepower it made when first introduced. In the Thirties, the classic Offy size was 255 cubic inches (4.18-liters). This grew to 270 cubic inches (4.43-liters) when the Indianapolis rules changed to 4.5-liters in 1938. The Offy 270 was extensively modernized between 1946 and 1952, under the direction of Louie Meyer and Dale Drake.

With the advent of the "laydown" roadster in the late-Fifties—in which the Offy was literally laid on its side—Leo Goossen made more modifications so that the engine would work in this position. He provided a new sump that was angled 72 degrees, plus new oil lines and cam covers to keep the oil in the right place. Hilborn's fuel-injection units needed to be kept level, so they were mounted on long, curving inlet manifolds above the horizontal engine.

A neat feature of the Offy is that by simply redrilling a few oil holes, the block can be turned completely around. This means you can have the exhaust headers and intake manifold on whichever side you want. That's wonderful if you're a chassis engineer and you want to run the exhaust out the opposite side from everyone else, for example.

When newly-formed USAC reduced the displacement limit to 256 cubic inches (4.2-liters) for 1957, most mechanics simply used a slightly smaller bore in their big Offy 270s to reverse the process that got them from the Offy 255 to 270 in 1938. A.J. Watson was much more clever. He got Leo Goossen to help him assemble a "composite" engine by using the 270 block and head to keep the big-breathing valves, milling 0.625 inch off the bottom of the block, then using a new crankshaft with the shorter rods and gear-drive from the small Offy 220 cubic inch engine used in Sprint cars.

The result was a 252 cubic inch Offy with only 10 hp less than the 270, but an extra 800 rpm. Within a year or two, every car was powered by the "Watson" Offy 252. By using an aluminum block and magnesium cam and gear covers, Meyer-Drake got the weight of a ready-to-run Offy 252 down to 355 lbs. Such an engine would put out 450 hp at 6500 rpm, better than 1.26 hp per pound of engine. And all for $7000 in the late-Fifties. No wonder the Offy was so popular. ∎

(left) Incredibly complicated but dead reliable, the Offy's gear-drive transfers rotary motion from the crankshaft to the twin overhead cams without the use of belts, chains or shafts. The front-mounted, aircraft-style magneto is also gear-driven. This type of design minimizes friction losses but costs a bundle to build. (below) Harry Miller's basic Offy is still recognizable, despite three decades of changes. This is the 252 cubic inch Meyer-Drake version as used between 1957 and 1966. A sharp tuner could see 450 hp at 6500 rpm; 410 lbs-ft of torque at 5000 rpm. That's 1.8 hp per cubic inch, normally aspirated.

to be. Then he moved it as far to the left as possible. This got *all* the engine weight to the left side, not just some of it. Then he moved the whole frame to the left on the axles, and made the body as narrow and aerodynamic as possible. He also made the track narrower for better weight transfer. By using fiberglass and magnesium body panels, he brought his cars in as light as 1550 lbs., when other builders were doing well to get their machines under 1700 lbs. Watson's well-balanced roadsters were so easy on tires that they could go 500 miles at Indianapolis Motor Speedway on three pits stops, while other cars needed four. That's the difference between winning and losing.

INCREMENTAL CHANGES

In 1951, driving J.C. Agajanian's dirt car, fastest qualifier Walt Faulkner averaged 136.872 mph, with one lap at 138.122 mph. In 1952, Bill Vukovich could go only about 2 mph faster in the first Kurtis roadster. But 2 mph at Indianapolis is enough to start a revolution. Over the next decade, the roadsters got another 12 mph faster in qualifying. How? Well, figure 3 mph for Firestone's better tires. Figure another 2 mph for the 50 hp one got by using nitromethane in the fuel. Add another 2 mph because of the stiffer, more balanced chassis that could utilize better shock absorbers and finer suspension tuning. Even the new lightweight magnesium wheels and disc brakes helped by reducing unsprung weight and keeping the tires in better contact with the surface.

The short-stroke 252 cubic inch Offy used after 1957 could safely be run approximately 800 rpm higher down the straights than the old long-stroke 270 cubic inch engine. This means the cars could pull a numerically higher gear ratio, which improved acceleration out of the corners with no loss of top speed. You could get up to top speed more quickly, and stay pegged at the redline longer. Figure another 2 mph.

Actually, the biggest single improvement in lap times came in 1956. Why? Because Tony Hulman repaved most of the track after the 1955 race. This new asphalt—with only the front straight left in brick—had more to do with increasing lap speeds than any of A.J. Watson's "demon tweaks." Figure the track repaving was worth 3 mph in qualifying speed, all by itself. The new asphalt provided better grip, a smoother ride...and finally eliminated most of the bumpy brick. There was no science to it, just a lot of money.

POP

In the Forties, California drag racers discovered that an explosive compound of nitrogen, oxygen and hydrogen called nitromethane—nitro, like the "N" in TNT—would add additional oxygen to the mix in an engine's combustion chamber. They called it *pop.* Even an 85/15 mix of methanol and nitro would add about 50 hp to the old Offy, but it would also detonate a $7000 engine like a hand grenade if everything wasn't *precisely* right. After a lot of expensive trial and error, it became pretty common for crew chiefs in the Fifties to mix 15 or 20 percent pop into their fuel for qualifying, but not for the race itself. That's why there's often a 3 mph discrepancy between qualifying and the fastest lap in the race.

TIRES

There was also a dramatic change to wider, nylon-cord tires that could handle

(above) The first crash helmet to really offer protection to a driver's head was developed by racer Hal Minyard. It's a fiberglass globe filled with leather-covered foam, not all that different from today's helmets but a quantum leap forward from the peaked Cromwell, Herbert Johnson or "puddin' bowl" helmets used before then. Those were made of not much more than *papier mache* layers of canvas lined with cork and were originally intended for polo players. The new Bell, McHal and Buco helmets offered real energy-absorption and were designed especially for motor racing. Johnnie Parsons wore the first fiberglass helmet at Indianapolis in 1953; hold-out Dick Rathmann wore the last Cromwell at Indianapolis in 1964. The helmet above is the one Sam Hanks wore in 1955, '56 and '57.

the higher speeds produced by roadsters running on pop. Firestone Tire and Rubber Company was the only tire supplier in those days. And their basic Indy tire hadn't changed since 1936, when Eddie Rickenbacker paved the corners and the abrasive asphalt ate the tires faster than the previous bricks had done.

In 1953 and '54, Firestone starting building tires based on their World War II aircraft technology. This meant bias-ply nylon cord construction plus softer compound tires inflated to 50 psi. The new tires were a full 1.5 inches wider than before. Everything is relative. Most Indianapolis cars in those days were set up with 8.00-18 tires on the back; 7.60-16s on the front. These put about 5 inches of tread on the asphalt. The Novi used super-tall 20 inch wheels which must have fed a tremendous amount of centrifugal force into the suspension at 180 mph.

These improved tires were still the weak link in the Fifties. Indeed, most of the chassis fiddling was to try balancing the chassis and equalizing tire wear left and right. If the tires had been more durable to start with, most of this feverish activity wouldn't have gone on at all. Still, thanks to the new tires and better chassis, in the mid-Fifties most drivers were hitting over 130 mph in the corners and higher speeds on the straights as well. The new tires were said to be worth 300 to 500 rpm on the straights thanks to their better traction.

THE TURNING POINT

When Tony Hulman spent his millions to improve the Indianapolis Motor Speedway in the mid-Fifties—repaving most of the track in 1955, organizing the Speedway Museum and incorporating it into a new office/museum building complex in 1956, erecting a new control tower in 1957—it was an act of faith. Why? Because worldwide, 1955 was probably the worst year in the history of motor racing. On May 26, 1955, Formula One World Champion Alberto Ascari was killed at Monza. Four days later, Bill Vukovich was killed at Indianapolis.

And then came June 11, 1955. Pierre Bouillion-Levegh, driving a factory Mercedes-Benz 300SLR, catapulted through the crowd of spectators lining the pit straight at LeMans, his magnesium-bodied sports/racer exploding like burning

(below) Johnny Boyd in the Bowes Seal Fast Special was the top-finishing Kurtis/ Offy in 1958...third behind the laydown Epperlys of Jimmy Bryan and George Amick. You can see from the names on the body that Boyd's crew chief was the legendary George Bignotti, just starting his fabulous career. The crew still doesn't have any sort of protection in case of fire, though Boyd is wearing an early fiberglass helmet and gloves. Thanks to his third at Indianapolis and fifth at Milwaukee two weeks later, Boyd was fighting for the National Championship until his hands were seriously burned when his Champ car caught fire at Langhorne. He never had as good a chance at either the 500 or the USAC championship, before or after 1958.

Faces Behind the
Scenes, 1960:
(above) Well-
known starter Pat
Vidan is color-
coordinated to
match his flag.
(above right)
Smokey Yunick,
proprietor of the
"Best Damn Garage
in Town" (Daytona
Beach, Florida) and
probably the
canniest crew chief
ever to confront a
USAC official.

(above) Not another overnight engine change! Norm Demler's 1959 team pulled themselves together and put Paul Goldsmith's Epperly laydown roadster into fifth on Memorial Day. (left) The classic Offy roadster. Rodger Ward won in A.J. Watson's Leader Card Special in 1959 and '62,

1957

Winner: Sam Hanks, Salih/Offy, 135.601 mph
Winner's Purse: $103,844
Total Purse: $300,252
Pace Car: F.C. "Jack" Reith, Mercury Turnpike Cruiser

George Salih prepared the radical "laydown" roadster with which Sam Hanks easily won. Hanks tearfully retired from racing in Victory Lane after the race. Veteran Paul Russo jammed a Novi into fourth, its best performance since finishing fourth in 1941 and 1947, third in 1948.

Number	Driver	Sponsor/Team	Engine Type/Displacement	Chassis	Qualifying	Start/Finish	Laps
9	Sam Hanks	Belond Exhaust/George Salih	Offy I-4/250 cu.in.	Salih	142.812	13/1	200
26	Jim Rathmann	Chiropractic/Lindsey Hopkins	Offy I-4/255 cu.in.	Epperly	139.806	32/2	200
1	Jimmy Bryan	Dean Van Lines	Offy I-4/252 cu.in.	Kuzma	141.188	15/3	200
54	Paul Russo	Novi Auto/Novi Racing	Novi V-8/169 cu.in.	KK500F	144.817	10/4	200
73	Andy Linden	McNamara/Kalamazoo Sports	Offy I-4/255 cu.in.	KK500G	143.244	12/5	200
6	Johnny Boyd	Bowes Seal Fast/Bignotti	Offy I-4/252 cu.in.	KK500G	142.10	5/6	200
48	Marshall Teague	Sumar/Chapman Root	Offy I-4/255 cu.in.	KK500D	140.329	28/7	200
12	Pat O'Connor	Sumar/Chapman Root	Offy I-4/255 cu.in.	KK500G	143.948	1/8	200
7	Bob Veith	Bob Estes	Offy I-4/255 cu.in.	Phillips	141.016	16/9	200
22	Gene Hartley	Massaglia Hotels	Offy I-4/252 cu.in.	Lesovsky	141.271	14/10	200
19	Jack Turner	Bardahl/Pat Clancy	Offy I-4/252 cu.in.	KK500G	140.367	19/11	200
10	Johnny Thomson	D-A Lubricant Racing	Offy I-4/252 cu.in.	Kuzma	143.529	11/12	199
95	Bob Christie	Jones & Maley/Cars	Offy I-4/252 cu.in.	KK500C	139.779	33/13	197
82	Chuck Weyant	Central Excavating/Pete Salemi	Offy I-4/252 cu.in.	Kuzma	141.105	25/14	196
27	Tony Bettenhausen	Novi Auto/Novi Racing	Novi V-8/169 cu.in.	KK500F	142.439	22/15	195
18	Johnnie Parsons	Sumar/Chapman Root	Offy I-4/255 cu.in.	KK500G	140.784	17/16	195
3	Don Freeland	Ansted Rotary	Offy I-4/252 cu.in.	KK500D	139.649	21/17	192
5	Jimmy Reece	Hoyt Machine/Sommer	Offy I-4/255 cu.in.	KK500C	142.006	6/18	182
92	Don Edmunds	Roy McKay	Offy I-4/251 cu.in.	KK500G	140.449	27/19	170
28	Johnnie Tolan	Greenman-Casale	Offy I-4/252 cu.in.	Kuzma	139.844	31/20	138
89	Al Herman	Dunn Engineering	Offy I-4/251 cu.in.	Dunn	140.007	30/21	111
14	Fred Agabashian	Bowes Seal Fast/Bignotti	Offy I-4/252 cu.in.	KK500G	142.557	4/22	107
88	Eddie Sachs	Peter Schmidt	Offy I-4/251 cu.in.	Kuzma	143.872	2/23	105
77	Mike Magill	Dayton Steel Foundry/Walther	Offy I-4/252 cu.in.	KK500G	140.411	18/24	101
43	Eddie Johnson	H.A. Chapman	Offy I-4/252 cu.in.	KK500G	140.171	20/25	93
31	Bill Cheesbourg	Schildmeier Seal/Donaldson	Offy I-4/251 cu.in.	KK500G	141.565	23/26	81
16	Al Keller	Bardahl/Pat Clancy	Offy I-4/252 cu.in.	KK500G	141.398	8/27	75
57	Jimmy Daywalt	Helse/H.H. Johnson	Offy I-4/252 cu.in.	KK500C	140.203	29/28	53
83	Ed Elisian	McNamara/Kalamazoo Sports	Offy I-4/255 cu.in.	KK500D	141.777	7/29	51
8	Rodger Ward	Roger Wolcott	Offy I-4/166 cu.in.	Lesovsky	141.321	24/30	27
52	Troy Ruttman	John Zink	Offy I-4/252 cu.in.	Watson	142.772	3/31	13
55	Eddie Russo	Sclavi & Amos	Offy I-4/252 cu.in.	KK500C	140.862	26/32	0
23	Elmer George	Travelon Trailer/Ernest Ruiz	Offy I-4/252 cu.in.	KK500B	140.729	9/33	0

shrapnel. At least eighty-one spectators were killed, hundreds more were injured. LeMans 1955 was the worst accident in racing history, far worse than anything that had happened during Paris-Madrid in 1903.

Coming on top of the deaths of Ascari and Vukovich, all within a period of two weeks, the public reaction was understandable. All over the world—including America—there were calls for a ban on racing. Mercedes withdrew from LeMans immediately and from all racing at the end of the year. Lancia sold their Formula One cars to Ferrari. Switzerland, once the home of innumerable hillclimbs, banned all motor racing permanently. The Grand Prix season was shortened, and many tracks closed.

The following year, LeMans was postponed from June until the summer while safety changes were made to the track and pits. Englishman Mike Hawthorn had been blamed by many people—especially the French—for causing Frenchman Levegh's accident. Hawthorn was driving a Jaguar. Jaguar gave it one more year to show that they wouldn't be bullied by the French newspapers, but after LeMans in 1956, Jaguar retired from racing, too.

THE FOUNDING OF USAC

In America in 1955, the American Automobile Association—which had been sanctioning auto racing since before World War I—decided that it was bad for their image to be associated with such a dangerous sport. The AAA abruptly stopped all racing activities. Tony Hulman, more power to him, never considered turning the Indianapolis Motor Speedway into a shopping mall. Instead, he re-paved and refurbished the track to make it as safe as possible, including a new pit apron first used in the 1957 race, separated from the track by a concrete wall. This was one of the first separate pit lanes at any race track in the world.

At the same time, in September of 1955, Hulman organized the United States Auto Club to take over the AAA's sanctioning function. Former driver Duane Carter was elected USAC Director of Competition. Even more than the AAA, USAC was associated with Indianapolis, since many of the officers and aims of the two organizations were the same. USAC not only provided a smooth transition at the Speedway, but got involved in areas, such as sports car racing, that the AAA had rarely touched. Auto racing had become professional enough by 1956 that it really deserved its own full-time sanctioning body, not a group to whom racing was only a sideline. USAC was the right group at the right time.

When USAC took over, the Indianapolis formula was still for 270 cubic inch (4.42-liters) unsupercharged—the Offy—or 183 cubic inches (3.0-liters) super-charged—the Novi. USAC decreed that for 1957, unsupercharged engines would be reduced in size to 256 cubic inches (4.2-liters) and supercharged engines to 171 cubic inches (2.8-liters). This modest cut in displacement had virtually no effect

(below) Ecstatic Sam Hanks retired in Victory Lane after winning the 1957 500, seventeen years after his first Speedway attempt. He was AAA Midget National Champion twice, and AAA National Champion in 1953. Financially secure thanks to wise investments, he came back as a volunteer Indianapolis official for many years afterward. "If I had it to do over again," he said. "I'd still go racing."

on horsepower or lap speeds at the Speedway, and could even be met with inexpensive modifications to the existing engines. You can think of it more as public relations than a genuine attempt to make the cars go slower.

THE RACE OF TWO WORLDS

Except for responding to mutual tragedy, there was very little communication between American and European racers throughout most of the Fifties. American racing had become essentially a "spec" formula for similar cars all using the same Firestone tires and Offy engines. There were many changes during this decade, but all within the existing framework. Not so in Europe.

Grands Prix stayed with the 1.5-liter supercharged/4.5-liter unsupercharged Formula One through 1951. In 1952 and '53, Grand Prix races were run using 2.0-liter unsupercharged Formula Two cars, for the simple reason that there were no factories willing to campaign the costly supercharged 1.5-liter machines.

From 1954 through 1960, Grand Prix races were conducted using new Formula One cars with 2.5-liter engines, unsupercharged. This was a grand formula that brought such memorable front-engine racing cars as the W-196 Mercedes, Maserati 250F, Lancia D50 and Tony Vandervell's gorgeous Vanwall. These Formula One cars of the late-Fifties were actually somewhat similar in size and performance to Indianapolis cars, and so communications were re-established between Europe and America. Some European cars and drivers showed up at the Speedway, and some American racers went to Europe.

There were two unique meetings between the USAC racers and the Grand Prix stars. In 1955, the Monza Autodromo outside Milan was rebuilt. The existing road racing course was maintained, but within it was built a 2.5-mile oval, with turns banked at 38 degrees. This was construction that had been planned long before the dreadful events of May and June, and, by the end of the summer, it was essentially finished. Like the old Brooklands track rendered unusable during World War

THE LAYDOWN

Frank Kurtis' revolutionary rear-drive roadster angled the old Offy 36 degrees from the vertical and put the driveshaft down the left side of the car. Crew chief George Salih figured if a little is good, a lot should be just enough. For the 1957 race, he got Leo Goossen to rework the Offy so it could be laid almost horizontal, 72 degrees from the vertical.

Then Salih had Lawndale, California, car builder Quin Epperly build a new chassis that placed this "laydown" engine even further to the left, to shift as much weight to the inside of the turns as possible. Over this, Epperly put the lowest, slipperiest body ever seen at Indianapolis. The cowl was only 21 inches off the ground. Epperly also added a tall tailfin to the rear for stability, something that Frank Kurtis had introduced on the new Novi the year before.

The rest is history. Veteran Sam Hanks won with Salih's car in 1957, Jimmy Bryan repeated with the same car in 1958. By then, Epperly had built two more cars to the same design, but with even lower bodywork. George Amick was second behind Bryan; Tony Bettenhausen was fourth. For 1959, there were two more. George Amick set a track record at the new Daytona Speedway at 176.887 mph, then crashed. The car was rebuilt, and Johnny Boyd took it to sixth at the Speedway. Tony Bettenhausen was fourth again and Paul Goldsmith fifth. The cars remained competitive in the Top Five at Indianapolis for years. Bill Cheesbourg took the last one to sixteenth in 1964.

Kurtis, Kuzma and Lesovsky copied the laydown Salih-Epperly as early as 1958, and their cars also ran near the top for years. But they were already also-rans. The incredible A.J. Watson steam-roller was already moving, and his cars would win the 500 six years in a row starting in 1959. Watson's cars looked tall, heavy and old-fashioned compared to the laydowns. But they were actually lighter, more aerodynamic and better balanced. The extreme laydowns were a short-lived phenomenon. But in their day, they were simply unbeatable. ■

(left) Dancer Cyd Charisse and Alice Hanks hold red and white carnations, 1957 500 winner Sam Hanks holds a quart of milk while Speedway owner Tony Hulman, crew chief George Salih and sponsor Sandy Belond enjoy the crush in Victory Lane. The grimy yellow Belond Exhaust Special "Experimental" is literally knee-high to a celebrity and carries early sponsor decals. These decals started to appear on Indianapolis cars only around 1951. (below) Scrubbed up and presented to the Speedway Museum, the laydown roadster shows its best angle. Low nose reduced drag, tall fin was intended to move center of pressure rearward for better stability at high speeds. Knock-off Halibrand "beanhole" magnesium wheels hold Firestone Deluxe Champions, larger in the rear. Notice how the exhaust pipe is neatly routed along the rocker and all body panels are snugly held by Dzus fasteners.

1958

Winner: Jimmy Bryan, Salih/Offy, 133.791 mph
Winner's Purse: $105,574
Total Purse: $305,217
Pace Car: Sam Hanks, Pontiac Bonneville

A first lap accident fatally injured Pat O'Connor and destroyed seven cars. On the restart, Eddie Sachs, George Amick, Tony Bettenhausen and Jimmy Bryan dueled for the lead, with Bryan finally winning out in the same Belond Exhaust Special with which Sam Hanks won in 1957.

Number	Driver	Sponsor/Team	Engine Type/Displacement	Chassis	Qualifying	Start/Finish	Laps
1	Jimmy Bryan	Belond AP/George Salih	Offy I-4/252 cu.in.	Salih	144.185	7/1	200
99	George Amick	Norman Demler	Offy I-4/255 cu.in.	Epperly	142.710	25/2	200
9	Johnny Boyd	Bowes Seal Fast	Offy I-4/252 cu.in.	KK500G	144.023	8/3	200
33	Tony Bettenhausen	Jones & Maley/Cars Inc.	Offy I-4/252 cu.in.	Epperly	143.919	9/4	200
2	Jim Rathmann	Leader Card 500/Hopkins	Offy I-4/252 cu.in.	Epperly	143.147	20/5	200
16	Jimmy Reece	John Zink	Offy I-4/252 cu.in.	Watson	145.513	3/6	200
26	Don Freeland	Bob Estes	Offy I-4/252 cu.in.	Phillips	143.033	13/7	200
44	Jud Larson	John Zink	Offy I-4/252 cu.in.	Watson	143.512	19/8	200
61	Eddie Johnson	Bryant Heating/Donaldson	Offy I-4/251 cu.in.	KK500G	142.670	26/9	200
54	Bill Cheesbourg	Novi Auto/Novi Racing	Novi V-8/169 cu.in.	KK500F	142.546	33/10	200
52	Al Keller	Bardahl/Pat Clancy	Offy I-4/252 cu.in.	KK500G-2	142.931	21/11	200
45	Johnnie Parsons	Fred Gerhardt	Offy I-4/252 cu.in.	Kurtis	144.683	6/12	200
19	Johnnie Tolan	Greenman-Casale	Offy I-4/252 cu.in.	Kuzma	142.309	30/13	200
65	Bob Christie	Federal Engineering	Offy I-4/251 cu.in.	KK500C	142.253	17/14	189
59	Dempsey Wilson	Bob Sorenson	Offy I-4/252 cu.in.	Kuzma	134.272	32/15	151
29	A.J. Foyt	Dean Van Lines	Offy I-4/252 cu.in.	Kuzma	143.130	12/16	148
77	Mike Magill	Dayton Steel Foundry/Walther	Offy I-4/255 cu.in.	KK500G	142.276	31/17	136
15	Paul Russo	Novi Auto/Novi Racing	Novi V-8/169 cu.in.	KK500F	142.959	14/18	122
83	Shorty Templeman	McNamara/Kalamazoo Sports	Offy I-4/255 cu.in.	KK500D	142.817	23/19	116
8	Rodger Ward	Wolcott Fuel Injection	Offy I4/252 cu.in.	Lesovsky	143.266	11/20	93
43	Billy Garrett	H.A. Chapman	Offy I-4/252 cu.in.	KK500G	142.778	15/21	80
88	Eddie Sachs	Peter Schmidt	Offy I-4/255 cu.in.	Kuzma	144.660	18/22	68
7	Johnny Thomson	D-A Lubricant/Racing	Offy I-4/251 cu.in.	Kurtis	142.908	22/23	52
89	Chuck Weyant	Dunn Engineering	Offy I-4/251 cu.in.	Dunn	142.608	29/24	38
25	Jack Turner	Massaglia Hotels	Offy I-4/252 cu.in.	Lesovsky	143.438	10/25	21
14	Bob Veith	Bowes Seal Fast	Offy I-4/252 cu.in.	KK500G	144.881	4/26	1
97	Dick Rathmann	McNamara/Kalamazoo Sports	Offy I-4/255 cu.in.	Watson	145.974	1/27	0
5	Ed Elisian	John Zink/Ellen McKinney Zink	Offy I-4/252 cu.in.	Watson	145.926	2/28	0
4	Pat O'Connor	Sumar/Chapman Root	Offy I-4/255 cu.in.	KK500G	144.823	5/29	0
31	Paul Goldsmith	City of Daytona/Smokey Yunick	Offy I-4/255 cu.in.	KK500G	142.744	16/30	0
92	Jerry Unser	Roy McKay	Offy I-4/251 cu.in.	KK500G	142.755	24/31	0
68	Len Sutton	Jim Robbins	Offy I-4/255 cu.in.	KK500G	142.653	27/32	0
57	Art Bisch	Helse/H.H. Johnson	Offy I-4/251 cu.in.	Kuzma	142.631	28/33	0

II, the Monza oval was paved in concrete and, like Brooklands, turned out to be *very* bumpy right from the beginning.

Having built this showplace, nobody in Italy seems to have known what to do with it. The oval sat idle for two years, though most of the banking was incorporated into the road course for the Italian Grand Prix. Finally, on June 29, 1957, Monza hosted The Race of Two Worlds, meant to be a showdown between European drivers and American drivers in comparable equipment. It was hoped that this would get the ball rolling at Monza by introducing European spectators to the excitement of high-speed oval track racing.

Monza paid for ten USAC stars, their cars and crews to fly to Milan. Tony

Bettenhausen, Jimmy Bryan, Ray Crawford, Andy Linden, Pat O'Connor, Johnnie Parsons, Troy Ruttman, Paul Russo, Eddie Sachs and Bob Veith made a pretty good cross-section of American racers, including three Indianapolis 500 winners and three National Champions.

The Europeans failed to show. Finally, the Scots Ecurie Ecosse team, who had finished first and second at LeMans the weekend before, agreed to bring their three Jaguar D-type sports/racers. These were all the wrong kind of car for the oval. Jean Behra brought an old Maserati 250F. It, too, was slow.

The Monza track was so rough that the cars simply shook apart. The "race" consisted of three 63 lap heats. Tony Bettenhausen set a new closed-course World Speed Record of 176.818 mph in his Novi. But the star was Jimmy Bryan, who won two of the three heats, and The Race of Two Worlds overall. He took home $35,000, which was a tidy sum in those days.

In 1958, a number of top-rank European drivers were attracted by this prize money. Ferrari sent Luigi Musso, Phil Hill and Mike Hawthorn. Maserati built the bizarre Eldorado Ice Cream Special for Stirling Moss. Jack Fairman came in a Lister/Jag, Masten Gregory and Ivor Bueb in Jaguar D-types. The Americans brought two extra cars with them, one for Juan Manuel Fangio and one for Maurice Trintignant.

Most of the Americans from the previous year returned, plus Jim Rathmann, Rodger Ward, Johnny Thomson, Don Freeland, Jimmy Reece and A.J. Foyt. Jim Rathmann and Jimmy Bryan were first and second, with a Ferrari shared by Musso, Hawthorn and Hill in third. Poor Stirling Moss ran third most of the time, until the Maserati's steering broke at 170 mph on the banking and slammed him into the guardrail. Moss was lucky to walk away.

The Race of Two Worlds had virtually no effect on European racing. The one interesting result is that the Eldorado Special came to Indianapolis, as well as

(above) Signor Zanetti of the Italian Eldorado ice cream company hired Maserati to assemble this one-off from 250F GP car and 450S sports/racing car pieces. Stirling Moss drove it at Monza in the June, 1958 "Race of Two Worlds," but crashed when the steering broke. Ralph Liguori tried to qualify it at Indianapolis in 1959. His 136.395 mph was too slow. **(below)** Rodger Ward #1 and Jim Rathmann #4 in matching Watson roadsters dueled for the lead in 1959 and '60. Ward won the first year, Rathmann second. The positions were reversed the next time out.

World Champions Nino Farina and Juan Manuel Fangio. None of them did anything memorable at Indianapolis, however.

THE NEW PROFESSIONALS

The fundamental change in American racing during the Fifties is that it became a business again. Back in the Twenties, racing was for professionals. Then in the Thirties and Forties, it became a little more laid-back. In the Fifties, Tony Hulman was the acknowledged leader of American racing, and he was emphatically *not* a car nut with gasoline in his veins who'd do anything to hang around a race track. Hulman was an impeccably dressed, successful Midwest businessman who tried to run American racing like any other profit-making division of Hulman and Company.

To accomplish that, he poured money into the Indianapolis Motor Speedway, making it a showplace. Like his predecessor Carl Fisher, he deliberately made the Indy purse so large that it was always the biggest payout in sports. That was just good business. The excellent track and large purse attracted both spectators and racers, and they attracted sponsors. So the competition became more keen, which attracted more spectators and more sponsors. It was a classic business school example of how to make your company grow.

It wouldn't have worked without an influx of wealthy sponsors to fund all these new cars filled with new ideas. In the Thirties and Forties, progress was so slow that you could race a given car for years, decades even. By the mid-Fifties, competition was so stiff that even the best cars stayed competitive for no more than three years. Top teams bought a new car every year. In 1956, author Vic Roberts figured that to "take at crack at the $270,000 offered as Indy prize money," it would cost $8000 for a chassis, $2500 for a body and $6600 for an engine.

That was just for starters, of course. Even a mid-pack team running on the thin-

(right) In 1956, Dr. George Snively started the Snell Memorial Foundation to test crash helmets. Lightweight helmets that "crush" to absorb impact were found to be safer than the heavy helmets then in vogue. By the end of the decade, smart drivers were using a "Snell Approved" Bell 500 TX like Freddie Agabashian wore to qualify at Indianapolis in 1958. Poor Fred didn't make the cut.
(below) Neither did five-time Formula One World Champion Juan Manuel Fangio, who tried George Walther's Dayton Steel Foundry Kurtis 500G in 1958. Mike Magill finally qualified it on the last row and finished seventeenth. That's a pretty nice '58 Ford Thunderbird being used as a camera car.

NOVI

Lou Welch came back to the Speedway every year with his front-wheel drive Kurtis/Novis. They were great crowd favorites because of their obvious horsepower, the incredible noise they made and, well, because while definitely underdogs, they were just so *neat*. But they were also hopelessly outclassed.

So in 1956, Welch had Frank Kurtis build him three new chassis, two race cars and a spare. Based on the current KK500E, these were rear-wheel drive, with tubular space frame, cross-chassis torsion bars and the engine/drivetrain offset to the left with the driver on the right. The thirsty supercharged, 3.0-liter V-8 made 500 hp at 7000 rpm, but still required 82 gallons of fuel on board. Kurtis got the car weight down under 1900 lbs. Not bad, considering the engine alone weighed 575 lbs.

Paul Russo qualified eighth in 1956, but blew a tire while leading and was the first car out. In 1957, he kept it all together and finished fourth with Tony Bettenhausen back in fifteenth in the second car. The next year, Bill Cheesbourg was tenth, Russo eighteenth. In 1959, neither car was fast enough to qualify, since even in three years, the "bump speed" had increased from 138 mph to 141 mph and the Novis were becoming obsolete again. Welch finally gave up in 1960 and sold the whole team to Andy Granatelli.

Andy Granatelli owned Paxton Products, which made superchargers. By redesigning the supercharger, Paxton's engineers boosted the Novi to 640 hp at 7600 rpm, the most powerful engine to run at the Speedway up to that point. Top speed on the straights zoomed from 167 mph to 180 mph. That was mind-boggling performance at the time. It took two years to get the cars sorted out, but Jim Hurtubise, Art Malone and Bobby Unser all made the field in 1963. All were out by lap 102. Jim McElreath replaced Hurtubise in '64 and Malone got a Novi into eleventh. Granatelli fitted Unser's car with Ferguson four-wheel drive for 1964, but he never got past the first lap. In 1965 he started eighth and finished nineteenth. Hurtubise broke his transmission on the first lap in 1965.

Andy Granatelli finally got fed up with the Novi, and went off with his turbine cars. And that was that. After twenty-four years, no wins, a few hits, uncounted errors and a million heartbreaks, the Novi was done at Indianapolis. Nobody who ever heard one will ever forget the sound, a penetrating roar that went right to your heart. Novi. Now *that* was a racing car. ∎

(above) Last gasp of the Novi, 1965. Young Bobby Unser qualified at 157.467 mph in this Ferguson four-wheel drive, supercharged 640 hp monster, just 4 mph off the pole. As always, the Novi showed great potential, accomplished nothing. As Charles Schultz's Charlie Brown once lamented, "There's no heavier burden than a great potential."
(left) Befinned mid-Fifties Novi is Frank Kurtis' rear-drive version. Bill Cheesbourg got this one into tenth in 1958. As always, the Novi made more power than the Offy, but its extra weight and thirst wore out tires and required extra pit stops. If the race had been the Indianapolis 100, the Novi would have been unbeatable.

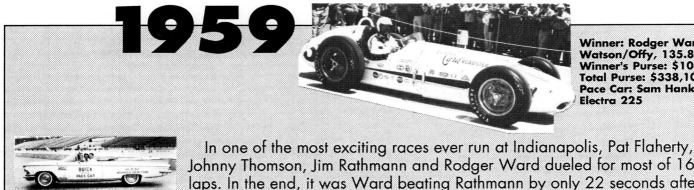

1959

Winner: Rodger Ward,
Watson/Offy, 135.857 mph
Winner's Purse: $106,850
Total Purse: $338,100
Pace Car: Sam Hanks, Buick
Electra 225

In one of the most exciting races ever run at Indianapolis, Pat Flaherty, Johnny Thomson, Jim Rathmann and Rodger Ward dueled for most of 163 laps. In the end, it was Ward beating Rathmann by only 22 seconds after Flaherty hit the Turn Four wall on lap 163 and Thomson suffered car trouble.

Number	Driver	Sponsor/Team	Engine Type/Displacement	Chassis	Qualifying	Start/Finish	Laps
5	Rodger Ward	Leader Card 500 Roadster	Offy I-4/252 cu.in.	Watson	144.035	6/1	200
16	Jim Rathmann	Simoniz/Lindsey Hopkins	Offy I-4/252 cu.in.	Watson	144.433	3/2	200
3	Johnny Thomson	Racing Associates	Offy I-4/252 cu.in.	Lesovsky	145.908	1/3	200
1	Tony Bettenhausen	Hoover Motor Express/Wills	Offy I-4/252 cu.in.	Epperly	142.721	15/4	200
99	Paul Goldsmith	Norman Demler	Offy I-4/255 cu.in.	Epperly	142.670	16/5	200
33	Johnny Boyd	Bowes Seal Fast/Bignotti	Offy I-4/252 cu.in.	Epperly	142.812	11/6	200
37	Duane Carter	Smokey Yunick	Offy I-4/252 cu.in.	Kurtis	142.795	12/7	200
19	Eddie Johnson	Bryant Heating/Donaldson	Offy I-4/251 cu.in.	KK500G	144.000	8/8	200
45	Paul Russo	Bardahl/Fred Gerhardt	Offy I-4/252 cu.in.	KK500G	142.383	27/9	200
10	A.J. Foyt	Dean Van Lines	Offy I-4/252 cu.in.	Kuzma	142.648	17/10	200
88	Gene Hartley	Drewry's/R.T. Marley	Offy I-4/255 cu.in.	Kuzma	143.575	9/11	200
74	Bob Veith	John Zink Heater	Offy I-4/252 cu.in.	Moore	144.023	7/12	200
89	Al Herman	Dunn Engineering	Offy I-4/251 cu.in.	Dunn	141.939	23/13	200
66	Jimmy Daywalt	Federal Engineering	Offy I-4/251 cu.in.	Kurtis	144.683	13/14	200
71	Chuck Arnold	Hall-Mar	Offy I-4/255 cu.in.	Curtis	142.118	21/15	200
58	Jim McWithey	Ray Brady	Offy I-4/252 cu.in.	KK500C	141.215	33/16	200
44	Eddie Sachs	Peter Schmidt	Offy I-4/252 cu.in.	Kuzma	145.425	2/17	182
57	Al Keller	Helse/H.H. Johnson	Offy I-4/251 cu.in.	Kuzma	142.057	28/18	163
64	Pat Flaherty	John Zink Heater	Offy I-4/252 cu.in.	Watson	142.399	18/19	162
73	Dick Rathmann	McNamara/Kalamazoo Sports	Offy I-4/255 cu.in.	Watson	144.248	4/20	150
53	Bill Cheesbourg	Greenman-Casale	Offy I-4/252 cu.in.	Kuzma	141.788	30/21	147
15	Don Freeland	Jim Robbins	Offy I-4/255 cu.in.	KK500G	143.056	25/22	136
49	Ray Crawford	Meguiar's Mirror/Crawford	Offy I-4/255 cu.in.	Elder	141.348	32/23	115
9	Don Branson	Bob Estes	Offy I-4/253 cu.in.	Phillips	143.312	10/24	112
65	Bob Christie	Federal Engineering	Offy I-4/251 cu.in.	KK500C	143.244	24/25	109
48	Bobby Grim	Sumar/Chapman Root	Offy I-4/255 cu.in.	KK500G	144.225	5/26	85
24	Jack Turner	Travelon Trailer/Ernest Ruiz	Offy I-4/252 cu.in.	Christensen	143.478	14/27	47
47	Chuck Weyant	Roy McKay	Offy I-4/252 cu.in.	KK500G	141.950	29/28	45
7	Jud Larson	Bowes Seal Fast/Bignotti	Offy I-4/252 cu.in.	Kurtis	142.298	19/29	45
77	Mike Magill	Dayton Steel Foundry/Walther	Offy I-4/255 cu.in.	Sutton	141.482	31/30	45
87	Red Amick	Wheeler-Foutch	Offy I-4/255 cu.in.	KK500C	142.925	26/31	45
8	Len Sutton	Wolcott Memorial Racing	Offy I-4/168 cu.in.	Lesovsky	142.107	22/32	34
6	Jimmy Bryan	Belond AP Muffler/Salih	Offy I-4/249 cu.in.	Salih	142.118	20/33	1

nest shoestring had to figure on spending $25,000 for the month of May, and that's if they used only one engine and had no trouble at all. Realistically, competing at the 500 cost twice that. Winning, even more. In the Fifties, when schoolteachers earned $3500 a year and a mechanical engineer started at IBM for $100 a week, $50,000 for one four-hour race was a heck of a lot of money.

Every successful racer *had* to have a wealthy patron, and that permanently changed the whole structure of racing in America. The way racing developed in the Fifties—with sponsors, car owners, hired drivers and crew chiefs, independent car builders, independent engine suppliers, small aftermarket makers of exotic racing parts—is the way racing is still organized today.

THE OLD PRO

Young Rodger Ward graduated as a P-38 jockey just as World War II ended. He started racing Midgets in 1946, while still stationed in Texas. By 1950, he was good enough to win the feature at Gilmore Stadium driving a Kurtis powered by a flathead Ford 60. Everybody else had an Offy Midget that normally ran in a faster class. "I feel ready for Indy after that," Ward told the crowd.

Good as his word, he first ran at the Speedway in 1951. Unfortunately, he soon earned an undeserved reputation as a dangerous driver to be around. In 1954, Ward touched wheels with Chuck Stevenson at the DuQuoin, Illinois, dirt track and catapulted into the pits, killing his friend and former crew chief, Clay Smith. Smith was now Stevenson's crew chief and a genius mechanic revered by the close-knit racing fraternity. Wrongly, Rodger was blamed for something that was "just racing."

Then at the Speedway in 1955 Ward was about to be lapped by a four-car group containing race leader Bill Vukovich. At just that moment, Ward's car broke its front axle, causing him to veer into the backstretch wall and tumble upside down into the middle of the track. That set off the four-car accident in which Vukovich was killed. Ward was wrongly blamed again. "The night after Vuky's accident," he later said, "I became a man."

The chance of a lifetime came in 1959. Bob Wilke and A.J. Watson were looking for a driver for their Leader Cards Special. They asked Rodger Ward. The "Three Flying Ws" won both the Indianapolis 500 and USAC National Championship in 1959.

In 1960, Ward was second in the 500 and in the Championship. He was third in both in '61, then won both the 500 and the National Championship again in 1962. He was fourth at Indianapolis, second in the Championship the next year, then second on Memorial Day in 1964.

When he retired after the 500 in 1966, forty-four-year-old Rodger Ward had enjoyed one of the greatest runs ever in American racing: two wins, two seconds, a third and a fourth at Indianapolis plus two National Championships, three seconds and a third in just six years. It couldn't have happened to a nicer guy. ■

(above) May, 1962. Rodger Ward with his sons and his parents in Victory Lane.
(left) Proudly carrying #1 in recognition of his USAC National Championship in 1959, Ward lines up on the front row at the 1960 500. Crew chief A.J. Watson leans on the car. By the way, that big tube projecting from the grille is actually a guide to line up the auxiliary starter with the Offy's crankshaft. The crew would jam the starter motor shaft through that tube, engage a spring-loaded rachet and start the engine. Then they'd pull it back out and jump out of the way as the car accelerated out of the pits. Anyway, in 1960, after a fierce battle with Jim Rathmann, Rodger Ward wisely settled for second when the cord showed through a tire three laps from the finish. As Ward said at the time, "In the old days, I would have gone for it. Now I'm smarter."

1960

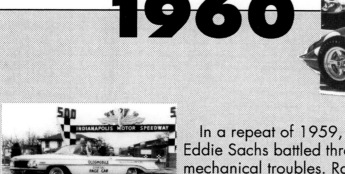

Winner: Jim Rathmann, Watson/Offy, 138.767 mph
Winner's Purse: $110,000
Total Purse: $369,150
Pace Car: Sam Hanks, Oldsmobile "98"

In a repeat of 1959, Johnny Thomson, Jim Rathmann, Rodger Ward and Eddie Sachs battled throughout the race until Sachs and Thomson slowed with mechanical troubles. Rathmann and Ward raced wheel to wheel until three laps from the end, when Ward's tires wore through to the cord and he slowed.

Number	Driver	Sponsor/Team	Engine Type/Displacement	Chassis	Qualifying	Start/Finish	Laps
4	Jim Rathmann	Ken-Paul	Offy I-4/252 cu.in.	Watson	146.371	2/1	200
1	Rodger Ward	Leader Card 500 Roadster	Offy I-4/252 cu.in.	Watson	145.560	3/2	200
99	Paul Goldsmith	Norman Demler	Offy I-4/255 cu.in.	Epperly	142.783	26/3	200
7	Don Branson	Bob Estes	Offy I-4/252 cu.in.	Phillips	144.753	8/4	200
3	Johnny Thomson	Adams Quarter Horse Racing	Offy I-4/252 cu.in.	Lesovsky	146.443	17/5	200
22	Eddie Johnson	Jim Robbins	Offy I-4/252 cu.in.	Trevis	145.003	7/6	200
98	Lloyd Ruby	J.C. Agajanian	Offy I-4/252 cu.in.	Watson	144.208	12/7	200
44	Bob Veith	Peter Schmidt	Offy I-4/252 cu.in.	Meskowski	143.363	25/8	200
18	Bud Tingelstad	Jim Robbins	Offy I-4/252 cu.in.	Trevis	142.354	28/9	200
38	Bob Christie	Federal Engineering	Offy I-4/255 cu.in.	KK500C	143.638	14/10	200
27	Red Amick	King O'Lawn/Leonard Faas	Offy I-4/252 cu.in.	Salih	143.084	22/11	200
17	Duane Carter	Thompson/Ensley & Murphy	Offy I-4/252 cu.in.	Kuzma	142.631	27/12	200
39	Bill Homeier	Ridgewood Builders/Hall	Offy I-4/252 cu.in.	Kuzma	141.248	31/13	200
48	Gene Hartley	Sumar/Chapman Root	Offy I-4/252 cu.in.	KK500G	143.896	24/14	196
65	Chuck Stevenson	Leader Card 500 Roadster	Offy I-4/252 cu.in.	Watson	144.665	9/15	196
14	Bobby Grim	William Forbes	Offy I-4/252 cu.in.	Meskowski	143.158	21/16	194
26	Shorty Templeman	Federal Engineering	Offy I-4/255 cu.in.	KK500C	143.856	19/17	191
56	Jim Hurtubise	Travelon Trailer/Ernest Ruiz	Offy I-4/252 cu.in.	Christensen	149.056	23/18	185
10	Jimmy Bryan	Metal-Cal/George Salih	Offy I-4/252 cu.in.	Epperly	144.532	10/19	152
28	Troy Ruttman	John Zink Heater	Offy I-4/252 cu.in.	Watson	145.366	6/20	134
6	Eddie Sachs	Dean Van Lines Racing	Offy I-4/252 cu.in.	Ewing	146.592	1/21	132
73	Don Freeland	Ross-Babcock Traveler/Racing	Offy I-4/252 cu.in.	KK550H	144.352	11/22	129
2	Tony Bettenhausen	Dowgard/Lindsey Hopkins	Offy I-4/252 cu.in.	Watson	145.214	18/23	125
32	Wayne Weiler	Ansted Rotary	Offy I-4/252 cu.in.	Epperly	143.512	15/24	103
5	A.J. Foyt	Bowes Seal Fast/Bignotti	Offy I-4/252 cu.in.	KK500J	143.466	16/25	90
46	Eddie Russo	Go-Kart/C.O. Prather	Offy I-4/255 cu.in.	KK500G	142.203	29/26	84
8	Johnny Boyd	Bowes Seal Fast/Bignotti	Offy I-4/252 cu.in.	Epperly	143.770	13/27	77
37	Gene Force	Roy McKay	Offy I-4/255 cu.in.	KK500J	143.472	20/28	74
16	Jim McWithey	Hoover Motor Express	Offy I-4/252 cu.in.	Epperly	140.378	32/29	60
9	Len Sutton	S-R Racing/Salemi & Rini	Offy I-4/252 cu.in.	Watson	145.443	5/30	47
97	Dick Rathmann	Jim Robbins	Offy I-4/255 cu.in.	Watson	145.543	4/31	42
76	Al Herman	Joe Hunt Magneto	Offy I-4/252 cu.in.	Ewing	141.838	30/32	34
23	Dempsey Wilson	Bryant Heating/Donaldson	Offy I-4/251 cu.in.	KK500G	143.215	33/33	11

THE ULTIMATE ROADSTER

The high-point of the classic front-engine roadster was in 1962, when Parnelli Jones put himself on the pole with the first 150 mph qualifying lap. But despite all the changes that had gone on during that decade, Parnelli only went 12 mph faster than Bill Vukovich had gone in 1952 with the first Kurtis KK500A. There were incremental improvements everywhere...Kurtis, Watson and their rivals had made a lot of changes over ten years. But the changes that the roadster builders made were *little* changes. Those little changes weren't enough. In the great scheme of things, the roadsters turned out to be an expensive engineering *cul de sac* of monumental proportions. The time was ripe for revolution.

THE MID-ENGINE REVOLUTION 1961-1968

The arrival of Jack Brabham's Cooper in 1961 didn't *cause* the mid-engine revolution at the Indianapolis Speedway, just as the Boston Tea Party of 1773 didn't *cause* the American Revolution. A revolution *happens*, spontaneously, because any number of unrelated influences converge upon a single point in time and place. Throwing taxable tea in the harbor was just a symbol of myriad problems between Britain and America; the low-slung Cooper was just a symbol that the front-engine Offy roadster was becoming *passe*. Putting the engine behind the driver wasn't even a new idea.

Way back in 1885, when they independently built the world's first two automobiles, both Gottlieb Daimler and Karl Benz put their engines behind the seats, driving the rear wheels through what we would now call a transaxle. It seemed more logical and convenient to them to place the engine and the driven wheels next to each other. It wasn't until around 1900 that more powerful engines became too large to squeeze between the seats and the rear wheels. Only then did

(below) Jack Brabham's tiny green 1961 Cooper/Climax initiated the radical changes that completely altered racing at Indianapolis during the early-Sixties. This makes it one of the most significant cars ever to run at the Speedway.

1961

Winner: A.J. Foyt,
Watson/Offy, 139.130
mph
Winner's Purse: $117,975
Total Purse: $400,000
Pace Car: Sam Hanks,
Ford Thunderbird

Speedway connoisseurs consider this one of the best 500s ever. Seven different drivers led the tight contest, and there were twenty lead changes. In the end, it was young A.J. Foyt chasing Eddie Sachs, but Sachs had to pit with three laps to go and Foyt flashed by to win the "Golden Anniversary 500."

Number	Driver	Sponsor/Team	Engine Type/Displacement	Chassis	Qualifying	Start/ Finish	Laps
1	A.J. Foyt	Bowes Seal Fast/Bignotti	Offy I-4/252 cu.in.	Trevis	145.903	7/1	200
12	Eddie Sachs	Dean Van Lines	Offy I-4/252 cu.in.	Ewing	147.481	1/2	200
2	Rodger Ward	Webb's Sun City/Leader Card	Offy I-4/252 cu.in.	Watson	146.187	4/3	200
7	Shorty Templeman	Bill Forbes Racing Team	Offy I-4/252 cu.in.	Watson	144.341	18/4	200
19	Al Keller	Konstant Hot/Bruce Homeyer	Offy I-4/253 cu.in.	Phillips	146.157	26/5	200
18	Chuck Stevenson	Met-Cal/C&H Supply	Offy I-4/252 cu.in.	Epperly	145.191	28/6	200
31	Bobby Marshman	Hoover Motor Express	Offy I-4/252 cu.in.	Epperly	144.293	33/7	200
5	Lloyd Ruby	Autolite/Lindsey Hopkins	Offy I-4/254 cu.in.	Epperly	146.909	25/8	200
17	Jack Brabham	Cooper-Climax	Climax I-4/168 cu.in.	Cooper	145.144	13/9	200
34	Norm Hall	Federal Engineering	Offy I-4/255 cu.in.	KK500C	144.555	32/10	200
28	Gene Hartley	John Chalik	Offy I-4/252 cu.in.	Trevis	144.817	15/11	198
98	Parnelli Jones	Agajanian Willard Battery	Offy I-4/252 cu.in.	Watson	146.080	5/12	192
97	Dick Rathmann	Jim Robbins	Offy I-4/252 cu.in.	Watson	146.033	6/13	164
10	Paul Goldsmith	Racing Associates	Offy I-4/252 cu.in.	Lesovsky	144.741	17/14	160
15	Wayne Weiler	Lindsey Hopkins	Offy I-4/252 cu.in.	Watson	145.349	12/15	147
35	Dempsey Wilson	Lysle Greenman	Offy I-4/252 cu.in.	Kuzma	144.202	31/16	145
32	Bob Christie	North Electric/William Tucker	Offy I-4/252 cu.in.	Kurtis	144.782	16/17	132
33	Eddie Johnson	Jim Robbins	Offy I-4/252 cu.in.	Kuzma	145.843	10/18	127
8	Len Sutton	Bryant Heating/Salemi & Rini	Offy I-4/252 cu.in.	Watson	145.897	8/19	110
52	Troy Ruttman	John Zink Trackburner	Offy I-4/252 cu.in.	Moore	144.799	22/20	105
41	Johnny Boyd	Leader Card 500 Roadster	Offy I-4/252 cu.in.	Watson	144.092	20/21	105
99	Jim Hurtubise	Norm Demler	Offy I-4/256 cu.in.	Epperly	146.306	3/22	102
86	Ebb Rose	Meyer Speedway/Racing	Offy I-4/252 cu.in.	Porter	144.338	19/23	93
26	Cliff Griffith	McCullough/Edgar Elder	Offy I-4/252 cu.in.	Elder	145.038	30/24	55
45	Jack Turner	Bardahl/Fred Gerhardt	Offy I-4/252 cu.in.	KK500J	144.904	21/25	52
73	A.J. Shepherd	Travelon Trailer/Ernest Ruiz	Offy I-4/252 cu.in.	Watson	144.954	14/26	51
22	Roger McCluskey	Racing Associates	Offy I-4/252 cu.in.	Moore	145.068	29/27	51
14	Bill Cheesbourg	Dean Van Lines	Offy I-4/252 cu.in.	Kuzma	145.873	9/28	50
83	Don Davis	Dart-Kart/Trevis & Morcroft	Offy I-4/252 cu.in.	Trevis	145.349	27/29	49
4	Jim Rathmann	Simoniz/Ken-Paul	Offy I-4/252 cu.in.	Watson	145.413	11/30	48
55	Jimmy Daywalt	Schultz Fueling/C.O. Prather	Offy I-4/251 cu.in.	KK500G	144.219	23/31	27
16	Bobby Grim	Thompson Industries	Offy I-4/252 cu.in.	Watson	144.029	24/32	26
3	Don Branson	Hoover Motor Express	Offy I-4/252 cu.in.	Epperly	146.843	2/33	2

early automobile designers move the engine to the front, up ahead of the dashboard, leaving more room for passengers in the center of the chassis.

There were occassional attempts to build a mid-engine race car over the decades—most famously the streamlined Benz *Tropfenwagen* of 1923—but the first successful mid-engine racer was Ferdinand Porsche's 1934 Auto Union. This effectively packaged a huge twin-supercharged 4.0-liter (244 cubic inch) V-16 ahead of the rear wheels, with the driver located at the extreme front. These Auto Unions earned a reputation as being difficult to drive, and about the only car they inspired was Harry Miller's even more radical but considerably less successful Gulf-Miller Indianapolis car of the late-Thirties.

THE MID-ENGINE REVOLUTION

The revolution at Indianapolis really started in 1946 in England, when John Cooper and his father Charles built a tiny racing car in their garden shed in Surbiton, a suburb of London. This first Cooper was a crude home-built, with Fiat suspension and a JAP 500cc (30 cubic inch) motorcycle engine mounted behind the driver's seat so that the chain drive could directly reach the rear axle. Cooper's little cars rapidly improved, and in the hands of young drivers like Stirling Moss, Peter Collins and Bernie Ecclestone, came to dominate European Formula Three in the early-Fifties.

By 1957, the mid-engine Cooper/Climax was the class of European Formula Two. It used a Coventry-Climax SOHC Four originally designed to power a portable water pump for fire brigades and a proper rear transaxle rather than a motorcycle gearbox and chain drive. By 1958, Stirling Moss and Maurice Trintignant were winning races in Formula One with these curious machines, despite having 2.0-liter (122 cubic inch) engines that developed 100 hp less than the 2.5-liter (152.5 cubic inch) competition. In 1959 and 1960, Australian Jack Brabham ran away with the Formula One World Championship in his Cooper, now fitted with a "full-size" 2495cc four-cylinder Coventry-Climax.

At the time, most European Formula One cars were very traditional front-engine/rear-drive machines, comparatively large and heavy and not unlike contemporary Indianapolis roadsters. The tiny, lightweight, aerodynamic Coopers handled so well they simply drove rings around the old Ferrari, Vanwall and BRM designs, despite having 50 hp less. By 1960, Lotus and BRM were also building mid-engine cars for Formula One, while Lotus and many other smaller constructors copied the mid-engine Cooper not only for Formula One, but also for Formula Two and the new "starter" class that had replaced Formula Three, Formula Junior. It was this welter of mid-engine Formula cars in Europe which led directly to the mid-engine revolution that changed the shape of the Indianapolis 500 for the next three decades. The importance of these seemingly unrelated happenings in Europe cannot be overstated. It was truly the start of a worldwide revolution.

A NEW FORMULA ONE

For 1961, the CSI decreed that Grands Prix would be contested in 1.5-liter (91.5 cubic inch) cars. Superchargers were not allowed, fuel was 100 octane gasoline—no more Avgas—and the minimum weight was 450 kg (990 lbs.). In effect, the FIA abandoned Formula One and decided to use 1.5-liter Formula Two rules for Grands Prix, just as they had done in 1952, '53 and '54. The reason? The FIA was coming under a lot of political pressure to make racing safer, and requiring smaller cars with less powerful engines seemed the quickest way to accomplish that elusive goal.

The British manufacturers—who were winning everything under the 2.5-liter formula—wasted their time lobbying the FIA to retain the old formula, with the

Indianapolis 500 purses sky-rocketed under Tony Hulman's care. The total prize money was only $115,450 in 1946. Ten years later, Sam Hanks was the first driver to win more than six figures. He took home $103,844 for less than four hours work in 1957. In 1964, A.J. Foyt earned $153,650 for winning. How much money was $150,000 in 1964? Well, in February, young "Dick" Petty won his first Daytona 500 NASCAR race and a *big* prize of $35,300. A few months later Parnelli Jones won the professional USRRC sports car race at Riverside, the richest road race in the world thanks to sponsorship by the *L.A. Times*. The purse was big enough to attract international stars like Roger Penske, Jimmy Clark, Dan Gurney, Bruce McLaren, Bob Bondurant and yes, A.J. Foyt. Parnelli won $10,000 plus a Pontiac Grand Prix worth $3400. How big was the 500 purse back then? Big.

1962

Winner: Rodger Ward, Watson/Offy, 140.293 mph
Winner's Purse: $125,015
Total Purse: $426,152
Pace Car: Sam Hanks, Studebaker Lark Daytona

Parnelli Jones started from the pole thanks to the first 150 mph qualifying speed and led until a brake line let go. Rodger Ward and his teammate Len Sutton then held off Eddie Sachs to put their Leader Card Roadsters 1-2. The future was still back in twentieth place, with Dan Gurney.

Number	Driver	Sponsor/Team	Engine Type/Displacement	Chassis	Qualifying	Start/Finish	Laps
3	Rodger Ward	Leader Card 500 Roadster	Offy I-4/252 cu.in.	Watson	149.371	2/1	200
7	Len Sutton	Leader Card 500 Roadster	Offy I-4/252 cu.in.	Watson	149.328	4/2	200
2	Eddie Sachs	Dean-Autolite	Offy I-4/252 cu.in.	Ewing	146.431	27/3	200
27	Don Davis	J.H. Rose Truck/Bob Phillip	Offy I-4/252 cu.in.	Lesovsky	147.209	12/4	200
54	Bobby Marshman	Bryant Heating	Offy I-4/252 cu.in.	Epperly	149.347	3/5	200
15	Jim McElreath	Schulz Fueling/C.O. Prather	Offy I-4/252 cu.in.	Kurtis	149.025	7/6	200
98	Parnelli Jones	Agajanian Willard Battery	Offy I-4/252 cu.in.	Watson	150.370	1/7	200
12	Lloyd Ruby	Thompson Industries/Ansted	Offy I-4/253 cu.in.	Watson	146.520	24/8	200
44	Jim Rathmann	Simoniz Vista/Smokey Yunick	Offy I-4/252 cu.in.	Watson	146.610	23/9	200
38	Johnny Boyd	Metal-Cal/C&H Supply	Offy I-4/252 cu.in.	Epperly	147.047	28/10	200
4	Shorty Templeman	Bill Forbes Racing Team	Offy I-4/252 cu.in.	Watson	149.050	6/11	200
14	Don Branson	Mid-Continent/Hopkins	Offy I-4/252 cu.in.	Epperly	147.312	11/12	200
91	Jim Hurtubise	Jim Robbins/John Pusilo	Offy I-4/252 cu.in.	Watson	146.963	29/13	200
86	Ebb Rose	J.H. Rose Truck/Herb Porter	Offy I-4/252 cu.in.	Porter	146.336	32/14	200
5	Bud Tingelstad	Konstant Hot/Bruce Homeyer	Offy I-4/252 cu.in.	Phillips	147.753	10/15	200
17	Roger McCluskey	Bell Lines Trucking/Sclavi	Offy I-4/252 cu.in.	Watson	147.759	9/16	168
21	Elmer George	Sarkes Tarzian/Mari George	Offy I-4/252 cu.in.	Lesovsky	146.092	17/17	146
26	Troy Ruttman	Jim Robbins	Offy I-4/252 cu.in.	Kuzma	146.765	30/18	140
18	Bobby Grim	Gilbert Morcroft	Offy I-4/252 cu.in.	Trevis	146.604	15/19	96
34	Dan Gurney	Harvey Aluminum	Buick V-8/256 cu.in.	Thompson	147.886	8/20	92
19	Chuck Hulse	Federal Engineering	Offy I-4/252 cu.in.	KK500C	146.377	16/21	91
79	Jimmy Daywalt	Albany, NY/Tassi Vatis	Offy I-4/252 cu.in.	KK500J	146.318	33/22	74
1	A.J. Foyt	Bowes Seal Fast/Bignotti	Offy I-4/252 cu.in.	Trevis	149.074	5/23	69
9	Dick Rathmann	H.A. Chapman	Offy I-4/252 cu.in.	Watson	147.161	13/24	51
32	Eddie Johnson	Polyaire Foam/Peter Torosian	Offy I-4/252 cu.in.	Trevis	146.592	18/25	38
53	Paul Goldsmith	American Rubber/Bignotti	Offy I-4/252 cu.in.	Epperly	146.437	26/26	26
88	Gene Hartley	Drewry's/M&W Racing	Offy I-4/252 cu.in.	Watson	146.969	20/27	23
62	Paul Russo	Denver-Chicago Truck/Osborn	Offy I-4/252 cu.in.	Watson	146.687	14/28	20
45	Jack Turner	Bardahl/Fred Gerhardt	Offy I-4/252 cu.in.	KK500J	146.496	25/29	17
29	Bob Christie	North Electric/William Tucker	Offy I-4/252 cu.in.	KK500J	146.341	31/30	17
83	Allen Crowe	S-R Racing/Salemi & Rini	Offy I-4/252 cu.in.	Trevis	146.831	22/31	17
67	Chuck Rodee	Travelon Trailer/Ernest Ruiz	Offy I-4/252 cu.in.	Watson	146.969	21/32	17
96	Bob Veith	Meguiar's Mirror/Crawford	Offy I-4/252 cu.in.	Elder	146.157	19/33	12

inevitable result that when the 1.5-liter formula went into effect, there wasn't one British car competitive with the new mid-engine V-6 Ferrari 156. Significantly, the new Ferrari, and every other 1961 Formula One car, was mid-engine.

The last Formula One Grand Prix race ever won by a front-engine car was at Monza in 1960, when American Phil Hill beat a mediocre field with his old-fashioned Ferrari 256. All the British teams had stayed home because of a fight with the Italian organizers, so the front-engine Ferrari team finished one-two-three. It was the only race they won all year. In Grand Prix racing, the mid-engine revolution was already complete long before the first mid-engine car appeared at the Indianapolis Motor Speedway. In that sense, the Europeans were five years ahead.

In 1950, the FIA had actually made the 500 a World Championship race; a driver could earn points towards the Formula One Championship by doing well at the Indianapolis 500. There was only a smattering of interest from the European drivers, and only Alberto Ascari ever qualified. When Formula One was revised for 1961, European and American racing had grown so far apart that there was no attempt to develop a formula that would accommodate both Grand Prix and Speedway cars. The Atlantic might just as well have stretched to the moon.

THE REVOLUTION SPREADS TO INDIANAPOLIS

And then, suddenly, there was a mid-engine Grand Prix car circling the Indianapolis Speedway. The Speedway regulars looked at it with the same amazement they would have shown if Flash Gordon had entered his rocketship for the 500. The legend has it that wealthy American sports car racer Jim Kimberly—as in Kimberly-Clark—first suggested to John Cooper that he bring one of his obsolete 2.5-liter Formula One cars to the Speedway and see what it could do. What it could do was 144.8 mph, which would have put test driver Jack Brabham eighth on the grid in 1960.

John Cooper was so encouraged that he modified the car by canting the engine slightly to the left and boring it out to 2.7-liters (168 cubic inches)—the USAC limit was still 4.2-liters (255 cubic inches)—and fitting bigger gas tanks. The result was a 260 hp, 1200 lb. roller skate that could circle the Speedway literally flat-out at 145.1 mph. That was only 2 mph off Eddie Sachs' pole-winning speed in his Offy roadster. The little Cooper was dwarfed by the giant roadsters, but no matter. World Champion Jack Brabham cruised easily into ninth place in the 1961 Indianapolis 500.

Brabham's Cooper was successful because while it could only go 150 mph on the straights at Indianapolis—a good Watson/Offy roadster could top 160 mph—the Cooper could zip through the corners at 145 mph versus about 140 mph for the roadsters. The Cooper also got better fuel economy and better tire wear. It was also a lot less tiring to drive, which is an important consideration in a 500 mile endurance race.

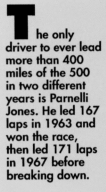

The last team to finish first *and* second at the 500? No, not one of Roger Penske's all-conquering crews, but Rodger Ward and Len Sutton, both driving for Leader Cards back in 1962.

The only driver to ever lead more than 400 miles of the 500 in two different years is Parnelli Jones. He led 167 laps in 1963 and won the race, then led 171 laps in 1967 before breaking down.

(left) Modified for British car importer Kjell Qvale, this is Jack Brabham's '61 Cooper fitted with an Aston Martin DOHC 4.2-liter six-cylinder and driven by Mexican Grand Prix star Pedro Rodriguez. He missed qualifying for the 1963 500 by 1 mph. The team tried again the next year with a similar car, now Offy-powered, but with MG "hydrolastic" suspension units. Walt Hansgen qualified tenth and finished thirteenth.

1963

Winner: Parnelli Jones,
Watson/Offy, 143.137 mph
Winner's Purse: $148,513
Total Purse: $494,030
Pace Car: Sam Hanks,
Chrysler 300J Convertible

The "mid-engine revolution" was in full swing; Scots Formula One star Jimmy Clark was second in his Lotus, Dan Gurney was seventh. But Parnelli Jones was the pole-sitter with his old Watson roadster named "Calhoun." Despite a leaking oil tank and pitside protest, Jones was allowed to keep running and win.

Number	Driver	Sponsor/Team	Engine Type/Displacement	Chassis	Qualifying	Start/ Finish	Laps
98	Parnelli Jones	J.C. Agajanian/Willard Battery	Offy I-4/252 cu.in.	Watson	151.153	1/1	200
92	Jim Clark	Lotus powered by Ford	Ford V-8/256 cu.in.	Lotus	149.750	5/2	200
2	A.J. Foyt	Sheraton-Thompson/Ansted	Offy I-4/252 cu.in.	Trevis	150.615	8/3	200
1	Rodger Ward	Kaiser Aluminum/Leader Cards	Offy I-4/252 cu.in.	Watson	149.800	4/4	200
4	Don Branson	Leader Card 500 Roadster	Offy I-4/252 cu.in.	Watson	150.188	3/5	200
8	Jim McElreath	Bill Forbes Racing Team	Offy I-4/252 cu.in.	Watson	149.744	6/6	200
93	Dan Gurney	Lotus powered by Ford	Ford V-8/256 cu.in.	Lotus	149.019	12/7	200
10	Chuck Hulse	Dean Van Lines	Offy I-4/252 cu.in.	Ewing	149.340	11/8	200
84	Al Miller	Thompson/Harvey Aluminum	Chevy V-8/255 cu.in.	Thompson	149.613	31/9	200
22	Dick Rathmann	Harry Allen Chapman	Offy I-4/252 cu.in.	Watson	149.130	17/10	200
29	Dempsey Wilson	Vita Fresh OJ/Gordon Van Liew	Offy I-4/252 cu.in.	Kuzma	147.832	30/11	200
17	Troy Ruttman	Robbins Autocrat/Jim Robbins	Offy I-4/252 cu.in.	Kuzma	148.374	33/12	200
65	Bob Christie	Travelon Trailer/Ernest Ruiz	Offy I-4/252 cu.in.	Watson	149.123	18/13	200
32	Ebb Rose	Sheraton-Thopson/Ansted	Offy I-4/252 cu.in.	Watson	148.545	32/14	200
14	Roger McCluskey	Konstant Hot/Bruce Homeyer	Offy I-4/252 cu.in.	Watson	148.680	14/15	198
5	Bobby Marshman	Econo-Car Rental/Hopkins	Offy I-4/252 cu.in.	Epperly	149.458	7/16	196
9	Eddie Sachs	Bryant Heating/D.V.S.	Offy I-4/252 cuin.	Watson	149.570	10/17	181
99	Paul Goldsmith	Norm Demler	Offy I-4/252 cu.in.	Watson	150.163	9/18	149
52	Lloyd Ruby	John Zink Trackburner	Offy I-4/252 cu.in.	Moore	149.123	19/19	126
88	Eddie Johnson	Drewry's/M&W Racing	Offy I-4/252 cu.in.	Watson	148.509	21/20	112
45	Chuck Stevenson	Bardahl/Fred Gerhardt	Offy I-4/252 cu.in.	Watson	148.386	22/21	110
56	Jim Hurtubise	Hotel Tropicana/Novi	Novi V-8/166 cu.in.	KK500K	150.257	2/22	102
83	Duane Carter	Thompson Harvey Aluminum	Chevy V-8/255 cu.in.	Thompson	148.002	15/23	100
16	Jim Rathmann	Coral Harbour/Lindsey Hopkins	Offy I-4/252 cu.in.	Watson	147.838	29/24	99
26	Bobby Grim	Gilbert Morcroft	Offy I-4/252 cu.in.	Trevis	148.717	20/25	79
86	Bob Veith	Racing Associates	Offy I-4/252 cu.in.	Porter	148.289	24/26	74
35	Allen Crowe	Gabriel Shocker/Salemi & Rini	Offy I-4/252 cu.in.	Trevis	148.877	13/27	47
54	Bud Tingelstad	Hoover/Tidewater Associates	Offy I-4/252 cu.in.	Epperly	148.227	25/28	46
37	Johnny Rutherford	US Equipment/Ed Kostenuk	Offy I-4/252 cu.in.	Watson	148.063	26/29	43
21	Elmer George	Sarkes Tarzian/Mari George	Offy I-4/252 cu.in.	Lesovsky	147.893	28/30	21
75	Art Malone	STP/Novi	Novi V-8/166 cu.in.	KK500F	148.343	23/31	18
23	Johnny Boyd	Bowes Seal Fast/Salih-Paddock	Offy I-4/252 cu.in.	Epperly	148.038	27/32	12
6	Bobby Unser	Hotel Tropicana/Novi	Novi V-8/166 cu.in.	KK500K	149.421	16/33	2

AMERICAN REACTION

It didn't take a genius to figure out that if you could preserve the Cooper's inherent balance, light weight, good handling and superior aerodynamics, but add another 150 hp by using a full 4.2-liter engine, you could run so fast they'd *never* catch you. It took a year or two for this to fully sink in, and four years to complete the transition from roadsters to mid-engine roller skates. But from the very beginning, the issue was never in doubt. It was just a matter of adapting the basic mid-engine concept to the special requirements of a high-speed oval.

The American with the quickest reaction time was hot-rodder Mickey Thompson, probably because he wasn't already part of the Speedway Establishment with

$100,000 worth of potentially worthless Offy roadsters sitting in his garage. In 1962, maverick Thompson showed up with radical mid-engine cars that were at least one step ahead of even the Coopers. John Cooper, after all, had barely changed his cars since 1957. Typical of most revolutionaries, he had become already tied to his own tradition as soon as the fight was over.

Mickey Thompson was never tied down to anything. His first-ever Speedway cars weren't particularly successful, but with their aluminum chassis/body and Buick aluminum 255 cubic inch V-8s, right off the trailer the Thompson cars were faster than Brabham's Cooper, which of course was the product of literally years of development on the same basic design. In 1963, Thompson showed up with even more radical cars built around an aluminum smallblock Chevrolet V-8. These were handsomely aerodynamic machines, 200 lbs. lighter than the Cooper, and, among other things, introduced the first Firestone low-profile, wide oval racing tires. If Mickey Thompson could have concentrated on one thing long enough to develop these cars, who knows what they might have accomplished.

LADDERS, TUBES AND SPACE FRAMES

Most early automobiles were built like a nineteenth-century farm wagon with a heavy "ladder" frame made from two parallel U-shaped rails connected by cross-members. The separate body was bolted on top of this frame. Up until the mid-Fifties, there were still dirt cars running at Indianapolis built this way, and indeed, there are still passenger cars, not to mention nearly all trucks, built with this primitive body-on-frame construction.

Back in 1885, however, when Karl Benz built his first three-wheeler, he had the chassis built like a bicycle's, out of steel tubing. Many small cars used similar

(left) Energetic whirlwind Mickey Thompson was a California hot-rodder just brimming with new ideas. He set records at Bonneville and drag strips all over the west coast. In 1962, he built a mid-engine car with a Buick V-8 that Dan Gurney qualified eighth at Indianapolis. For 1963, Thompson built three ultra-lightweight "skates" designed by Lotus' John Crosthwaite. The skates weighed only 1050 lbs. and were just 33 inches high to the top of the rollbar. An aluminum small-block Chevy V-8 lived behind the driver. Firestone had to make special tires to fit Thompson's 12 inch wheels... the first "wide oval" tires. The skates never handled very well—designers were still learning about independent rear suspension and how to make it work on a high-speed oval—and only Duane Carter managed to qualify, though solidly in fifteenth. Expatriate American Grand Prix star Masten Gregory came close to qualifying. Indeed, Gregory was just .3 mph too slow in the titanium-chassis skate shown here.

1964

Winner: A.J. Foyt, Watson/Offy, 147.350 mph
Winner's Purse: $153,650
Total Purse: $506,575
Pace Car: Benson Ford, Ford Mustang Convertible

Popular Eddie Sachs and rookie Dave MacDonald were killed in a lap 2 accident. During the somberly restarted race, Jimmy Clark led till a disintegrating tire wrecked his suspension. Parnelli Jones led until his car caught fire in the pits. A.J. Foyt soldiered on to win in his old Watson roadster.

Number	Driver	Sponsor/Team	Engine Type/Displacement	Chassis	Qualifying	Start/Finish	Laps
1	A.J. Foyt	Sheraton-Thompson/Ansted	Offy I-4/252 cu.in.	Watson	154.672	5/1	200
2	Rodger Ward	Kaiser Aluminum/Leader Cards	Ford V-8/255 cu.in.	Watson	156.406	3/2	200
18	Lloyd Ruby	Bill Forbes Racing Team	Offy I-4/252 cu.in.	Watson	153.932	7/3	200
99	Johnny White	Norm Demler	Offy I-4/252 cu.in.	Watson	150.893	21/4	200
88	Johnny Boyd	Vita Fresh OJ/Gordon Van Liew	Offy I-4/252 cu.in.	Kuzma	151.835	13/5	200
15	Bud Tingelstad	Federal Engineering	Offy I-4/252 cu.in.	Trevis	151.210	19/6	198
23	Dick Rathmann	Harry Allen Chapman	Offy I-4/252 cu.in.	Watson	151.860	12/7	197
4	Bob Harkey	Wally Weir Mobilgas	Offy I-4/252 cu.in.	Watson	151.573	27/8	197
68	Bob Wente	Morcroft-Taylor	Offy I-4/252 cu.in.	Trevis	149.869	32/9	197
16	Bobby Grim	Konstant-Hot/Vatis Enterprises	Offy I-4/252 cu.in.	KK500J	151.038	20/10	196
3	Art Malone	Studebaker/STP	Novi I-4/168 cu.in.	KK500K	151.222	30/11	194
5	Don Branson	Wynn's Friction/Leader Cards	Offy I-4/252 cu.in.	Watson	152.672	9/12	187
53	Walt Hansgen	MG Liquid Suspension/Qvale	Offy I-4/252 cu.in.	Huffaker	152.581	10/13	176
56	Jim Hurtubise	Tombstone Life/DVS	Offy I-4/252 cu.in.	Hurtubise	152.542	11/14	141
66	Len Sutton	Bryant Heating/Vollstedt	Offy I-4/252 cu.in.	Vollstedt	153.813	8/15	140
62	Bill Cheesbourg	Arizona Apache Airlines/Osborn	Offy I-4/252 cu.in.	Epperly	148.711	33/16	131
12	Dan Gurney	Lotus Powered By Ford	Ford V-8/255 cu.in.	Lotus	154.487	6/17	110
14	Troy Ruttman	Dayton Steel Wheel/Walther	Offy I-4/252 cu.in.	Watson	151.292	18/18	99
54	Bob Veith	MG Liquid Suspension/Qvale	Offy I-4/252 cu.in.	Huffaker	153.381	23/19	88
52	Jack Brabham	Zink-Urschel Trackburner	Offy I-4/252 cu.in.	Brabham	152.504	25/20	77
28	Jim McElreath	Studebaker/STP	Novi V-8/168 cu.in.	KK500K	152.381	26/21	77
77	Bob Mathouser	Dayton Disc Brake/Walther	Offy I-4/252 cu.in.	Walther	151.451	28/22	77
98	Parnelli Jones	Agajanian/Bowes Seal Fast	Offy I-4/252 cu.in.	Watson	155.099	4/23	55
6	Jim Clark	Lotus Powered By Ford	Ford V-8/255 cu.in.	Lotus	158.828	1/24	47
51	Bobby Marshman	Pure Oil Firebird/Hopkins	Ford V-8/255 cu.in.	Lotus	157.857	2/25	39
84	Eddie Johnson	Thompson-Sears Allstate	Ford V-8/255 cu.in.	Thompson	152.905	24/26	6
86	Johnny Rutherford	Bardahl Racing	Offy I-4/252 cu.in.	Watson	151.400	15/27	2
95	Chuck Stevenson	Diet Rite Cola/Leader Cards	Offy I-4/252 cu.in.	Watson	150.830	29/28	2
83	Dave MacDonald	Thompson-Sears Allstate	Ford V-8/255 cu.in.	Thompson	151.464	14/29	1
25	Eddie Sachs	American Red Ball/D.V.S.	Ford V-8/255 cu.in.	Halibrand	151.439	17/30	1
64	Ronnie Duman	Clean Wear/Nicholas Fulbright	Offy I-4/252 cu.in.	Trevis	149.744	16/31	1
9	Bobby Unser	Studebaker/STP	Novi V-8/168 cu.in.	Ferguson	154.865	22/32	1
26	Norm Hall	Hurst/Pope-Hall	Offy I-4/252 cu.in.	Watson	150.094	31/33	1

frames until around 1900. But because they were untriangulated, these early bicycle-style frames were too flimsy to carry large engines at high speeds on rough roads. The bicycle-style frame died out completely before World War I. The conventional ladder frame remained the norm.

Then in the early-Thirties, the all-conquering Auto Union and Mercedes-Benz Silver Arrows used ladder-type frames in which the longitudinal rails were made from large diameter steel tubing that was stronger and lighter than U-shaped channel. Only a few years later, Frank Kurtis was building Speedway cars this way, using large diameter chrome-moly tubing that was even lighter and stronger. This type of frame built from steel tubing was still around in the Sixties on some race cars and many high-performance street machines. Carroll Shelby's famous Cobra, for example, has this type of longitudinal large tube frame.

But there is a much better way to build a frame from steel tubing. Starting with the Wright Brothers on, airplanes have always been built with what we would now call a space frame. Whether the tubes are wood, bamboo, aluminum or carbon fiber; whether the covering is doped linen, aluminum or nomex-reinforced resin, it matters little. The concept has remained the same until the present day. The tubular space frame is lightweight, easy to engineer, easy to build, easy to repair.

According to legend, ex-aircraft engineer Dante Giacosa designed the first automotive space frame for a Fiat-based 1945 Cisitalia racing car, mostly because Cisitalia was also a bicycle manufacturer and there was plenty of tubing in the shop. Tubular space frames—in which comparatively small tubes form a structure of immense strength by being triangularly braced in horizontal, vertical and diagonal axes—were the accepted norm for both Grand Prix and Speedway cars by the early-Fifties. Frank Kurtis first brought them to Indianapolis with his KK2000.

MONOCOQUE

One step beyond the tubular space frame is the one-piece monocoque chassis. The first airplane with a monocoque was a remarkably advanced French Deperdussin racer built in 1913. This utilized the aluminum-and-wood skin of the fuselage to handle aerodynamic loads. There was no separate frame. Monocoque

(below) In one of the worst accidents in Speedway history, Dave MacDonald and Eddie Sachs were killed on lap 2 of the 1964 race. MacDonald's ill-handling Mickey Thompson "skate"—which World Champion Graham Hill had already refused to drive because of its instability—hit the inside wall of Turn Four and burst into flames, setting off a chain reaction that wrecked seven cars and seriously injured Ronnie Duman as well as killing Sachs and MacDonald.

LOTUS/FORD

Californian Daniel Sexton Gurney is one of the most talented Americans ever to sit behind the wheel of a racing car. Also one of the nicest, and one of the sharpest. In 1962, he paid out of his own pocket for pound sterling millionaire Colin Chapman of Lotus to attend the 500—"Chunky" Chapman was notoriously tight with a quid—and introduced him to some folks from Ford Motor Company. Chapman flew back to England clutching a contract for three mid-engine cars to be delivered to Indianapolis by May of 1963. This was a real accomplishment for Gurney, seeing as how Ford hadn't wanted anything to do with the Indianapolis Motor Speedway since the ill-fated Miller-Ford of 1935.

A year later, Chapman delivered the Lotus 29, which was essentially a longer, beefier Formula One Lotus 25 with the body offset on the suspension. At the time, the monocoque-chassis Lotus was considered the most advanced racing car in the world. Simultaneously, Ford had produced a lightweight aluminum version of their 260 cubic inch passenger car V-8, reduced to 255 cubic inches (4.18-liters) for Indy. This neat pushrod V-8 developed 376 hp at 7200 rpm and only weighed 344 lbs. Ready to go, the Lotus/Ford weighed 1300 lbs.

There were two cars, one for Gurney and one for Lotus Grand Prix star Jimmy Clark. Gurney started twelfth and finished seventh; Clark started fifth and finished second behind Parnelli Jones' oil-spewing Watson. There was a great brouhaha over whether PJ should have been blackflagged, letting Clark win. In any case, it was obvious that the mid-engine revolution was more than a fad.

(below) Why are these men smiling? Well, they've just won the Indianapolis 500 in 1965, along with more money than they'll make for a whole season of Formula One races. Colin Chapman, on the left, owns the car and the team; Jimmy Clark has driven it to the first 150 mph race average in 500 history (just three years before, Parnelli Jones had made history by merely *qualifying* at 150). Clark is about to win five Grands Prix in a row, along with his second World Championship and eventually a total of 25 GPs. For a lot of people, the world stopped on April 7, 1968, when Clark was killed at Hockenheim. Colin Chapman died suddenly on December 16, 1982.

The next year, Ford designed new double-overhead cam heads for the V-8 that brought the fuel-injection intakes *between* the cams and put the exhausts on the *inside* of the V-8 heads where the headers could be grouped into a "bundle of snakes." This engine was good for 545 hp at 8200 rpm and 370 lbs-ft of torque at 7000 rpm, running on 80/20 methanol/nitro. That's 2.13 hp per cubic inch, from a normally-aspirated V-8 that started out in a Fairlane!

In 1964, Jimmy Clark and Bobby Marshman went fast at Indianapolis in their Lotus/Fords, but they both broke early. At the end, Rodger Ward drove the highest-placed Ford four-cam V-8, in second behind A.J. Foyt's old Watson roadster.

For 1965, Ford had seventeen of these four-cam V-8s in the starting lineup. Two-time World Champion Jimmy Clark beat Parnelli Jones and Mario Andretti; Ford V-8s were first through fourth, eight of the Top Ten. Ford four-cams won again only in 1966 and '67, before the smaller turbocharged Offys and turbo Ford/Foyts took over.

Clark finished second behind Graham Hill's Lola/Ford in 1966, and Colin Chapman produced the STP turbine cars for Andy Granatelli in 1968. But a Lotus never again was a significant factor at the 500. As for Dan Gurney, the one who started all this, his Eagles came to dominate the Speedway in the Seventies, but he himself never won the race though he was second twice, third once.

There is no more important postwar car than the Lotus/Ford of the mid-Sixties. It introduced monocoque construction, it validated the mid-engine concept begun by Brabham's Cooper in 1961 and it paved the way for the European designers, engineers and car builders who have ruled the Speedway ever since.

And perhaps most important of all, it got Ford Motor Company not only back to Indianapolis, but into racing everywhere from Bonneville to Le-Mans. The Lotus-Ford tie-up eventually led to the Cosworth-Ford engine, which came to dominate Formula One and later Indy car racing, too. And, because of Ford, other passenger car manufacturers—like Chevrolet—ended up visiting Indianapolis on Memorial Day.

Beyond all that, when Jimmy Clark's Lotus/Ford won the 500 in 1965, it was the first time since 1946 the race was won by something other than an Offy, the first time since 1940 by an engine not laid out by Leo Goossen, only the third time since 1927 by an engine not derived from those of Harry Miller, for the first time since 1916 by a foreign driver and for the first time since 1914 by someone who was not already part of the American oval track racing community. Lotus powered by Ford. It truly was a revolution. ■

(top) Quick evolution: Ford's 1963 pushrod V-8 developed 376 hp at 7200 rpm on 103 octane Avgas. (above) Ford's 1964 four-cam V-8—based on the same block—produced 440 hp at 8400 rpm on Avgas, 545 hp at 8200 rpm on 80/20 methanol/nitro.

1965

Winner: Jim Clark, Lotus/Ford, 150.686 mph
Winner's Purse: $166,621
Total Purse: $628,399
Pace Car: P.N. Buckminster, Plymouth Sport Fury

There were only six old roadsters in the starting field—the highest finisher was Gordon Johncock in fifth—as the mid-engine "revolution" was now the norm. Jimmy Clark won in a walk-away, with Parnelli Jones and rookie Mario Andretti behind him. Happily, there were virtually no "incidents" at all.

Number	Driver	Sponsor/Team	Engine Type/Displacement	Chassis	Qualifying	Start/Finish	Laps
82	Jim Clark	Lotus powered by Ford	Ford V-8/255 cu.in.	Lotus	160.729	2/1	200
98	Parnelli Jones	Agajanian/Hurst	Ford V-8/255 cu.in.	Kuzma-Lotus	158.625	5/2	200
12	Mario Andretti	Dean Van Lines/Auto Technics	Ford V-8/255 cu.in.	Brawner	158.849	4/3	200
74	Al Miller	Jerry Alderman Ford-Lotus	Ford V-8/255 cu.in.	Lotus	157.805	7/4	200
76	Gordon Johncock	Weinberger Homes/Wilseck	Offy I-4/251 cu.in.	Watson	155.012	14/5	200
81	Mick Rupp	G.C. Murphy/Pete Salemi	Offy I-4/251 cu.in.	Gerhardt	154.839	15/6	198
83	Bobby Johns	Lotus powered by Ford	Ford V-8/255 cu.in.	Lotus	155.481	22/7	197
4	Don Branson	Wynn/Leader Cards	Ford V-8/255 cu.in.	Watson	155.501	18/8	197
45	Al Unser	Sheraton-Thompson/Ansted	Ford V-8/255 cu.in.	Lola	154.440	32/9	196
23	Eddie Johnson	H. Allen Chapman	Offy I-4/251 cu.in.	Watson	153.998	28/10	195
7	Lloyd Ruby	Dupont Golden 7/McManus	Ford V-8/255 cu.in.	Haliband	157.246	9/11	184
16	Len Sutton	Bryant/Robbins & Vollstedt	Ford V-8/255 cu.in.	Vollstedt	156.121	12/12	177
14	Johnny Boyd	George Bryant Racing	Ford V-8/255 cu.in.	BRP	155.172	29/13	140
53	Walt Hansgen	MG-Liquid Suspension/Qvale	Offy I-4/251 cu.in.	Huffaker	155.662	21/14	117
1	A.J. Foyt	Sheraton-Thompson/Ansted	Ford V-8/255 cu.in.	Lotus	161.233	1/15	115
5	Bud Tingelstad	American Red Ball/Hopkins	Ford V-8/255 cu.in.	Lola	154.672	24/16	115
66	Billy Foster	Jim Robbins & Vollstedt	Offy I-4/251 cu.in.	Vollstedt	158.416	6/17	85
18	Arnie Knepper	Konstant Hot/Vatis	Offy I-4/251 cu.in.	Kurtis	154.513	19/18	80
9	Bobby Unser	STP Gas Treatment	Novi V-8/167 cu.in.	Ferguson	157.467	8/19	69
52	Jim McElreath	Zink-Urschel Trackburner	Offy I-4/251 cu.in.	Brabham	155.878	13/20	66
94	George Snider	Gerhardt Offy	Offy I-4/251 cu.in.	Gerhardt	154.825	16/21	64
65	Ronnie Duman	Travelon Trailer/Ruiz	Offy I-4/251 cu.in.	Gerhardt	154.533	25/22	62
41	Masten Gregory	George Bryant Racing	Ford V-8/255 cu.in.	BRP	154.540	31/23	59
54	Bob Veith	MG-Liquid Suspension/Qvale	Offy I-4/251 cu.in.	Huffaker	156.427	10/24	58
88	Chuck Stevenson	Vita Fresh OJ/Van Liew	Offy I-4/251 cu.in.	Kuzma	154.725	26/25	50
17	Dan Gurney	Yamaha/All American Racers	Ford V-8/255 cu.in.	Lotus	158.898	3/26	42
48	Jerry Grant	Bardahl MG/Kjell Qvale	Offy I-4/251 cu.in.	Huffaker	154.606	17/27	30
19	Chuck Rodee	Wally Weir's Mobilgas	Offy I-4/251 cu.in.	Halibrand	154.546	30/28	28
29	Joe Leonard	All American Racers	Ford V-8/255 cu.in.	Halibrand	154.268	27/29	27
25	Roger McCluskey	All American Racers	Ford V-8/255 cu.in.	Halibrand	155.186	23/30	18
24	Johnny Rutherford	Racing Associates	Ford V-8/255 cu.in.	Halibrand	156.291	11/31	15
47	Bill Cheesbourg	WIFE GoodGuy/Lane-Fulbright	Offy I-4/251 cu.in.	Gerhardt	153.774	33/32	14
59	Jim Hurtubise	STP-Tombstone Life/Chemical	Novi V-8/168 cu.in.	Kurtis	156.863	23/33	1

construction can be time-consuming and difficult to produce, which is why there were few other monocoque airplanes until the late Thirties. But virtually every aircraft since World War II has been monocoque, because the airframe can be lighter and more rigid than with any other construction method.

The first automobile with a monocoque chassis was Louis Chevrolet's innovative Cornelian that raced at Indianapolis in 1915. The Cornelian's body sides were also the frame. The first monocoque passenger car was the 1923 Lancia Lambda. Lancia was joined by other manufacturers over the decades, until now all passenger cars except for a few big luxury models use a unitized body/chassis in which there is no frame per se. All loads are distributed throughout the structure.

Surprisingly, the monocoque 1915 Cornelian was not copied by other racing car designers for nearly fifty years. Then in 1962, Colin Chapman introduced the first modern monocoque racing car, the Formula One Lotus 25. Chapman used hollow boxes made of aluminum sheet held together with rivets. The fuel tanks went inside these boxes, the driver sat between them, the engine bolted on behind. Despite its flimsy appearance, the monocoque had greater torsional rigidity than a tubular space frame, was lighter, and, surprisingly enough, provided more protection in case of an accident. The aluminum monocoque came to Indianapolis in 1963 with the Lotus 29, and quickly became the norm.

TIRE WARS

Lightweight, mid-engine, monocoque cars were simply too small for the traditional 18 inch rear and 16 inch front tires that Firestone had been supplying for the Offy roadsters

since the early-Fifties. Firestone had enjoyed a tire monopoly at Indianapolis since the mid-Twenties when they introduced the first balloon tire, and while not exactly complacent, they hadn't made many changes over the years.

Conversely, Firestone's arch-rival Goodyear had gotten excited about racing in the Fifties, supplying tires for sports cars and NASCAR stock cars. The 3500 lb. stockers were lapping the high banks of the Daytona International Speedway faster than the 1700 lb. roadsters could go on the comparatively shallow banking of the Indianapolis Motor Speedway. For example, Paul Goldsmith qualified at 174.91 mph for the 1964 Daytona 500, 16 mph faster than pole-sitter Jim Clark's Lotus/Ford at Indianapolis three months later. Goodyear rightly figured that their 15 inch stock car tires would probably hold up alright at Indianapolis fitted to a 1200 lb. Lotus.

In 1963, Firestone made special 15 inch tires for the mid-engine Lotus/Fords. It shows how little they knew in those days about how a racing tire works...Firestone made their 15 inch tires with a 1.5 inch wider tread than that on their old 16 inch tires. This was supposed to compensate for the shorter contact patch of the smaller-diameter tire. Of course, if you put these new 15 inch tires on an old roadster, it immediately went 3 mph faster around the Speedway because the wide tread had so much more traction in the turns. Because of a shortage of tires and wheels, only about half the teams in the 1963 500 got the fast Firestone tires. As you can imagine, some of these disgruntled racers were ready to listen when Goodyear came a courtin' in 1964. The tire war was on.

Between 1962 and 1968, tread widths increased from 6.5 inches to 12.0 inches, while aspect ratios dropped from 85 percent to 40 percent. Not only did

(above) Dan Gurney in his 1964 Lotus 34. It was withdrawn halfway through the 500 after Clark's sister car broke its suspension thanks to disintegrating Dunlop tires. That was typical of Dan's luck. He'd do everything right, then something dumb would go wrong. Still, in his fifteen-year career he won races in Grand Prix, Can-Am, Trans-Am, NASCAR and Champ cars. He won LeMans, the Daytona Continental and Sebring. He also won the 1967 Belgian GP driving his own Eagle, the first American car and driver to win a Grand Prix since Jimmy Murphy's Duesenberg in 1921. Truly a great and versatile champion.

A.J.

Is Anthony Joseph Foyt, Jr., the best racing driver in history? Well, he has won more races—and more major championships—over a longer period of time than anybody else. Ever. He has won on ovals, on road courses, in stock cars, sports cars and Indy cars.

Even at the height of his powers, when he was already rich and famous, A.J. would still go back to the bullrings of Middle America and race Sprint cars on the dirt. Not because he had something to prove, but because The Dirt is *real* racing. And A.J. Foyt is a *real* racing driver. There's never been anyone like him.

Just listing all the things "Super Tex" has done would take a book. He is the only man to win seven National Championships: 1960, 1961, 1963, 1964, 1967, 1975, 1979. What's most striking about this? A.J. Foyt won those National Championships over a period of two decades. Nobody's ever done that, either.

He also won the USAC National Dirt Championship in 1972, and the USAC Stock Car Championship in 1968, 1978 and 1979. That's right, he won both the

(above) A.J. in 1967, winner of the Indianapolis 500 and USAC National Championship. You can feel the intensity from here. (right) 1960 National Champion A.J. Foyt, on his way to winning his first 500 in 1961. One secret to Foyt's early success was crew chief George Bignotti, at right.

Champ car and Stock car championships in the same year, 1979. Nobody else has done that. Few men have even tried.

He is one of only two drivers to win the Indianapolis 500 four times: 1961, 1964, 1967, 1977. There are men who are considered great racing drivers—and they are—who've never won the 500 once.

He has won 67 Champ car races, more than anybody else. He has also started 359 Champ car races over 34 different seasons, and won at least one race in 18 of those years. Out of those 359 races, he finished in the Top Ten 194 times, an amazing batting average of .540. All of those are records, too. He has been in the Indianapolis 500 more times than any other driver, and started from the pole in Champ car races 53 times, more than anyone

except Mario Andretti. He's also started from the pole at Indianapolis four times, second only to Rick Mears.

A.J. is also the only driver to win the Indianapolis 500, the Daytona 500 and the 24-Hours of LeMans, the three most prestigious races in the world. A.J. is also the only modern driver to have won the Memorial Day Classic with a car and engine of his own manufacture, the Coyote/Foyt in 1977. Of course, he's in the IMS Hall of Fame.

The hard part is remembering that behind the Legend of Super Tex, behind the unbelievable lists of races and wins and purses won, there is also an extremely successful businessman, a down-to-earth 56-year-old grandfather and a canny thoroughbred horse breeder. The man is a phenomenon, but he is a man. Maybe the most interesting man you'll ever meet.

What's his secret? An intensity that radiates from him like waves of heat. You can almost see it in the air. Incredible powers of concentration, and an attention to detail that has driven equally legendary crew chiefs like George Bignotti and John Pouelsen to walk away from Foyt's team because they couldn't stand the pressure. But that's what it takes to win, and if there is one characteristic of A.J. Foyt, it is that he is a winner. He will do *anything* to win.

Born January 16, 1935, Foyt has been around racing all his life. His father built Midgets in Houston and built A.J. his first race car when he was three. For much of his career, A.J. had his father to run his race shop. He was already racing as a teenager; he was in the Indianapolis 500 when he was just twenty-three. This man raced and beat legends like Rodger Ward, Jim Rathmann and Johnny Thomson. You would think that after four decades, he'd be tired of racing. But you don't understand. A.J. Foyt is a *racer*.

Twenty years ago, he was already a phenomenon. Back then, somebody asked George Bignotti what he thought. "A.J. will quit when he knows that he, not his car, lost a race he should have won." That hasn't happened yet, though A.J. is talking about retiring in 1992. ∎

(left) Second row at the 500 start in 1964: A.J. #1 is flanked by Parnelli Jones #98 and Dan Gurney #12. Clark, Marshman and Ward are out of the picture ahead of them. A.J. will inherit the win, the last for a roadster. (below) A.J. and his family in Victory Lane after winning their third 500 in 1967. A.J.'s wife Lucy is the pretty blonde, son Tony (A.J. III) holds the traditional milk next to A.J.'s father and his tearful mother.

(above) Fifty years of Speedway tires and drivers: Ray Harroun, Pete DePaolo, Earl Cooper and Eddie Sachs pose in 1961 as part of the Golden Anniversary celebration. If they'd waited two more years, they could have shown the first Wide Ovals.

(above) Pre-race Golden Anniversary celebration in 1961 featuring The Purdue University Band and the world's largest drum.
(left) The Eagle/Offy with which Bobby Unser won the 500 and $175,139 in 1968, bringing Bob Wilke of Leader Cards yet another victory.

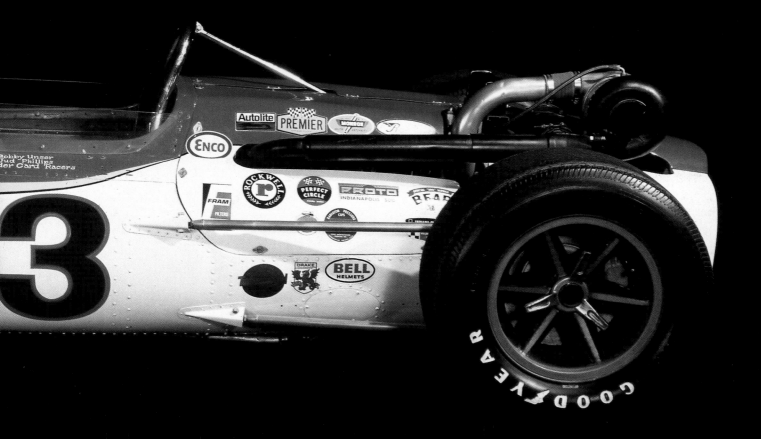

1966

Winner: Graham Hill, Lola/
Ford, 144.317 mph
Winner's Purse: $156,297
Total Purse: $691,808
Pace Car: Benson Ford,
Mercury Comet Cyclone GT

An eleven-car accident at the start and another crash on lap 5 got this 500 off to a slow beginning. Scot Jackie Stewart worked his way through the depleted pack to lead, but lost oil pressure with just 10 laps to go. His teammate, Graham Hill, was the surprise winner for Texan John Mecom's team.

Number	Driver	Sponsor/Team	Engine Type/Displacement	Chassis	Qualifying	Start/Finish	Laps
24	Graham Hill	American Red Ball/Mecom	Ford V-8/255 cu.in.	Lola	159.243	15/1	200
19	Jim Clark	STP Gas Treatment	Ford V-8/255 cu.in.	Lotus	164.114	2/2	200
3	Jim McElreath	Zink-Urschel-Slick	Ford V-8/255 cu.in.	Brabham	160.908	7/3	200
72	Gordon Johncock	Weinberger Homes	Ford V-8/255 cu.in.	Gerhardt	161.059	6/4	200
94	Mel Kenyon	Gerhardt Offy	Offy I-4/251 cu.in.	Gerhardt	158.555	17/5	198
43	Jackie Stewart	Bowes Seal Fast/Mecom	Ford V-8/255 cu.in.	Lola	159.972	11/6	190
54	Eddie Johnson	Valvoline II/Vatis	Offy I-4/251 cu.in.	Huffaker	158.898	29/7	175
11	Bobby Unser	Vita Fresh/Gordon Van Liew	Offy I-4/168 cu.in.	Huffaker	159.109	28/8	171
6	Joe Leonard	Yamaha/All American Racers	Ford V-8/255 cu.in.	Eagle	159.560	20/9	170
88	Jerry Grant	Bardahl-Pacesetter Homes	Ford V-8/255 cu.in.	Eagle	160.335	10/10	167
14	Lloyd Ruby	Bardahl/All American Racers	Ford V-8/255 cu.in.	Eagle	162.433	5/11	166
18	Al Unser	STP Oil Treatment	Ford V-8/255 cu.in.	Lotus	162.372	23/12	161
8	Roger McCluskey	G.C. Murphy/Hopkins	Ford V-8/255 cu.in.	Eagle	159.271	21/13	129
98	Parnelli Jones	Agajanian's Rev 500	Offy I-4/168 cu.in.	Shrike	162.484	4/14	87
26	Rodger Ward	Bryant Heating/John Mecom	Offy I-4/168 cu.in.	Lola	159.468	13/15	74
77	Carl Williams	Dayton Steel Wheel/Walther	Ford V-8/255 cu.in.	Gerhardt	159.645	25/16	38
56	Jim Hurtubise	Gerhardt Offy	Offy I-4/168 cu.in.	Gerhardt	159.208	22/17	29
1	Mario Andretti	Dean Van Lines	Ford V-8/255 cu.in.	Brawner	165.849	1/18	27
82	George Snider	Sheraton-Thompson/Ansted	Ford V-8/255 cu.in.	Coyote	162.521	3/19	22
12	Chuck Hulse	Wynn's/Leader Cards	Ford V-8/255 cu.in.	Watson	160.844	8/20	22
22	Bud Tingelstad	Federal Engineering	Offy I-4/168 cu.in.	Gerhardt	159.144	27/21	16
28	Johnny Boyd	Prestone/George Bryant	Ford V-8/255 cu.in.	B.R.P.	159.384	14/22	5
4	Don Branson	Leader Cards Racing	Ford V-8/255 cu.in.	Gerhardt	160.385	9/23	0
27	Billy Foster	Jim Robbins	Ford V-8/255 cu.in.	Vollstedt	149.490	12/24	0
53	Gary Congdon	Valvoline/Vatis Enterprises	Offy I-4/251 cu.in.	Huffaker	158.688	16/25	0
2	A.J. Foyt	Sheraton-Thompson/Ansted	Ford V-8/255 cu.in.	Lotus	161.355	18/26	0
31	Dan Gurney	All American Racers Eagle	Ford V-8/255 cu.in.	Eagle	160.499	19/27	0
66	Cale Yarborough	Jim Robbins	Ford V-8/255 cu.in.	Vollstedt	159.794	24/28	0
37	Arnie Knepper	Sam Liosi/D.V.S.	Ford V-8/255 cu.in.	Cecil	159.440	26/29	0
75	Al Miller	Jerry Alderman Ford-Lotus	Ford V-8/255 cu.in.	Lotus	158.681	30/30	0
39	Bobby Grim	Racing Associates/Porter	Offy I-4/168 cu.in.	Watson	158.367	31/31	0
34	Larry Dickson	Michner Petroleum	Ford V-8/255 cu.in.	Lola	159.144	32/32	0
96	Ronnie Duman	J. Frank Harrison	Ford V-8/255 cu.in.	Eisert	158.646	33/33	0

the tires get shorter and wider, but tread compounds got much softer, too. Tire technology in 1962 was essentially the same as it had been in 1953. Tire technology in 1968 was essentially the same as it is today.

By 1968, tires were capable of generating 1.5 times the force of gravity in a corner, which was simply unheard of six years before. Tire adhesion had nearly doubled, seemingly overnight. As a consequence, turn speeds at Indianapolis rose from around 140 mph in 1962 to 160 mph in 1968. And, of course, lap speeds rose from 150 mph to 170 mph during the same period. All of that increase wasn't due to tires, but certainly tires were a major factor in this astonishing progress. They were an integral part of the ongoing revolution.

FORD COMES HOME TO INDIANAPOLIS

The abortive Miller-Ford of 1935 drove Ford Motor Company away from the 500 for three decades. In November of 1960, however, flamboyant Lee Iacocca replaced conservative Robert McNamara as head of Ford Division when the chief "whiz kid" went to Washington with JFK.

Years later, Iacocca recalled, "It had really built up inside of me that we were going to go racing on all fronts." Iacocca believed totally in the youth-oriented "total performance" image that Ford publicized throughout the Sixties, and he got Ford into racing in the biggest possible way.

Iacocca was not a racer, but he was a consummate car salesman. He knew that "Win on Sunday, sell on Monday" was a valid way to sell new cars. But on December 10, 1969, Henry Ford II announced that Ford was getting out of racing, "Because we think we spent too much." Still, from 1962 to 1969, Ford Motor Company kept international racing alive. In addition to the three different engines they developed for Indianapolis, Ford bankrolled the Twin-Cam engine that powered so many small race cars, the Cosworth-Ford V-8, NASCAR sedans, drag cars, Shelby's Cobras, Trans-Am sedans and even the LeMans GT-40s and Mark IVs.

The centerpiece of Ford's racing effort was the Indianapolis 500, however, and they spent literally millions to win. In 1963, they showed up with the first cars

(left) Thanks mostly to accidents, there were only seven cars still running when marvelously handsome and drily humorous Grand Prix World Champion Graham Hill won the 1966 500 in John Mecom's Lola/Ford. It was Hill's first try, making him the first "rookie" to win since George Souders in 1927. Hill was hardly a rookie, of course. He first drove a car in 1953, at age 24. He drove in his first race in 1954, was a Lotus factory driver by 1956, on the Lotus Grand Prix team by 1958. In 1962, he was World Champion, bringing BRM its first Constructors Championship. Hill was second in the World Championship in 1963, '64 and '65, then won it again in 1968. He also won LeMans in 1972, by which time he was already running his own Grand Prix team. Hill retired from active driving in 1975, having competed in 176 Grands Prix. Among his many victories were an unprecedented five wins at Monaco, generally considered the toughest Grand Prix race. Hill was killed on November 29, 1975, when he crashed his private plane in fog, returning from a test session at Le Castellet with his new driver Tony Brise, who was also killed along with GH-1 designer Andy Smallman.

ODDIES

Every revolution brings a period of confusion while new ideas get tried out. Some of them are good ideas and work; some of them are bad ideas and don't work; some of them are good ideas, but don't work anyway. The mid-engine revolution was no different. It got everybody thinking about alternatives, only some of which were viable. Here are some of the ones that weren't.

SEARS ALLSTATE SPECIAL

In 1962, Mickey Thompson brought two mostly aluminum, mid-engine cars designed by John Crosthwaite and powered by the little Buick aluminum V-8 that had just been introduced. They did surprisingly well at Indianapolis, right out of the box. The next year, he came back with aluminum smallblock Chevy V-8s in these cars, plus three new Chevy-powered "skates" that were even smaller and lighter and rolled on low-profile 12 inch tires.

For 1964, Thompson replaced the Chevys with Ford four-cam V-8s, then clipped new aerodynamic body panels over the old bodies. USAC made him run 15 inch wheels, which exacerbated already iffy handling problems. Only Eddie Johnson and Dave MacDonald were able to qualify, though at 4 mph faster than the cars had gone with the Chevys a year before. Poor MacDonald was killed when his car hit the wall on the second lap and burst into flame. Eddie Johnson retired his sister car on lap 6 with fuel feed problems.

M/T CHALLENGER

You've got to give him credit for guts. Blackballed by the Indianapolis Establishment because of the deaths of MacDonald and Sachs, unable even to find a sponsor, Mickey Thompson came back in 1965 with his challenge to the naysayers. If the "experts" thought mid-engine cars were dangerous, by God he'd give them a front-engine, front-wheel drive machine, the modern equivalent of the Miller 91. Driver Bob Mathouser sat right over the rear axle, like the driver of a slingshot dragster, with a smallblock Chevy converted to double-overhead cams mounted at the extreme front and driving the front wheels. The chassis was a single titanium tube, a foot in diameter and running down the right side, with the V-8 canted 30 degrees and mounted on the left. Mathouser unfortunately threw a rod during his qualifying session, but he still holds the one-lap Speedway record for a front-wheel drive car at 153.374 mph.

HURST FLOOR SHIFT SPECIAL

Easily the most bizarre "car" ever to appear at Indy, this 1964 Smokey Yunick creation placed the mid-mounted Offy in a tubular space frame with four-wheel independent suspension and Buick Alfin drum brakes. The fuel tanks are in the center, ahead of the radiator. What's that? No place for driver Bobby Johns? No problem. We'll just hang a motorcycle sidecar pod here on the left side, with a big Hurst shifter—George Hurst is paying for this, after all—outside the body where everybody can see it. Mercifully, the unhappy Johns crashed in practice, and the car was never rebuilt.

VALVOLINE SPECIAL

Inspired by Lou Fageol's famous twin-engined Porsche sports car—not to mention, his Twin Coach Special of 1946—Al Stein put one air-cooled, fuel-injected Flat-6 Porsche engine in the rear, driving the rear wheels and another identical Porsche engine in the front, driving the front wheels. Twin engines; four-wheel drive. The rest of the car was a conventional tubular space frame. As in Fageol's cars, the only connection between the two engines was the throttle linkage. Driver Bill Cheesbourg couldn't get it going fast enough to qualify in 1966, though in concept it should have been as successful as the front row-starting Twin Coach Special.

SHELBY-WALLIS SPECIAL

Ken Wallis—designer of the 1967 STP turbine car which came within a whisker of winning at Indy—returned in 1968 with two new turbine-powered machines for Grand Prix and Can-Am teammates Bruce McLaren and Denis Hulme. Thanks to around $250,000 in sponsorship put up by Botany 500 Men's Wear, the two cars were beautifully turned-out. The General Electric turbine was on the left, enclosed in a form-fitting bulbous pod; the driver was next to it on the right. Four-wheel drive, excellent aerodynamics and the leadership of Carroll Shelby should have made these cars winners. Except that, well...the new GE turbine wasn't as powerful as the Pratt & Whitney Wallis had used the year before, and the car was heavier. They also arrived at the Speedway so late that there was no time to look for more speed. Embarrassingly, the Shelby-Wallis Specials were withdrawn before they ever got a chance to qualify. ■

1967

Winner: A.J. Foyt, Coyote/Ford, 151.207 mph
Winner's Purse: $171,527
Total Purse: $734,834
Pace Car: Mauri Rose, Chevrolet Camaro SS

Parnelli Jones in the innovative STP gas-turbine led most of the first 196 laps, spread over two days thanks to a race-stopping rain storm. When Parnelli lost a gearbox bearing, A.J. Foyt inherited the lead but had to pick his way through a last lap, four-car accident to reach the checker flag.

Number	Driver	Sponsor/Team	Engine Type/Displacement	Chassis	Qualifying	Start/ Finish	Laps
14	A.J. Foyt	Sheraton-Thompson/Ansted	Ford V-8/255 cu.in.	Coyote	166.289	4/1	200
5	Al Unser	Retzloff Chemical/Mecom	Ford V-8/255 cu.in.	Lola	164.594	9/2	198
4	Joe Leonard	Sheraton-Thompson/Foyt	Ford V-8/255 cu.in.	Coyote	166.098	5/3	197
69	Denis Hulme	City of Daytona Beach/Yunick	Ford V-8/255 cu.in.	Eagle	163.376	24/4	197
2	Jim McElreath	John Zink Trackburner	Ford V-8/255 cu.in	Moore	164.241	11/5	197
40	Parnelli Jones	STP Oil Treatment	Pratt & Whitney turbine	Granatelli	166.075	6/6	196
8	Chuck Hulse	Hopkins/Interstate Racer	Offy I-4/168 cu.in.	Lola	162.925	27/7	195
16	Art Pollard	Thermo King/Gerhardt & Casey	Offy I-4/168 cu.in.	Gerhardt	163.897	13/8	195
6	Bobby Unser	Rislone/Leader Cards	Ford V-8/255 cu.in.	Eagle	164.752	8/9	193
41	Carl Williams	George Bryant Racing Team	Ford V-8/255 cu.in.	B.R.P.	163.696	23/10	189
46	Bob Veith	Thermo King/Fred Gerhardt	Offy I-4/168 cu.in.	Gerhardt	162.580	28/11	189
3	Gordon Johncock	Gilmore Broadcasting/Johncock	Ford V-8/255 cu.in.	Gerhardt	166.559	3/12	188
39	Bobby Grim	Racing Associates	Offy I-4/168 cu.in.	Gerhardt	164.084	12/13	187
10	Bud Tingelstad	Federal Engineering	Ford V-8/255 cu.in.	Gerhardt	163.228	25/14	182
22	Larry Dickson	Vita Fresh OJ/Gordon Van Liew	Ford V-8/255 cu.in.	Lotus	162.543	21/15	180
15	Mel Kenyon	Thermo King/Fred Gerhardt	Offy I-4/168 cu.in.	Gerhardt	163.778	14/16	177
21	Cale Yarborough	Bryant Heating/Vollstedt	Ford V-8/255 cu.in.	Vollstedt	162.830	20/17	176
24	Jackie Stewart	Bowes "Seal Fast"/Mecom Racing	Ford V-8/255 cu.in.	Lola	164.099	29/18	168
12	Roger McCluskey	G.C. Murphy/Lindsey Hopkins	Ford V-8/255 cu.in.	Eagle	165.563	22/19	165
42	Jerry Grant	All American Racers Eagle	Ford V-8/255 cu.in.	Eagle	163.808	30/20	162
74	Dan Gurney	Wagner Lockheed/All American	Ford V-8/255 cu.in.	Eagle	167.224	2/21	160
19	Arnie Knepper	M.V.S. Racers	Ford V-8/255 cu.in.	Cecil	162.900	18/22	158
98	Ronnie Duman	Agajanian's Rev 500	Offy I-4/168 cu.in.	Shrike	162.903	17/23	154
48	Jochen Rindt	Wagner Lockheed/All American	OHV Ford V-8/303 cu.in.	Eagle	163.051	32/24	108
45	Johnny Rutherford	Weinberger Homes/WW Ent.	Ford V-8/255 cu.in.	Eagle	162.859	19/25	103
26	George Snider	Wagner Lockheed/Vel's Racing	Ford V-8/255 cu.in.	Mongoose	164.256	10/26	99
67	L.R. Yarbrough	Jim Robbins Seat Belt	Ford V-8/255 cu.in.	Vollstedt	163.066	26/27	87
32	Al Miller	Cleaver-Brooks/Walter Weir	Ford V-8/255 cu.in.	Gerhardt	162.602	33/28	74
53	Wally Dallenbach	Valvoline/Vatis Enterprises	Offy I-4/168 cu.in.	Huffaker	163.540	15/29	73
1	Mario Andretti	Dean Van Lines	Ford V-8/255 cu.in.	Hawk	168.982	1/30	58
31	Jim Clark	STP Oil Treatment	Ford V-8/255 cu.in.	Lotus	163.213	16/31	35
81	Graham Hill	STP Oil Treatment	Ford V-8/255 cu.in.	Lotus	163.317	31/32	23
25	Lloyd Ruby	American Red Ball/Gene White	Offy I-4/168 cu.in.	Mongoose	165.229	7/33	3

supported by an American car manufacturer since, well...Ford in 1935 (if you don't count Preston Tucker putting his name on the side of the Gulf-Miller in the late-Forties). In 1964, Ford came to the Speedway with the fabulous four-cam V-8, which was later turbocharged and stayed competitive until the late-Seventies under the guidance of A.J. Foyt. Ford suddenly had, as they say, a *presence* in racing.

THE BLOWN OFFY

Louie Meyer went to work for Ford in 1965. That left his partner Dale Drake and Leo Goossen—who'd devoted his whole life to the engines of Harry Miller—just about out of business. Luckily, the USAC formula was still for 256 cubic inch (4.2-

liter) engines, normally-aspirated, or 171 cubic inch (2.8-liter) engines, supercharged. Dick Jones of Champion Spark Plug helped Drake and Goossen fit a GMC 4-71 supercharger to a 168 cubic inch Offy. To get this new displacement, Leo Goossen completely redesigned the old engine, giving it a short stroke and an aluminum block. This blown Offy was capable of 540 hp at 7800 rpm, which was more than competitive with the Ford four-cam V-8. Three of these supercharged Offys ran in the 500 of 1966. Bobby Unser drove one to eighth.

At the same time, Stu Hilborn, Herb Porter and Bob DeBisschop of Garrett-AiResearch fitted an AiResearch TE06 turbocharger to an Offy 168. Like a supercharger, a turbocharger is a pump which forces more air/fuel mixture into the engine than it can suck in itself. A supercharger is mechanically-driven by the engine, and in the case of the Offy-GMC, used up about 85 hp just to drive the supercharger. The clever secret of a turbocharger is that the rotary compressor is spun by another turbine wheel mounted in the exhaust. The extra boost is "free," since the exhaust gases are rushing out anyway.

Turbochargers had been used on aircraft and diesel trucks for a decade before the first one appeared at Indianapolis on the Kurtis/Cummins diesel roadster which Freddie Agabashian put on the pole in 1952. Cummins engineers didn't know a whole lot about turbos in those days, so they used a huge turbo and no wastegate. Poor Freddie had to suffer serious turbo lag coming off the corners before the boost would go positive and rocket him down the straights.

Fifteen years later, the AiResearch engineers knew a lot more about turbos. On the Offy 168 they reduced turbo lag to less than 1 second by using a small turbine and a wastegate to protect the engine from receiving too much boost. This first turbo Offy produced 625 hp at 8000 rpm, with 17 psi of boost. After a year of teething troubles—Goossen had to redesign the head and block and go back to a cast-iron block instead of aluminum—the $17,000 Offy was as reliable as ever and more powerful than a $23,000 Ford four-cam. Bobby Unser won the 500 with a turbo Offy in 1968, and Dale Drake was back in the engine business.

RETURN OF THE STOCK-BLOCK...BUT ONLY BRIEFLY

Second behind Bobby Unser in 1968 was Dan Gurney, driving one of his own Eagles powered by something called a Gurney-Weslake. A Gurney-Weslake was Ford's 5.0-liter (302 cubic inch) Trans-Am pushrod V-8 fitted with Lucas fuel-injection and a set of racing cylinder heads designed by British engineer Harry Weslake. This inexpensive engine produced 535 hp at 7800 rpm. What was it doing at Indianapolis? Well, in 1966 USAC raised the stock-block displacement limit to 5.0-liters, up from 4.2-liters. For 1969, they raised it even further, to 320 cubic inches (5.25-liters). With all the other changes going on, they wanted to lure more passenger car manufacturers back to the Speedway.

The only significant stock-block was Gurney's, but it worked wonderfully. He qualified tenth and finished second two years in a row, 1968 and '69. By 1970, however, Gurney figured the turbocharged Ford four-cams and Offys were going

*B*ack Home Again In Indiana has been sung before the 500 by a variety of entertainers. Among the famous names are Mel Torme, Vic Damone, Dinah Shore, Morton Downey, Sr., James Melton and Phil Harris. Jim Nabors has done the honors nearly every year for two decades. Thousands of balloons are released when Nabors sings the line about "the smell of new-mown hay."

to be too fast, and switched to an Offy. This time he qualified eleventh and finished third. But his qualifying speed with the Offy was actually 1 mph slower than it had been the year before with his own V-8. *Sic transit gloria.*

GAS TURBINES

We take jet engines for granted, archaic technology compared to VCRs and digital audio tape. But, in the Fifties, if you wanted to show something was futuristic, you called it a Jet...car wash, street gang, breakfast cereal. Jets were good. Now a jet engine burns fuel to spin a turbine, which pushes air out the back and shoves your vehicle ahead. If you mechanically take the power from this turbine and use it to propel your vehicle, we call this a gas turbine. And in the Fifties and Sixties, nearly every passenger car company developed a gas turbine. Compared to a piston engine, the gas turbine is light, powerful, simple, smooth...and will run on virtually anything from vodka to kerosene. Problems with fuel consumption, emissions, manufacturing and price kept gas turbines out of passenger cars.

Way back in 1950, Rover set a world's record for a gas turbine car at 151.965 mph, and in 1963 Graham Hill and Richie Ginther drove a turbine Rover-BRM at the 24 Hours of LeMans, completing the race at an average of 107.8 mph. In the mid-Fifties, some engineers from Boeing put a gas turbine in a Kurtis and tested at Indy, and in 1962 John Zink brought a mid-engine car to the Speedway with a 375 hp Boeing gas turbine. It never really got up to speed.

In 1966, Jack Adams put a General Electric gas turbine into an old laydown roadster owned by long-time entrant Norm Demler. Driver Bill Cheesbourg went rocketing down the straights, but was too slow through the corners. Faced with the possibility of actually having a gas turbine qualify for the 500, USAC figured they better have some rules. The easiest way to restrict the power of a gas turbine is to limit the air inlet size. Think of it as the equivalent of restricting the bores on a carburetor. USAC settled on 23.99 square inches of inlet area for 1967.

Flamboyant STP entrepreneur Andy Granatelli found a Pratt & Whitney Model ST6 helicopter gas turbine that made 550 hp, weighed only 260 lbs. and was small enough to fit in a car. Designer Ken Wallis literally built the car around the engine and the Ferguson four-wheel drive system that Granatelli had been using with his Novi. The result was the most high-tech machine to run at the Speedway in that era, perhaps forever. It was almost like a two-seater, one seat for Parnelli Jones, one seat for the Pratt & Whitney. Parnelli has a weakness for naming his racing cars. He called the turbine "Silent Sam," the press dubbed it the Whooshmobile. Afraid of raising an outcry, Parnelli and Silent Sam modestly qualified in 1967, then blew by everyone else at the start and were leading when the gearbox failed on lap 197.

Silent Sam garnered STP and Andy Granatelli more publicity than he possibly could have dreamed about. So for 1968, he had Lotus build three new four-wheel drive cars. These were more conventional, with the engine behind the driver in the center of the chassis. These were the first cars with an aerodynamic wedge shape, rather than the tube shape of most mid-engine cars. Because Silent Sam had obviously been faster than the reciprocating engine competition, USAC reduced the air inlet area to 15.99 square inches. Predictably, Andy Granatelli took them to court, predictably the court said USAC could write its own rules for its own race. So Granatelli spent a rumored $200,000 to redesign the Pratt & Whitney.

SAFETY

The only good result of the 1964 MacDonald/Sachs catastrophe was that USAC was moved to legislate even more stringent safety requirements. Understandably, the emphasis was on fuel and fuel handling. Most importantly, Firestone came up with a variation of the fuel cell used in military helicopters that has since become standard equipment in every type of racing car all over the world.

The fuel cell is a steel or aluminum box containing a thick rubber bladder to hold the fuel. Inside the bladder is a low-density plastic foam that is 96 percent void. If the fuel tank is ruptured in an accident, the rubber bladder keeps the fuel from spilling. If the bladder is ripped, the foam keeps the fuel from spraying all over and exploding. It has been remarkably effective in preventing the spectacular and dangerous fires that were an accepted hazard in every type of motor racing in the old days.

USAC also imposed a minimum weight rule for the first time in decades. Thanks to lightweight titanium and magnesium, innovators like Mickey Thompson and Ted Halibrand had been able to build cars that weighed 1100 lbs. or less, ready to go except for fuel and driver. Starting in 1965, Indy cars had to weigh 1250 lbs. In 1966, that was raised to 1350 lbs. The idea was to force car builders to make their chassis stronger and, hopefully, more crashworthy.

In addition, USAC limited fuel tank capacity to 75 gallons and required two mandatory pit stops during the 500. They also banned the pressurized fuel rigs that could pump 50 or 60 gallons of fuel under pressure into a car in 10 seconds. Instead, every team was given a standardized 400 gallon, gravity-feed tank. Volatile and dangerous gasoline was banned, and the standard fuel for the Indianapolis Motor Speedway became safe and clean-burning methanol, as it remains today.

By modern standards these safety rules seem rudimentary at best, but they worked. The last serious fire at Indianapolis was the MacDonald/Sachs inferno, despite dozens of cars which have whacked the Speedway's unyielding walls in the past three decades. Indeed, the Indianapolis Motor Speedway is probably the safest race course in the world, considering the speeds involved. ∎

(left) A major culprit in the MacDonald/Sachs fire of 1964 was explosive gasoline used in the Ford V-8s to enable them to go 500 miles with just one pitstop. After '64, gasoline was outlawed in favor of less dangerous methanol.
(below) Crowd favorite Eddie Sachs shows other hazards common in 1964. His gas tanks are mounted outboard, without even bodywork to protect them. Flimsy cars would tear apart in a crash, while the unstayed rollbar is little more than decoration. Sachs' open-face helmet and leather gloves offered only rudimentary protection, too.

(above) Andy Granatelli's 1967 STP gas turbine. Ken Wallis literally designed the chassis around the Pratt & Whitney gas turbine...bulky, but capable of 550 hp from an engine weighing only 260 lbs. The whole car only weighed 1400 lbs., even with Ferguson four-wheel drive. Rufus Parnelli Jones quietly qualified "Silent Sam" on the second row, then whooshed past everyone on the first lap, dominating the race. He was 43 seconds ahead of A.J. Foyt with only 3 laps to go when a transmission bearing failed. Parnelli was one of the best USAC drivers of his era, unbeatable on the dirt, equally skilled in stock cars, sports cars, off-road pickups and Champ cars. He won two poles and the 1963 Indianapolis 500 with his Watson roadster, Ol' Calhoun. He retired after 1967, but his Vel's Parnelli Colt/ Ford won the 500 in 1970 and '71 with Al Unser driving.

Whether it was the four-wheel drive, the aerodynamics, the good Lotus handling, the fatter tires or the redesigned turbine, Joe Leonard set a new lap record of 171.95 mph, with Graham Hill next to him on the front row and Art Pollard three rows behind. Unfortunately, Hill crashed and both other cars broke the same fuel pump shaft within three laps of each other. Leonard was leading at the time, with only 9 laps to go. Once again the gas turbine had come within a whisper of winning the Memorial Day Classic. As a result of this success, USAC reduced the air inlet area to 11.99 square inches starting in 1969. This effectively limited a gas turbine to about 400 hp, which wasn't enough to be competitive. There hasn't been a gas turbine in the Indianapolis 500 since.

THE FRUITS OF REVOLUTION

What did the revolution accomplish? Well, in 1961, a good front-engine Watson/Offy roadster weighed 1600 lbs., developed 400 hp, could hit 160 mph on the Speedway straights and 140 mph through the corners. A record-breaking lap was 149 mph. In 1968, a good mid-engine Eagle/Offy turbo weighed 1400 lbs., developed 650 hp, could hit 200 mph on the straights and 155 mph through the corners. A record-breaking lap was 170 mph. The car itself was also much easier and safer to drive, even though speeds were higher.

Between 1951 and 1961, lap speeds at Indianapolis increased only about 1 mph per year, even though there had been major changes with the introduction of the roadster, the new Offy 252, better tires, disc brakes and a repaved track. Between 1961 and 1968, lap speeds increased by 3.2 mph per year. It may not sound like much, but this was the greatest leap in speeds at Indianapolis Motor Speedway since they first started racing there in 1909.

It wasn't easy. Switching from quiet development of the familiar roadsters to a mad scramble to out-think competitors from all over the world broke up established teams, severed friendships and destroyed business associations that went back decades. Some racers died trying new ideas, and some took early retirement when they couldn't adapt to the new way of doing things.

Things changed financially, too. Ford Motor Company, STP and Studebaker spent millions to develop new cars and engines for the 500, most of which were obsolete within a year. For the first time ever, Indianapolis changed so quickly that

MR. 500

Andy, Vince and Joe Granatelli were hot-rodders in Chicago in the Forties...tough, streetwise kids who ran their own gas station during

the day and street-raced half the night. By 1947, they were running the Hurricane Racing Association, an outlaw oval track group that gave drivers like Pat Flaherty and Jim Rathmann their starts.

They came to Indianapolis for the first time in 1946, a bunch of hot-rodders with an old Miller-Ford that lasted 46 laps. But the Granatellis were hooked. They've come back to Indianapolis almost every year since.

(above) Already a Speedway fixture, young Andy Granatelli with winner Mauri Rose and Carol Landis in 1948.
(left) Andy poses with his driver Pat Flaherty and Clark Gable in 1950. Flaherty finished tenth. Vince and Joe are standing in the background.
(below) Parnelli Jones—who always named his cars—Silent Sam and the STP crew in 1967. Andy is flanked by his brothers Joe and Vince. Andy also had a suit made of that STP material, which led some fashion critic to label him "The Second Greatest Spectacle in Racing."

Grancor Automotive made the brothers millionaires selling hop-up equipment to speed-hungry kids in the Fifties. Then in 1957 Andy bought Paxton Products and put together a deal with his old friend Sherwood Egbert of Studebaker. Paxton-supercharged Studebakers and Avantis set Bonneville records, Paxton-supercharged Novi V-8s with Studebaker painted on the side showed up at Indy. On the nose was an old-fashioned corporate logo for an oil additive called Scientifically Treated Petroleum, or STP. Beginning with 1963, STP has turned into one of the longest-running sponsors, second only to Leader Cards.

Within a few years, rotund petroleum billboard Andy Granatelli would be claiming "They call me Mr. 500." Andy made STP one of the best-known consumer products in the world and made himself yet another fortune. He garnered tremendous publicity for the Novis, STP turbine cars and finally, in 1969, for kissing Mario Andretti in Victory Lane after their old Hawk/Ford finally put the STP logo across the finish line on the nose of the winning car. It had taken him more than two decades, but Mr. 500 had finally won the 500.

Andy later took over Tuneup Masters, building himself yet a third fortune and a fourth or fifth career. Or is it his sixth? Or tenth? Of all the personalities who've come through the gates of Gasoline Alley, the irrepressible Andy Granatelli—not to mention Vince and Joe—has been one of the most colorful. From the very beginning, Andy has always had the Midas touch, as well as the knack of generating publicity for himself and his products...but also for racing in general and Indy in particular. ■

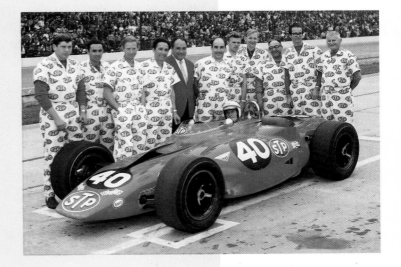

1968

Winner: Bobby Unser,
Eagle/Offy, 152.882 mph
Winner's Purse: $175,139
Total Purse: $712,269
Pace Car: William C. Ford,
Ford Torino GT

Popular "Pelican Joe" Leonard qualified one of Andy Granatelli's gas-turbines on the pole and was leading during a caution period 9 laps from the end. When the green came out and Leonard punched the throttle, his turbine stalled in a "flame-out" and Bobby Unser ripped past to win.

Number	Driver	Sponsor/Team	Engine Type/Displacement	Chassis	Qualifying	Start/Finish	Laps
3	Bobby Unser	Rislone/Leader Cards	Offy I-4/168 cu.in.	Eagle	169.507	3/1	200
48	Dan Gurney	Olsonite/All American Racers	Ford-Weslake V-8/305 cu.in.	Eagle	166.512	10/2	200
15	Mel Kenyon	City of Lebanon/Gerhardt	Offy I-4/168 cu.in.	Gerhardt	165.191	17/3	200
42	Denis Hulme	Olsonite/All American Racers	Ford V-8/255 cu.in.	Eagle	164.189	20/4	200
25	Lloyd Ruby	Gene White Company	Offy I-4/168 cu.in.	Mongoose	167.613	5/5	200
59	Ronnie Duman	Cleaver-Brooks/Hayhoe	Offy I-4/168 cu.in.	Brabham	162.338	26/6	200
98	Billy Vukovich	Wagner Lockheed/Agajanian	Offy I-4/168 cu.in.	Shrike	163.510	23/7	198
90	Mike Mosley	Zecol-Lubaid/Leader Cards	Offy I-4/168 cu.in.	Watson	162.499	27/8	197
94	Sam Sessions	Valvoline/Vatis Enterprises	Offy I-4/168 cu.in.	Finley	162.118	31/9	197
6	Bobby Grim	Gene White Company	Offy I-4/168 cu.in.	Mongoose	162.866	25/10	196
16	Bob Veith	Thermo-King/Don Gerhardt	Offy I-4/168 cu.in.	Gerhardt	163.495	24/11	196
60	Joe Leonard	STP Oil Treatment	Pratt & Whitney turbine	Lotus	171.599	1/12	191
20	Art Pollard	STP Oil Treatment	Pratt & Whitney turbine	Lotus	166.297	11/13	188
82	Jim McElreath	James Greer	Ford V-8/255 cu.in.	Coyote	165.327	13/14	179
84	Carl Williams	Sheraton-Thompson/Ansted	Ford V-8/255 cu.in.	Coyote	162.323	28/15	163
10	Bud Tingelstad	Federal Engineering	Ford V-8/255 cu.in.	Gerhardt	164.444	18/16	158
54	Wally Dallenbach	Valvoline/Vatis Enterprises	Offy I-4/168 cu.in.	Finley	165.548	12/17	148
18	Johnny Rutherford	City of Seattle/Alan Green	Ford V-8/255 cu.in.	Eagle	163.830	21/18	125
70	Graham Hill	STP Oil Treatment	Pratt & Whitney turbine	Lotus	171.208	2/19	110
1	A.J. Foyt	Sheraton-Thompson/Ansted	Ford V-8/255 cu.in.	Coyote	166.821	8/20	86
45	Ronnie Bucknum	Weinberger Homes	Ford V-8/255 cu.in.	Eagle	164.211	19/21	76
27	Jim Malloy	Jim Robbins	Ford V-8/255 cu.in.	Vollstedt	165.032	14/22	64
78	Jerry Grant	Bardahl Eagle/Friedkin	Ford V-8/168 cu.in.	Eagle	164.782	15/23	50
11	Gary Bettenhausen	Thermo-King/Gerhardt	Offy I-4/168 cu.in.	Gerhardt	163.562	22/24	43
21	Arnie Knepper	Bryant Heating/Vollstedt	Ford V-8/168 cu.in.	Vollstedt	161.900	32/25	42
24	Al Unser	Retzloff Chemical	Ford V-8/168 cu.in.	Lola	167.069	6/26	40
4	Gordon Johncock	Gilmore/Johncock Racing	Offy I-4/168 cu.in.	Gerhardt	166.775	9/27	37
64	Larry Dickson	Overseas National/Andretti	Ford V-8/255 cu.in.	Hawk II	161.124	33/28	24
8	Roger McCluskey	G.C. Murphy/Hopkins	Offy I-4/168 cu.in.	Eagle	166.976	7/29	16
56	Jim Hurtubise	Pepsi-Frito Lay/Hurtubise	Offy I-4/168 cu.in.	Mallard	162.191	30/30	9
29	George Snider	Vel's Parnelli Jones	Ford V-8/255 cu.in.	Mongoose	162.264	29/31	9
35	Jochen Rindt	Repco-Brabham/Motor Racing	Repco V-8/254 cu.in.	Brabham	164.144	16/32	5
2	Mario Andretti	Overseas National/Andretti	Ford V-8/168 cu.in.	Kuzma	167.691	4/33	2

it was just about impossible to get more than one race out of a car. Things just changed too fast. Old-timers fondly remembered the days when you could build a car for Indianapolis, also race it on the AAA National Championship circuit, and be competitive for years, perhaps even for a decade.

Not in the Sixties. The Indianapolis 500 had become the most expensive, most competitive, most exciting event in motor sports. No longer a bastion of tradition, the Speedway was where you went to try the latest ideas, ideas you couldn't try anywhere else. The fruit of the revolution? Not just cars with the engine in a different place, but a whole new way of thinking about racing as a business, a sport and a place to showcase new ideas.

THE AERO ERA 1969-1978

Every revolution has been followed by a period of consolidation during which the new ideas are assimilated into the mainstream and become, in turn, orthodoxy. Just as the Depression naturally followed the Roaring Twenties, the recession/inflation "stagflation" of the Seventies followed the revolutionary Sixties. Motor racing is a mirror of society, so of course these economic hard times had an effect on racing.

Free-spending Ford Motor Company was gone from competition and no other passenger car company entered Big Time racing in a significant way for over a decade. They were all too busy engineering solutions to the fuel economy, safety and emissions problems handed them by government regulations.

In 1975, Goodyear replaced Firestone as the sole supplier of tires for not only the Indianapolis 500, but most other worldwide racing series, too. This helped reduce the costs of racing during these hard times because tire design became stable. Starting in 1969, USAC essentially froze the rules for racing at Indianapolis, rules that are still mostly the same today. And that reduced the costs of racing as well.

In every class of worldwide racing—including Indianapolis—mid-engine cars designed by European designers were the norm by 1970. Just as in the Fifties, when every car was a variation on Frank Kurtis' roadster, in the Seventies every car was a variation on the winged-wedge theme begun in 1971 by McLaren designer Gordon Coppuck. After a decade of intense innovation in the Sixties, the Indianapolis 500 was almost "one-design" racing again.

(below) Bobby Unser salutes the crowd before winning the 1975 500 with his Dan Gurney Eagle/Offy. Half the starting grid was filled by winged Eagles, the first serious domination of the Speedway by one chassis in fifteen years.

1969

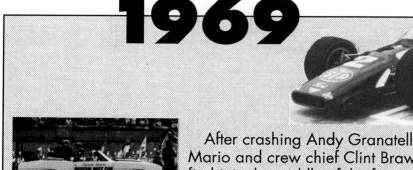

Winner: Mario Andretti,
Hawk/Ford, 156.867 mph
Winner's Purse: $206,727
Total Purse: $805,127
Pace Car: Jim Rathmann,
Chevrolet Camaro SS
Convertible

After crashing Andy Granatelli's new four-wheel drive Lotus in practice, Mario and crew chief Clint Brawner resurrected their old Hawk. Andretti qualified it in the middle of the front row, then cruised to an easy victory. It was Andy Granatelli's first Indianapolis 500 victory in three decades of trying.

Number	Driver	Sponsor/Team	Engine Type/Displacement	Chassis	Qualifying	Start/Finish	Laps
2	Mario Andretti	STP Oil Treatment	Ford V-8/159 cu.in.	Hawk III	169.851	2/1	200
48	Dan Gurney	Olsonite/All American Racers	Weslake-Ford V-8/319 cu.in.	Eagle	167.341	10/2	200
1	Bobby Unser	Bardahl/Leader Cards	Offy I-4/159 cu.in.	Lola	169.683	3/3	200
9	Mel Kenyon	Krohne Grain/3-K Racing	Offy I-4/159 cu.in.	Gerhardt	165.426	24/4	200
92	Peter Revson	Repco-Brabham	Repco V-8/254 cu.in.	Brabham	160.851	33/5	197
44	Joe Leonard	City of Daytona Beach/Yunick	Ford V-8/159 cu.in.	Eagle	167.240	11/6	193
66	Mark Donohue	Sunoco-Simoniz/US Racing	Offy I-4/159 cu.in.	Lola	168.903	4/7	190
6	A.J. Foyt	Sheraton-Thompson/Ansted	Ford V-8/159 cu.in.	Coyote	170.568	1/8	181
21	Larry Dickson	Bryant Heating/Vollstedt	Ford V-8/159 cu.in.	Vollstedt	163.014	31/9	180
97	Bobby Johns	Wagner-Lockheed/Agajanian	Offy I-4/159 cu.in.	Shrike	160.901	32/10	171
10	Jim Malloy	Jim Robbins	Offy I-4/159 cu.in.	Vollstedt	167.092	13/11	165
11	Sam Sessions	Valvoline/Vatis Enterprises	Offy I-4/159 cu.in.	Finley	165.434	23/12	163
90	Mike Mosley	Zecol-Lubaid/Leader Cards	Offy I-4/159 cu.in.	Eagle	166.113	22/13	162
82	Roger McCluskey	G.C. Murphy/Foyt & Greer	Ford V-8/159 cu.in.	Coyote	168.350	6/14	157
15	Bud Tingelstad	Vel's/Parnelli Jones	Offy I-4/159 cu.in.	Lola	166.597	18/15	155
84	George Snider	Sheraton-Thompson/Ansted	Ford V-8/159 cu.in.	Coyote	166.914	15/16	152
59	Sonny Ates	Krohne Grain/3-K Racing	Offy I-4/159 cu.in.	Brabham	166.968	14/17	146
42	Denis Hulme	Olsonite/All American Racing	Ford V-8/159 cu.in.	Eagle	165.092	25/18	145
12	Gordon Johncock	Gilmore/Johncock Racing	Offy I-4/159 cu.in.	Gerhardt	168.626	5/19	137
4	Lloyd Ruby	Wynn's Spitfire/Gene White	Offy I-4/159 cu.in.	Mongoose	166.428	20/20	105
22	Wally Dallenbach	Sprite/Lindsey Hopkins	Offy I-4/159 cu.in.	Eagle	166.497	19/21	82
29	Arnie Knepper	M.V.S.	Ford V-8/159 cu.in.	Cecil	166.220	21/22	82
67	Lee Roy Yarbrough	Jim Robbins	Ford V-8/159 cu.in.	Vollstedt	168.075	8/23	65
95	Jack Brabham	Repco-Brabham	Repco V-8/254 cu.in.	Brabham	163.875	29/24	58
57	Carl Williams	STP Gas Treatment	Offy I-4/159 cu.in.	Gerhardt	163.265	30/25	50
8	Gary Bettenhausen	Thermo King Auto/Gerhardt	Offy I-4/159 cu.in.	Gerhardt	167.777	9/26	35
62	George Follmer	Retzloff Chemical	Ford V-8/159 cu.in.	Gilbert	164.286	27/27	26
38	Jim McElreath	Adams Airplanes/Two Jacks	Offy I-4/159 cu.in.	Hawk II	168.224	7/28	24
36	Johnny Rutherford	Patrick Petroleum/Michner	Offy I-4/159 cu.in.	Eagle	166.628	17/29	24
45	Ronnie Bucknum	Weinberger Homes	Offy I-4/159 cu.in.	Eagle	166.636	16/30	16
40	Art Pollard	STP Oil Treatment	Offy I-4/159 cu.in.	Lotus	167.123	12/31	7
98	Billy Vukovich	Wagner-Lockheed/Agajanian	Offy I-4/159 cu.in.	Mongoose	165.843	26/32	1
16	Bruce Walkup	Thermo King Auto/Gerhardt	Offy I-4/159 cu.in.	Gerhardt	163.942	28/33	0

REVAMPING THE SPEEDWAY

Tony Hulman started making mammoth investments in the Indianapolis Motor Speedway from the day he bought it, and, if anything, the pace of his spending increased during the late-Sixties and early-Seventies. He built more and more new grandstands, new entrance tunnels and additional garages. Hospitality suites went up in Turn Two, new safety fences along the front straight, and then in 1975 the fancy Hall of Fame Museum. In 1969, most of the track was resurfaced, and in 1976 the entire 2.5-mile oval was repaved. It was the first time since the original bricks were laid in 1909 that the whole track was redone at once.

All this is evidence of how successful the Speedway had become under

Hulman's care. From a derelict wreck at the end of World War II, he rebuilt it into the finest motor racing facility anywhere in the world. Not just the physical plant, but the race itself got bigger and better. The total purse broke $1 million in 1970, then climbed steadily to $2 million by 1982. Despite economic hard times, the 500 continued to boom, growing richer and better every year.

The Speedway's success carried the USAC National Championship along with it. There were no longer any Champ car races still run on the dangerous dirt ovals. One-mile paved ovals and expensive 2.5-mile Super-Speedways were the latest things. In addition to Indianapolis, the banked Super-Speedways at Ontario, Pocono and Michigan joined the Championship Trail.

All this had a couple of important effects. Despite the stagnant economy, there was more money than ever in Speedway racing, which attracted more world-class drivers and teams, and created more intense competition. And that, of course, brought more media and sponsor attention, and even more prestige. The Indianapolis 500 remained not only the biggest and richest race in the world, but also the best known. It was older and more famous than its only rivals in prestige, the Monaco Grand Prix and LeMans.

THE SHAPE OF CARS TO COME

In the early-Seventies, the new emphasis on high-speed paved tracks also changed the shape of Speedway cars in very basic ways. There hadn't been a "dual purpose" Speedway/dirt car at Indianapolis since the early-Fifties, but the addition of other 500 mile races meant that high-speed performance became more important than ever. And that intensified the search for more horsepower, reliable horsepower and sleeker air penetration. For the first time, the teams started wind-tunnel testing, and the remarkably narrow-focus job description of "racing aerodynamicist" entered the Speedway lexicon.

There were outside influences at work, too, most especially the wings which appeared on Formula One cars in 1968 and '69. The huge inverted airfoils worked like an airplane wing in reverse. Instead of lift, they provided "downforce," literally pressing the tires to the pavement so that the cars had better traction. But the wings also created a tremendous amount of aerodynamic drag, enough to knock 20 mph off the top speed. It was obvious that wings were a tremendous aid on a Grand Prix road racing course, since by definition road courses consist mostly of corners with only a few high-speed straights.

At first, Indianapolis racers didn't think wings were applicable to them. But that was a basic misunderstanding of the Indianapolis Motor Speedway. Despite those 5/8th-mile straights, the key to the Speedway is its four 1/4-mile corners. Out of the 46 seconds it took to complete a lap in the early-Seventies, 22 of those seconds were spent actually negotiating a corner and the remainder exiting one corner and getting ready for the next. At lap speeds approaching 195 mph, Indianapolis is no longer four corners linked by straights. It becomes one large left turn, albeit of variable radius as you rocket around it.

Once they understood that the key to the Speedway is the corners, it was obvi-

(above) The innovative Bell Star first appeared in 1969; within four years, every racer was wearing a full-face helmet like this. There were many advantages. The lower portion protected your chin and face in an accident, and could be fitted with a Nomex skirt for fire protection. So the Star was safer. It was also more comfortable, because the airflow at 200 mph tended to lift an open-face helmet and pull against your neck. The Star slipped easily through the air. So easily, that it actually helped the aerodynamic penetration of a race car by reducing drag. This simple yet perfect shape is considered such a classic example of industrial design that a Bell Star is in the permanent collection of New York's Museum of Modern Art.

MARIO

No wonder the crowds love him. Mario Andretti is about as honest and decent a man as you'd ever want to meet, inside or outside racing. He enjoys a marvelous combination of skill and determination, blended with innate modesty. And after 35 years spent behind the wheel of hundreds of different racing cars, he is, if anything, better than ever. Winston Churchill's definition of courage as "grace under pressure" could have been written to describe this wonderfully engaging personality, already a racing legend like his boyhood idol, Alberto Ascari.

Mario and his twin brother, Aldo, were born in Montona on February 28, 1940, in that part of Italy which is now annexed to Yugoslavia. In 1955, their family moved to Nazareth, PA, where Mario still lives today down the street from his parents. The twins started racing with a '48 Hudson on the local dirt track, on the same ground that decades later became Roger Penske's Pennsylvania International Raceway. Aldo had a bad accident early on, and never seriously went racing again. But Mario turned out to be a natural. He started driving USAC Sprint cars and met legendary chief mechanic Clint Brawner and car owner Al Dean of Dean Van Lines. The two became his mentors in 1964 and taught him the ropes.

(above) Mario at fifty-one. A grandfather now with a touch of gray, he's still competitive with youngsters half his age, not to mention his son Michael, now twenty-eight. (right) Mario's medallion from Auto Racing's Hall of Fame, just one of hundreds of awards he's won over the past three decades. (bottom right) Racing is tougher than it looks. Mario gets a kiss from ebullient sponsor Andy Granatelli in Victory Lane after winning the 500 in 1969. Ironically, it was the only Indianapolis win for both of them, despite decades of trying and coming *this* close over and over.

In 1965, Andretti burst upon Indianapolis, qualifying fourth, finishing third and going on to win the National Championship, the first rookie champion in decades. He repeated as National Champion in 1966, and sat on the pole at Indy. In 1967 and '68, he was second in the National Championship, first again in 1969, when he also won the 500. Add his fourth National Championship in 1984, and Mario becomes second only to his great rival A.J. Foyt in the number of championships he has won. And, like Foyt's, they are spread over two decades, a true sign of greatness.

Already, in 1965, Mario was driving for Ferrari and Ford in sports car endurance races, winning Sebring. Since then, he has won dozens of sports car endurance races. In '67, he won the Daytona

500 NASCAR race. Like the other drivers of his generation to whom he is often compared—A.J. Foyt, Dan Gurney and Parnelli Jones—Mario excels in a variety of types of racing.

But Mario has some special distinctions. In 1968, he ran his first Formula One race—he took the pole at Watkins Glen—and unlike any of his American rivals, was immensely successful in Grands Prix. He won the World Championship in 1978, only the second American to do so (Phil Hill was the first, in 1961). Mario and Emerson Fittipaldi are also the only men who have been both World Champion and National Champion. With Fittipaldi, Jimmy Clark and Graham Hill, Mario is one of four men to win both a World Championship and the 500.

Over the years, Mario has started 343 Champ car races and won 51 of them, second only to A.J. Foyt. He has finished in the Top Three 132 times, in the Top Ten 218 times, for a phenomenal Top Ten Average of .636. The only place Mario hasn't been able to consistently win is at the Indianapolis Motor Speedway. In twenty-six seasons, he has started from the pole three times, but aside from his hard-fought win in 1969, has mostly suffered appalling luck. He's finished second two times, third once and fourth once. But he's also finished in the bottom half at the Speedway sixteen heartbreaking times.

Mario and his son Michael also share the distinction of being the only father/son team-mates to ever run at the Speedway, and, with the addition of son Jeff and nephew John at Milwaukee in 1990, the only family to put four relatives in one CART race. And that's typical of Mario, too. A dedicated American racer, but also possessed of that wonderful Italian sense of family. Not just a wonderful racing driver, but an admirable man, too. Just as Mario idolized Alberto Ascari, there are boys who idolize Mario Andretti. And with good reason. ■

(above) Legends at speed, 1969. A.J. Foyt and Mario Andretti started first and second in their similar turbocharged Coyote/Ford and Hawk/Ford. A.J. finished eighth with turbo problems, Mario went on to win his only Speedway victory. Mario was supposed to drive a new four-wheel drive Lotus 64, but he destroyed it against the wall in practice when the right rear hub broke. Chief mechanic Clint Brawner dragged out his old Hawk/Ford with which Mario qualified first in 1967. A quick brush-up, and they had a winner. Nobody was more surprised than the driver and mechanic.

1970

Winner: Al Unser, Colt/
Ford, 155.749 mph
Winner's Purse: $271,697
Total Purse: $1,000,002
Pace Car: Rodger Ward,
Oldsmobile 442

Completely dominating the race, Al Unser started on the pole and led a total of 190 laps to win easily from Mark Donohue and Dan Gurney. The only real excitement was caused by a rain delay and then a red flag when Jim Malloy hit the wall on the start, which necessitated yet another delay and a restart.

Number	Driver	Sponsor/Team	Engine Type/Displacement	Chassis	Qualifying	Start/Finish	Laps
2	Al Unser	Johnny Lightning/Parnelli Jones	Ford V-8/159 cu.in.	P.J. Colt	170.221	1/1	200
66	Mark Donohue	Sunoco/US Racing	Ford V-8/159 cu.in.	Lola	169.911	5/2	200
48	Dan Gurney	Olsonite Eagle	Offy I-4/159 cu.in.	Eagle	166.860	11/3	200
83	Donnie Allison	Foyt & Greer	Ford V-8/159 cu.in.	Eagle	165.662	23/4	200
14	Jim McElreath	Sheraton-Thompson/Ansted	Ford V-8/159 cu.in.	Coyote	166.821	33/5	200
1	Mario Andretti	STP Oil Treatment	Ford V-8/159 cu.in.	McNamara	168.209	8/6	199
89	Jerry Grant	Nelson Iron Works/Jerry Grant	Offy I-4/159 cu.in.	Eagle	165.983	29/7	198
38	Rick Muther	The Tony Express/Two Jacks	Offy I-4/159 cu.in.	Hawk II	165.654	15/8	197
75	Carl Williams	Bruce McLaren	Offy I-4/159 cu.in.	McLaren	166.590	19/9	197
7	A.J. Foyt	Sheraton-Thompson/Ansted	Ford V-8/159 cu.in.	Coyote	170.004	3/10	195
3	Bobby Unser	Wagner-Lockheed/Leader Cards	Ford V-8/159 cu.in.	Eagle	168.508	7/11	192
67	Sam Sessions	Jim Robbins	Ford V-8/159 cu.in.	Vollstedt	163.373	32/12	190
32	Jack Brabham	Brabham-Gilmore/Motor Racing	Offy I-4/159 cu.in.	Brabham	166.397	26/13	175
44	Dick Simon	Bryant Heating	Ford V-8/159 cu.in.	Vollstedt	165.548	31/14	168
19	Ronnie Bucknum	M.V.S.	Ford V-8/159 cu.in.	Morris	166.136	27/15	162
23	Mel Kenyon	Sprite/Lindsey Hopkins	Offy I-4/159 cu.in.	Coyote	165.906	22/16	160
22	Wally Dallenbach	Sprite/Lindsey Hopkins	Ford V-8/159 cu.in.	Eagle	165.601	24/17	143
18	Johnny Rutherford	Patrick Petroleum/Michner	Offy I-4/159 cu.in.	Eagle	170.213	2/18	135
27	Lee Roy Yarbrough	Jim Robbins	Ford V-8/159 cu.in.	Vollstedt	166.559	13/19	107
84	George Snider	Sheraton-Thompson/Ansted	Ford V-8/159 cu.in.	Coyote	167.660	10/20	105
9	Mike Mosley	G.C. Murphy/Leader Cards	Offy I-4/159 cu.in.	Eagle	166.651	12/21	96
73	Peter Revson	Bruce McLaren	Offy I-4/159 cu.in.	McLaren	167.942	16/22	87
58	Billy Vukovich	Sugaripe Prune/Jerry O'Connell	Offy I-4/159 cu.in.	Brabham	165.753	30/23	78
15	Joe Leonard	Johnny Lightning/Parnelli Jones	Ford V-8/159 cu.in.	P.J. Colt	166.898	18/24	73
11	Roger McCluskey	Quickick/Hayhoe Racing	Ford V-8/159 cu.in.	Scorpion	169.213	4/25	62
16	Gary Bettenhausen	Thermo King Auto Air/Gerhardt	Offy I-4/159 cu.in.	Gerhardt	166.451	20/26	55
25	Lloyd Ruby	Daniels Cablevision/Gene White	Offy I-4/159 cu.in.	Mongoose	168.895	25/27	54
5	Gordon Johncock	Gilmore Broadcasting/Johncock	Ford V-8/159 cu.in.	Gerhardt	167.015	17/28	45
97	Bruce Walkup	Wynn's Spit-Fire/Agajanian-Faas	Offy I-4/159 cu.in.	Mongoose	166.459	14/29	44
10	Art Pollard	Art Pollard Car Wash/Race-Go	Offy I-4/159 cu.in.	Kingfish	168.595	6/30	28
20	George Follmer	STP Oil Treatment	Ford V-8/159 cu.in.	Hawk III	166.052	21/31	18
93	Greg Weld	Art Pollard Car Wash/Race-Go	Offy I-4/159 cu.in.	Gerhardt	166.121	28/32	12
31	Jim Malloy	Stearns Mfg/Federal Automotive	Offy I-4/159 cu.in.	Gerhardt	167.895	9/33	0

ous to designers in the early Seventies that wings were the way to go. Of course, wings reduced straightaway speeds, but they more than made up for it in cornering ability. And so beginning in 1969, Speedway cars sprouted wings. Lots of wings, some of them, in sets of two or three. They were still feeling their way compared to the sophisticated aerodynamicists of a decade later, but even at the beginning, it was obviously only a matter of time before designers went to the inverted airfoils on stilts that the Formula One teams had begun using in 1968.

THE RETURN OF POWER TO EUROPE

Back in the Fifties, Formula One and Indianapolis cars, while not identical, were

actually quite similar. It was possible to bring a modified Grand Prix car to the Indianapolis 500 and earn World Championship points. And technically it was possible to race Formula One with an Indianapolis car in the Fifties. Barbara Hutton's wealthy son, Lance Reventlow, even bankrolled an American Formula One car called the Scarab, which challenged the Grand Prix circuits in 1960 with a sleeved-down Offy engine, albeit unsuccessfully.

Then from 1961 through 1965, Grands Prix were contested in little 1.5-liter racers that weren't much more than Formula Juniors with 1.5-liter instead of 1.1-liter engines. The original intention of the CSI was to make Formula One safer by going to these small cars. Of course, the little cars turned out to be faster than the previous Formula One cars, and even more dangerous. The little cars had virtually nothing to do with Indianapolis cars—or much else—and turned out to be a monumental cul de sac disliked by drivers and spectators alike.

So for the 1966 season, the CSI decreed a 3.0-liter Formula One, which turned out to be as popular as the previous formula had been unpopular. This required a maximum displacement of 3.0-liters (183 cubic inches) unsupercharged or 1.5-liters (91 cubic inches) supercharged. Minimum weight was now 500 kg (1100 lbs.), and the engines had to run on commercially available gasoline. Originally, this Formula was supposed to run only through 1970, but it proved so popular with drivers, engineers and spectators that it was kept in effect—though with many minor changes—up until 1985.

From our point of view, what was important about this new Formula One is that it once again brought the Grand Prix rules into a rough equivalency with USAC rules. A difference of 200cc (12 cubic inches) and a turbocharger is no great difference, and as early as 1969, Lotus was racing essentially the same four-wheel drive car in both Formula One and USAC, labelled the Model 63 and 64, respectively. That this particular Lotus was a bomb no matter where you raced it is beside

(below) Texan Jim McElreath qualified seventh in his Hawk/Offy in 1969, but jumped out early when his turbo caught fire. Steady McElreath never won the 500, but he finished in the Top Ten six times in his twenty-year career. Teams like John Zink and A.J. Foyt eagerly employed him year after year as their steady "Number Two" driver. McElreath's Hawk II is typical of cars of this period...low nose with radiator air intake, wedge shape, "ducktail" rear. Note how wide the tires have become compared to just a few years earlier.

1971

Winner: Al Unser, Colt/
Ford, 157.735 mph
Winner's Purse: $238,454
Total Purse: $1,001,604
Pace Car: Eldon Palmer,
Dodge Challenger

Peter Revson qualified on the pole, setting a new track record in the process. Mark Donohue was next to him on the front row and both were driving new McLaren M16s. In the race itself, however, Al Unser cruised to his second runaway win in a row, taking charge after lap 118.

Number	Driver	Sponsor/Team	Engine Type/Displacement	Chassis	Qualifying	Start/ Finish	Laps
1	Al Unser	Johnny Lightning/Parnelli Jones	Ford V-8/158 cu.in.	P.J. Colt	174.522	5/1	200
86	Peter Revson	McLaren Cars	Offy I-4/159 cu.in.	McLaren	178.696	1/2	200
9	A.J. Foyt	ITT/Thompson	Ford V-8/159 cu.in.	Coyote	174.317	6/3	200
42	Jim Malloy	Olsonite Eagle/Dan Gurney	Offy I-4/158 cu.in.	Eagle	171.838	10/4	200
32	Billy Vukovich	Sugaripe Prune/Jerry O'Connell	Offy I-4/158 cu.in.	Brabham	171.674	11/5	200
84	Donnie Allison	Purolator/Foyt & Greer	Ford V-8/159 cu.in.	Coyote	171.903	20/6	199
58	Bud Tingelstad	Sugaripe Prune/Jerry O'Connell	Offy I-4/158 cu.in.	Brabham	170.156	17/7	198
43	Denny Zimmerman	Frank Fiore	Offy I-4/159 cu.in.	Vollstedt	169.755	28/8	189
6	Roger McCluskey	Sprite/Lindsey Hopkins	Ford V-8/159 cu.in.	Kuzma	171.241	22/9	188
16	Gary Bettenhausen	Thermo King/Don Gerhardt	Offy I-4/159 cu.in.	Gerhardt	171.233	13/10	178
12	Lloyd Ruby	Utah Stars/Gene White Racing	Ford V-8/159 cu.in.	Mongoose	173.821	7/11	174
2	Bobby Unser	Olsonite Eagle/Dan Gurney	Offy I-4/158 cu.in.	Eagle	175.816	3/12	164
4	Mike Mosley	G.C. Murphy/Leader Cards	Ford V-8/159 cu.in.	Eagle	169.579	19/13	159
44	Dick Simon	TraveLodge Sleeper/Dick Simon	Ford V-8/159 cu.in.	Vollstedt	170.164	33/14	151
41	George Follmer	Grant King Racers	Offy I-4/158 cu.in.	Kingfish	169.205	29/15	147
21	Cale Yarborough	Gene White Racing	Ford V-8/159 cu.in.	Mongoose	170.156	14/16	140
85	Denis Hulme	McLaren Cars	Offy I-4/159 cu.in.	McLaren	174.910	4/17	137
18	Johnny Rutherford	Patrick Petroleum/Michner	Offy I-4/159 cu.in.	Eagle	171.151	24/18	128
15	Joe Leonard	Samsonite/Parnelli Jones Ford	Ford V-8/158 cu.in.	P.J. Colt	172.761	8/19	123
68	David Hobbs	Penske Products/US Racing	Ford V-8/160 cu.in.	Lola	169.571	16/20	107
38	Rick Muther	Arkansas Aviation/Two Jacks	Offy I-4/159 cu.in.	Hawk II	169.972	18/21	85
99	Bob Harkey	Joe Hunt Magneto	Offy I-4/159 cu.in.	Gerhardt	169.197	32/22	77
95	Bentley Warren	Classic Wax/Vatis Enterprises	Offy I-4/159 cu.in.	Eagle	169.627	15/23	76
22	Wally Dallenbach	Sprite/Lindsey Hopkins	Offy I-4/159 cu.in.	Kuzma	171.160	23/24	69
66	Mark Donohue	Sunoco/US Racing	Offy I-4/159 cu.in.	McLaren	177.087	2/25	66
64	Art Pollard	Gilmore Champion Racing	Ford V-8/159 cu.in.	Scorpion	169.500	31/26	45
98	Sam Sessions	Wynn's Kwik-Kool/Agajanian	Ford V-8/159 cu.in.	Lola	170.358	25/27	43
45	Larry Dickson	Grant King Racers	Offy I-4/159 cu.in.	Kingfish	170.285	26/28	33
7	Gordon Johncock	Norris Industries	Ford V-8/159 cu.in.	McLaren	171.388	12/29	11
5	Mario Andretti	STP Oil Treatment	Ford V-8/159 cu.in.	McNamara	172.612	9/30	11
20	Steve Krisiloff	STP Gas Treatment	Ford V-8/159 c.in.	McNamara	169.835	27/31	10
23	Mel Kenyon	Sprite/Lindsey Hopkins	Ford V-8/159 cu.in.	Kuzma	170.205	30/32	10
80	George Snider	G.C. Murphy/Leader Cards	Offy I-4/159 cu.in.	Eagle	171.600	21/33	6

the point. For the first time in a decade, it was now possible to race the same car on either side of the Atlantic and, for the first time since the Thirties, with a fair prospect of success in both places.

USAC CHANGES THE RULES

Anticipating the arrival of Formula One cars—and dreading the arrival of Formula One cars wearing dangerous inverted airfoils on stilts—in 1969 USAC promulgated the first serious rewrite of the Speedway rules since the safety restrictions of 1965. USAC wisely limited the height of the bodywork, which effectively banned wings on stilts without actually coming out and banning wings on stilts.

They also reduced the displacement of turbocharged, double-overhead cam engines from 171 cubic inches (2.8-liters) to 162 cubic inches (2.65-liters). Normally-aspirated engines remained at 256 cubic inches (4.2-liters) and stock-blocks at 320 cubic inches (5.25-liters). In addition, there was a specification for turbocharged stock-blocks, allowed 209 cubic inches (3.42-liters).

As it turned out, the only viable engines during the Seventies were DOHC, 2.65-liter turbos. Dan Gurney ran his Ford-based Eagle/Gurney-Weslake engines with great success at the beginning of this era, and Fred Carrillo built some AMC-based stock-block engines in 1976 and '77. But neither of these engines could compete with "real" racing engines, designed from the ground up for competition. Only three engines were factors at the Speedway in this period: the Offy, the four-cam Foyt (Ford) V-8 and the Cosworth-Ford V-8.

LAST DAYS OF THE WINNINGEST ENGINE IN HISTORY

The venerable four-cylinder Offy, now fitted with an AiResearch TEO67 or TEO9 turbocharger, was capable of producing over 1000 hp when boosted over 100 in/Hg. That was good for qualifying, but too short-fused for 500 miles. For the race itself, the Offy was usually run at about 85 in/Hg in the early-Seventies before USAC started restricting boost pressures. Under those conditions, the Offy would reliably make 820 hp at 9000 rpm and about 560 lbs-ft of torque at 7000 rpm. And that was enough to beat the four-cam Foyts.

Still, the Offy had just about reached the limits of its development. Then Art Sparks, the engineer who had built the six-cylinder Sparks-Thorne engine in the Thirties—essentially an Offy with two more cylinders—got together with Dale Drake, who was still building Offys. Sparks recommended that Drake design a new cylinder head, with a narrow 44 degree angle between the valves rather than the wide 72 degree angle. High-performance European engines, including the all-conquering Formula One Cosworth, used narrow-angle valves.

(below) Mark Donohue's M16 McLaren/Offy sat on the front row and handily won the 1972 500. These McLarens—and the similar Eagles—were responsible for the incredible rise in qualifying speeds, from 170 mph in 1970 to 195 mph in 1972...the biggest jump in Speedway history.

(left) Faces Behind
the Scenes, 1973:
Cadillac dealers
take delivery of
white Eldorado
Convertible Pace
Car Replicas before
a spin around the
Speedway. Those
big Eldos are
collector's items
today.

1972

Winner: Mark Donohue, McLaren/Offy, 162.962 mph
Winner's Purse: $218,767
Total Purse: $1,011,845
Pace Car: Jim Rathmann, Hurst/Olds Cutlass

Gary Bettenhausen led 138 laps, then Jerry Grant had it in the bag until he stopped for fuel with 12 laps to go. His crew used the wrong fuel tank. Bettenhausen's team-mate Mark Donohue passed Grant on the track, then USAC officials dropped him to twelfth because of his illegal fuel stop.

Number	Driver	Sponsor/Team	Engine Type/Displacement	Chassis	Qualifying	Start/Finish	Laps
66	Mark Donohue	Sunoco McLaren/Penske	Offy I-4/159 cu.in.	McLaren	191.408	3/1	200
4	Al Unser	Viceroy/Parnelli Jones	Offy I-4/158 cu.in.	Parnelli	183.617	19/2	200
1	Joe Leonard	Samsonite/Parnelli Jones	Offy I-4/158 cu.in.	Parnelli	185.223	6/3	200
52	Sam Sessions	Gene White Racing	Ford V-8/159 cu.in.	Lola	180.415	24/4	200
34	Sam Posey	Norris Eagle/Champ Carr	Offy I-4/158 cu.in.	Eagle	184.379	7/5	198
5	Lloyd Ruby	Wynn's/Gene White Racing	Ford V-8/159 cu.in.	Atlanta	181.415	11/6	196
60	Mike Hiss	STP Pylon Blade/Page Racing	Offy I-4/158 cu.in.	Eagle	179.015	25/7	196
9	Mario Andretti	Viceroy/Parnelli Jones Racing	Offy I-4/158 cu.in.	Parnelli	187.617	5/8	194
11	Jimmy Caruthers	US Armed Forces/Quality Racing	Ford V-8/159 cu.in.	Scorpion	178.909	31/9	194
21	Cale Yarborough	Bill Daniels GOP/Gene White	Ford V-8/159 cu.in.	Atlanta	178.864	32/10	193
84	George Snider	ITT-Thompson/A.J. Foyt, Jr.	Ford V-8/159 cu.in.	Coyote	181.855	21/11	190
48	Jerry Grant	Mystery/All American Racers	Offy I-4/158 cu.in.	Eagle	189.294	15/12	188
44	Dick Simon	TraveLodge Sleeper/Dick Simon	Foyt V-8/159 cu.in.	Lola	180.424	23/13	186
7	Gary Bettenhausen	Sunoco McLaren/Penske	Offy I-4/158 cu.in.	McLaren	188.877	4/14	182
40	Wally Dallenbach	STP Oil Treatment	Foyt V-8/159 cu.in.	Lola	181.626	33/15	182
89	John Martin	Automotive Technology	Offy I-4/158 cu.in.	Brabham	179.614	14/16	161
37	Lee Kunzman	Caves Buick Company	Offy I-4/158 cu.in.	Gerhardt	179.265	30/17	131
23	Mel Kenyon	Gilmore Racing/Lindsey Hopkins	Ford V-8/159 cu.in.	Coyote	181.388	12/18	126
17	Denny Zimmerman	Bryant Heating/Vollstedt	Offy I-4/159 cu.in.	Coyote	180.027	28/19	116
24	Gordon Johncock	Gulf McLaren	Offy I-4/162 cu.in.	McLaren	188.511	26/20	113
15	Steve Krisiloff	Ayr-Way Lloyds/Grant King	Offy I-4/158 cu.in.	Kingfish	181.433	10/21	102
31	John Mahler	Harbor Fuel Oil/Vanguard	Offy I-4/158 cu.in.	McLaren	179.497	29/22	99
56	Jim Hurtubise	Miller High Life/M.V.S.	Foyt V-8/158 cu.in.	Coyote	181.050	13/23	94
14	Roger McCluskey	American Underwriters/Hopkins	Offy I-4/158 cu.in.	Antares	182.676	20/24	92
2	A.J. Foyt	ITT-Thompson/A.J. Foyt	Foyt V-8/159 cu.in.	Coyote	188.996	17/25	60
98	Mike Mosley	Vivitar/Leader Cards	Offy I-4/159 cu.in.	Eagle	189.145	16/26	56
18	Johnny Rutherford	Patrick Petroleum/Michner	Offy I-4/158 cu.in.	Brabham	183.234	8/27	55
3	Billy Vukovich	Sugaripe Prune/Jerry O'Connell	Offy I-4/158 cu.in.	Eagle	184.814	18/28	54
95	Carl Williams	Vatis Enterprises	Offy I-4/158 cu.in.	Eagle	180.469	22/29	52
6	Bobby Unser	Olsonite Eagle	Offy I-4/158 cu.in.	Eagle	195.940	1/30	31
12	Peter Revson	Gulf McLaren	Offy I-4/162 cu.in.	McLaren	192.885	2/31	23
42	Swede Savage	Michner/Patrick Racing	Offy I-4/158 cu.in.	Eagle	181.726	9/32	5
33	Salt Walther	Dayton Disc Brakes/Walmotor	Foyt V-8/159 cu.in.	P.J. Colt	180.542	27/33	0

This improved combustion and breathing of the mixture into the cylinder.

Leo Goossen was still working for Drake—he'd been drawing the Miller and Offy engines for over 50 years—and he modified his beloved Offy for the last time, making Sparks' recommended changes. As it turned out, both Dale Drake and Leo Goossen died in the middle of this project. Goossen, in particular, had presided over the Miller legacy his entire working life and taken the original Offy concept from 220 hp to 1100 hp. When he presented this new engine in 1975, Dale Drake's son John called it an SGD, which stood for Sparks-Goossen-Drake. It was a fitting tribute to three men that most people have never heard of, but who won more races than anybody else.

MCLAREN VS EAGLE

The "wedge shape" first appeared on a racing car at the Indianapolis 500 in 1968, the Lotus 56 STP turbine designed by Maurice Phillippe. This was so fast, albeit ultimately unsuccessful, that Colin Chapman and Phillippe copied it for the Lotus 72 Grand Prix car. This won for the first time at the Dutch Grand Prix in 1970. Jochen Rindt then went on to win the World Championship posthumously, since he had already been killed in his 72 practicing for the Italian Grand Prix. The Lotus 72 was obviously so superior that it became one of the most-copied race cars of all time: no grille opening, a wedge-shaped body, side radiators, a separate rear wing set far back.

One of the most successful Lotus 72 clones was McLaren's M16. Company founder Bruce McLaren had recently been killed, testing the M8D Can-Am car at Goodwood on June 2, 1970, and McLaren's famous designer Robin Herd had left to start March Racing in 1968. That left McLaren's American partner Teddy Mayer and Herd's assistant Gordon Coppuck to carry on. Coppuck's first car had been the 1970 McLaren M15, which he called "a single-seat Can-Am car." Peter Revson and Carl Williams ran them in the Indianapolis 500, with Williams finishing ninth.

For 1971, Coppuck came back with the Lotus-like M16 and set Indianapolis on its ear. The M16 looked like a Lotus 72—no grille, wedge shape, side radiators—and it also introduced the concept of "low polar moment of inertia" to Indy car racing. This is just a fancy way of saying something most people could figure out intuitively: if you put the weight in your car out at the ends, it will be harder to turn it than if you concentrate all the weight near the middle. Coppuck used a longer wheelbase than his competitors, grouped all the heavy components in the center, created a suspension that worked beautifully and overlaid the whole thing with that Lotus-style body. The M16s were the class of Indianapolis racing in 1971, even though Al Unser's Parnelli Colt beat Peter Revson at the 500. McLaren opened a shop in Detroit to supply the demand.

Dan Gurney drove Can-Am for McLaren in 1970. Then he retired, and along with engineer Roman Slobodynskj, came out with a new Eagle that was virtually a copy of the McLaren M16. In 1972, the new Eagle was even faster than the McLaren, and the two brands dominated the 500. Indeed, Eagle and McLaren cars made up the bulk of USAC grids until 1977, and the design of the M16 stayed competitive for nearly a decade. In the fast-paced world of USAC racing as it developed throughout the Seventies, that was simply remarkable. But the concept was a valid one. Even the Lotus 72, which started it all, was raced for five years in Formula One. Incredible. ∎

(below) Handsome Peter Revson in the trend-setting 1971 McLaren M16. You can see the chisel nose, wedge shape, smallish wings and side-mounted radiators next to the cockpit. Revson set a new qualifying record at 178.696 mph, started on the pole, but finished second behind Al Unser. In 1972, he started second but broke early; in '73 he qualified tenth and crashed. He was killed in a Shadow DN3 before the South African GP of 1974.

(bottom) Jerry Grant in his McLaren-like 1972 Eagle. He started fifteenth and finished twelfth. Sam Posey's similar Eagle was the top finisher that year, in fifth.

WINGS 'N THINGS

DeHavilland Aircraft engineer Frank Costin blended art and aerodynamics in the design of exquisite Lotus, Vanwall and Lister racing cars in the late-Fifties, but Ferrari's early-Sixties 250 GTO was one of the first racing cars actually developed in a wind-tunnel. Most other racing cars of that time were intuitively drawn to be "racy," and only coincidentally to have low drag. The first glimmer of how beneficial body shape could be to handling came in 1961 when Ferrari driver Richie Ginther invented the rear "spoiler" to keep the rear of his Testa Rossa from lifting on the long straight at LeMans.

But it wasn't until 1968, when the Lotus 49B Formula One racer appeared sporting inverted front and rear airfoils, that automotive engineers began to really appreciate what aerodynamics could do for them. The Lotus 49—and most other Grand Prix and USAC cars of that era—was essentially an aluminum monocoque tube, open at the front end to flow cooling air to the front-mounted radiator, open at the rear to hold the engine. Aerodynamically, it was hopefully neutral, though most of these cars tended to lift at high speeds because of the low-pressure area formed over the top of the body.

For the 1968 season and the beginning of 1969, Formula One cars sprouted inverted airfoils mounted high above the front and rear on stilts attached directly to the suspension. These monstrous wings pushed the tires on the pavement in the corners, then were automatically adjusted from the cockpit for minimum air resistance on the long straights. At Barcelona in 1969, Graham Hill and Jochen Rindt destroyed their Lotuses when their rear wings folded up going over a 150 mph bump. Wings acting directly on the suspension were banned by the CSI before the next race.

To its credit, USAC never did allow these crazy wings. The first aerodynamic aids appeared on cars at the 500 in 1969, small tabs and spoilers on the fronts, modest ducktails on the back. All were intended to provide downforce to stick the cars to the pavement. At this time, the leaders in aerodynamic development worldwide were definitely Colin Chapman and Maurice Phillippe of Lotus, and their Lotus 56 was state-of-the-art.

(above) Art Pollard failed to qualify this "Super Wedge" in 1969. Underneath is one of the Lotus 56B four-wheel drive turbine chassis, but now fitted with a stock-block 305 cubic inch Plymouth. Over that, Vince Granatelli has put this boldly streamlined body with front wings, NACA ducts, rear "fenders" and integrated rear wing. Notice how Pollard is snugly tucked out of the airstream in the tall cockpit. A very innovative, if unsuccessful, machine for its day.
(right) A.J. Foyt finished third in 1971 with this Coyote/Foyt. Notice its small wings, lumpy air-catching surface, unnecessary front grille. A real transition design.

The breakthrough machine in Formula One was the 1970 Lotus 72; the breakthrough machine in USAC was the 1971 McLaren M16, followed by the 1972 Eagle. All three used a chisel nose, wedge profile, side-radiators, adjustable front wings and a wide rear wing attached to the bodywork rather than the suspension. In broad concept, these wedge cars had a slight amount of downforce designed into the body, with the wings used to fine tune the amount. The wings were so effective that by 1974, most cars were fitted with "wickerbills," or small tabs on the wings that could be adjusted by tenths of an inch. At 220 mph, such minute adjustments have a tremendous effect.

In 1969, USAC decided to limit total body height to 28 inches from top to chassis bottom, which effectively ruled out the dangerous Grand Prix-style wings of that era. The front spoilers were limited to 9 inches wide on either side of the nose, and couldn't extend past the center of the tire treads. The M16 McLaren met these rules, but, by lowering the rear body, the rear wing was given airflow both above and below, so it could act as a wing, not a spoiler. Total aerodynamic downforce of a 1971 M16 was about 700 lbs. at 200 mph.

For 1972, USAC said rear wings had to be within the centers of the tire treads—a car's "track"—within 32 inches of the bottom of the bodywork and extend no more than 42 inches behind the centerline of the rear wheels. This allowed a real wing, mounted on stilts, but fastened to the bodywork. With this new setup, the 1972 Eagles and McLarens had about 1500 lbs. of downforce at 200 mph. In other words, the effective weight of the car was literally doubled. Speeds got so high so quickly that USAC reduced the wing size starting in 1974. Wings could only be 36 inches wide. The rules remained stable until 1979, and lap speeds at Indianapolis stayed in the 185 to 190 mph range.

What a difference a wing makes! In 1970, Indy pole-sitter Al Unser qualified his Colt/Ford at 170.221 mph. He was hitting about 158 mph in the corners, about 200 mph on the straights. In 1971, Peter Revson's qualifying speed was 178.696 mph in an M16 McLaren/Offy. He was hitting about 163 mph in the corners, 215 mph on the straights. In 1972, Bobby Unser qualified at an astounding 195.940 mph in an Eagle/Offy. He was hitting 183 mph in the corners, but because of the aerodynamic drag from his wings, only 206 mph on the Speedway straights.

Between 1970 and 1972, lap speeds at Indianapolis went up by 25.71 mph, or 12.85 mph per year! Never in the history of racing has there been such a leap in lap speeds, not even with the introduction of the Miller 91, the Kurtis roadster or the mid-engine Lotus/Ford. After all the changes during the Sixties, they didn't think of the wings as a revolution, but merely a continuation of the incredible changes of an incredible decade. From our contemporary perspective, however, nothing changed the shape of racing as much as the discovery of aerodynamic downforce and how to use it. ∎

(below) One of the few successful alternates to the winged-wedge of the McLarens and Eagles was this 1972 Maurice Phillippe creation for Vel's Parnelli Jones Racing. Not only does it have a shovel nose with horizontal wings, but also diagonal wings used to cover the front upper control arms. Body sides are also diagonal, with large NACA ducts used to feed the mid-mounted radiators. Behind the turbo Offy is a wide, high-mounted wing. Al Unser, shown here, finished second behind Mark Donohue's McLaren in 1972, with Joe Leonard third and Mario Andretti eighth in matching Parnellis. The next year, Phillippe created McLaren/Eagle clones for Parnelli that weren't successful at all. But nobody tried to copy his clever diagonal car.

1973

Winner: Gordon Johncock,
Eagle/Offy, 159.036 mph
Winner's Purse: $236,022
Total Purse: $1,006,105
Pace Car: Jim Rathmann,
Cadillac Eldorado

One of the most dismal Mays in Speedway history. Art Pollard and Swede Savage were both killed, Salt Walther caused a red flag at the start and two race days were rained out before the race was finally run and then stopped because of yet more rain. Everybody was glad to finally go home.

Number	Driver	Sponsor/Team	Engine Type/Displacement	Chassis	Qualifying	Start/ Finish	Laps
20	Gordon Johncock	STP Double Oil Filter/Patrick	Offy I-4/157 cu.in.	Eagle	192.555	11/1	133
2	Billy Vukovich	Sugaripe Prune/Jerry O'Connell	Offy I-4/161 cu.in.	Eagle	191.103	16/2	133
3	Roger McCluskey	Lindsey Hopkins Buick	Offy I-4/159 cu.in.	McLaren	191.928	14/3	131
19	Mel Kenyon	Atlanta Falcons/Lindsey Hopkins	Foyt V-8/159 cu.in.	Eagle	190.225	19/4	131
5	Gary Bettenhausen	Sunoco DX/Roger Penske	Offy I-4/159 cu.in.	McLaren	195.599	5/5	130
24	Steve Krisiloff	Elliott-Norton Spirit/King Racers	Offy I-4/158 cu.in.	Kingfish	194.932	7/6	129
16	Lee Kunzman	Ayr-Way/Lloyd's/Hopkins	Offy I-4/159 cu.in.	Eagle	193.092	25/7	127
89	John Martin	Automotive Technology	Offy I-4/156 cu.in.	McLaren	194.384	24/8	124
7	Johnny Rutherford	Gulf McLaren	Offy I-4/159 cu.in.	McLaren	198.413	1/9	124
98	Mike Mosley	Lodestar/Leader Cards	Offy I-4/161 cu.in.	Eagle	189.753	21/10	120
73	David Hobbs	Carling Black Label/Woods	Offy I-4/158 cu.in.	Eagle	189.454	22/11	107
84	George Snider	Gilmore Racing/A.J. Foyt, Sr.	Foyt V-8/159 cu.in.	Coyote	190.355	30/12	101
8	Bobby Unser	Olsonite Division	Offy I-4/159 cu.in.	Eagle	198.183	2/13	100
44	Dick Simon	TraveLodge/Dick Simon	Ford V-8/160 cu.in.	Eagle	191.276	27/14	100
66	Mark Donohue	Sunoco DX/Roger Penske	Offy I-4/159 cu.in.	Eagle	197.412	3/15	92
60	Graham McRae	STP Gas Treatment	Offy I-4/159 cu.in.	Eagle	192.031	13/16	91
6	Mike Hiss	Thermo King/Don Gerhardt	Offy I-4/159 cu.in.	Eagle	191.939	26/17	91
1	Joe Leonard	Samsonite/Parnelli Jones Racing	Offy I-4/159 cu.in.	Parnelli	189.954	29/18	91
48	Jerry Grant	Olsonite/All American Racers	Offy I-4/159 cu.in.	Eagle	190.235	18/19	77
4	Al Unser	Viceroy/Parnelli Jones Racing	Offy I-4/159 cu.in.	Parnelli	194.879	8/20	75
21	Jimmy Caruthers	Cobre/Robert Fletcher	Offy I-4/159 cu.in.	Eagle	194.217	9/21	73
40	Swede Savage	STP Oil Treatment/Patrick Racing	Offy I-4/157 cu.in.	Eagle	196.582	4/22	57
35	Jim McElreath	Norris Eagle/Champ Carr	Offy I-4/159 cu.in.	Eagle	188.640	33/23	54
62	Wally Dallenbach	Olsonite/All American Racers	Offy I-4/159 cu.in.	Eagle	190.194	20/24	48
14	A.J. Foyt	Gilmore Racing/A.J. Foyt, Sr.	Foyt V-8/159 cu.in.	Coyote	188.927	23/25	37
30	Jerry Karl	Oriente Express/Smokey Yunick	Chevy V-8/208 cu.in.	Eagle	190.799	28/26	22
18	Lloyd Ruby	Commander Motor Homes/Slater	Offy I-4/159 cu.in.	Eagle	191.622	15/27	21
9	Sam Sessions	M.V.S.	Foyt V-8/159 cu.in.	Eagle	188.986	32/28	17
28	Bob Harkey	Bryant Heating/Lindsey Hopkins	Foyt V-8/159 cu.in.	Ken-Eagle	189.733	31/29	12
11	Mario Andretti	Viceroy/Parnelli Jones Racing	Offy I-4/159 cu.in.	Parnelli	159.059	6/30	4
15	Peter Revson	Gulf McLaren	Offy I-4/159 cu.in.	McLaren	192.606	10/31	3
12	Bobby Allison	Sunoco DX/Roger Penske	Offy I-4/159 cu.in.	McLaren	192.308	12/32	1
77	Salt Walther	Dayton-Walther/Walmotor	Offy I-4/159 cu.in.	McLaren	190.739	17/33	0

Wally Dallenbach almost won the 500 in 1975 with an SGD, so for 1976, John Drake reduced the valve angle to 38 degrees to make even more horsepower and renamed the engine the Drake-Offy. Unfortunately, USAC instituted a fuel economy rule beginning in 1974, and, as the power of the Offy went up, its fuel consumption went up, too. Even more unfortunately, the new Cosworth-Ford V-8 returned better fuel economy than the Offy at these higher power levels. The Drake-Offy died with a whimper in 1979, a victim not of younger competitors with more strength, but rules that stressed frugality over prowess. It was an ignominious end for a glorious engine that had brought the Indianapolis Motor Speedway so many memorable moments.

MR. FOYT'S OWN V-8

The second engine of the Seventies was the turbocharged version of the four-cam V-8 that Ford had designed specifically for Indianapolis in 1964. This engine, like the Offy, had been originally designed as a normally-aspirated, 255 cubic inch (4.2-liter) engine. When the turbochargers took over, the four-cam was reduced to 159 cubic inches (2.6-liters) to fit the USAC rules.

Then in 1970, when Henry Ford II pulled his company out of racing, the entire Ford four-cam engine operation was presented on a platter to A.J. Foyt. By the early-Seventies, the turbocharged Foyt V-8 was reliably producing around 825 hp at 9600 rpm with a turbocharger boost of 80 in/Hg. Any more boost and the engines would blow up like a hand-grenade.

This put the Foyt-powered cars about 10 mph down from the 1000 hp, 100 in/Hg Offys in the early-Seventies. But after 1974, when USAC instituted a cap on turbo boost at 80 in/Hg and a minimum fuel consumption limit of 1.8 mpg during the race, the Foyt V-8 was suddenly competitive again. Indeed, it was now about 50 hp ahead of the Offy, and 3 mph faster. A.J. Foyt finished third in 1975, second in 1976 and first in 1977. A simple revision in the maximum turbocharger boost pressure—a difference of about 10 psi—was enough to put Super Tex into the record books with four 500 wins and the Offy out of business after fifty years. Who ever could have guessed?

And who could have guessed that by 1978 the Foyt V-8 would be obsolete, and that in 1979 A.J. Foyt would just barely miss winning his fifth 500...driving a Parnelli chassis powered by a Cosworth. And who could have guessed that for the next decade, the Formula One Cosworth-Ford would dominate Speedway racing as thoroughly as had the Offy in its day. Times truly had changed.

THE FIRST TIRE RESTRICTIONS

Starting in 1969 and continuing up until today, USAC has restricted wheel widths to 10 inches front, 14 inches rear. This was an easy way to control tire sizes, since modern racing tires are designed with a tread width equal to the wheel width. According to Leo Mehl, Competition Director of Goodyear, the tire companies were in favor of this restriction in width because even in the late-Sixties it was already technically feasible to make tires with such sticky compounds that drivers would be able to circle the Speedway literally foot-to-the-floor all the way around.

At the time, Goodyear was even planning tires that would be so wide they'd function like one large rubber roller across the full width of the car. The problem, according to Leo Mehl, is that such tires would have allowed virtually anyone to drive flat-out around the Speedway, disregarding the line, other race traffic or anything else. "The tires would have been so good they would have stifled competition," he says, "and we didn't want that."

As it turned out, even on narrow tires the best drivers of the early-Seventies could charge around the Speedway flat-out, only scrubbing off a little speed in the

Between 1975 and 1982, Rick Mears was the only Indianapolis 500 winner who hadn't already won the race at least once before. He was also the first 500 winner to be born after World War II, on December 3, 1951.

1974

Winner: Johnny Rutherford, McLaren/Offy, 158.589 mph
Winner's Purse: $245,031
Total Purse: $1,015,686
Pace Car: Jim Rathmann, Hurst/Oldsmobile Cutlass W30

"Lonestar J.R." rocketed from the ninth row to the lead within 65 laps, then battled with fellow Texan A.J. Foyt until Foyt's scavenger pump broke. Rutherford finished 22 seconds ahead of Bobby Unser who had run up front all day, but never quite far enough up front.

Number	Driver	Sponsor/Team	Engine Type/Displacement	Chassis	Qualifying	Start/Finish	Laps
3	Johnny Rutherford	McLaren Cars	Offy I-4/159 cu.in.	McLaren	190.446	25/1	200
48	Bobby Unser	Olsonite/All American Racers	Offy I-4/159 cu.in.	Eagle	185.176	7/2	200
4	Billy Vukovich	Sugaripe Prune/O'Connell	Offy I-4/159 cu.in.	Eagle	182.500	16/3	199
20	Gordon Johncock	STP Double Oil Filter/Patrick	Offy I-4/157 cu.in.	Eagle	186.287	4/4	198
73	David Hobbs	Carling Black Label/McLaren	Offy I-4/159 cu.in.	McLaren	184.833	9/5	196
45	Jim McElreath	Thermo King/Fred Gerhardt	Offy I-4/159 cu.in.	Eagle	177.279	30/6	194
11	Pancho Carter	Cobre Firestone/R.L. Fletcher	Offy I-4/159 cu.in.	Eagle	180.605	21/7	191
79	Bob Harkey	Peru Circus/Lindsey Hopkins	Foyt V-8/158 cu.in.	Kenyon	176.687	31/8	189
9	Lloyd Ruby	Unlimited Racing Team	Offy I-4/159 cu.in.	Eagle	181.699	18/9	187
55	Jerry Grant	Cobre Firestone/R.L. Fletcher	Offy I-4/159 cu.in.	Eagle	181.781	17/10	175
89	John Martin	Sea Snack/Automotive Tech.	Offy I-4/159 cu.in.	McLaren	180.406	22/11	169
27	Tom Bigelow	Bryant Heating/Vollstedt	Offy I-4/159 cu.in.	Vollstedt	180.144	23/12	166
18	Bill Simpson	American Kids Racer/Beith	Offy I-4/159 cu.in.	Eagle	181.041	20/13	163
68	Mike Hiss	Norton Spirit/Penske Racing	Offy I-4/159 cu.in.	McLaren	187.490	3/14	158
14	A.J. Foyt	Gilmore Racing/A.J. Foyt, Sr.	Foyt V-8/160 cu.in.	Coyote	191.632	1/15	142
1	Roger McCluskey	English Leather/Hopkins	Offy I-4/159 cu.in.	Riley	181.005	27/16	141
77	Salt Walther	Dayton-Walther/Walmotor	Offy I-4/159 cu.in.	McLaren	183.927	14/17	141
15	Al Unser	Viceroy/Parnelli Jones	Offy I-4/160 cu.in.	Eagle	183.889	26/18	131
42	Jerry Karl	Ayr-Way/Lloyd's/Hopkins	Offy I-4/159 cu.in.	Eagle	181.452	19/19	115
24	Tom Sneva	Raymond Companies/King	Offy I-4/159 cu.in.	Kingfish	185.149	8/20	94
51	Jan Opperman	Viceroy/Parnelli Jones	Offy I-4/159 cu.in.	Parnelli	176.186	32/21	85
60	Steve Krisiloff	STP Gas Treatment/Patrick	Offy I-4/157 cu.in.	Eagle	182.519	15/22	72
21	Jimmy Caruthers	Cobre Firestone/R.L. Fletcher	Offy I-4/159 cu.in.	Eagle	184.049	12/23	64
59	Larry Cannon	American Financial/Hoffman	Offy I-4/159 cu.in.	Eagle	173.963	33/24	49
56	Jim Hurtubise	Miller High Life/Gohr	Offy I-4/159 cu.in.	McLaren	180.288	28/25	31
94	Johnny Parsons	Vatis Enterprises	Offy I-4/159 cu.in.	Finley	180.252	29/26	18
61	Rick Muther	Eisenhour-Brayton Racing	Foyt V-8/161 cu.in.	Coyote	179.991	24/27	11
82	George Snider	Gilmore Racing/J.H. Greer	Foyt V-8/160 cu.in.	Atlanta	183.993	13/28	7
98	Mike Mosley	Lodestar/Agajanian-Leader	Offy I-4/159 cu.in.	Eagle	185.319	6/29	6
40	Wally Dallenbach	STP Oil Treatment/Patrick	Offy I-4/157 cu.in.	Eagle	189.683	2/30	3
5	Mario Andretti	Viceroy/Parnelli Jones	Offy I-4/160 cu.in.	Eagle	186.027	5/31	2
8	Gary Bettenhausen	Score/Penske Racing	Offy I-4/159 cu.in.	McLaren	184.492	11/32	2
44	Dick Simon	TraveLodge/Dick Simon	Foyt V-8/160 cu.in.	Eagle	184.502	10/33	1

corners...just as their grandfathers had done on the banked board tracks of the Twenties. Remarkably, for the past twenty years there have been almost no significant changes in Speedway tire design with the exception of the switch from bias ply to radial tires in the late-Eighties.

The most important factor in terms of tire design was when USAC demanded a switch to 40 gallon fuel tanks, maximum, in 1974. This meant that every car in the 500 would have to stop at least six times during the 500 miles. And since a good pit crew could change tires as quickly as the required gravity feed storage tanks could fill a 40 gallon tank, everybody would now change tires at every fuel stop. And that meant there was no reason for an Indianapolis tire to have to last longer

TURBO

Any heat engine is simply a way of converting stored energy into useful work. A reciprocating, internal combustion heat engine converts the energy released by exploding fuel in the combustion chamber into linear motion which is converted to rotary motion by the crankshaft. And that drives Rick Mears at 240 mph. There are many ways to increase the amount of energy released. We can use fuel with more btu-per-liter, we can increase the swept volume of the cylinders—in other words, bigger displacement—and we can use more intake valve area and hold the valves open longer to allow more mixture into the cylinders.

Or we can *compress* the fuel/air mixture so more fits into the cylinders. If we drive this compressor mechanically with gears, a chain or a belt, it's called a *supercharger*. If we drive it with a turbine blade placed in the rush of spent gases out the exhaust pipe, it's called a *turbocharger*. The turbo is really a small, high-speed rotary vane compressor, usually running at 80,000 to 100,000 rpm.

When you compress air, the molecules heat up and expand, exactly the opposite of what we're trying to do. An *intercooler* is simply a heat exchanger—a radiator—placed between the turbo and the cylinder to recool the fuel/air mix.

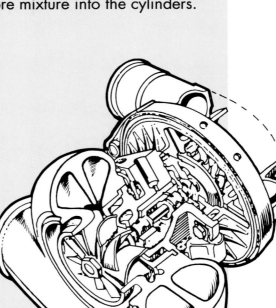

The first turbos at Indy compressed the mixture at about 17 psi for Offys and 25 psi for Ford four-cams. Tuners very quickly discovered that the turbo had to be carefully matched to the engine for the best performance, and that there had to be a waste-gate or "pop-off valve" that would release the pressure if it got too high for safety. Engineers call this pressure "manifold absolute pressure." MAP is properly measured, not in psi, but in Inches of Mercury. At sea level, barometric pressure will maintain a column of mercury at 29.92 inches, equivalent to 14.7 psi of atmospheric pressure.

USAC officials finally figured out that they could control the incredible horsepower of turbo engines by simply setting the pop-off valve at whatever limit they wanted. In the late-Seventies, they tried 80 in/Hg, which is 39 psi. Later on, they went to 48 in/Hg. Now it's 45 in/Hg, or 22 psi. What's amazing is how much horsepower the turbos gave in the Seventies—USAC stepped in when good tuners were getting 1000 hp out of 161 cubic inches (2.6-liters), or better than 6 hp per cubic inch! With the 45 in/Hg pop-offs in place, they're back up to around 760 hp, or 4.7 hp per cubic inch. That's nearly double what these engines would make without a turbo. It's easy to see why racers like turbochargers so much. ■

(left) A turbocharger is a simple rotary vane pump placed in the exhaust stream. The hot gases from the exhaust manifold spin the pump by pushing against the exhaust turbine. The principle is the same as a tiny water wheel. An identical turbine wheel is thus spun, and it pumps air under pressure back into the intake manifold. A typical turbo spins at about 100,000 rpm and pumps air into the cylinders at between 8 and 15 psi, maximum. This is enough to double the amount of air/fuel mixture being burned, and thus double the amount of power being released.

1975

Winner: Bobby Unser, Eagle/Offy, 149.213 mph
Winner's Purse: $214,031
Total Purse: $1,001,321
Pace Car: James Garner, Buick Century Custom

Starting on the seventh row, Wally Dallenbach zoomed to the front and was leading on lap 161 when he blew a piston. Bobby Unser, Johnny Rutherford and A.J. Foyt then battled for the lead until a freak rain storm caused the race to be red-flagged after 174 laps with Unser out front in Dan Gurney's Eagle.

Number	Driver	Sponsor/Team	Engine Type/Displacement	Chassis	Qualifying	Start/ Finish	Laps
48	Bobby Unser	Jorgensen/All American Racers	Offy I-4/159 cu.in.	Eagle	191.073	3/1	174
2	Johnny Rutherford	Gatorade/McLaren Cars	Offy V-8/159 cu.in.	McLaren	185.998	7/2	174
14	A.J. Foyt	Gilmore Racing	Foyt V-8/161 cu.in.	Coyote	193.976	1/3	174
11	Pancho Carter	Cobre Tire/Fletcher Racing	Offy I-4/159 cu.in.	Eagle	183.449	18/4	169
15	Roger McCluskey	Silver Floss/Hopkins Racing	Offy I-4/159 cu.in.	Riley	183.964	22/5	167
6	Billy Vukovich	Cobre Tire/Fletcher Racing	Offy I-4/159 cu.in.	Eagle	185.845	8/6	166
83	Bill Puterbaugh	McNamara-D.I.A./McNamara	Offy I-4/159 cu.in.	Eagle	183.833	15/7	165
97	George Snider	Leader Card Lodestar	Offy I-4/159 cu.in.	Eagle	182.918	24/8	165
40	Wally Dallenbach	Sinmast Wildcat/Patrick	SGD I-4/159 cu.in.	Wildcat	190.648	21/9	162
33	Bob Harkey	Dayton-Walther/Walmotor	Offy I-4/159 cu.in.	McLaren	183.786	23/10	162
98	Steve Krisiloff	Leader Card Lodestar	Offy I-4/159 cu.in.	Eagle	182.408	29/11	162
19	Sheldon Kinser	Spirit of Indiana/King Racing	Offy I-4/159 cu.in.	Kingfish	182.389	26/12	161
30	Jerry Karl	Jose Johnson/Smokey Yunick	Chevy V-8/207 cu.in.	Eagle	182.537	20/13	161
78	Jimmy Caruthers	Alex Foods	Offy I-4/159 cu.in.	Eagle	185.615	10/14	161
45	Gary Bettenhausen	Thermo King/Fred Gerhardt	Offy I-4/159 cu.in.	Eagle	182.611	19/15	158
4	Al Unser	Viceroy/Vel's-Parnelli Jones	Offy I-4/159 cu.in.	Eagle	185.452	11/16	157
36	Sammy Sessions	Commander/Unlimited Racing	Offy I-4/159 cu.in.	Eagle	182.750	25/17	155
17	Tom Bigelow	Bryant Heating/Vollstedt	Offy I-4/159 cu.in.	Vollstedt	181.864	33/18	151
93	Johnny Parsons	Ayr-Way WNAP Buzzard/Vatis	Offy I-4/159 cu.in.	Eagle	184.521	12/19	140
73	Jerry Grant	Spirit of Orange/Fred Carrillo	Offy i-4/159 cu.in.	Eagle	184.266	14/20	137
44	Dick Simon	Bruce Cogle Ford/Dick Simon	Foyt V-8/161 cu.in.	Eagle	181.892	30/21	133
68	Tom Sneva	Norton Spirit/Penske Racing	Offy I-4/159 cu.in.	McLaren	190.094	4/22	125
24	Bentley Warren	THE BOTTOMHALF/King Racing	Offy I-4/159 cu.in.	Kingfish	183.589	17/23	120
58	Eldon Rasmussen	Anacomp-Wild Rose/Rasmussen	Foyt V-8/161 cu.in.	Rascar	181.910	32/24	119
16	Bobby Allison	CAM2 Motor Oil/Penske Racing	Offy I-4/159 cu.in.	McLaren	184.398	13/25	112
12	Mike Mosley	Sugaripe Prune/Jerry O'Connell	Offy I-4/159 cu.in.	Eagle	187.822	5/26	94
89	John Martin	Automotive Technology	Offy I-4/159 cu.in.	McLaren	183.655	16/27	61
21	Mario Andretti	Viceroy/Vel's-Parnelli Jones	Offy I-4/159 cu.in.	Eagle	186.480	27/28	49
94	Mike Hiss	Ayr-Way WNAP Buzzard/Vatis	Offy I-4/159 cu.in.	Finley	181.754	31/29	39
63	Larry McCoy	Shurfine/Bidwell & McCoy	Offy I-4/159 cu.in.	Rascar	182.760	28/30	24
20	Gordon Johncock	Sinmast Wildcat/Patrick Racing	SGD I-4/159 cu.in.	Wildcat	191.652	2/31	11
7	Lloyd Ruby	Allied Polymer/McLaren Cars	Offy I-4/159 cu.in.	McLaren	186.984	6/32	7
77	Salt Walther	Dayton-Walther/Walmotor	Offy I-4/159 cu.in.	McLaren	185.701	9/33	2

than about 80 miles. This, in turn, meant that Goodyear could develop super-sticky tires with great adhesion but a relatively short life.

Every tire design is a compromise. A short sidewall gives a harsher ride. A wider tread nibbles and aquaplanes. A soft tread compound gives better traction, but wears out more quickly. Starting in 1975, Goodyear was able to use soft compounds that raised cornering grip from around 1.3G to 1.6G, all other factors—such as wings—being equal. For a while, there were even super-soft "gum-balls" that would last only six laps before wearing out: one lap to get up to speed, four laps to qualify, one lap to cool off and come into the pits. At that level, supplying tires as Goodyear has done for decades becomes *very* expensive.

INCREASING SPEEDS

The history of racing is a series of battles between the organizers and the engineers. The organizers want to have all the cars roughly equal, so that the drivers can show their skill and the race is between men, not money. The engineers, of course, just want *their* car to go fast; they're not worried about anybody else. So the organizers have to walk a fine line between maintaining competition and not stifling innovation. At no time in Indianapolis history was this balance more delicate than in the Aero Era, mostly because simply bolting on a new wing design could make one car suddenly 10 mph faster than all the rest.

In 1969, when we entered this period, the Speedway field of thirty-three starters all qualified between 160 mph and 170 mph. A few of them were using rudimentary ducktail spoilers and tabs, but no wings. They were no faster in 1970, and the cars were still mostly "hollow tubes" with front-mounted radiators and minimal aerodynamic add-ons.

The first big change was the 1971 McLaren M16, the first winged-wedge. Peter Revson's pole-sitting McLaren was almost 10 mph faster than Al Unser's pole-sitter of 1970. Indeed, Dick Simon's four-year-old Vollstedt that was the last-place qualifier in 1971 would have been on the pole in 1970. This was thanks to unregulated turbochargers and small wings. The best cars were now lapping at 180 mph, with straightaway speeds over 220 mph thanks to a combination of better aerodynamics, better handling and unbelievable amounts of power.

(below) Start of the pace lap, 1973. Johnny Rutherford is on the pole in his orange McLaren/ Offy #7, Bobby Unser in the middle in his Eagle/Offy #8, Mark Donohue on the outside in the blue and yellow Eagle/Offy #66. Rutherford's 199.071 mph lap will stand as a record until 1977, thanks to new rules which will slow the cars in the mid-Seventies. Not long after this photo was taken, Swede Savage in the fluorescent orange STP Eagle/ Offy #40—starting fourth—hit the Turn Four wall. Then it rained, and Gordon Johncock won.

1976

Winner: Johnny Rutherford, McLaren/Offy, 149.213 mph
Winner's Purse: $255,321
Total Purse: $1,037,776
Pace Car: Marty Robbins, Buick Century V-6 Turbo

For the third time in four years, the race was shortened because of rain, at 255 miles becoming the shortest "500" in history. Johnny Rutherford continued his incredible McLaren hot streak: ninth in 1973, first in 1974, second in 1975, first in 1976. Al Unser brought the first Cosworth V-8 home in seventh.

Number	Driver	Sponsor/Team	Engine Type/Displacement	Chassis	Qualifying	Start/Finish	Laps
2	Johnny Rutherford	Hy-Gain/McLaren	Offy I-4/159 cu.in.	McLaren	188.957	1/1	102
14	A.J. Foyt	Gilmore Racing/A.J. Foyt	Foyt V-8/161 cu.in.	Coyote	185.261	5/2	102
20	Gordon Johncock	Sinmast/Patrick Racing	D.G.S. I-4/159 cu.in.	Wildcat	188.531	2/3	102
40	Wally Dallenbach	Sinmast/Patrick Racing	D.G.S. I-4/159 cu.in.	Wildcat	184.455	7/4	101
48	Pancho Carter	E.M. Jorgensen	Offy I-4/159 cu.in.	Eagle	184.824	6/5	101
68	Tom Sneva	Norton Spirit/Penske Racing	Offy I-4/159 cu.in.	McLaren	186.355	3/6	101
21	Al Unser	American Racing/Parnelli Jones	Cosworth V-8/161 cu.in.	Parnelli	186.258	4/7	101
6	Mario Andretti	Cam2 Oil/Penske Racing	Offy I-4/159 cu.in.	McLaren	189.404	19/8	101
77	Salt Walther	Dayton-Walther/Walmotor	Offy I-4/159 cu.in.	McLaren	182.797	22/9	100
3	Bobby Unser	Cobre Tire/Robert Fletcher	Offy I-4/159 cu.in.	Eagle	187.520	12/10	100
51	Lloyd Ruby	Fairco Drugs/Michael Devin	Offy I-4/159 cu.in.	Eagle	186.480	30/11	100
93	Johnny Parsons	Ayr-Way/WIRE/Vatis	Offy I-4/159 cu.in.	Eagle	182.843	14/12	98
23	George Snider	Hubler Chevy/Leader Cards	Offy I-4/159 cu.in.	Eagle	181.141	27/13	98
24	Tom Bigelow	Leader Card Racers	Offy I-4/159 cu.in.	Eagle	181.965	32/14	98
12	Mike Mosley	Sugaripe Prune/O'Connell	Offy I-4/159 cu.in.	Eagle	187.888	11/15	98
8	Jan Opperman	Routh Meat Packing/Routh	Offy I-4/159 cu.in.	Eagle	181.717	33/16	97
69	Larry Cannon	American Financial/Hoffman	Offy I-4/159 cu.in.	Eagle	181.388	10/17	97
9	Vern Schuppan	E.M. Jorgensen	Offy I-4/159 cu.in.	Eagle	182.011	17/18	97
97	Sheldon Kinser	THE BOTTOMHALF/King Racing	Offy I-4/159 cu.in.	Dragon	181.114	29/19	97
96	Bob Harkey	McIntire Ford/Agajanian/King	Offy I-4/159 cu.in.	Kingfish	181.141	28/20	97
98	John Martin	Genesse/Agajanian/King	Offy I-4/159 cu.in.	Dragon	182.417	15/21	96
83	Bill Puterbaugh	McNamara Motor Express	Offy I-4/159 cu.in.	Eagle	182.002	18/22	96
28	Billy Scott	Spirit of Public Ent./Hodgdon	Offy I-4/159 cu.in.	Eagle	183.383	21/23	96
92	Steve Krisiloff	First National City/Vatis	Offy I-4/159 cu.in.	Eagle	182.131	23/24	95
86	Al Loquasto	Frostie Root Beer/Loquasto, Sr.	Offy I-4/159 cu.in.	McLaren	182.002	24/25	95
63	Larry McCoy	Shurfine/Spirit of America	Offy I-4/159 cu.in.	Ras-Car	181.388	26/26	91
73	Jerry Grant	California-Oklahoma/Carrillo	AMC V-8/208 cu.in.	Eagle	183.617	20/27	91
45	Gary Bettenhausen	Thermo-King/Gerhardt Racers	Offy I-4/159 cu.in.	Eagle	181.791	8/28	52
33	David Hobbs	Dayton-Walther/Walmotor	Offy I-4/159 cu.in.	McLaren	183.580	31/29	10
7	Roger McCluskey	Lindsey Hopkins	Offy I-4/159 cu.in.	Lightning	186.500	13/30	8
5	Billy Vukovich	Alex Foods	Offy I-4/159 cu.in.	Eagle	181.433	9/31	2
17	Dick Simon	Bryant Heating/Vollstedt	Offy I-4/159 cu.in.	Vollstedt	182.343	16/32	1
19	Spike Gehlhausen	Spirit of Indiana/C. Gehlhausen	Offy I-4/159 cu.in.	McLaren	181.717	25/33	0

But this was just the beginning. The difference from 1971 to 1972 was an incredible 17 mph. Bobby Unser sat on the pole with his Eagle/Offy at an average of 195.940 mph, and Wally Dallenbach's last-place Lola/Foyt was 3 mph faster than Revson's pole-sitting McLaren the year before. This was the year that designers discovered that if you put the rear wing as far back as the rules would allow, it made a tremendous difference in downforce because of simple leverage.

By 1973, Johnny Rutherford's McLaren was averaging 199 mph thanks to even bigger wings and yet more horsepower. Indeed, he was only 0.30 mph away from breaking the legendary 200 mph mark with his McLaren/Offy. Incredible. Between 1970 and 1973, lap speeds at Indy increased 30 mph. It was the most dramatic increase ever. For most of its history, speeds at Indianapolis had increased about 1 mph per year. That was a nice steady, controllable progression. And then here was McLaren condensing three decades of progress into as many years. It was too much, too soon.

PUTTING ON THE BRAKES

For 1974, USAC did another major rewrite of the rules. This is when the 80 in/ Hg popoff valve was mandated on a turbo, the rear wing width reduced and fuel capacity reduced to 40 gallons. More importantly, all fuel had to be carried on the left side of the car, away from the outside walls of the Speedway. This particular rule was in response to Swede Savage's fatal accident, the first serious fire at Indianapolis since the Sachs/MacDonald explosion a decade before.

All these changes combined to knock nearly 10 mph off of Speedway lap speeds; A.J. Foyt qualified on the pole at 191.632 mph in 1974 in his Coyote/

(left) History in the making, 1977. A.J. Foyt stops on the way to his fourth 500 victory. It will make him the first four-time winner of the Memorial Day Classic. Even from here, you can see the shape of the mid-Seventies car...shovel nose, footwell lower than the wheel centers, high cockpit, "running boards" with side radiators, rear wing mounted on struts as far back as the rules allow.

Foyt. As you can see, these new rules also made the Foyt V-8 more competitive with the Offy, though it took A.J. three more years to find Victory Lane again. From 1974 through 1978, speeds at Indianapolis climbed gradually as the winged-wedges were progressively refined. Finally, in 1977, Tom Sneva took one of Roger Penske's McLaren/Cosworths around at 200.535 mph to finally break the infamous 200 mph barrier.

The next year Sneva came back to run 203.620 mph with his Penske/Cosworth. That was only 4 mph quicker than Johnny Rutherford had gone in 1973. The difference?

131

COSWORTH-FORD

In November, 1963, the CSI announced that Formula One would change to 3.0-liters (183 cubic inches) for the 1966 season. In 1965, Ford Motor Company belatedly decided to finance a new engine for this formula. They contracted with Mike Costin and Keith Duckworth of Cosworth Engineering in England to design and build it. Colin Chapman of Lotus was given exclusive use of this Cosworth-Ford engine for the first season, so Lotus designer Maurice Phillipe literally designed his new 49 around the Cosworth engine, using it as a stressed member to which he attached the Hewland transaxle and rear suspension. The monocoque ended behind the driver.

Costin and Duckworth took two of their 1.5-liter (91 cubic inch), double-overhead cam, four-valve-per-cylinder conversions for the four-cylinder Ford Cortina passenger car engine and put them together to form a 90 degree V-8. They called the four-cylinder the FVA, and it had already become the backbone of Formula Two as well as small-bore sports/racers and numerous Lotus street models. The new V-8 was called the DFV and, fitted with Lucas fuel-injection, was said to produce 405 hp at 8600 rpm.

The DFV Cosworth took Formula One by storm. Jim Clark won at Zandvoort on June 4, 1967, the very first race for both the Cosworth V-8 and the Lotus 49. The combination was literally an overnight success. Clark led almost every Grand Prix that year, and won four. In 1968, Colin Chapman's exclusive contract with Cosworth was up, which meant that half the Grand Prix teams instantly switched to the Cosworth-Ford.

The DFV won eleven of twelve Formula One races in 1968. Eventually, twelve drivers won World Championships with this remarkable engine between 1968 and 1982. By the end, it was producing 520 hp at 9000 rpm in short-stroke DFY configuration. When the 1.5-liter turbocharged engines finally displaced it in 1983, the Cosworth had won an unprecedented 155 Grand Prix races in sixteen years, making it far and away the most successful racing engine in history. Its last win, fittingly enough, was when Michele Alboreto outlasted the fragile turbos at the Detroit Grand Prix, not 50 yards from the Renaissance Center offices of the Ford Motor Company which had bankrolled this engine two decades earlier.

(right) The fifth Indianapolis engine from Ford in a decade—pushrod Ford, Ford four-cam, turbo four-cam (since called the Foyt), Gurney-Weslake—and now this Cosworth-Ford. European in origin and concept, the Cosworth was very different from any engine that had ever run at Indy up to that time, though today it's the accepted way to build a high-performance racing powerplant. What's most amazing is that this compact, complicated but lightweight design was actually produced by putting two Cosworth FVA four-cylinder engines on a common crankcase to make a V-8. It sounds like something Harry Miller and Leo Goossen would do, with equally fortuitous results. The lesson is that good engineering is both timeless and versatile.

COSWORTH AT INDIANAPOLIS

By the mid-Seventies, the USAC formula and Formula One were surprisingly similar. In 1972, Maurice Phillippe had left Lotus to work for Parnelli Jones, and in 1974 he designed the Parnelli VPJ4 Formula One car for Mario Andretti. This unsuccessful effort lasted only through 1975.

But when Parnelli abandoned Grands Prix, he and his partner Vel Melitich realized that with only minor changes their car could be perfect for Indianapolis. So they built a short-stroke, 162 cubic inch (2.65-liter) version of the DFV, lowered the compression ratio to 8.5:1 and engineered a turbo installation. This simple conversion more than doubled the horsepower of the Formula One Cosworth, producing 885 hp at 9200 rpm. Parnelli knew he had a winner. Cosworth soon went into production with a modified version of the DFV which they called the DFX, specifically designed for Indianapolis.

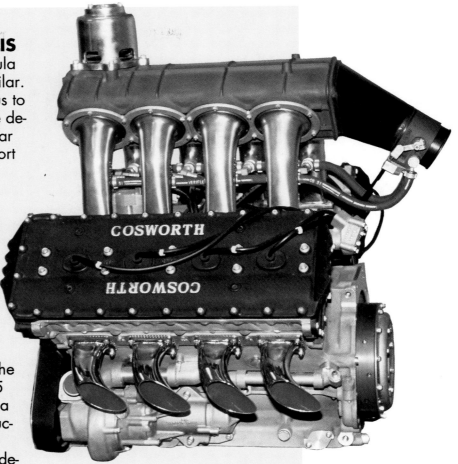

Al Unser drove the first Parnelli/Cosworth at Indianapolis in 1976, and qualified on the second row. He finished seventh in the rain-shortened event. In 1977, Tom Sneva and Unser finished second and third in the 500 with Cosworth DFX power. By 1978, there were ten Cosworths in the starting field...Unser and Sneva finished one-two. After that, the Cosworth DFX ruled Indianapolis as completely as it ruled Formula One, eventually winning ten Indianapolis 500s.

What makes the Cosworth so good? Well, thanks to excellent cylinder head and valve design, the Cosworth has a comparatively flat torque curve for a racing engine, which means it's quick out of the Indy corners. It's very economical with fuel, thanks to the precise fuel-injection system. It's durable, thanks to wet cylinder liners and a strong crankcase design, and strong enough to use as the main structural support for the rear suspension in the Lotus 49 and subsequent Formula One cars. And, compared to the tall Offy or wide Ford four-cam/Foyt, the Cosworth-Ford is surprisingly small. That means you can wrap the bodywork tightly around it, for less frontal area.

The Cosworth has also had a tremendous influence on other engine designers all over the world. The all-conquering Chevrolet Indy V-8—developed by two former Cosworth engineers—is virtually identical in concept, as are all the other narrow-angle, DOHC V-8s currently wrangling over the 500. Without a doubt, there will still be engines racing at Indianapolis in 2001 directly based on the complicated, expensive, but oh-so-effective Cosworth-Ford. ■

(above) You can see many of the elements which made the Cosworth-Ford distinct...narrow-angle valves beneath double-overhead cams, Lucas sequential port fuel injection, a ribbed crankcase strong enough to be used as a supporting member for the transaxle, extremely compact size, and reversible cam covers that are "right reading" on either side. Externally, the Grand Prix DFV and later DFY are identical to the USAC DFX except for the turbo and attendant hardware.

1977

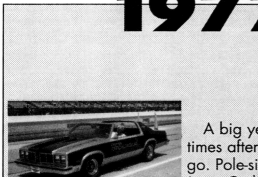

Winner: A.J. Foyt, Coyote/Foyt, 161.331 mph
Winner's Purse: $259,791
Total Purse: $1,116,807
Pace Car: James Garner, Oldsmobile Delta 88 Royale

A big year for records. A.J. Foyt became the first driver to win the 500 four times after leader Gordon Johncock broke a crankshaft with just sixteen laps to go. Pole-sitter Tom Sneva turned the first 200 mph lap in Speedway history; Janet Guthrie became the first woman to qualify and race in the 500.

Number	Driver	Sponsor/Team	Engine Type/Displacement	Chassis	Qualifying	Start/Finish	Laps
14	A.J. Foyt	Gilmore Racing/A.J. Foyt	Foyt V-8/161 cu.in.	Coyote	194.563	4/1	200
8	Tom Sneva	Norton Spirit/Penske Racing	Cosworth V-8/158 cu.in.	McLaren	198.884	1/2	200
21	Al Unser	American/Vel's-Parnelli	Cosworth V-8/159 cu.in.	Parnelli	195.950	3/3	199
40	Wally Dallenbach	STP/Patrick Racing	DGS I-4/159 cu.in.	Wildcat	189.563	10/4	199
60	Johnny Parsons	STP/Patrick Racing	DGS I-4/159 cu.in.	Wildcat	189.255	11/5	193
24	Tom Bigelow	Thermo King/Leader Card	Offenhauser I-4/159 cu.in.	Watson	186.471	22/6	192
65	Lee Kunzman	City of Syracuse/Santello	Offenhauser I-4/159 cu.in.	Eagle	186.384	24/7	191
11	Roger McCluskey	First National City/Hopkins	Offenhauser I-4/159 cu.in.	Lightning	190.992	18/8	191
92	Steve Krisiloff	Dave McIntire Chevy/Vatis	Offenhauser I-4/159 cu.in.	Eagle	184.691	25/9	191
36	Jerry Sneva	21st Amendment/Bidwell	Offenhauser I-4/159 cu.in.	McLaren	186.616	16/10	187
20	Gordon Johncock	STP/Patrick Racing	DGS I-4/159 cu.in.	Wildcat	193.517	5/11	184
16	Bill Puterbaugh	Dayton-Walther/Lee Elkins	Offenhauser I-4/159 cu.in.	Eagle	186.800	28/12	170
58	Eldon Rasmussen	Rent-a-Racer/Rasmussen	Foyt V-8/161 cu.in.	Ras-Car	185.119	32/13	168
42	John Mahler	20th Century/Mergard	Offenhauser I-4/159 cu.in.	Eagle	185.242	31/14	157
48	Pancho Carter	Jorgensen/Dan Gurney	Offenhauser I-4/159 cu.in.	Eagle	192.452	8/15	156
98	Gary Bettenhausen	Knievel/Agajanian/King	Offenhauser I-4/159 cu.in.	Kingfish	186.596	21/16	138
84	Billy Vukovich	Gilmore Racing/A.J. Foyt	Foyt V-8/161 cu.in.	Coyote	186.393	23/17	110
6	Bobby Unser	Cobre Tire/Fletcher Racing	Offenhauser I-4/159 cu.in.	Lightning	197.618	2/18	94
5	Mike Mosley	Sugaripe Prune/O'Connell	Offenhauser I-4/159 cu.in.	Lightning	190.069	9/19	91
25	Danny Ongais	Interscope/Ted Fields	Cosworth V-8/158 cu.in.	Parnelli	193.040	7/20	90
72	Bubby Jones	Bruce Cogle Ford/Hillin's	Offenhauser I-4/159 cu.in.	Eagle	184.938	33/21	78
29	Cliff Hucul	Team Canada/Hunter-Arndt	Offenhauser I-4/159 cu.in.	McLaren	187.198	27/22	72
73	Jim McElreath	Carrillo Rods/Fred Carrillo	AMC V-8/208 cu.in.	Eagle	187.715	20/23	71
18	George Snider	Dick Simon/Hillin's	DGS I-4/159 cu.in.	Wildcat	188.976	13/24	65
78	Bobby Olivero	Alex Foods/Alex Morales	Offenhauser I-4/159 cu.in.	Lightning	188.452	14/25	57
9	Mario Andretti	Cam2 Oil/Penske Racing	Offenhauser I-4/159 cu.in.	McLaren	193.351	6/26	47
10	Lloyd Ruby	First National City/Hopkins	Offenhauser I-4/159 cu.in.	Lightning	190.840	19/27	34
86	Al Loquasto	Frostie Root Beer/Loquasto	Offenhauser I-4/159 cu.in.	McLaren	187.647	15/28	28
27	Janet Guthrie	Bryant Heating/Vollstedt	Offenhauser I-4/159 cu.in.	Lightning	188.403	26/29	27
38	Clay Regazzoni	Theodore Racing/Simpson	Offenhauser I-4/159 cu.in.	McLaren	186.047	29/30	25
17	Dick Simon	Bryant Heating/Vollstedt	Offenhauser I-4/159 cu.in.	Vollstedt	185.615	30/31	24
97	Sheldon Kinser	Genesee/Agajanian/King	Offenhauser I-4/159 cu.in.	Kingfish	189.076	12/32	14
2	Johnny Rutherford	First National City/McLaren	Cosworth V-8/158 cu.in.	McLaren	197.325	17/33	12

Well, on the negative side, Sneva's car probably had only around 850 hp from his Cosworth fitted with an 80 in/Hg popoff valve, a narrow 36 inch rear wing and a car weight of around 1550 lbs. On the positive side compared to Rutherford's earlier car, Sneva's small rear wing created a lot less drag, so his straightaway speeds were almost 15 mph faster. He also had the new softer, stickier Goodyears, which compensated for less wing when it came to cornering traction. Sneva was clocked at 190 mph in the turns and 220 mph on the straight.

There was one other thing. When Tony Hulman had the track completely repaved in 1976, it was done with almost unbelievable care. Indianapolis would be no Monza, where there were bumps large enough to bounce you into the guard

rail. At Indianapolis, the entire oval was leveled to within 1/4 inch in 10 feet, then paved with very fine—and very sticky—asphalt. And then it was allowed to "cure" for ten months before qualifying in 1977. This fresh track surface was claimed to add 4 mph to lap speeds, all by itself.

THE AERO ERA

The Seventies weren't exciting and revolutionary like the Sixties, yet quietly, without a lot of fuss, USAC racing—and the Indianapolis Motor Speedway—entered modern times. In terms of speed, the early-Seventies saw the fastest rise in lap speeds ever, and if USAC hadn't restricted design, surely the cars would have gone much faster still. But the Seventies marked a new era in yet another way, too.

For the first time, aside from the obvious things like suspending the 500 during

Three heroes of the late-Seventies: (top left) In 1977, Rolla Vollstedt put Janet Guthrie into his Lightning/Offy. She became the first woman to qualify for the 500. It wasn't too many years since women weren't even allowed in the pits, let alone the race cars. Janet's car broke early, but in 1978 she came back with a Wildcat/DGS and Texaco sponsorship to finish ninth. (bottom left) Even in 1977, A.J. Foyt was already considered an old-timer when he won his unprecedented fourth 500. (below) Ever the gentleman, A.J. invited Tony Hulman to ride in the pace car with him during his Lap of Honor. This was Tony's last public appearance at the Speedway, since he died the following October, at seventy-six.

1978

Winner: Al Unser, Lola/ Cosworth, 161.363 mph
Winner's Purse: $290,363
Total Purse: $1,145,225
Pace Car: Jim Rathmann, Chevrolet Corvette

Tom Sneva was the first driver to qualify at over 200 mph, but he finished second for the second year in a row as Al Unser won his third 500. Unser's Lola/Cosworth was the first 500 entry from Jim Hall of Chaparral. Janet Guthrie finished ninth, the only time a woman driver has finished the race.

Number	Driver	Sponsor/Team	Engine Type/Displacement	Chassis	Qualifying	Start/ Finish	Laps
2	Al Unser	First National City/Chaparral	Cosworth V-8/161 cu.in.	Lola	196.474	5/1	200
1	Tom Sneva	Norton Spirit/Penske Racing	Cosworth V-8/161 cu.in.	Penske	202.156	1/2	200
20	Gordon Johncock	N. American Van Lines/Patrick	DGS I-4/159 cu.in.	Wildcat	195.833	6/3	199
40	Steve Krisiloff	Foreman Industries/Patrick	DGS I-4/159 cu.in.	Wildcat	191.255	13/4	198
6	Wally Dallenbach	Sugaripe Prune/O'Connell	Cosworth V-8/161 cu.in.	McLaren	195.228	7/5	195
48	Bobby Unser	ARCO Graphite/Dan Gurney	Cosworth V-8/161 cu.in.	Eagle	194.658	19/6	195
14	A.J. Foyt	Gilmore Racing/Citicorp/Foyt	Foyt V-8/161 cu.in.	Coyote	200.122	20/7	191
84	George Snider	Gilmore Racing/Citicorp/Foyt	Foyt V-8/161 cu.in.	Coyote	192.627	23/8	191
51	Janet Guthrie	Texaco Star/Janet Guthrie	DGS I-4/159 cu.in.	Wildcat	190.325	15/9	190
16	Johnny Parsons	First National City/Hopkins	Offy I-4/159 cu.in.	Lightning	194.280	8/10	186
35	Larry Rice	Bryant Heating/WIBC/Hedback	Offy I-4/159 cu.in.	Lightning	187.393	30/11	186
7	Mario Andretti	The Gould Charge/Penske	Cosworth V-8/161 cu.in.	Penske	194.647	33/12	185
4	Johnny Rutherford	First National City/McLaren	Cosworth V-8/161 cu.in.	McLaren	197.098	4/13	180
88	Jerry Karl	Machinists Union/Frank Fiore	Offy I-4/159 cu.in.	McLaren	187.549	28/14	176
69	Joe Saldana	Mr. WizeBuys Carpet/Hoffman	Offy I-4/159 cu.in.	Eagle	190.809	24/15	173
98	Gary Bettenhausen	Oberdorfer/Agajanian/King	Offy I-4/159 cu.in.	Kingfish	187.324	31/16	147
78	Mike Mosley	Alex XLNT Foods	Offy I-4/159 cu.in.	Lightning	188.719	25/17	146
25	Danny Ongais	Interscope Racing	Cosworth V-8/161 cu.in.	Parnelli	200.122	2/18	145
17	Dick Simon	La Machine/Vollstedt	Offy I-4/159 cu.in.	Vollstedt	192.967	10/19	138
26	Jim McElreath	Circle City Coal/Jim McElreath	Offy I-4/159 cu.in.	Eagle	188.058	26/20	132
43	Tom Bigelow	Armstrong Mould	DGS I-4/159 cu.in.	Wildcat	189.115	18/21	107
80	Larry Dickson	Polak/Stay-on Car Glaze	Cosworth V-8/159 cu.in.	McLaren	193.434	9/22	104
71	Rick Mears	CAM2 Motor Oil/Penske	Cosworth V-8/161 cu.in.	Penske	200.078	3/23	103
8	Pancho Carter	Budweiser/Fletcher Racing	Cosworth V-8/161 cu.in.	Lightning	196.829	21/24	92
11	Roger McCluskey	National Engineering/Hodgdon	AMC V-8/207 cu.in.	Eagle	192.256	11/25	82
39	John Mahler	Tibon/Carl Gelhausen	Offy I-4/159 cu.in.	Eagle	189.773	17/26	58
22	Tom Bagley	Kent Oil/Leader Cards	Offy I-4/159 cu.in.	Watson	190.941	14/27	25
77	Salt Walther	Dayton-Walther/Walmotor	Cosworth V-8/161 cu.in.	McLaren	193.226	22/28	24
19	Spike Gehlhausen	Hubler Chevy/WIRE/Gehlhausen	Offy I-4/159 cu.in.	Eagle	190.325	16/29	23
47	Phil Threshie	Circle Chevy/Tutweiler/Threshie	Offy I-4/159 cu.in.	Lightning	187.520	29/30	22
30	Jerry Sneva	Smock Materials/Freeman	Offy I-4/159 cu.in.	McLaren	187.266	32/31	18
24	Sheldon Kinser	Thermo-King/Leader Cards	Offy I-4/159 cu.in.	Watson	192.051	12/32	15
29	Cliff Hucul	Wendy's Hamburgers/Hucul	Offy I-4/159 cu.in.	McLaren	187.803	27/33	4

World Wars I and II, Indianapolis Speedway racing was socially responsible. During the Energy Crisis, they started restricting fuel at the Speedway, despite the fact that Indianapolis cars raced on methanol, not gasoline. And there was an abudance of methanol. Still, restricting fuel and restricting speeds in the Seventies was a symbol. A symbol that the Indianapolis Motor Speedway is an integral part of American society, and that if Indianapolis racers could drive more safely and more economically, so could the people in the stands. Motor racing had never really seen itself as a public opinion leader, and it was a new feeling. Most importantly, these new attitudes of the Seventies set the stage for the incredible racing boom of the next decade.

THE INTERNATIONAL ERA 1979-1991

In his book *Civilisation*, Lord Kenneth Clark writes, "Where some way of thought or human activity is really vital to us, internationalism is accepted unhesitatingly." His examples are the medieval church and modern science, but he might just as well have been talking about the Indianapolis 500. Where else can you find drivers, engineers, mechanics and sponsors from a dozen different countries on five continents? The Indianapolis 500 has become so important—not just to Americans, but all over the world—that talented people come here every May from just about everywhere.

Take the drivers, for example. Of the four dozen men currently capable of competing at this incredibly rarefied level, seventeen are originally from a foreign country and six more from California. Five of the six engines used in Indianapolis car racing during the Eighties were designed and built overseas; all three chassis-builders are in England. The Speedway has never been this international before, not even in the halcyon years preceding World War I.

This global trend began in the Sixties, with the first mid-engine cars from England. But it has become more and more pervasive as the decades zoom by. Partly, this is an economic discussion. Skilled labor to build cars or make patterns for engine castings was cheaper in England than in America. The European founda-

(below) One of the dominant combinations of the Eighties...a March/Cosworth owned by Roger Penske...here driven by Al Unser on his way to fourth in 1985. Compared to Indianapolis cars of the Seventies, the driver now sits far forward inside a tall cockpit. The "Concorde" nose is very pointed and flanked by wings, while the bodywork slopes smoothly down towards the back, allowing air to reach the tall wing unimpeded.

1979

Winner: Rick Mears, Penske/Cosworth, 158.899 mph
Winner's Purse: $270,401
Total Purse: $1,271,954
Pace Car: Jackie Stewart, Ford Mustang

Due to qualifying irregularities, two extra cars swelled the field to thirty-five starters. Al and Bobby Unser dominated the race, but Rick Mears held on to win in only his second start. A.J. Foyt continued a great streak—third in 1975, second in '76, first in '77, seventh in '78, second in 1979.

Number	Driver	Sponsor/Team	Engine Type/Displacement	Chassis	Qualifying	Start/Finish	Laps
9	Rick Mears	The Gould Charge/Penske	Cosworth V-8/161 cu.in.	Penske	193.736	1/1	200
14	A.J. Foyt	Gilmore Racing/Foyt/Vel's-P.J.	Cosworth V-8/161 cu.in.	Parnelli	189.613	6/2	200
36	Mike Mosley	Theodore Racing/Gurney	Cosworth V-8/161 cu.in.	Eagle	186.278	12/3	200
25	Danny Ongais	Interscope/Panasonic	Cosworth V-8/161 cu.in.	Penske	188.009	27/4	199
12	Bobby Unser	The Norton Spirit/Penske	Cosworth V-8/161 cu.in.	Penske	189.913	4/5	199
3	Gordon Johncock	N. American Van Lines/Patrick	Cosworth V-8/161 cu.in.	Penske	189.753	5/6	197
46	Howdy Holmes	Armstrong Mould/Jiffy	Cosworth V-8/159 cu.in.	Wildcat	185.864	13/7	195
22	Billy Vukovich	Hubler/WNDE/Thermo-King	Offy I-4/160 cu.in.	Watson	187.042	34/8	194
11	Tom Bagley	Dairy Queen/Kent Oil/Hillin	Cosworth V-8/160 cu.in.	Penske	185.514	15/9	193
19	Spike Gehlhausen	Sta-On Glaze/WIRE/Patrick	Cosworth V-8/160 cu.in.	Wildcat	185.061	31/10	192
7	Steve Krisiloff	Frosty Acres/Winton/Fletcher	Offy I-4/159 cu.in.	Lightning	186.287	28/11	192
77	Salt Walther	Dayton-Walther/Walmotor	Cosworth V-8/161 cu.in.	Penske	184.162	16/12	191
72	Roger McCluskey	National Engineering	Cosworth V-8/161 cu.in.	McLaren	183.908	25/13	191
44	Tom Bigelow	Armstrong Mould	Cosworth V-8/161 cu.in.	Lola	185.147	30/14	190
1	Tom Sneva	Sugaripe Prune/Jerry O'Connell	Cosworth V-8/161 cu.in.	McLaren	192.998	2/15	188
69	Joe Saldana	KBHL/Nebraska/Hoffman	Offy I-4/159 cu.in.	Eagle	188.778	26/16	186
97	Phil Threshie	Guiffre/Agajanian/King	Chevy V-8/347 cu.in.	King	185.854	29/17	172
4	Johnny Rutherford	Budweiser/Team McLaren	Cosworth V-8/161 cu.in.	McLaren	188.137	8/18	168
31	Larry Rice	S&M Electric	Offy I-4/159 cu.in.	Lightning	184.219	23/19	142
10	Pancho Carter	Alex XLNT Foods	Offy I-4/159 cu.in.	Lightning	185.806	17/20	129
34	Vern Schuppan	Wysard Motor	DGS I-4/159 cu.in.	Wildcat	184.341	22/21	111
2	Al Unser	Pennzoil/Chaparral Racing	Cosworth V-8/161 cu.in.	Chaparral	192.503	3/22	104
50	Eldon Rasmussen	Vans by Bivouac/WFMS/BFM	Offy I-4/159 cu.in.	Antares	183.927	33/23	89
80	Larry Dickson	Russell Polak	Cosworth V-8/161 cu.in.	Penske	184.181	24/24	86
92	John Mahler	Intercomp/Sports Magazine	Offy I-4/161 cu.in.	Eagle	184.322	32/25	66
17	Dick Simon	Sanyo/Vollstedt	Offy I-4/159 cu.in.	Vollstedt	185.071	20/26	57
6	Wally Dallenbach	Foreman Industries/Patrick	Cosworth V-8/161 cu.in.	Penske	188.285	7/27	43
24	Sheldon Kinser	Genesee Beer/Leader Cards	Offy I-4/159 cu.in.	Watson	186.674	10/28	40
29	Cliff Hucul	Hucul/Hunter & Arndt	Offy I-4/159 cu.in.	McLaren	186.200	18/29	22
89	Lee Kunzman	Vetter Windjammer/Conqueste	Cosworth V-8/161 cu.in.	Parnelli	186.403	11/30	18
73	Jerry Sneva	National Engineering AMC	AMC V-8/208 cu.in.	Spirit	184.379	21/31	16
15	Johnny Parsons	Lindsey Hopkins	Offy I-4/159 cu.in.	Lightning	187.813	9/32	16
59	George Snider	KBHL/Nebraska/Hoffman	Offy I-4/159 cu.in.	Lightning	185.319	35/33	7
45	Janet Guthrie	Texaco Star/Armstrong	Cosworth V-8/161 cu.in.	Lola	185.720	14/34	3
23	Jim McElreath	Amax Coal/Shirley McElreath	Cosworth V-8/161 cu.in.	Penske	185.883	18/35	0

(opposite page) 1981 winner Bobby Unser in Penske/Cosworth #3 leads second place Mario Andretti's Wildcat/Cosworth #40 and A.J. Foyt's Coyote/Cosworth #14.

tion of worldwide racing also has to do with the staggering amount of money that was tossed into Formula One in the Seventies and Eighties.

Back in the Sixties, Grand Prix teams were only too happy to visit Indianapolis, where the prize money for four hours work was more than they could win all season in Europe. But during the past decade, thanks to incredibly generous sponsors, Formula One teams with annual budgets of $50 million or even $100 million a year are common. Driver salaries in Formula One ballooned throughout the Eighties; $1 million a race is now the going rate for a World Champion.

TUNNELS AND SKIRTS

(below) A.J. Foyt in his 1981 Coyote/Cosworth. You can clearly see the air intakes for the ground effects underwings which flank the narrow cockpit. The external wings, front and rear, were now used for minor aerodynamic "tuning" rather than providing the major amount of downforce. This was the last of Foyt's Coyotes; in 1982 he switched to a March/Cosworth pretty much like the ones everybody else was driving.

In the Seventies, when they saw racing cars festooned with wings and airfoils, any number of clever pundits made cute remarks about "flying on the ground." There was some truth to their conceit. Because it is basically flat on the bottom and rounded over the top, almost any automobile has vaguely the same profile as an airplane's wing. And that means that the air traveling over the top of it must move faster than the air traveling under it, which creates a low-pressure area at the top, or *lift*. Lift is good for an airplane but bad for an automobile, because it will cause both to take off and fly. And, of course, the faster you go, the more lift you create.

So the whole thrust of racing car design since the Sixties has been trying to counteract the natural tendency of a car shaped like an airfoil to want to fly at high speeds. In the early days, this effort consisted mostly of adding spoilers, bits of wing that stick up from the body to interrupt the air flow only on their top surface. Spoilers are excellent for modifying the aerodynamic performance of a car body, but not for creating large aerodynamic forces.

Experimentation with wings mounted away from the body showed that an airfoil which can direct the air flow both above and below it is much more effective than a simple spoiler. There was also internal ducting. If you draw air in the nose to cool the radiator, for example, and let it out the top of the hood—and connect the two openings with spoiler-shaped ducting—you could use that to counteract lift, too. Similar ducting could go in the rear bodywork.

The next logical step was to start thinking about the shape of the whole car as an aerodynamic device. Once they got into it, these early racing car aerodynamicists discovered that a car, even though it's shaped like an airfoil, doesn't *act* like a pure airfoil. There is something called the *ground effect*, caused by squeezing the air between the bottom of the car and the surface of the asphalt.

Immediately, it was apparent that if you could create a *venturi* under the car—a place where the air is squeezed and therefore accelerates—you could create a low-pressure area *beneath* the car. If this low-pressure area was stronger than the low-pressure area above the car, then the car would be sucked down onto the track with incredible force. And the faster you went, the more *downforce* you'd create.

One of the leaders in all this was Texan Jim Hall, who we now know was aided by Chevrolet. Chevrolet's engineers had worked out most of the wing, airfoil and internal ducting problems by 1966, on the Chaparral 2E Can-Am car. These were refined on the 1967 2G. Then in 1970, Hall presented the famous 2J, which had a 45 hp snowmobile engine mounted in the rear, driving a pair of huge fans which sucked air from beneath the boxy Chaparral. Lexan plastic skirts dragged on the track, sealing the ground effects area. The Chaparral "vacuum cleaner" was so effective that this type of self-powered ground effects system was banned by the FIA.

The next innovative step came in 1978, when Mario Andretti won the Formula One World Championship driving a Lotus 78 "ground effects" car. Developed by Colin Chapman and Ralph Bellamy, the new Lotus had a very narrow cockpit sandwiched between wide body sides. The bottom of the body on either side was shaped like an inverted airfoil, while moveable Lexan skirts sealed the gap between the edge of the body and the track. The next year, Chapman moved the fuel cells from the body sides into the monocoque between the engine and the driver, so that the ground effects wings could be even larger. The Lotus 79 was soon copied by every other Formula One designer.

Full ground effects came to Indianapolis in 1979 on the Chaparral 2K and Penske PC-7, essentially copies of the Lotus 79. Compared to earlier Indy cars, the driver now sat up between the front wheels, tucked into a narrow monocoque. Behind him was the 40 gallon fuel cell, behind that the engine and transaxle. The entire space between the wheels was occupied by the inverted airfoils which acted as a venturi to create a low-pressure area between the bottom of the car and the asphalt and "glue" the chassis to the track. In the most effective ground effects cars, these airfoil tunnels extended past the rear wheels to form "expansion cones" which accelerate the air even more. The expansion cones then force the air to exit beneath the rear-mounted wing.

(below) Johnny Rutherford won the 1980 500 with this Chaparral/ Cosworth, the same car Al Unser had qualified on the front row in 1979 before having a transmission seal let go half-way through the race. This Chaparral 2K was the first full ground effects car in the Indianapolis 500. With its pointed nose, narrow cockpit and wide underwings, it set the style for every car that has run there since.

For the 1981 season, both Formula One and Indy car organizers banned moveable skirts and specified that the lowest point on the car had to be 60cm (2.4 inches) above the ground. After two years of fiddling around, in 1983 the CSI finally outlawed ground effects on Formula One cars in favor of "flat bottom" chassis. Since then, most Formula One designers have fitted expansion cones at the back of the chassis to achieve some limited venturi effect.

In 1991, Indy cars still use ground effects chassis not all that different from the 1979 Chaparral 2K, Jim Hall's brilliant design that brought ground effects to America. In addition to outlawing moveable skirts, CART and USAC over the years have limited the size of wings and underwings in order to control downforce. But a good Indy car still has about 3.0-4.0G of downforce.

In other words, at speed, the force pushing an Indy car against the track is four times the weight of the car itself. Once you got them started, if you could turn the entire Indianapolis Motor Speedway upside down, today's cars would happily continue to circle at 225 mph, securely glued to the ceiling. At least until the first pit stop. ■

1980

Winner: Johnny Rutherford, Chaparral/Cosworth, 142.862 mph
Winner's Purse: $318,819
Total Purse: $1,503,225
Pace Car: Johnnie Parsons, Sr., Pontiac Trans Am

Tom Sneva started last and finished second behind pole-sitter Johnny Rutherford, who dominated the race with fellow-Texan Jim Hall's Chaparral. Rutherford became only the sixth three-time winner, with the unusual 1974-1980 record of three wins, one second and one last place in seven 500s.

Number	Driver	Sponsor/Team	Engine Type/Displacement	Chassis	Qualifying	Start/ Finish	Laps
4	Johnny Rutherford	Pennzoil/Chaparral Racing	Cosworth V-8/161 cu.in.	Chaparral	192.526	1/1	200
9	Tom Sneva	Bon Jour Jeans/O'Connell	Cosworth V-8/161 cu.in.	McLaren	185.290	33/2	200
46	Gary Bettenhausen	Armstrong Mould	DGS I-4/160 cu.in.	Wildcat II	182.463	32/3	200
20	Gordon Johncock	N. American Van Lines/Patrick	Cosworth V-8/160 cu.in.	Penske	186.075	17/4	200
1	Rick Mears	The Gould Charge/Penske	Cosworth V-8/158 cu.in.	Penske	187.490	6/5	199
10	Pancho Carter	Alex XLNT Foods	Cosworth V-8/161 cu.in.	Penske	186.480	8/6	199
25	Danny Ongais	Interscope/Panasonic	Cosworth V-8/161 cu.in.	Parnelli	186.606	16/7	199
43	Tom Bigelow	Armstrong Mould/Jiffy Mix	Cosworth V-8/161 cu.in.	Lola	182.547	31/8	198
21	Tim Richmond	UNO/Q95 Starcruiser/MACH 1	Cosworth V-8/161 cu.in.	Penske	188.334	19/9	197
44	Greg Leffler	Starcraft R.V./Armstrong	Cosworth V-8/161 cu.in.	Lola	183.748	23/10	197
29	Bill Engelhart	Master Lock/Beaudoin Racing	Cosworth V-8/161 cu.in.	McLaren	184.237	22/11	193
2	Billy Vukovich	Hubler Chevy/WFMS/Leader	Offy I-4/160 cu.in.	Watson	182.741	30/12	192
96	Don Whittington	Sun System/Whittingtons	Cosworth V-8/161 cu.in.	Penske	183.927	18/13	178
14	A.J. Foyt	Gilmore Racing/A.J. Foyt	Cosworth V-8/161 cu.in.	Parnelli	185.500	12/14	173
16	George Snider	Gilmore Racing/A.J. Foyt	Cosworth V-8/161 cu.in.	Parnelli	185.385	21/15	169
18	Dennis Firestone	Scientific Drilling/Jack Rhoades	Cosworth V-8/161 cu.in.	Penske	183.702	24/16	137
7	Jerry Sneva	Hugger's Holders/AMI	Cosworth V-8/161 cu.in.	Lola	187.852	5/17	130
99	Hurley Haywood	Sta-On/Guarantee/Hopkins	Chevy V-6/207 cu.in.	Lightning	183.561	25/18	127
11	Bobby Unser	The Norton Spirit/Penske	Cosworth V-8/161 cu.in.	Penske	189.994	3/19	126
12	Mario Andretti	Essex/Penske Racing	Cosworth V-8/161 cu.in.	Penske	191.012	2/20	71
38	Jerry Karl	Tonco Trailer/Willie Compton	Chevy V-8/351 cu.in.	McLaren	183.011	28/21	64
8	Dick Simon	Vermont American/Simon	Offy I-4/160 cu.in.	Vollstedt	182.788	29/22	58
66	Roger Rager	Advance/Carpenter/Rager	Chevy V-8/357 cu.in.	Wildcat	186.374	10/23	55
23	Jim McElreath	Shirley McElreath	Cosworth V-8/161 cu.in.	Penske	186.249	11/24	54
70	Gordon Smiley	Valvoline/Patrick Racing Team	Cosworth V-8/161 cu.in.	Phoenix	186.948	20/25	47
15	Johnny Parsons	Wynn's/Lindsey Hopkins	Offy I-4/160 cu.in.	Lightning	187.412	7/26	44
5	Al Unser	Longhorn Racing/Bobby Hillin	Cosworth V-8/161 cu.in.	Longhorn	186.442	9/27	33
40	Tom Bagley	Kent Oil/Patrick Racing Team	Cosworth V-8/161 cu.in.	Wildcat	185.405	13/28	29
35	Spike Gehlhausen	Winton Sales/Fletcher Racing	Cosworth V-8/161 cu.in.	Penske	188.344	4/29	20
94	Bill Whittington	Sun System/Whittingtons	Cosworth V-8/161 cu.in.	Parnelli	183.262	27/30	9
26	Dick Ferguson	AMS/Oil/Sanett	Cosworth V-8/161 cu.in.	Penske	182.880	15/31	9
48	Mike Mosley	Theodore Racing/Gurney	Chevy V-8/355 cu.in.	Eagle	183.449	26/32	5
95	Larry Cannon	Kraco Car Stereos	DGS I-4/160 cu.in.	Wildcat	183.253	14/33	2

Surprisingly, these unlimited budgets did not create a tremendous leap in Grand Prix technology, but rather a long series of tiny, very costly changes. Those big budgets also created a tremendous pool of people with knowledge expensively acquired. To apply this hard-won expertise to Indy cars was the work of a moment. The infrastructure was already in place, and since the two types of cars are so similar, it was no big deal to transfer what had been learned in Formula One into building a car to run at Indianapolis.

The result? Though they were built to completely different rules, the Grand Prix and Indy cars of the Eighties were virtually identical, with the critical difference that the CSI outlawed "ground effects" chassis in Formula One as of 1983, while

LONESTAR JR

Johnny Rutherford's career started out fast enough. Born in 1938, he began racing Modifieds on the dangerous Texas dirt "bullrings" in 1959. By 1963, he was at Indianapolis and running a full season of Champ car races. He was a young driver on his way up.

He was also amazingly versatile, able to drive almost anything with four wheels. JR was the fastest qualifier at the Daytona 500 NASCAR race in 1963, for example, and 1965 USAC Sprint Car Champion. He even won the Atlanta 250-miler in 1965. Then he had to sit out a season after breaking both arms at Eldora, Ohio in 1966. In 1968, he sat out some more races after burning both hands at Phoenix.

In 1973, JR picked a plum, a ride in the overwhelming new McLaren winged-wedge at Indianapolis. He rose to the occasion and put his McLaren/Offy on the pole with a new track record of 198.413 mph and a one-lap record at 199.071 mph. That was the turning point for Johnny Rutherford. Filled with new confidence, he was third in the National Championship in 1973. At the Speedway in 1974, he was the second-fastest qualifier but had to start twenty-fifth because he qualified on the second day. He worked his way through the pack like a master to win the 500. He won three more USAC races that year and was second in the Championship behind Bobby Unser. His streak continued in 1975, with a second at Indianapolis and another second in the Championship, this time behind A.J. Foyt.

The next year was even better. "Lonestar JR" started on the pole and won the 500, then lost the National Championship in a heartbreaker at season-ending Phoenix when a broken oil line let Gordon Johncock beat him by 20 points for the season. In 1977, he was third in the Championship, fourth in '78 and '79. In 1980, he won his third Indianapolis 500 and his first National Championship. JR was forty-two and at the very top of his chosen profession.

The next two years were mediocre at best. Then in 1983 JR crashed twice at Indianapolis, the second time breaking both feet. He came back from serious injuries yet again, winning the CART race at Michigan in 1986 and finishing twenty-second at Indy in 1988. His twenty-seven victories to date make him fifth on the list of all-time Champ car winners. He's sixth in pole positions with twenty-three, and ninth in total laps led since World War II. He's also one of only two drivers to win the 500 twice starting from the pole, a three-time pole sitter and, with a total of $4,209,232 in winnings, eleventh on the list of all-time Champ car winners. ∎

(left) Johnny Rutherford qualified at Indianapolis in 1989, but was bumped from the field for the first time in twenty-five years. He was first alternate on race day.
(below) Lonestar JR heads out for qualifying in his 1989 Lola/Cosworth.

1981

Winner: Bobby Unser, Penske/Cosworth, 139.029 mph
Winner's Purse: $299,124
Total Purse: $1,605,375
Pace Car: Duke Nalon, Buick Regal

Bobby Unser and Mario Andretti raced for the flag, with Unser getting there first. Steward Tom Binford then penalized Unser a lap for incorrectly exiting the pits. In court, it turned out Mario had made the same mistake. Unser was fined $40,000, but declared the winner.

Number	Driver	Sponsor/Team	Engine Type/Displacement	Chassis	Qualifying	Start/Finish	Laps
3	Bobby Unser	The Norton Spirit/Penske	Cosworth V-8/161 cu.in.	Penske	200.545	1/1	200
40	Mario Andretti	STP Oil Treatment/Patrick	Cosworth V-8/160 cu.in.	Wildcat	193.040	32/2	200
33	Vern Schuppan	Red Roof Inns/Theodore Racing	Cosworth V-8/161 cu.in.	McLaren	186.548	18/3	199
32	Kevin Cogan	Jerry O'Connell Racing	Cosworth V-8/161 cu.in.	Phoenix	189.444	12/4	197
50	Geoff Brabham	Psachie/Garza Esso	Cosworth V-8/161 cu.in.	Penske	187.990	15/5	197
81	Sheldon Kinser	Sergio Valente Jeans/Hillin	Cosworth V-8/161 cu.in.	Longhorn	189.454	23/6	195
16	Tony Bettenhausen	Provimi Veal/H&R Racing	Cosworth V-8/161 cu.in.	McLaren	187.013	16/7	195
53	Steve Krisiloff	Psachie/Garza Esso	Cosworth V-8/161 cu.in.	Penske	186.722	17/8	194
20	Gordon Johncock	STP Oil Treatment/Patrick	Cosworth V-8/160 cu.in.	Wildcat	195.429	4/9	194
4	Dennis Firestone	Rhoades Aircraft Sales	Cosworth V-8/160 cu.in.	Patrick	187.784	28/10	193
7	Bill Alsup	AB Dick Pacemaker/Alsup	Cosworth V-8/161 cu.in.	Penske	193.154	7/11	193
74	Michael Chandler	National/Warner Hodgdon	Cosworth V-8/161 cu.in.	Penske	187.568	25/12	192
14	A.J. Foyt	Valvoline-Gilmore/Foyt	Cosworth V-8/161 cu.in.	Coyote	196.078	3/13	191
84	Tim Richmond	UNO/WTTV/Guarantee/MACH1	Cosworth V-8/161 cu.in.	Parnelli	189.255	33/14	191
38	Jerry Karl	Tonco Trailer/Jerry Karl	Chevy V-8/351 cu.in.	McLaren	186.008	31/15	189
37	Scott Brayton	Forsythe Industries	Cosworth V-8/161 cu.in.	Penske	187.774	29/16	173
88	Al Unser	Valvoline-Longhorn/Hillin	Cosworth V-8/161 cu.in.	Longhorn	192.719	9/17	166
31	Larry Dickson	Machinist Union/I.A.M.A.W.	Cosworth V-8/161 cu.in.	Penske	186.278	19/18	165
35	Bob Lazier	Montgomery Ward/Fletcher	Cosworth V-8/161 cu.in.	Penske	189.424	13/19	154
56	Tom Bigelow	Genesee Beer/Gohr Distributing	Chevy V-8/351 cu.in.	Penske	188.294	14/20	152
90	Bill Whittington	Kraco Car Stereo/Whittington	Cosworth V-8/161 cu.in.	March	197.098	27/21	146
60	Gordon Smiley	Intermedics/Patrick Racing	Cosworth V-8/161 cu.in.	Wildcat	192.988	8/22	141
55	Josele Garza	Psachie/Garza Esso	Cosworth V-8/161 cu.in.	Penske	195.101	6/23	138
79	Pete Halsmer	Hubler Chevy/KISS 99/Arciero	Cosworth V-8/161 cu.in.	Penske	181.919	24/24	123
2	Tom Sneva	Blue Poly/Bignotti-Cotter	Cosworth V-8/161 cu.in.	March	200.691	20/25	96
8	Gary Bettenhausen	Lindsey Hopkins	Cosworth V-8/161 cu.in.	Lightning	190.870	11/26	69
25	Danny Ongais	Interscope Racing	Cosworth V-8/161 cu.in.	Interscope	197.694	21/27	64
5	Pancho Carter	Alex Foods	Cosworth V-8/161 cu.in.	Penske	191.022	10/28	63
51	Tom Klausler	IDS Idea/Douglas Schulz	Chevy V-8/208 cu.in.	Schkee	186.732	30/29	60
6	Rick Mears	The Gould Charge/Penske	Cosworth V-8/161 cu.in.	Penske	194.018	22/30	58
91	Don Whittington	Whittington Brothers	Cosworth V-8/161 cu.in.	March	187.237	26/31	32
1	Johnny Rutherford	Pennzoil/Chaparral Racing	Cosworth V-8/161 cu.in.	Chaparral	195.387	5/32	25
48	Mike Mosley	Pepsi Challenger/All-American	Chevy V-8/351 cu.in.	Eagle	197.141	2/33	16

Indianapolis cars have continued to use sophisticated ground effects "underwings" since 1979.

INSTABILITY ABROAD, STABILITY AT HOME

Despite the huge amount of money available—or perhaps, because of it—Formula One has been a maelstrom of controversy for the past decade. Ground effects, no ground effects, fuel restrictions, tighter fuel restrictions, 3.0-liter non-turbos, 1.5-liter turbos, 3.5-liter non-turbos; and always accompanied by strident shouting and ever-rising costs. In the end, the result has been confusion for the fans and stressful hard feelings for the drivers and crews. This aggravation and fighting

THE GUNSLINGER

Bobby's nephew, Al Unser, Jr., once was asked what he would have done if his father had been in a different business. "Followed my dad," said Little Al. "If he still had his auto parts store, I suppose I'd be driving the wrecker today." Luckily, the Unsers are *racers*. It's what they do.

OLSONITE EAGLE

The best known are Bobby and his brother Al, but their father and two uncles were racers before them. Uncle Louis won the Pikes Peak hillclimb nine times. Bobby's older brother Jerry was killed during practice at Indianapolis in 1959, by which time Bobby had already been racing for a decade.

Bobby first ran at the Speedway in 1963. He hit the wall on his third lap and was the first car out. The next year, he crashed into the Sachs/MacDonald accident and completed only one lap. Things got better—they couldn't get much worse—until in 1968 there was this rangy cowboy-looking guy from Albuquerque standing in Victory Lane with Bob Wilke from Leader Cards. Bobby went on to win the National Championship and return the next year to finish third on Memorial Day.

After a long stretch of fast qualifying but poor finishes with Dan Gurney's Eagles, in 1974 Bobby finished second to Johnny Rutherford, only 22 seconds behind. The next year he beat Rutherford by about the same margin for his last year with All-American racers. He finished third in the Championship, too. After another long dry spell, Bobby joined Roger Penske to finish fifth in 1979, then first again in 1981. He then wisely retired at the top, one of only eight men to win the Indianapolis 500 three times.

He's also fourth in all-time Indy car victories, with thirty-five. Add in some eleven wins at Pikes Peak and a bunch of other racing successes, and Bobby Unser has to be considered one of the best racing drivers of all time.

He was always exciting to watch, too, with a forceful, dynamic style. Nowadays, of course, he brings the same style to his authoritative racing commentary on television. The man knows whereof he speaks. ■

(left) Bobby Unser in 1972, after capturing the Indianapolis 500 pole with his radical Eagle/Offy. He averaged 195.540 mph for four laps, a phenomenal speed in those days. Unfortunately, he was out on lap 31 with a broken distributor rotor. (below) In 1975, Unser started on the front row and went on to win the 500. He's shown here with his son, Robby, who's grown into a successful racing driver in his own right.

(extreme left) Paul Newman has been a partner in Newman-Haas Racing since 1983, supplying cars for his friend Mario Andretti and now Mario's son Michael as well.

(far left) Joseph Cloutier was Tony Hulman's "right hand man" for five decades. At his death on December 11, 1989, he was President of the Indianapolis Motor Speedway.

(left) Changing four tires every pitstop takes a lot of wheels. These are for Michael Andretti's March in 1985.

(below) Johnny Rutherford won the 500 in 1980 with this year-old Chaparral 2K/Cosworth. It was the first of the full ground effects cars in the 500 when it appeared in 1979.

1982

Winner: Gordon Johncock, Wildcat/Cosworth, 162.029 mph
Winner's Purse: $290,606
Total Purse: $2,067,475
Pace Car: Jim Rathmann, Chevrolet Camaro Z-28

Rick Mears and Gordon Johncock raced wheel to wheel, until Johncock pulled ahead after their final pit stops. Mears began to catch up, but fell just 0.16 second short of victory in the closest Indianapolis 500 finish ever. Johncock's Wildcat was also the last American-built chassis to win the race.

Number	Driver	Sponsor/Team	Engine Type/Displacement	Chassis	Qualifying	Start/Finish	Laps
20	Gordon Johncock	STP Oil Treatment/Patrick	Cosworth V-8/161 cu.in.	Wildcat	201.884	5/1	200
1	Rick Mears	The Gould Charge/Penske	Cosworth V-8/160 cu.in.	Penske	207.004	1/2	200
3	Pancho Carter	Alex Foods	Cosworth V-8/161 cu.in.	March	198.950	10/3	199
7	Tom Sneva	Texaco Star/Bignotti-Cotter	Cosworth V-8/161 cu.in.	March	201.027	7/4	197
10	Al Unser	Longhorn Racing	Cosworth V-8/161 cu.in.	Longhorn	195.567	16/5	197
91	Don Whittington	Simoniz Finish/Whittington	Cosworth V-8/161 cu.in.	March	200.725	8/6	196
42	Jim Hickman	Stroh's/Schwartz	Cosworth V-8/161 cu.in.	March	196.217	24/7	189
5	Johnny Rutherford	Pennzoil/Chaparral Racing	Cosworth V-8/161 cu.in.	Chaparral	197.066	12/8	187
28	Herm Johnson	Menard Cashway Lumber	Chevy V-8/355 cu.in.	Eagle	195.929	14/9	186
30	Howdy Holmes	Domino's Pizza/Shierson	Cosworth V-8/161 cu.in.	March	194.468	18/10	186
19	Bobby Rahal	Red Roof Inns/Truesports	Cosworth V-8/161 cu.in.	March	194.700	17/11	174
8	Gary Bettenhausen	Kraco Stereo/Lindsey Hopkins	Cosworth V-8/161 cu.in.	Lightning	195.673	30/12	158
52	Hector Rebaque	Carta Blanca/Forsythe Racing	Cosworth V-8/161 cu.in.	March	195.684	15/13	150
53	Danny Sullivan	Forsythe-Brown Racing	Cosworth V-8/161 cu.in.	March	196.292	13/14	148
12	Chip Ganassi	First Commercial/Rhoades	Cosworth V-8/161 cu.in.	Wildcat	197.704	11/15	147
94	Bill Whittington	Whittington/Hodgdon	Cosworth V-8/161 cu.in.	March	201.658	6/16	121
68	Michael Chandler	Freeman/Gurney Eagle	Chevy V-8/355 cu.in.	Eagle	198.042	22/17	104
27	Tom Bigelow	H.B.K. Racing/Hall Brothers	Chevy V-8/355 cu.in.	Eagle	194.784	31/18	96
14	A.J. Foyt	Valvoline/Gilmore/Foyt	Cosworth V-8/161 cu.in.	March	203.332	3/19	95
34	Johnny Parsons	Silhouette Spas/WIFE/Wysard	Cosworth V-8/161 cu.in.	March	195.929	25/20	92
35	George Snider	Cobre Tire/Robert Fletcher	Cosworth V-8/161 cu.in.	March	195.493	26/21	87
25	Danny Ongais	Interscope Racing	Cosworth V-8/161 cu.in.	Interscope	199.948	9/22	62
69	Jerry Sneva	Great American/Hoffman	Cosworth V-8/161 cu.in.	March	195.270	28/23	61
39	Chet Fillip	Circle Bar Truck Corral	Cosworth V-8/161 cu.in.	Eagle	194.879	29/24	60
66	Pete Halsmer	Col. Bread Pay Less/Arciero	Chevy V-8/208 cu.in.	Eagle	194.295	32/25	38
16	Tony Bettenhausen	Provimi Veal/H&R Racing	Cosworth V-8/161 cu.in.	March	195.429	27/26	37
75	Dennis Firestone	B.C.V. Racing	Cosworth V-8/355 cu.in.	Eagle	197.217	21/27	37
21	Geoff Brabham	Pentax Super/Bignotti-Cotter	Cosworth V-8/161 cu.in.	March	198.906	20/28	12
55	Josele Garza	Schlitz Gusto/Garza Racing	Cosworth V-8/161 cu.in.	March	194.500	33/29	1
4	Kevin Cogan	The Norton Spirit/Penske	Cosworth V-8/161 cu.in.	Penske	204.082	2/30	0
40	Mario Andretti	STP Oil Treatment/Patrick	Cosworth V-8/161 cu.in.	Wildcat	203.172	4/31	0
31	Roger Mears	Machinist's Union/I.A.M.A.W.	Cosworth V-8/161 cu.in.	Penske	194.154	19/32	0
95	Dale Whittington	Whittington/Hodgdon	Cosworth V-8/161 cu.in.	March	197.694	23/33	0

is a far cry from the glory days of the Fifties, further still from the halcyon era of the Silver Arrows of Mercedes-Benz and Auto Union.

"Formula One today is politics, fighting and aggravation all the time," explains two-time World Champion Emerson Fittipaldi. "Indy car racing is like a big, happy family having a good time together every weekend. Indy car racing is a sport *and* a business; Grand Prix has become only business. Crazy business."

By comparison to the zaniness of Formula One, Speedway rules over the past two decades have been a very model of thoughtful sanity, and one of the few constants in racing. The rules have gotten progressively stricter over the years, but they have not changed in any dramatic way since 1969.

THE MOST PERFECT RULES IN RACING HISTORY?

Not only have the Indy rules not changed, they've been mostly popular with designers, drivers and team owners. They haven't been changed, because nobody can find a reason why they should be changed. That's never happened before in the hundred years that people have been racing motorcars. Somebody always wants to change *something*, but the Indy car rules are so even, so balanced, so fair, there's no reason why they shouldn't last in essentially the same form for another decade.

Throughout this period, DOHC engines have been restricted to 2.65-liters (162 cubic inches) turbocharged. Cars are a maximum of 185 inches long, minimum weight 1550 lbs. (705 kg). They have to carry a 40 gallon fuel cell between the driver and engine and burn methanol rather than gasoline. Even the wheel widths are still restricted to 10 inches front, 14 inches rear. But over that two-decade period without dramatic rules changes, lap speeds at Indianapolis increased from 170 mph to 225 mph. Obviously, something has been going on.

(above) The closest finish in Speedway history: Gordon Johncock's STP Wildcat/Cosworth edges Rick Mears' Penske/Cosworth by 0.16 second in 1982. This was the same year that front-row qualifier Kevin Cogan ran into A.J. Foyt at the start and was rammed by Mario Andretti from behind. Ironically, Cogan was Mears' Penske teammate and Andretti was Johncock's STP teammate.

UNFAIR ADVANTAGE?

Since 1970, cars entered by Roger Penske have won 64 Indy car races and seven Indianapolis 500s. His nearest competitor is Al Dean, whose cars won 39 Indy car races between 1953 and 1967. In addition, Penske Racing dominated the Trans-Am series in the 1967-1972 period, the USRRC and the Can-Am. Penske built his own successful Formula One cars in the mid-Seventies and was even able to make a NASCAR winner out of an AMC Matador, which is performing miracles indeed. Roger also owns Michigan International Speedway and Pennsylvania International Speedway, started the IROC series and was one of the founders of CART.

In his spare time, in less than thirty years, starting virtually from scratch, Roger

(above) The Captain in 1972, just after Mark Donohue had won Penske Racing's first Indianapolis 500.

Penske also amassed a personal fortune in the $300 million range. His $2.5 billion Penske Corporation is the forty-eighth largest privately held company in the country. It owns dozens of car dealerships—including Longo Toyota, the largest dealer in the country—Penske/Hertz truck leasing and GM/Allison Diesel. He's very low-key about it, but that distinguished-looking fellow wearing headphones and an immaculate windbreaker in the pits is one of the richest people in America...and one of the rare members of the *Forbes 400* who didn't inherit most of what he has.

All of which brings up the obvious question: What makes Roger Penske so successful?

Well, there is no "unfair advantage," at least not the way you mean. Instead: *Professionalism. Hard Work. Determination. Organization. Self-Confidence. Attention to Detail.*

According to his former driver Danny Sullivan, Roger Penske will do whatever it takes to win. "If that means sweeping the floors at 5 am," says Danny, "Roger will be there sweeping the garage when the crew arrives. If it means going testing at 6 am the morning before the Indianapolis 500, he'll find a way. Roger will literally do whatever it takes. Most people won't. If anything, that's his 'unfair advantage.'"

There are people who criticize this obsessiveness, mostly people whom Roger has beaten. And there are rumors that Penske is the very devil to work for. "That's nonsense," says Sullivan. "If Roger were so terrible to work for, why would so many of his people still be with him after twenty or thirty years? If you do your job, you'll have no trouble with Roger. If you don't do your job, you'll be out. That's fair."

Penske's family wasn't exactly poor—he grew up in the fancy Shaker Heights suburb of Cleveland and his first wife was Lissa Stouffer, as in the restaurants—but they were never "Big Money," as they say in Texas. Roger put himself through Lehigh by buying, restoring and reselling sports cars, then in 1959 got his SCCA license and started racing with a Corvette, followed by a Porsche. He won an SCCA National Championship in 1960. In 1961 he started running Grand Prix races in a Cooper/Climax. Later, he rebuilt a crashed Formula One Cooper/Climax into the famous Zerex Special sports/racer with which he dominated professional American road racing for two years. By 1964, he had worked his way up to one of the factory Corvette Grand Sports and a Chaparral ride for 1965. In sports cars, Penske was quite capable of beating Dan Gurney and A.J. Foyt head to head in equal machinery. He was that good.

Instead, Penske retired as a driver in 1965 when he bought his first Chevrolet dealership. In 1966, he put together Sunoco sponsorship, a Chevy-powered Lola and a young driver/engineer named Mark Donohue to form Penske Racing and win the USRRC. And thus is immortality born. Mark was a brilliant development engineer and behind that engaging grin, a deceptively-competitive racer. Penske was the most professional team manager in racing. Between 1966 and 1975, when Mark was killed practicing for the Grand Prix at Zeltweg, Penske Racing succeeded at almost everything they touched. Roger Penske and Mark Donohue were generally considered the best American racers of their day.

When Mark was killed, a lot of people figured Roger would quit. But by then, Penske Racing had far outgrown one driver. Penske continued with Formula One through 1976—John Watson even won a Grand Prix—but then switched back to Indy car racing exclusively.

Tom Sneva and Mario Andretti drove for Penske Racing in 1976 and '77, then were joined by Rick Mears in 1978. Mears won Penske's second Indianapolis 500 in 1979 on only his second try—Mark Donohue had won on his fourth try in 1972.

Mears was fifth in 1980, Bobby Unser first in 1981, Mears second in 1982 after teammate Kevin Cogan crashed at the start. Al Unser and Mears were second and third in 1983, Mears and Unser were first and third the next year. In '85, Danny Sullivan and Unser were first and fourth, Mears was third the next year, then Al Unser won his fourth Indianapolis 500 in a Penske team car in 1987, followed by a third in 1988, with Mears first. After a bad Indy in 1989, Emerson Fittipaldi and Mears were third and fifth in 1990. No other team in history has enjoyed such a winning streak, nor so many finishers in the Top Five, consistently, year after year. Penske is the *best*.

The difference between Penske Racing and other teams is that around Roger such overwhelming excellence is not just the norm, it's *expected*. Roger Penske, more than any other individual, has turned racing from an exciting sport into a rewarding business. Penske's drivers—like Penske himself in his racing days—aren't out there to "win, blow or put a hole in the fence." They are professional, competent, analytical drivers, *thinking* drivers who will ultimately beat any hot-headed kid with a heavy throttle foot. That's the way Roger Penske runs his racing, his business, his *life*—cool, competent, controlled and *very* successful. ■

(above) History in the making, 1988: Rick Mears #5, Danny Sullivan #9 and Al Unser #1 form an all-Penske front row, the only time that one team has qualified one-two-three at the Speedway. 500 miles later, Mears was still first and Unser third, but Sullivan had dropped out halfway through. Still, two out of three ain't bad.

1983

Winner: Tom Sneva, March/Cosworth, 162.117 mph
Winner's Purse: $385,886
Total Purse: $2,411,450
Pace Car: Duke Nalon, Buick Riviera

Rookie Teo Fabi qualified on the pole, but Al Unser seemed headed for victory until Tom Sneva passed him—and Al, Jr., who was blocking for his father—late in the race and held on to win by only 11.175 seconds. It was Sneva's first victory after a decade of trying.

Number	Driver	Sponsor/Team	Engine Type/Displacement	Chassis	Qualifying	Start/ Finish	Laps
5	Tom Sneva	Texaco Star/Bignotti-Cotter	Cosworth V-8/161 cu.in.	March	203.687	4/1	200
7	Al Unser	Hertz/Penske	Cosworth V-8/161 cu.in.	Penske	201.954	7/2	200
2	Rick Mears	Pennzoil/Penske	Cosworth V-8/161 cu.in.	Penske	204.301	3/3	200
12	Geoff Brabham	UNO/British Sterling/VDS	Cosworth V-8/161 cu.in.	Penske	198.613	26/4	199
16	Kevin Cogan	Caesar's Palace	Cosworth V-8/161 cu.in.	March	201.528	22/5	198
30	Howdy Holmes	Domino's Pizza/Shierson	Cosworth V-8/161 cu.in.	March	199.295	12/6	198
21	Pancho Carter	Alex Foods Pinata	Cosworth V-8/161 cu.in.	March	198.207	14/7	197
60	Chip Ganassi	Sea Ray Boats/Patrick Racing	Cosworth V-8/161 cu.in.	Wildcat	197.608	16/8	195
37	Scott Brayton	SME Cement/Brayton	Cosworth V-8/161 cu.in.	March	196.713	29/9	195
19	Al Unser, Jr.	Coors Light/Galles/Roman	Cosworth V-8/161 cu.in.	Eagle	202.146	5/10	192
56	Steve Chassey	Genesee/Sizzler/WLNH/Gohr	Chevy V-8/355 cu.in.	Eagle	195.108	19/11	191
72	Chris Kneifel	Primus/C.F.I.	Cosworth V-8/161 cu.in.	Primus	198.625	25/12	191
18	Mike Mosley	Kraco Car Stereo	Cosworth V-8/161 cu.in.	March	205.372	2/13	169
20	Gordon Johncock	STP Oil Treatment/Patrick	Cosworth V-8/161 cu.in.	Wildcat	199.748	10/14	163
22	Dick Simon	Vermont American/Simon	Cosworth V-8/161 cu.in.	March	192.993	20/15	161
29	Mike Chandler	Agajanian/Curb/Rattlesnake	Cosworth V-8/161 cu.in.	Rattlesnake	194.934	30/16	153
10	Tony Bettenhausen	Provimi Veal	Cosworth V-8/161 cu.in.	March	199.893	9/17	152
94	Bill Whittington	Whittington Brothers	Cosworth V-8/161 cu.in.	March	197.755	15/18	144
34	Derek Daly	Wysard Motor	Cosworth V-8/161 cu.in.	March	197.658	28/19	126
4	Bobby Rahal	Red Roof Inns/Truesports	Cosworth V-8/161 cu.in.	March	202.005	6/20	110
25	Danny Ongais	Interscope Racing	Cosworth V-8/161 cu.in.	March	202.320	21/21	101
66	Johnny Parsons	Colonial Bread/Arciero Racing	Cosworth V-8/161 cu.in.	Penske	199.984	23/22	80
3	Mario Andretti	Newman/Haas/Budweiser	Cosworth V-8/161 cu.in.	Lola	199.404	11/23	79
90	Dennis Firestone	Simpson/Jones/Hackman	Cosworth V-8/161 cu.in.	March	190.888	33/24	77
55	Josele Garza	Machinists Union/I.A.M.A.W.	Cosworth V-8/161 cu.in.	March	195.671	18/25	64
33	Teo Fabi	Skoal Bandit/Forsythe Racing	Cosworth V-8/161 cu.in.	March	207.395	1/26	47
91	Don Whittington	Simoniz Finish/Whittington	Cosworth V-8/161 cu.in.	March	198.597	27/27	44
9	Roger Mears	Machinists Union/I.A.M.A.W.	Cosworth V-8/161 cu.in.	March	200.108	8/28	43
43	Steve Krisiloff	Armstrong Mould/AMI Racing	Cosworth V-8/161 cu.in.	Lola	191.192	31/29	42
35	Patrick Bedard	Escort Radar Warning/Brayton	Cosworth V-8/161 cu.in.	March	195.941	17/30	25
14	A.J. Foyt	Valvoline-Gilmore/A.J. Foyt	Cosworth V-8/161 cu.in.	March	199.557	24/31	24
1	George Snider	Calumet Farm/A.J. Foyt	Cosworth V-8/161 cu.in.	March	198.544	13/32	22
38	Chet Fillip	Circle Bar Truck Corral	Cosworth V-8/161 cu.in.	Eagle	183.146	32/33	11

It hasn't been horsepower. In the unlimited era of the early Seventies, there were Indy cars with 1000 or even 1100 hp. Turbo boost and fuel consumption restrictions reduced that to about 850 hp in the late-Seventies and to around 725-750 hp throughout the Eighties. Without these restrictions on horsepower, Indy cars would no doubt be lapping the Speedway at 250 mph. *Plus.*

Racing regulations have gotten so sophisticated that the organizers can now write the rules to keep speeds at whatever level they want, or allow slow increases each year as USAC has done. NHRA currently limits Top Fuel to about 300 mph; NASCAR limits Winston Cup to 200 mph, USAC and CART limit Indy cars to around 225 mph.

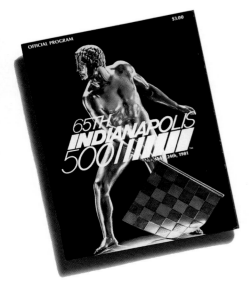

The purpose? Not only to make racing safer, but to make it more interesting. Spectators come to watch *racing*, not speed per se. As long as the rules are the same for everyone, whether the cars are lapping at 225 mph or 250 mph really doesn't matter. Racing is ultimately about people, about competition, not about going fast.

SPEC RACERS

The Indy cars of the Eighties and Nineties are so similar they almost constitute a "spec class" like ARS or the SCCA's Shelby Can Am. Goodyear supplies all the tires, all of identical hardness and consequently of identical grip. Engines are virtually interchangeable in design and power, whether they say Cosworth, Chevrolet, Alfa or Judd on the cam covers. Today's engines are even designed with the mounts in the same place, so that a Chevy can be bolted in place of a Cosworth, for example, without welding on the frame. And for much of this period, there have been only three chassis builders: March, Lola and Penske.

The last revolutionary Indy car was the Chaparral 2K of 1979 which introduced "ground effects." A ground effects car has a very narrow central body which holds the driver, the fuel cell, the engine and the transaxle, in that order. On either side of this core is a huge "underwing" enclosed in bodywork. Air is drawn in the front of each side-pod, through a radiator on either side, then out the back of the car. As it goes, the air is directed past the underwing, creating a low-pressure area that literally sucks the car to the pavement. Compared to the 1.0G or 1.5G of downforce created by the huge wings of the early-Seventies, a ground effects Indy car creates between 3.0G and 4.0G of downforce.

Downforce itself is of no importance. But as the tires are forced against the pavement for better traction, cornering speeds soar dramatically. A typical Indy car of the late-Eighties can generate side loads of 3.5G. Cornering speeds at Indianapolis have risen from about 185 mph in 1978 to about 220 mph in 1990. Virtually all of that improvement is the result of increased downforce from ground effects.

The overall width of an Indy car is restricted by the rules. So the only way to find room for larger underwings is to make the cockpit narrower. Progressively through the Eighties, Indy cars became smoother and cleaner. But there were no radical changes.

Following Formula One design, Indy cars went to the pointed "Concorde" nose, named after the long, pointy nose of the supersonic airliner. After Rick Mears' crash at Montreal in 1984, the Indy car rules were changed demanding a much stronger footwell to protect

One of the greatest brother acts in history was the 1982 500. One-third of the drivers in the entire field were racing against their own brothers. They were Rick and Roger Mears, Tom and Jerry Sneva, Gary and Tony Bettenhausen, plus Don, Bill and Dale Whittington. Half-brothers Johnny Parsons and Pancho Carter make eleven out of thirty-three starters...their mother was married to both 1950 Indy 500 winner Johnnie Parsons and Duane Carter, whose best finish was third in 1953 (he relieved Sam Hanks). In 1982, his son Pancho (Duane, Jr.) finished third behind Gordon Johncock and Rick Mears, *his* best finish.

Rick Mears is just 2.06 seconds short of being the only five-time 500 winner. In 1982, he was second by just 0.16 second behind Gordon Johncock; in 1986 he was third behind Bobby Rahal by 1.88 seconds with Kevin Cogan in between them.

GOTTA HAVE A V-8

The time-honored Offy won its last 500 in 1976. Behind Johnny Rutherford the entire grid was also all Offy, with the exceptions of a single Foyt (Ford four-cam), two Drake-Goossen-Sparks versions of the Offy, an AMC stock-block and a sole Cosworth-Ford. The next year, a Foyt four-cam won, with Cosworths second and third. Most of the rest were Offys and DGS Offys. The Cosworth first won in 1978, and by then, fourteen out of thirty-three Indy racers had broken away from the Offy. By '79, the field was mostly Cosworth; by 1981, there were only four non-Cosworths, and those were Chevrolet stock-blocks. After more than fifty years, the Offy was gone from Indy.

For nearly a decade, the Cosworth replaced the Offy as the standard Indy car engine. The Cosworth set the basic design parameters of the Indy Engine of the Eighties...a very compact, all-alloy, 2.65-liter V-8 with double-overhead camshafts, four-valves-per-cylinder, central sparkplugs, narrow-angle valve layout, fuel-injection and a Borg-Warner IHI turbocharger limited to 45 in/Hg (22 psi). Power of such a Cosworth-Ford DFX is somewhere between 750 and 900 hp at 11,000 rpm, depending on whose dynamometer you believe.

In 1986, Al Unser showed up with a new engine in his Penske. This was essentially a second-generation Cosworth designed by two former Cosworth engineers, Mario Ilien and Paul Morgan. Called the Chevrolet Indy V-8—Chevy and Penske put up the money for Ilmor Engineering to develop this new engine—it was slightly lighter than the Cosworth and had superior acceleration out of the corners, though about the same amount of horsepower. By 1987, the Chevy Indy V-8 was winning races. By 1988 it was winning everything including Indy. By 1989 it was the only engine capable of winning an Indy car race. That is still true in 1991...the Chevrolet Indy V-8 now dominates Indy car racing as completely as the Offy or Cosworth ever did.

Not that there aren't challengers. A few years ago, Englishman John Judd developed an Indy engine based on the 3.0-liter V-8 Honda designed for European Formula 3000. The Judd looks and acts exactly like a Cosworth or

(above) John Judd's V-8 is based on a 3.0-liter Honda designed for Formula 3000 and reduced in size to fit the Indy car rules.
(top right) The similar Alfa Romeo Indy V-8.
(bottom right) Although virtually identical to the others, the Porsche Indy V-8 was never as successful.
All these engines are very similar in engineering, size, weight and power output: around 750 hp at 11,000 rpm with a 45 Hg/in popoff valve. That's an output of about 4.6 hp per cubic inch or about three times the power/displacement of even the hottest passenger car engines.

Chevy, and even the engineering drawings look identical. It's the very model of a modern Indy engine. Bobby Rahal put a Judd into fifth at Indy in 1988. Raul Boesel got one into third in 1989. Those have been the Judd's best finishes so far.

At the end of the 1987 season, Germany's Porsche showed up with a factory-built Indy car that was embarassingly uncompetitive. The DOHC V-8—another Cosworth clone—was popped into a March chassis. That was better, but Teo Fabi and John Andretti were never able to qualify or finish higher than mid-pack at Indy. At the end of the 1990 season, Porsche announced that they were retiring from Indy car racing having met none of their goals.

Part way through the 1989 season, Italy's Alfa Romeo also started racing a Cosworth-like DOHC V-8 in a March chassis. Al Unser and Roberto Guerrero qualified and finished in mid-pack at Indy in 1990, then Guerrero finished no higher than fifth during the remainder of the season. He has been replaced by Danny Sullivan for 1991, but Indy insiders expect that still won't make the March/Alfa competitive with Lola and Penske chassis powered by the Chevrolet Indy V-8.

CONTEMPORARY STOCK-BLOCKS

You can have up to 390 cubic inches (6.4-liters) if you run your stock-block engine normally-aspirated (355 cubic inches up until 1987), but the last big stock-block in the race was Kevin Cogan's Eagle/Pontiac entered by Dan Gurney in 1984. It qualified and finished well off the pace. In 1982 and '83, Herm Johnson and Steve Chassey finished ninth and eleventh respectively using a 355 cubic inch Chevrolet smallblock that was essentially a 600 hp NASCAR Winston Cup V-8. And that is the best performance from a non-turbo at Indy in this era.

There is also a more tantilizing provision in the Indy car rules that allows you an extra 48 cubic inches (0.8-liter) of displacement and more turbo boost if you start with a passenger car stock-block to build your racing engine. Both Chevrolet and Buick turbocharged V-6s were used in the late-Eighties. Pancho Carter put one of these Buicks on the Indy pole in 1985, and Jim Crawford actually led the 1988 Indy 500 for a while before finishing sixth with his Lola/Buick. He qualified fourth in 1989, while Scott Brayton qualified and finished sixth with a similar car. There were actually eleven out of thirty-three Indy starters powered by Buick in 1990, though none of them qualified near the front and the highest finisher was Kevin Cogan in ninth. The lesson? If you want to win at Indy, your chances are better with a real racing engine than one modified from a passenger car. That's been true since Jules Goux arrived with his Peugeot in 1913, and it's still true today. ∎

(top) The Ilmor-designed, Chevrolet Indy V-8 replaced the Cosworth as the engine to beat in the late-Eighties. In design terms, think of it as a second-generation Cosworth-Ford. (above) The trend-setting Cosworth DFX.
(left) Buick's compact turbo V-6 stock-block has qualified on the pole but never won at Indianapolis.

1984

Winner: Rick Mears, March/Cosworth, 163.612 mph
Winner's Purse: $434,060
Total Purse: $2,795,899
Pace Car: John Callies, Pontiac Fiero

Front-row rivals Tom Sneva and Rick Mears ran nose to tail until Sneva's March broke a CV joint with 32 laps to go. Mears went on to win from rookie Roberto Guerrero at a record-breaking average speed thanks to a minimum of race-slowing accidents. Not since Miller had one chassis so filled the field.

Number	Driver	Sponsor/Team	Engine Type/Displacement	Chassis	Qualifying	Start/ Finish	Laps
6	Rick Mears	Pennzoil Z-7/Penske	Cosworth V-8/161 cu.in.	March	207.847	3/1	200
9	Roberto Guerrero	Master Mechanics/Bignotti-Cotter	Cosworth V-8/161 cu.in.	March	205.707	7/2	198
2	Al Unser	Miller High Life/Penske	Cosworth V-8/161 cu.in.	March	204.441	10/3	198
21	Al Holbert	C.R.C. Chemical/Alex Morales	Cosworth V-8/161 cu.in.	March	203.016	16/4	198
99	Michael Andretti	Electrolux/Kraco	Cosworth V-8/161 cu.in.	March	207.805	4/5	198
14	A.J. Foyt	Gilmore/Foyt	Cosworth V-8/161 cu.in.	March	203.860	12/6	197
5	Bobby Rahal	7 Eleven/Red Roof Inns/Truesport	Cosworth V-8/161 cu.in.	March	202.203	18/7	197
28	Herm Johnson	3M/Menard Cashway	Cosworth V-8/161 cu.in.	March	204.618	9/8	194
25	Danny Ongais	Interscope Racing	Cosworth V-8/161 cu.in.	March	203.978	11/9	193
55	Josele Garza	Schaefer/Machinists/I.A.M.A.W.	Cosworth V-8/161 cu.in.	March	200.615	24/10	193
4	George Snider	Calumet Farm/A.J. Foyt	Cosworth V-8/161 cu.in.	March	201.860	31/11	193
50	Dennis Firestone	Hoosier Transport/Purcell Racing	Cosworth V-8/161 cu.in.	March	201.217	32/12	186
41	Howdy Holmes	"Jiffy" Mixes/Mayer Motor	Cosworth V-8/161 cu.in.	March	207.977	2/13	185
77	Tom Gloy	The Simoniz Finish/Rick Galles	Cosworth V-8/161 cu.in.	March	203.758	13/14	179
73	Chris Kneifel	Spa Erobics/Living Well/Primus	Cosworth V-8/161 cu.in.	Primus	199.831	33/15	175
1	Tom Sneva	Texaco Star/Mayer Motor	Cosworth V-8/161 cu.in.	March	210.019	1/16	168
3	Mario Andretti	Budweiser Lola/Newman/Haas	Cosworth V-8/161 cu.in.	Lola	207.467	6/17	153
37	Scott Brayton	Buick Dealers/Brayton	Buick V-6/208 cu.in.	March	203.637	26/18	150
10	Pancho Carter	American Dream R.T.	Cosworth V-8/161 cu.in.	March	201.820	21/19	141
98	Kevin Cogan	Dubonnet/Curb Records/Gurney	Pontiac V-8/356 cu.in.	Eagle	203.622	27/20	137
7	Al Unser, Jr.	Coor Light Silver Bullet/Galles	Cosworth V-8/161 cu.in.	March	203.404	15/21	131
84	Johnny Rutherford	Gilmore/Greer/Foyt	Cosworth V-8/161 cu.in.	March	202.062	30/22	116
22	Dick Simon	Break Free/Dick Simon Racing	Cosworth V-8/161 cu.in.	March	201.834	20/23	112
33	Teo Fabi	Skoal Bandit/Forsythe Racing	Cosworth V-8/161 cu.in.	March	203.600	14/24	104
20	Gordon Johncock	STP Oil Treatment/Patrick Racing	Cosworth V-8/161 cu.in.	March	207.545	5/25	103
16	Tony Bettenhausen	Provimi Veal	Cosworth V-8/161 cu.in.	March	202.813	17/26	86
61	Derek Daly	Provimi Veal	Cosworth V-8/161 cu.in.	March	202.443	29/27	76
40	Chip Ganassi	Old Milwaukee/Patrick Racing	Cosworth V-8/161 cu.in.	March	201.612	22/28	61
30	Danny Sullivan	Domino's Pizza/Shierson Racing	Cosworth V-8/161 cu.in.	Lola	203.567	28/29	57
35	Patrick Bedard	Escort Radar/Brayton	Buick V-6/208 cu.in.	March	201.915	19/30	55
57	Spike Gehlhausen	Little Kings/Indy Auto Racing	Cosworth V-8/161 cu.in.	March	200.478	25/31	45
47	Emerson Fittipaldi	W.I.T. Promotions	Cosworth V-8/161 cu.in.	March	201.078	23/32	37
18	Geoff Brabham	Kraco Car Stereo	Cosworth V-8/161 cu.in.	March	204.931	8/33	1

the driver's feet and legs. In that sense, then, even the design of the Indy car nose is standardized.

The Marches, Lolas and Penskes of the early-Eighties typically have a low, wide nose flanked by short wings. The windshield rises rather abruptly from the cowl. The cars from the late-Eighties have a narrow, pointy nose flanked by long wings. The top of the nose is higher, forming an unbroken line with the windshield and bodywork. The result is a much more aerodynamic shape...plus more front wing area for greater downforce. For the whole decade of the Eighties, it has been this type of small, seemingly insignificant change which has occupied Indy designers. In a very real sense, design is even more fixed than it was during the Fifties, when

A RACER'S RACER

At some point, every racing driver has put in "sheet time" as A.J. Foyt calls those tedious hours laying in a hospital bed. But not many have endured three months between the sheets, another six months in a wheelchair, and then come back to win the Indy 500, racing better than ever. By the harsh standards of his peers, that makes Rick Mears a "real" racing driver; somebody who knows what racing can cost, physically and mentally, and who still holds the throttle down.

Rick started racing motorcycles as a kid in Bakersfield, California, in 1968, then joined his older brother Roger to form the off-road racing Mears Gang, supported by their family and friends. In 1976, California safety equipment manufacturer Bill Simpson sponsored Rick's first rides in an Indy car. His idea was to showcase how good young Mears really was, hoping that a major team would pick him up and make him a star.

It worked like a charm. In 1978, Rick went straight to the top when he signed with Roger Penske as Mario Andretti's understudy and promptly qualified on the front row at Indy. In his second Indy 500, Rick started on the pole and went on to win, then finished in the Top Ten at every Indy car race all season to win the National Championship in 1979. The next year he was fifth at Indy, fourth in the Championship. In 1981 and '82, he won back-to-back National Championships and missed winning Indianapolis in '82 by the closest margin in history.

In 1984, Rick won the 500 again, then was on his way to yet another Championship when he crashed at Montreal, crushing and nearly severing both feet. The doctors told him he'd never walk again. Instead, he ran five races in 1985 before giving up his car to Al Unser—who'd been fourth at Indy subbing for the wheelchair-bound Mears—so that Big Al could win the Championship.

Penske switched to the new Chevrolet Indy V-8 for 1986, and Rick failed to win an Indy car race for the first time in a decade as they sorted out the new engine. The next year was only slightly better, as the new Penske PC-16 wasn't competitive and Rick had to run his year-old March. In 1988, however, Penske Racing pulled it all together and Mears came back to win his third Indy 500 and post the first lap over 220 mph. He started on the pole again in 1989 before breaking, then started in the middle of the front row in 1990, finishing fifth.

Mears has started from the Indianapolis pole five times, which is more than anybody else. He is also fifth in all-time Indy car wins, with twenty-seven. And, of course, he is also a three-time Indy winner, three-time National Champion and, thanks to having spent his whole career in the high-paying modern era, is now the all-time money winner, with $8,268,565 as of 1990. Rick's a "real" racer, indeed. ∎

(above) Thanks to a combination of skill, luck and Roger Penske's unbeatable team work, Rick Mears has been the dominant Indy car driver of his generation. (below) Mears in his 1989 Penske/ Chevrolet Indy V-8 sat on the pole at Indianapolis for the fifth time. That is more Indy poles than any other driver since 1911.

1985

**Winner: Danny Sullivan,
March/Cosworth,
152.982 mph
Winner's Purse: $517,662
Total Purse: $3,217,025
Pace Car: James Garner,
Oldsmobile Calais 500**

Danny Sullivan and Mario Andretti raced wheel-to-wheel for most of the race, both skillfully avoiding a high-speed incident when Sullivan spun without damage just after passing Andretti in mid-race. At the checker, it was Sullivan by a scant 2.47 seconds over Andretti.

Number	Driver	Sponsor/Team	Engine Type/Displacement	Chassis	Qualifying	Start/ Finish	Laps
5	Danny Sullivan	Miller American/Penske	Cosworth V-8/161 cu.in.	March	210.298	8/1	200
3	Mario Andretti	Beatrice/Lola/Newman-Haas	Cosworth V-8/161 cu.in.	Lola	211.576	4/2	200
9	Roberto Guerrero	Master Mechanics/Bignotti-Cotter	Cosworth V-8/161 cu.in.	March	208.062	16/3	200
11	Al Unser	Hertz/Penske	Cosworth V-8/161 cu.in.	March	210.523	7/4	199
76	Johnny Parsons	Canadian Tire	Cosworth V-8/161 cu.in.	March	205.778	26/5	198
21	Johnny Rutherford	Vermont American/Morales	Cosworth V-8/161 cu.in.	March	208.254	30/6	198
61	Arie Luyendyk	Dutch Treat/Sports/Provimi Veal	Cosworth V-8/161 cu.in.	Lola	206.004	20/7	198
99	Michael Andretti	Electrolux/Kraco Enterprises	Cosworth V-8/161 cu.in.	March	208.185	15/8	196
98	Ed Pimm	Skoal Bandit/Gurney-Curb	Cosworth V-8/161 cu.in.	Eagle	205.724	22/9	195
33	Howdy Holmes	Jiffy Mix/Forsythe Racing	Cosworth V-8/161 cu.in.	Lola	206.372	19/10	194
18	Kevin Cogan	Kraco Stereo	Cosworth V-8/161 cu.in.	March	206.368	32/11	191
29	Derek Daly	Kapsreiter Bier/Tom Hess Racing	Cosworth V-8/161 cu.in	Lola	207.548	31/12	189
40	Emerson Fittipaldi	7 Eleven/STP-Patrick Racing	Cosworth V-8/161 cu.in.	March	211.322	5/13	188
12	Bill Whittington	B&B Properties/Arciero Racing	Cosworth V-8/161 cu.in.	March	209.006	12/14	183
43	John Paul, Jr.	Satellite Technology/AMI Racing	Cosworth V-8/161 cu.in.	March	206.340	24/15	164
34	Jim Crawford	Canadian Tire/Wysard	Cosworth V-8/161 cu.in.	Lola	205.525	27/16	142
25	Danny Ongais	Interscope Racing	Cosworth V-8/161 cu.in.	March	207.220	17/17	141
23	Raul Boesel	Break Free/Dick Simon Racing	Cosworth V-8/161 cu.in.	March	206.498	23/18	134
7	Geoff Brabham	Coors Light Silver Bullet/Galles	Cosworth V-8/161 cu.in.	March	210.074	9/19	130
2	Tom Sneva	Skoal Bandit/Gurney-Curb	Cosworth V-8/161 cu.in.	Eagle	208.927	13/20	123
1	Rick Mears	Pennzoil Z-7/Penske Cars	Cosworth V-8/161 cu.in.	March	209.796	10/21	122
84	Chip Ganassi	Calumet Farm/A.J. Foyt	Cosworth V-8/161 cu.in.	March	206.104	25/22	121
60	Rich Vogler	Kentucky Fried Chicken/Patrick	Cosworth V-8/161 cu.in.	March	205.653	33/23	119
20	Don Whittington	STP Oil Treatment/Patrick	Cosworth V-8/161 cu.in.	March	210.991	6/24	97
30	Al Unser, Jr.	Domino's Pizza/Shierson	Cosworth V-8/161 cu.in.	Lola	209.215	11/25	91
22	Dick Simon	Break Free/Dick Simon Racing	Cosworth V-8/161 cu.in.	March	208.536	14/26	86
10	Bobby Rahal	Budweiser/Truesports	Cosworth V-8/161 cu.in.	March	211.818	3/27	84
14	A.J. Foyt	Copenhagen-Gilmore/A.J. Foyt	Cosworth V-8/161 cu.in.	March	205.782	21/28	62
97	Tony Bettenhausen	Skoal Bandit/Gurney-Curb	Cosworth V-8/161 cu.in.	Lola	204.824	29/29	31
37	Scott Brayton	Hardee's #37/Brayton	Buick V-6/208 cu.in.	March	212.354	2/30	19
55	Josele Garza	Schaefer/Machinists Union	Cosworth V-8/161 cu.in.	March	206.677	18/31	15
44	George Snider	A.J. Foyt Chevrolet/Foyt	Chevy V-6/205 cu.in.	March	205.455	28/32	13
6	Pancho Carter	Valvoline Buick Hawk/Galles	Buick V-6/206 cu.in.	March	212.583	1/33	6

every car was an Offy-powered roadster. Unless you're a real connoisseur, you probably can't even tell a Penske from a Lola.

MARCH VS LOLA VS PENSKE

That's understandable, because the late-Eighties Penske and Lola were both designed by Nigel Bennett. Indy cars rapidly became standardized in the Eighties. In 1979, for example, there was a great variety of American-built and English chassis at Indy from thirteen different manufacturers. The first Adrian Reynard-designed March didn't appear until 1981, and then, back in the pack. In 1982, Pancho Carter put a March into third. In 1983, March abandoned Formula One to concentrate on Indy. Tom Sneva won with a March. There were twenty Marches

on the grid. By 1984, only four cars at Indianapolis were *not* Marches. Even Roger Penske, who'd been building his own cars for years, bowed to the inevitable. In 1984, the new March/Cosworth designed by Gordon Coppuck ruled Indy more completely than even his seminal McLaren M16 of 1971. Indeed, the '84 March dominated the Speedway more completely than any machine since Harry Miller's 91 of the late-Twenties.

What made the March so good? Nothing you could put your finger on. The March was a teensy bit faster on the straights, a twitch quicker out of the corners. Most of all, it was available. Rather than fuss around building your own car—which might or might not be

competitive—it was so much easier and cheaper to spend $140,000 and simply buy a March.

The glory days of March didn't last very long. After Mario Andretti did so well in 1984 with his Lola, there were seven Lolas at the Speedway in 1985, including Mario's in second. This ratio between March and Lola continued for two years. At the time, the two cars were so equal that well-financed Indy teams ordered a car from each chassis-builder, figuring to race whichever was faster that year and keep the other as a back-up. This went on until 1987 when Nigel Bennett designed a new Lola that was decisively faster than the March. At the same time, March raised their price to $230,000 for a rolling chassis, compared to $190,000 for the Lola. The Lola was a better car for $40,000 less.

(above) Incredibly lucky Danny Sullivan spun in front of Mario Andretti at over 200 mph, waited for it to come around 360 degrees, caught it all up again and went on to win the 1985 Indy 500 in his March/Cosworth. Andretti was second.

1986

Winner: Bobby Rahal, March/Cosworth, 170.722 mph
Winner's Purse: $581,062
Total Purse: $4,001,050
Pace Car: Chuck Yeager, Chevrolet Corvette Roadster

Kevin Cogan was leading Bobby Rahal and Rick Mears under yellow just a few laps from the end. When the green flag came out again, Rahal literally out-dragged Cogan to the checker with Mears just a second behind. Rahal's popular car owner, Jim Trueman, died of cancer two weeks later.

Number	Driver	Sponsor/Team	Engine Type/Displacement	Chassis	Qualifying	Start/Finish	Laps
3	Bobby Rahal	Budweiser/Truesports	Cosworth V-8/161 cu.in.	March	213.550	4/1	200
7	Kevin Cogan	7 Eleven/Patrick Racing	Cosworth V-8/161 cu.in.	March	211.922	6/2	200
4	Rick Mears	Pennzoil Z-7/Penske	Cosworth V-8/161 cu.in.	March	216.828	1/3	200
5	Roberto Guerrero	True Value/Team Cotter	Cosworth V-8/161 cu.in.	March	211.576	8/4	200
30	Al Unser, Jr.	Domino's Pizza/Shierson	Cosworth V-8/161 cu.in.	Lola	211.533	9/5	199
18	Michael Andretti	STP-Lean Machine/Kraco	Cosworth V-8/161 cu.in.	March	214.522	3/6	199
20	Emerson Fittipaldi	Marlboro/Patrick Racing	Cosworth V-8/161 cu.in.	March	210.237	11/7	199
21	Johnny Rutherford	Vermont American/Morales	Cosworth V-8/161 cu.in.	March	210.220	12/8	198
1	Danny Sullivan	Miller American/Penske	Cosworth V-8/161 cu.in.	March	215.382	2/9	197
12	Randy Lanier	Arciero Racing/Frank Arciero	Cosworth V-8/161 cu.in.	March	209.964	13/10	195
24	Gary Bettenhausen	Vita Fresh-Timex/Leader Cards	Cosworth V-8/161 cu.in.	March	209.756	29/11	193
8	Geoff Brabham	Valvoline Spirit/Rick Galles	Cosworth V-8/161 cu.in.	Lola	207.082	20/12	193
22	Raul Boesel	Duracell/Dick Simon Racing	Cosworth V-8/161 cu.in.	Lola	211.202	22/13	192
23	Dick Simon	Duracell/Dick Simon Racing	Cosworth V-8/161 cu.in.	Lola	204.978	33/14	189
61	Arie Luyendyk	MCI-Race For Life/Groenevelt	Cosworth V-8/161 cu.in.	Lola	207.811	19/15	188
15	Pancho Carter	Coors Light/Rick Galles	Cosworth V-8/161 cu.in.	Lola	209.635	14/16	179
66	Ed Pimm	Skoal-Pace/Curb Motorsports	Cosworth V-8/161 cu.in.	March	210.874	10/17	168
55	Josele Garza	Schaefer/Machinists Union	Cosworth V-8/161 cu.in.	March	208.939	17/18	167
9	Roberto Moreno	Valvoline Spirit/Rick Galles	Cosworth V-8/161 cu.in.	Lola	209.469	32/19	158
81	Jacques Villeneuve	Living Well/Hemelgarn Racing	Cosworth V-8/161 cu.in.	March	209.397	15/20	154
59	Chip Ganassi	Bryant/Machinists Union	Cosworth V-8/161 cu.in.	March	207.590	25/21	151
11	Al Unser	Hertz/Penske	Chevy Indy V-8/161 cu.in.	Penske	212.295	5/22	149
25	Danny Ongais	GM Goodwrench/Ongais	Buick V-6/208 cu.in.	March	209.158	16/23	136
14	A.J. Foyt	Gilmore-Copenhagen/Foyt	Cosworth V-8/161 cu.in.	March	213.212	21/24	135
6	Rich Vogler	Byrd's Chicken/Morales	Cosworth V-8/161 cu.in.	March	209.089	27/25	132
84	George Snider	Calumet Farm/A.J. Foyt	Cosworth V-8/161 cu.in.	March	209.025	31/26	110
95	Johnny Parsons	Pizza Hut/Machinists Union	Cosworth V-8/161 cu.in.	March	207.894	28/27	100
16	Tony Bettenhausen	Bettenhausen Racing	Cosworth V-8/161 cu.in.	March	208.933	18/28	77
31	Jim Crawford	Team ASC	Buick V-6/208 cu.in.	March	208.911	26/29	70
71	Scott Brayton	Hardee's/Hemelgarn Racing	Buick V-6/208 cu.in.	March	208.079	23/30	69
42	Phil Krueger	Squirt-Moran/Leader Cards	Cosworth V-8/161 cu.in.	March	207.948	24/31	67
2	Mario Andretti	Newman-Haas	Cosworth V-8/161 cu.in.	Lola	212.300	30/32	19
33	Tom Sneva	Skoal Bandit/Curb Motorsports	Cosworth V-8/161 cu.in.	March	211.878	7/33	0

In 1987, twenty-eight of the thirty-three Indy starters were Gordon Coppuck-designed Marches. In 1988, only twelve were Marches, mostly updated cars from the year before. By 1989, there were only four Marches at Indy. For 1990, March signed exclusive contracts to build chassis only for Porsche and Alfa Romeo. Neither was particularly successful in a sea of Lolas and Penskes designed by Nigel Bennett.

Of course, most years this rivalry between March and Lola was of little importance because the checker flag was often waved at a car owned by Roger Penske. The most important Penske model of the decade is probably the PC-18, designed by Nigel Bennett after he left Lola. Think of it as an improved Lola T8700. Compared to the Lola and March, the Penske is just a little bit lower, just a little bit sleeker, just a little bit more adjustable in both wings and suspension. According to Emerson Fittipaldi, who won an Indy 500 and a National Championship in one of these Penskes, "The Penske is consistent and easy to adjust. That's why it wins."

COMPOSITES/EXOTICS

Along with ground effects and computers, the biggest advance in Indy cars during the Eighties was in the use of advanced materials. You won't find much cast iron or steel on a modern-day race car. A goodly portion of the $300,000 a 1991 Indy car costs goes to pay for materials. The monocoque chassis is mostly aircraft-quality aluminum honeycomb, bonded together with high-strength adhesives and rivets. This is strengthened with Kevlar and carbon fiber-reinforced composite.

The bodywork is pure carbon fiber composite. It's light and strong, but stunningly expensive. On most Indy

(left) Bobby Rahal and car owner Jim Trueman in Victory Lane, 1986. Already ill, Mr. Trueman would die from cancer two weeks later, so his first Indy win was especially poignant. His wife Barbara and crew chief Steve Horne have kept Truesports in racing, though Rahal left at the end of the 1988 season after they'd had two National Championships and eighteen Indy car victories together. (below) Bobby salutes the crowd as he crosses the finish line in his winning 1986 March/Cosworth.

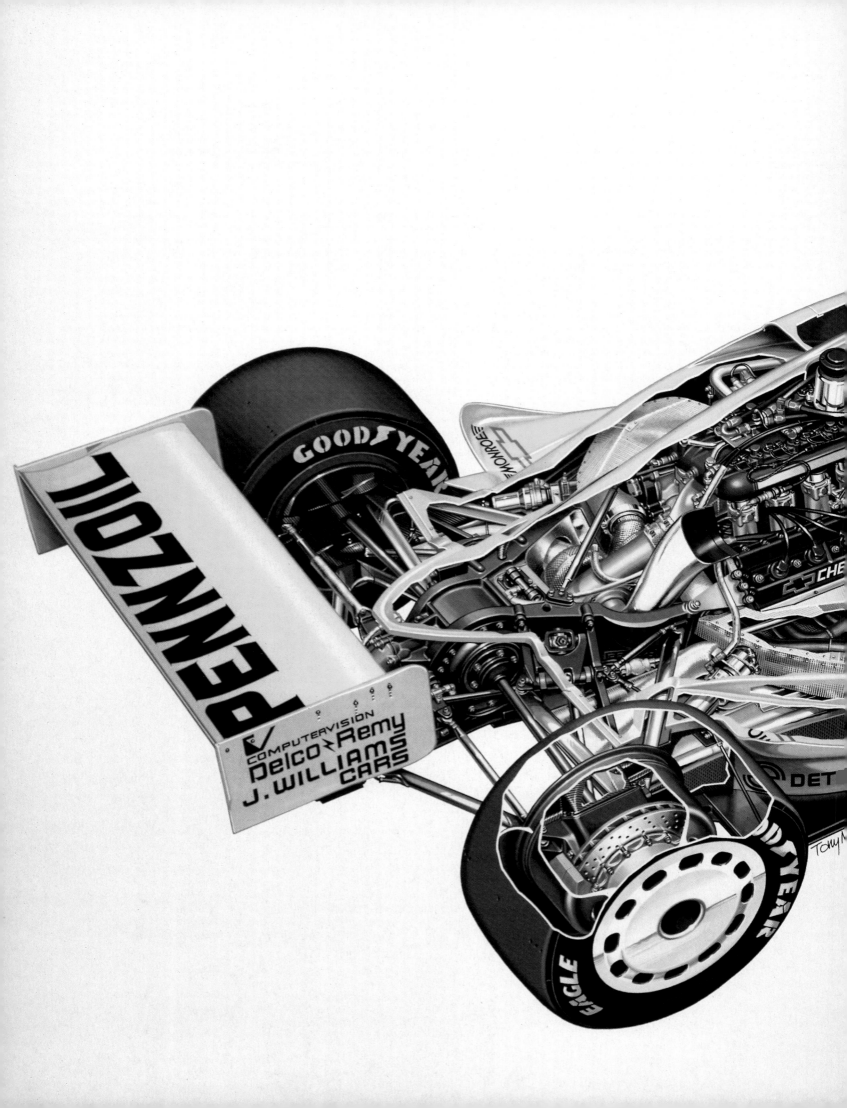

(left) Rick Mears' Penske/Chevrolet Indy V-8 finished fifth at Indy in 1990. Beneath the Pennzoil yellow paint lurks a sophisticated ground effects monocoque chassis made mostly of aluminum honeycomb strengthened with carbon fiber-reinforced resin. The bodywork is pure carbon fiber composite. Even from here you can see the incredibly intricate suspension, every part of which is adjustable.

1987

Winner: Al Unser, March/
Cosworth, 162.175 mph
Winner's Purse: $526,762
Total Purse: $4,490,375
Pace Car: Carroll Shelby,
Chrysler LeBaron

Originally without a ride, Big Al Unser teamed up with Roger Penske at the last minute and, in storybook fashion, motored through the pack to win his fourth 500. His car was a left-over March that Penske had been displaying in auto shows around the country.

Number	Driver	Sponsor/Team	Engine Type/Displacement	Chassis	Qualifying	Start/ Finish	Laps
25	Al Unser	Cummins-Holset/Penske	Cosworth V-8/160 cu.in.	March	207.423	20/1	200
4	Roberto Guerrero	True Value-STP/Granatelli	Cosworth V-8/161 cu.in.	March	210.680	5/2	200
12	Fabrizio Barbazza	Arciero Winery	Cosworth V-8/160 cu.in.	March	208.038	17/3	198
30	Al Unser, Jr.	Domino's Pizza/Shierson Racing	Cosworth V-8/161 cu.in.	March	206.752	22/4	196
56	Gary Bettenhausen	Genesee Beer/Gohr Distributing	Cosworth V-8/158 cu.in.	March	204.504	15/5	195
22	Dick Simon	Soundesign/Dick Simon Racing	Cosworth V-8/160 cu.in.	Lola	209.960	6/6	193
41	Stan Fox	Kerker Exhaust/A.J. Foyt	Cosworth V-8/160 cu.in.	March	204.518	26/7	192
11	Jeff MacPherson	Team MacPherson/Galles	Judd-Honda V-8/161 cu.in.	March	205.688	12/8	182
5	Mario Andretti	Hanna Auto/Newman-Haas	Chevy Indy V-8/161 cu.in.	Lola	215.370	1/9	180
16	Tony Bettenhausen	Nationwise/Bettenhausen	Cosworth V-8/160 cu.in.	March	203.892	27/10	171
21	Johnny Rutherford	Vermont American/Morales	Cosworth V-8/160 cu.in.	March	208.296	8/11	171
91	Scott Brayton	Amway-Livingwell/Hemelgarn	Cosworth V-8/161 cu.in.	March	205.647	13/12	167
3	Danny Sullivan	Miller American/Penske	Chevy Indy V-8/161 cu.in.	March	210.271	16/13	160
33	Tom Sneva	Skoal Bandit/Curb Motorsports	Buick V-6/208 cu.in.	March	207.254	21/14	143
77	Derek Daly	Scheid Tire/B.C. Pace Racing	Buick V-6/208 cu.in.	March	207.522	19/15	133
20	Emerson Fittipaldi	Marlboro/Patrick Racing Team	Chevy Indy V-8/161 cu.in.	March	205.584	33/16	131
55	Josele Garza	Bryant-Schaefer/Machinists	Cosworth V-8/160 cu.in.	March	205.692	25/17	129
71	Arie Luyendyk	Provimi Veal/Hemelgarn	Cosworth V-8/159 cu.in.	March	208.337	7/18	125
14	A.J. Foyt	Copenhagen-Gilmore/A.J. Foyt	Cosworth V-8/159 cu.in.	Lola	210.935	4/19	117
81	Rich Vogler	Kentucky Chicken/Hemelgarn	Buick V-6/208 cu.in.	March	205.887	11/20	109
98	Ed Pimm	Skoal Classic/Mike Curb	Cosworth V-8/160 cu.in.	March	203.284	30/21	109
2	Gordon Johncock	STP Oil/American Racing	Buick V-6/208 cu.in.	March	207.990	18/22	76
8	Rick Mears	Pennzoil Z-7/Penske	Chevy Indy V-8/161 cu.in.	March	211.467	3/23	75
15	Geoff Brabham	Team Valvoline/Galles Racing	Judd-Honda V-8/161 cu.in.	March	205.503	14/24	71
87	Steve Chassey	United Oil/Lydia Laughrey	Cosworth V-8/160 cu.in.	March	202.488	32/25	68
1	Bobby Rahal	Budweiser/Truesports	Cosworth V-8/160 cu.in.	Lola	213.316	2/26	57
29	Pancho Carter	Hardee's/Machinists Union	Cosworth V-8/160 cu.in.	March	205.154	29/27	45
44	Davy Jones	Skoal Classic/A.J. Foyt	Cosworth V-8/160 cu.in.	March	208.117	28/28	34
18	Michael Andretti	Kraco/STP	Cosworth V-8/160 cu.in.	March	206.129	9/29	28
23	Ludwig Heimrath, Jr.	Horton/MacKenzie/Dick Simon	Cosworth V-8/161 cu.in.	Lola	207.591	10/30	25
7	Kevin Cogan	Marlboro/Patrick Racing Team	Chevy Indy V-8/161 cu.in.	March	205.999	24/31	21
24	Randy Lewis	Toshiba-Altos/Leader Cards	Cosworth V-8/160 cu.in.	March	206.209	23/32	8
84	George Snider	Calumet Farm/A.J. Foyt	Chevy V-6/207 cu.in.	March	203.192	31/33	0

cars, the wings are still aluminum, though the entire underwing area is smoothly contoured composite.

Of course, the engine is almost totally aluminum and the wheels magnesium. But the suspension arms are mostly titanium these days, and virtually every ancilliary part like radiators, fuel cell enclosure and transaxle is aluminum. There are still steel gears in the transaxle. And the halfshafts and brake discs are still steel. But that's about all that's not made from a so-called "exotic" material, though certainly today's high-strength steels are really as exotic as any other alloy. Formula One cars are already using lightweight carbon fiber brake rotors. No doubt those will soon appear on Indy cars, too.

(left) Al Unser's storybook win almost didn't happen in 1987, when Josele Garza #55 spun in front of him on the first lap. Big Al #25 and Kevin Cogan #7 barely squeaked by. Unser was actually substituting for Danny Ongais who had crashed during practice. Al's car was a one-year-old March/Cosworth that Penske had been using as a display in auto shows. After starting back in twentieth, Al moved slowly through the field and finally zipped into the lead with just 18 laps to go. (below) Josele Garza in his March/Cosworth before the race. You can see how tightly the modern Indy car fits its driver.

As Dan Gurney puts it, "The biggest influence on modern race car design and construction has been the U.S. Space program." Indeed, most of these exotic materials—not to mention the way they are used—have come from either military aircraft or NASA. This is true of Formula One, too, of course. Ironically, some of the most advanced technology used to build European Grand Prix cars was paid for by American taxpayers.

SPORTY CAR TYPES

One of the most far-reaching effects of the mid-engine revolution during the Sixties was the introduction of a new type of driver to USAC racing. Traditionally, one got to Indianapolis by serving an apprenticeship that started with Midgets or Sprint cars on dirt ovals, then progressed through Champ cars on paved ovals until you were finally ready for the Big Leagues. In 1991, about the only CART/USAC drivers left who came up this way are A.J. Foyt, Mario Andretti, Al Unser, Sr., Tony and Gary Bettenhausen, Johnny Rutherford and Pancho Carter.

The typical Indy star of the Eighties and Nineties—drivers like Emerson Fittipaldi, Bobby Rahal, Al Unser, Jr., Michael Andretti, Arie Luyendyk, Danny Sullivan—started out racing go-karts, attended a road racing drivers school, then raced

BIG AL

"Racing is fun," says Al Unser. "I enjoy it. If you don't enjoy it, you won't last long. There are so many ups and downs. Racing is a very frustrating job. You get to the finish, and then you lose because some stupid part breaks. That's hard to deal with. But you have to put it behind you. If you pout over things, you'll be a very unhappy person. You always have to keep looking forward, not backward."

Big Al should know. He's been going through these cycles of ecstacy and despair, always looking forward, for over three decades. And, despite having some of the most humiliating lows any racer has ever had to suffer through, Al Unser is also the only racing driver who is ever mentioned in the same breath with A.J. Foyt and Mario Andretti.

Look at his amazing record. A.J. and Big Al are the only four-time winners of the Indianapolis 500, in Al's case over the impressively wide span of 1970, 1971, 1978 and 1987. He's also a three-time National Champion, in 1970, 1983 and 1985, behind only Mario's four Championships and A.J.'s seven. With 39 Indy car wins, he is also third behind Mario and A.J., and sixth in all-time earnings at $6,129,901 as of 1990. Big Al is also the only driver to win racing's "Triple Crown" of Indianapolis, Ontario and Pocono 500 mile races in the same season.

Back in 1957 when Al started racing Modifieds, he was best known around Albuquerque as the nephew of Louis Unser and the little brother of Jerry and Bobby. Like many little brothers, he didn't really care about beating anybody except his big brother Bobby. He started running USAC in 1964, then in 1965 went to Indianapolis for the first time. After the engine blew in the uncompetitive car Al was practicing, A.J. Foyt offered him his backup Lola/Ford. Al started in the last row, then slowly worked his way up to ninth at the end.

That was typical of Al's style. Bobby Unser is the original charger...exciting to watch, but all too often out early because the overstressed car couldn't keep up with him. Al is just the opposite...a master at gently bringing a fragile race car carefully through the field, almost unnoticed by the crowd, until he's suddenly leading the only lap that counts.

In 1966 he raced for Team Lotus, then in 1967 was hired by Texan John Mecom. Al was sec-

(above) The start of something big: Al Unser proudly sits in his first Indy 500 ride, the Lola/Ford he carefully brought into ninth place. From the left are his father Pop Unser, owner Bill Ansted, A.J. Foyt and master mechanic George Bignotti.
(right) Big Al in 1985, the year he won his third National Championship. Big Al and Little Al were racing for the title at the last race of the season in Miami. It was the first time in history that a father and son were in that position in any racing series. Big Al was only fourth at Miami, but Little Al was third to lose the title by one point. As Big Al said, "It was a no-lose situation for me. No matter which of us won, I'd be happy." Of course, deep in his heart, Big Al was happier that he was out front. He's a great father and a nice man, but he's still a *racer*.

ond on Memorial Day behind A.J. Foyt, but more importantly he once again teamed up with the legendary crew chief George Bignotti. Bignotti taught Al how to diagnose what his car was doing, then report back so the crew could get the proper set-up. Over the years, Al earned a reputation as the best development and set-up driver in Indy car racing.

After breaking his leg in a motorcycle accident, Al still finished second in the National Championship in 1969. In 1970, he and team owner Parnelli Jones picked up sponsorship from Johnny Lightning toys. Big Al went on a tear, winning ten out of eighteen USAC races, including Indy from the pole, and, of course, the National Championship. It was the greatest season in Indy car history. The streak continued in 1971, when Al finished first at the Speedway again (only the fourth driver to ever win back-to-back 500s), then won five of the first six USAC races. The streak ended as suddenly as it began, and the team failed to earn even one point for the whole second half of the 1971 season. It must have been pretty tough to "keep looking forward, not backward" that year.

For the next few years, Al's luck deserted him, and he just about abandoned Indy cars in favor of Formula 5000 and other lesser series. Then in 1976 Parnelli gave up on Formula One and Al drove the first Cosworth-powered car in USAC, a modified Parnelli Grand Prix car. He was seventh, then third the next year and second in the USAC Championship. In 1978, he won the 500 and was second in the National Championship. Then came another streak when Al couldn't do anything right.

Those hard times ended in 1983, when he joined Penske Racing. He won his second National Championship and was second at Indy, too. The next year he was third at Indy, then in 1985 won his third National Championship by one point...over Al Unser, Jr. "It was the most special season of my life," says Al. "For my boy to do what he did, and for the two of us to do what we did...well, very few fathers get to experience that."

Ironically, the defending National Champion was without a season ride in 1986 and '87, though he did win his fourth Indy in 1987, subbing for Danny Ongais. The next year, he was in the famous all-Penske front row at Indy and finished third. He qualified on the front row again in 1989, proof positive that even in his fifties and running only a limited schedule, Big Al Unser is still one of the best drivers in Indy car racing. And the proudest father you'd ever want to meet, now that Little Al has won his own National Championship in 1990. Going into its fifth decade, the Unser Dynasty is still alive and well. And still having fun. ■

(left) Big Al, his wife and mother, the famous Mom Unser, who started the annual Unser Green Chili Feast before the 500. Al has just won in 1970.
(below) Big Al's membership medallion from the Auto Racing's Hall of Fame.
(bottom) Al Unser becomes only the second man to win four Indianapolis 500s, as he salutes the crowd's standing ovation in 1987. His March/Cosworth was a Penske showcar hurriedly prepared after Danny Ongais crashed their intended race car.

AL UNSER

1988

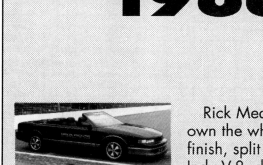

**Winner: Rick Mears,
Penske/Chevy Indy,
144.809 mph
Winner's Purse: $809,853
Total Purse: $5,025,400
Pace Car: Chuck Yeager,
Oldsmobile Cutlass
Supreme**

Rick Mears, Danny Sullivan and Al Unser were the first teammates ever to own the whole front row of the grid. Mears and Unser were still in front at the finish, split by hard-charging Emerson Fittipaldi. All three had the new Chevy Indy V-8, decidedly faster than the Cosworth that had ruled Indy for years.

Number	Driver	Sponsor/Team	Engine Type/Displacement	Chassis	Qualifying	Start/Finish	Laps
5	Rick Mears	Pennzoil Z-7/Penske	Chevy Indy V-8/161 cu.in.	Penske	219.198	1/1	200
20	Emerson Fittipaldi	Marlboro/Patrick Racing	Chevy Indy V-8/161 cu.in.	March	212.512	8/2	200
1	Al Unser	Hertz/Penske	Chevy Indy V-8/161 cu.in.	Penske	215.270	3/3	199
18	Michael Andretti	Kraco Enterprises	Cosworth V-8/161 cu.in.	March	210.183	10/4	199
4	Bobby Rahal	Budweiser/Truesports	Judd V-8/159 cu.in.	Lola	208.526	19/5	199
15	Jim Crawford	Mac Tools/Kenny Bernstein	Buick V-6/208 cu.in.	Lola	210.564	18/6	198
30	Raul Boesel	Domino's Pizza/Shierson	Cosworth V-8/161 cu.in.	Lola	211.058	20/7	198
97	Phil Krueger	CNC System Sales/Baker	Cosworth V-8/161 cu.in.	March	208.212	15/8	196
22	Dick Simon	Uniden-Soundesign/Dick Simon	Cosworth V-8/161 cu.in.	Lola	207.555	16/9	196
7	Arie Luyendyk	Provimi Veal/Dick Simon	Cosworth V-8/160 cu.in.	Lola	213.611	6/10	196
11	Kevin Cogan	Schaefer-Playboy/Machinists	Cosworth V-8/161 cu.in.	March	209.552	13/11	195
21	Howdy Holmes	Jiffy Mixes/Alex Morales	Cosworth V-8/160 cu.in.	March	206.970	33/12	192
3	Al Unser, Jr.	Team Valvoline/Galles	Chevy Indy V-8/161 cu.in.	March	214.186	5/13	180
56	Billy Vukovich III	Genesee Beer/Gohr	Cosworth V-8/161 cu.in.	March	208.545	23/14	179
24	Randy Lewis	Toshiba-Oracle/Leader Cards	Cosworth V-8/161 cu.in.	Lola	209.774	11/15	175
48	Rocky Moran	Skoal Classic/A.J. Foyt	Cosworth V-8/161 cu.in.	March	207.181	28/16	159
29	Rich Vogler	Byrd's Cafeteria/J.B.-Machinists	Cosworth V-8/161 cu.in.	March	207.126	32/17	159
92	Dominic Dobson	Moore-Columbia/Dobson	Cosworth V-8/161 cu.in.	Lola	210.096	21/18	145
23	Tero Palmroth	Bronson-Neste/Dick Simon	Cosworth V-8/160 cu.in.	Lola	208.001	25/19	144
6	Mario Andretti	Amoco/Kmart/Newman-Haas	Chevy Indy V-8/161 cu.in.	Lola	214.692	4/20	118
98	John Andretti	Skoal Bandit/Mike Curb	Cosworth V-8/161 cu.in.	Lola	207.894	27/21	114
17	Johnny Rutherford	Mac Tools/Kenny Bernstein	Buick V-6/208 cu.in.	Lola	208.442	30/22	107
9	Danny Sullivan	Miller High Life/Penske Racing	Chevy Indy V-8/161 cu.in.	Penske	216.214	2/23	101
35	Steve Chassey	Kasle Recycling/Gary Trout	Cosworth V-8/161 cu.in.	March	207.951	26/24	73
71	Ludwig Heimrath, Jr.	MacKenzie Funds/Hemelgarn	Cosworth V-8/161 cu.in.	Lola	207.215	31/25	59
14	A.J. Foyt	Copenhagen-Gilmore/Foyt	Cosworth V-8/161 cu.in.	Lola	209.696	22/26	54
81	Tom Sneva	Pizza Hut/WRTV/Hemelgarn	Judd V-8/159 cu.in.	Lola	208.659	14/27	32
8	Teo Fabi	Quaker State/Porsche	Porsche V-8/161 cu.in.	March	207.244	17/28	30
10	Derek Daly	Raynor Garage Doors	Cosworth V-8/161 cu.in.	Lola	212.295	9/29	18
84	Stan Fox	Calumet Farm/A.J. Foyt	Chevy V-6/207 cu.in.	March	208.578	29/30	2
91	Scott Brayton	Amway Spirit/Hemelgarn	Buick V-6/208 cu.in.	Lola	212.624	7/31	0
2	Roberto Guerrero	STP-Dianetics/Vince Granatelli	Cosworth V-8/161 cu.in.	Lola	209.633	12/32	0
16	Tony Bettenhausen	Sony-Hardee's/Bettenhausen	Cosworth V-8/161 cu.in.	Lola	208.342	24/33	0

Formula Ford, Super Vee and even Formula One before graduating to the Indianapolis Motor Speedway.

There are two reasons for this. One, the modern Indy car is much more like a road racing Formula car than it is like a Midget or Champ car. Logically enough, it makes sense to learn your trade in cars at least somewhat similar to what you'll be driving at Indy. And that means Super Vee or ARS.

Second, and perhaps more importantly, Indy car racing has changed almost out of recognition since the Sixties and Seventies. Instead of a National Championship based on the Indianapolis 500, various races on 1 mile paved ovals and a handful of Champ car races on the dirt, today's PPG Indy car World Series consists of

COMPUTERS

The biggest change in Indy cars during the Eighties was the introduction of sophisticated onboard computers to control and measure most engine functions. There are three basic computer systems on a typical Indy car from the era of 1985-1991. The simplest one is the ignition system. Ignition timing is taken off the crankshaft by a computer readout—a "crank-trigger ignition" in engineerese—which is much more accurate than using a distributor.

Next in complexity is the electronic fuel-injection system. This is a digitally-controlled, sequential-port injection system not all that different from the ones used on many new passenger cars. The computer controls the timing of the fuel-injection and also the pulse-width of the injection. It can even compensate for a drop in fuel pressure. The amount of fuel sprayed into the cylinders is controlled by the microprocessor and depends on engine speed, engine timing, throttle position, manifold pressure, coolant temperature and turbocharger air temperature. All these parameters are continuously monitored as the computer releases the proper amount of fuel for each cylinder.

Designing these fuel systems is diabolically difficult, mostly because of the tremendous volume and dynamic range that they must cover at Indy. The range is from about 5 lbs/hr of fuel at idle to 1000 lbs/hr at 240 mph. The hardest thing for the computer to handle, surprisingly enough, is a pit stop. The car is roaring flat-out at over 230 mph, then the engine is suddenly idled. Seconds later it is accelerated as fast as it will go to 230 mph. The poor engine management computer is humming away flat-out, trying to keep up.

Finally, every modern Indy car uses a "Black Box." The Black Box is a $30,000 data-logger that stores and displays information from thirty-two or even sixty-four onboard sensors. In Indy car racing, the Black Box is down-loaded into a portable computer at every pit stop, then the data is analyzed by the crew chief, aerodynamicist and engineer. What they learn is then used to tune the car at the next pit stop.

This same type of Black Box is used by Formula One and Group C teams in Europe, and by adding a $100,000 servo unit, it has the capability of on-board, interactive telemetry. The engine in Ayrton Senna's Honda-powered McLaren, for example, is actually tuned during every Formula One race by Honda engineers in Japan!

Engine data is transmitted via satellite directly from the car as it circles a track in Europe. The engineers decide whether the computer should be reprogrammed for best performance, then make their changes, which are instantly sent via satellite back to the car. Interactive telemetry should be on Indy cars within a few years, allowing engineers in the pits to change not only engine characteristics, but also suspension and aerodynamic parameters, too. That will open up a whole new era at Indy. ■

(above) The digital dash of Arie Luyendyk's 1990 winner. The Black Box not only controls his Chevrolet Indy V-8, but displays and remembers a wide range of information, including turbo boost pressure, fuel flow and, of course, rpm. Notice that the tachometer is essentially unreadable below 9000 rpm, with the important segment of the scale between 10,000 and 13,000 rpm! The button on the detachable steering wheel is the "push-to-talk" for his two-way radio. The big orange warning light blinks on in case of a sudden loss of engine oil pressure.

(below) Emerson Fittipaldi in his Penske/Chevrolet Indy V-8 on his way to winning the 1989 Indy 500. He joined Jimmy Clark, Graham Hill and Mario Andretti as the only winners of both the Formula One World Championship and the Indy 500. By going on to dominate and win the PPG/CART National Championship, he also became only the second driver in history—Mario is the other—to win both a National Championship and the World Championship.

two 500 mile races, one on the 2.5-mile oval at Indianapolis and one on the 2.0-mile oval of Michigan International Speedway, three races on short 1-mile paved ovals—Phoenix, Milwaukee and Nazareth—four races on permanent road courses—Portland, Mid-Ohio, Road America and Laguna Seca—and seven races on temporary road courses. These are created out of city streets in downtown Long Beach, Detroit, Denver and Vancouver, out of parks and parking lots at Toronto and the Meadowlands, out of airport runways at Cleveland. Sliding a Midget around Ascot isn't exactly the proper training for this kind of road racing.

TURBULENCE

During the Eighties, not only were Indy cars driven by a new type of driver at a new type of track, but the actual racing itself was different, too. A conventional racing car punches a hole through the air, leaving a low-pressure area behind it. If you are driving a second racing car, you can tuck your machine right behind the leading car and this low-pressure area will pull you along. It's just like sitting behind a big truck on the highway; you go just as fast while using lower rpms and thus less gas. Racers call this *drafting*, and NASCAR stars have refined it to an art. Even better, drafting makes both cars go faster, so when the second car pulls out to pass, the first car slows down while the follower sling-shots past. That's why so many NASCAR races are won in the last corner, by the guy who's been second.

When you use a ground effects chassis, however, funny things begin to happen. Instead of punching a whole through the air, the Indy cars of the Eighties slip through the air. Instead of forming a nice, stable low-pressure area behind the car, the ground effects underwings create a tremendous amount of turbulence that boils around behind the car. Instead of making a useful draft for the following car, this turbulence will literally throw the second car into the wall. So you'll rarely see cars

running nose to tail at Indy anymore. The turbulence from the first car destroys the ground effects of the following car, making it almost impossible to handle. Since engine cooling depends on this air flow, too, the following car will often overheat as well. That's why there's usually a couple of car lengths between racers when they head down the Indy straight. They're trying to stay out of each other's turbulence. You can't learn that racing Midgets at Ascot, either.

FISA AND FOCA AND CART

New drivers, new courses, new techniques—much of the change in modern-day Indy car racing is because of CART. The late-Seventies was a time of terrific upheaval in almost every sport. In baseball, for example, there was a huge wrangle which led to the establishment of "free agent" status. In 1978, all the change going on around them spurred the FIA to create a new governing body for international racing, called the *Federation Internationale du Sport Automobile.* FISA replaced the CSI and was headed by a French journalist named Jean-Marie Balestre, who still runs FISA today. At the same time, the various Formula One teams founded the Formula One Constructors Association. FOCA is still run by former Brabham team owner Bernie Ecclestone.

Inspired by FOCA, in 1978 Roger Penske and Pat Patrick founded Championship Auto Racing Teams as an organization of Indy car owners. They wanted USAC to give the team owners more control over Indy car rules much as FOCA has given Formula One team owners more power. As it turned out, USAC discontinued sanctioning Indy car racing except the Indy 500, while CART took over the job of running the National Championship. CART ran its first race at Phoenix in March of 1979 and today is in charge of the PPG Indy Car World Series, which includes the Indianapolis 500.

Fittipaldi Firsts: In 1989, Emerson became the first CART driver to win more than $2 million for a single season and the first Indy 500 winner to earn more than $1 million, the first foreign driver to win the National Championship since Dario Resta in 1916 and the first foreigner since Graham Hill in 1966 to win at Indianapolis. In 1990, he led the first 92 laps of the Indy 500...the previous record was 81 laps, by Frank Lockhart in 1927.

1989

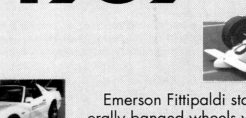

Winner: Emerson Fittipaldi, Penske/Chevy Indy, 167.581 mph
Winner's Purse: $1,001,640
Total Purse: $5,723,725
Pace Car: Bobby Unser, Pontiac Trans Am

Emerson Fittipaldi started on the front row, led 158 out of 198 laps, then literally banged wheels with challenger Al Unser, Jr., with two laps to go. "Little Al" spun out, Emmo held on to win the first million-dollar Indy purse and, at the end of the season, the CART PPG/Indy Car World Series.

Number	Driver	Sponsor/Team	Engine Type/Displacement	Chassis	Qualifying	Start/Finish	Laps
20	Emerson Fittipaldi	Marlboro/Patrick Racing	Chevy Indy V-8/160 cu.in.	Penske	222.329	3/1	200
2	Al Unser, Jr.	Valvoline-Stroh/Galles	Chevy Indy V-8/161 cu.in.	Lola	218.642	8/2	198
30	Raul Boesel	Domino's Pizza/Shierson	Judd V-8/159 cu.in.	Lola	218.288	9/3	194
5	Mario Andretti	Kmart/Newman-Haas	Chevy Indy V-8/161 cu.in.	Lola	220.486	5/4	193
14	A.J. Foyt	Copenhagen-Gilmore/Foyt	Cosworth V-8/161 cu.in.	Lola	217.136	10/5	193
22	Scott Brayton	Amway-Speedway/Simon	Buick V-6/208 cu.in.	Lola	220.459	6/6	193
50	Davy Jones	Euromotorsport Uno/A. Ferrari	Cosworth V-8/160 cu.in.	Lola	214.279	31/7	192
29	Rich Vogler	Byrd's Cafeteria-Bryant/Byrd	Cosworth V-8/160 cu.in.	March	213.239	33/8	192
69	Bernard Jourdain	Corona-Monarch/Andale	Cosworth V-8/160 cu.in.	Lola	213.105	20/9	191
3	Scott Pruett	Budweiser/Truesports	Judd V-8/158 cu.in.	Lola	213.955	17/10	190
65	John Jones	Labatts-Protofab	Cosworth V-8/161 cu.in.	Lola	214.028	25/11	189
81	Billy Vukovich III	Consani-Siera/Hemelgarn	Judd V-8/159 cu.in.	Lola	216.698	30/12	186
71	Ludwig Heimrath, Jr.	MacKenzie/Hemelgarn	Judd V-8/159 cu.in.	Lola	213.878	18/13	185
33	Rocky Moran	Skoal Bandit/A.J. Foyt	Cosworth V-8/161 cu.in.	March	214.212	28/14	181
10	Derek Daly	Raynor Garage Doors	Judd V-8/160 cu.in.	Lola	214.237	24/15	167
56	Tero Palmroth	Neste-Rotator-Nanso/Gohr	Cosworth V-8/161 cu.in.	Lola	214.203	16/16	165
6	Michael Andretti	Kmart/Newman-Haas	Chevy Indy V-8/161 cu.in.	Lola	218.774	21/17	163
86	Dominic Dobson	Texaco Havoline Star/Bayside	Cosworth V-8/161 cu.in.	Lola	213.590	29/18	161
15	Jim Crawford	Mac Tools-Planters/Bernstein	Buick V-6/208 cu.in.	Lola	221.450	4/19	135
12	Didier Theys	Arciero Wines	Cosworth V-8/161 cu.in.	Penske	213.120	19/20	131
9	Arie Luyendyk	Provimi/Dutch Boy/Simon	Cosworth V-8/161 cu.in.	Lola	214.883	15/21	123
24	Pancho Carter	Hardee's/Leader Card Racers	Cosworth V-8/160 cu.in.	Lola	214.067	32/22	121
4	Rick Mears	Pennzoil Z-7/Penske	Chevy Indy V-8/161 cu.in.	Penske	223.885	1/23	113
25	Al Unser	Marlboro/Penske	Chevy Indy V-8/160 cu.in.	Penske	223.471	2/24	68
70	John Andretti	Tuneup Masters/Granatelli	Buick V-6/208 cu.in.	Lola	215.611	12/25	61
18	Bobby Rahal	Kraco Racing Team	Cosworth V-8/161 cu.in.	Lola	219.530	7/26	58
7	Tom Sneva	STP/Vince Granatelli	Buick V-6/208 cu.in.	Lola	218.396	22/27	55
1	Danny Sullivan	Miller High Life/Penske	Chevy Indy V-8/161 cu.in.	Penske	216.027	26/28	41
28	Randy Lewis	Toshiba-Oracle/TEAMKAR	Cosworth V-8/160 cu.in.	Lola	214.212	11/29	24
8	Teo Fabi	Quaker State/Porsche	Porsche V-8/159 cu.in.	March	215.564	13/30	23
91	Gordon Johncock	STP-Pizza Hut/Hemelgarn	Buick V-6/208 cu.in.	Lola	215.072	23/31	19
11	Kevin Cogan	Schaefer-Playboy/Machinists	Cosworth V-8/161 cu.in.	March	214.569	27/32	2
99	Gary Bettenhausen	ATEC Environmental/Mann	Buick V-6/208 cu.in.	Lola	215.230	14/33	0

BIG MONEY

Since 1911, the Indianapolis Motor Speedway has always offered the biggest purse in motor sports. But since World War II, the total Indianapolis 500 purse has grown exponentially. From $115,450 in 1946, it went to $200,000 in 1950, $400,000 in 1961, $1 million in 1970, $2 million in 1982, $3 million in 1985, $4 million in 1986, $5 million in 1988 and $6 million in 1990. Emerson Fittipaldi, the 1989 winner, was the first man in history to win more than $1 million for one motor race. That's more than the total purse just twenty years before. Even though there are sixteen races in the National Championship, the Indy 500 purse

THE SOPHISTICATE

Probably the most cultured and sophisticated man in racing, Brazilian Emerson Fittipaldi has lived on three continents, speaks five languages and is almost intimidatingly bright and articulate. He's the son of famous racing journalist Wilson Fittipaldi; his brother Wilson, Jr., was also a Formula One driver in the Seventies. But it is Emerson who was the great success. You forget how young he was, and how good. Emerson left Brazil at 23 to race Formula Ford in Europe. A year later he was on the Lotus Formula One team, and in 1972 he won his first World Championship. He remains the youngest World Champion ever. He was second in 1973 for Lotus, World Champion again in 1974 for McLaren. He spent the rest of that decade and millions of cruzados trying to build his own Formula One cars. He finally retired in disgust in 1981.

Fittipaldi came to America in 1984 to start a new career. His first season was mixed while he learned the Indy car ropes. Then he teamed up with Pat Patrick. In 1985, he led the Indy 500 before fading and finished sixth in the PPG Indy Car World Series. The next year he was seventh at Indy and in the Championship, winning over $1 million. In 1987 and '88, he won races and lots of cash, including a second at Indy in 1988. It was a classic example of a highly intelligent and mature racing driver slowly learning a new skill.

It all came together in 1989, when Emmo won at Indy after banging wheels with Little Al Unser, then dominated the season to win the National Championship. His streak continued in 1990 after he switched to Penske Racing. He started on the pole and controlled the Indy 500 almost the whole way, only to be passed near the end by Arie Luyendyk and Bobby Rahal. He then finished fifth in the Championship. There is nobody else quite like Emmo, the thinking man's racing driver. As he says, "You can burn out on this sport. You must remember that racing is only part of life. Then you have the motivation to continue in racing for a long time. Otherwise, not so long." ■

(below) Emerson Fittipaldi, his 1989 Penske/Chevrolet Indy V-8 and over $1 million in cash...the first time time the Indy 500 winner took home over a million. In just six years, Emmo won $6,538,892, making him fifth in all-time Indy car earnings as of 1990. Unlike most racing drivers, Fittipaldi has had three distinct careers...as a Formula One champion, as a Grand Prix car constructor and team manager/driver, and as an Indy car driver. Unlike someone like Mario Andretti, Emerson didn't try to compete in different series simultaneously, but at different times in his career. Off the track, he designs Fittipaldi wheels and powerboats, owns a Mercedes-Benz dealership and a 200,000, acre orange plantation in Brazil.

1990

Winner: Arie Luyendyk, Lola/Chevy Indy, 185.981 mph (current track record)
Winner's Purse: $1,090,940
Total Purse: $6,325,803
Pace Car: Jim Perkins, Chevrolet Beretta Convertible

For the second year in a row, Emerson Fittipaldi dominated the race—the first qualifying average of over 225 mph and leader of the majority of laps—until his tires began to blister and he was forced to make an extra pit stop. Bobby Rahal passed, then Arie Luyendyk passed Rahal for the win.

Number	Driver	Sponsor/Team	Engine Type/Displacement	Chassis	Qualifying	Start/Finish	Laps
30	Arie Luyendyk	Domino's Pizza/Shierson	Chevy Indy V-8/160 cu.in.	Lola	223.304	3/1	200
18	Bobby Rahal	STP-Kraco/Galles-Kraco	Chevy Indy V-8/161 cu.in.	Lola	222.694	4/2	200
1	Emerson Fittipaldi	Marlboro/Penske	Chevy Indy V-8/160 cu.in.	Penske	225.301	1/3	200
5	Al Unser, Jr.	Valvoline/Galles-Kraco	Chevy Indy V-8/161 cu.in.	Lola	220.920	7/4	199
2	Rick Mears	Pennzoil Z-7/Penske	Chevy Indy V-8/160 cu.in.	Penske	224.215	2/5	198
14	A.J. Foyt	Copenhagen-Calumet/Foyt	Chevy Indy V-8/161 cu.in.	Lola	220.425	8/6	194
22	Scott Brayton	Amway-Speedway/Simon	Cosworth V-8/160 cu.in.	Lola	215.028	26/7	194
25	Eddie Cheever	Target Stores/Ganassi Racing	Chevy Indy V-8/161 cu.in.	Penske	217.926	14/8	193
11	Kevin Cogan	Tuneup Masters/Granatelli	Buick V-8/208 cu.in.	Penske	217.738	15/9	191
28	Scott Goodyear	MacKenzie-O'Donnell/Shierson	Judd V-8/158 cu.in.	Lola	213.622	21/10	191
70	Didier Theys	Tuneup Masters-RCA/Granatelli	Buick V-8/208 cu.in.	Penske	214.033	20/11	190
23	Tero Palmroth	Hoechst-Neste/Simon	Cosworth V-8/160 cu.in.	Lola	217.423	16/12	188
40	Al Unser	Miller High Life/Patrick Racing	Alfa Romeo V-8/160 cu.in.	March	212.087	30/13	186
12	Randy Lewis	AMP-Oracle-Samsung/Arciero	Buick V-6/208 cu.in.	Penske	218.412	12/14	186
15	Jim Crawford	Glidden Paints/Menard	Buick V-6/208 cu.in.	Lola	212.200	29/15	183
93	John Paul, Jr.	ATEC Environmental/Mann	Buck V-6/208 cu.in.	Lola	214.411	32/16	176
39	Dean Hall	(insight)/Dale Coyne Racing	Cosworth V-8/161 cu.in.	Lola	216.975	24/17	165
4	Teo Fabi	Foster's-Quaker State/Porsche	Porsche V-8/159 cu.in.	March	220.022	23/18	162
21	Geoff Brabham	Mac Tools/Truesports	Judd V-8/158 cu.in.	Lola	216.580	19/19	161
3	Michael Andretti	Kmart-Havoline/Newman-Haas	Chevy Indy V-8/161 cu.in.	Lola	222.055	5/20	146
41	John Andretti	Foster's-Quaker State/Porsche	Porsche V-8/159 cu.in.	March	219.484	10/21	136
86	Dominic Dobson	Texaco-Havoline Star/Leven	Cosworth V-8/160 cu.in.	Lola	219.230	11/22	129
20	Roberto Guerrero	Miller Genuine Draft/Patrick	Alfa Romeo V-8/160 cu.in.	March	212.652	28/23	118
81	Billy Vukovich III	Hemelgarn Racing	Buick V-6/208 cu.in.	Lola	211.389	31/24	102
56	Rocky Moran	Gohr-Glidden/Gohr Racing	Buick V-6/208 cu.in.	Lola	211.076	33/25	88
16	Tony Bettenhausen	AMAX/Bettenhausen	Buick V-6/208 cu.in.	Lola	218.368	13/26	76
6	Mario Andretti	Kmart-Havoline/Newman-Haas	Chevy Indy V-8/161 cu.in.	Lola	222.025	6/27	60
19	Raul Boesel	Budweiser/Truesports	Judd V-8/159 cu.in.	Lola	217.381	17/28	60
29	Pancho Carter	Hardee's-Machinists/Leader	Cosworth V-8/160 cu.in.	Lola	213.156	22/29	59
9	Tom Sneva	RCA/Vince Granatelli Racing	Buick V-6/208 cu.in.	Penske	216.142	25/30	48
51	Gary Bettenhausen	Glidden Paints/Menard	Buick V-6/208 cu.in.	Lola	217.264	18/31	39
7	Danny Sullivan	Marlboro/Penske	Chevy Indy V-8/160 cu.in.	Penske	220.310	9/32	19
97	Stan Fox	Miyano-CNC/Baker	Buick V-6/208 cu.in.	Lola	213.812	27/33	10

represents one-third of the $20 million total offered in 1991. As ever, the Indianapolis 500 is the biggest, richest, most important motor race in the world.

But Indy is more than a chance to win a lot of money, more than just another stop on the National Championship, more than a way to get your name in the record books, more than a pleasant way to spend the month of May. After seventy-five years, it has taken on a life, a momentum, an importance all its own. The Super Bowl? The Kentucky Derby? The World Series? You must be kidding. No other sporting event even comes close to the excitement, the wonder, the courage of watching thirty-three men do what they do better than anyone else in the world. Constantly changing, yet ever the same, the 500 is very special, indeed. *Indy.*

THE MONTH OF MAY

"You walk through the tunnel," says Emerson Fittipaldi, "and there are 500,000 people all around you. And the whole place is shaking. There is so much energy. The last five minutes before the start of the Indianapolis 500, everyone is so tense, the whole place is vibrating. There is nothing else like it in the whole world.

"If you are a driver, you have been here for the whole month of May, and you have gone to the track every day. And you have run, and run and run. And you go back to your garage, and then the next day you run, and run and run. And the next day, too.

"Every day there is more pressure, until you think you will burst. By race day, every person inside the race track feels this terrible pressure and is tense to bursting. It is incredible."

The pressure comes from everywhere, building and building for almost a year. Nearly every team starts planning for the 500 in June, as soon as the previous year's race is behind them. Barring an unexpected technological breakthrough, they can pretty much predict how fast they'll have to go to be competitive the following year.

Racers don't think in miles per hour; their cars don't even have speedometers. They think in terms of revolutions-per-minute and hundredths of a second. Ask a racer how fast he's going, and he'll reply something like "twelve-five into three" or "forty point seven."

What he means by the first is that his engine is turning 12,500 rpm at the fastest point on the Speedway. If

(below) Getting ready for the fray: Roberto Guerrero is buckled into his March/Alfa before the 1990 Indy 500.

PROFIT AND LOSS

As Indy car team owner Rick Galles puts it, "This is not a game. This is not a hobby. We don't spend money by the bucket, but by the wheelbarrow."

How many wheelbarrows?

Well, Galles and his partner Maurice Kraines of Galles/Kraco Racing own the cars driven by teammates Bobby Rahal and Al Unser, Jr. In 1990, Bobby was second at Indy, Little Al fourth. Unser, of course, then went on to win the 1990 PPG Indy Car World Series, with Bobby fourth. That made Galles/Kraco the most successful Indy car team of the year. Here's a condensation of their 1990 P&L statement, information that's normally as hush-hush as any CIA budget. And at $12-million a year, nearly as big.

CAPITAL INVESTMENT

5 Lola T9000 race cars, supplied without engine, but with "short track" bodywork for low-speed ovals and road courses: $230,000 each. Total: $1,150,000.

5 sets of "Indy kit" bodywork for use on high-speed ovals: $20,000 each. Total: $100,000.

20 Chevrolet Indy V-8 engines, not including computers: $100,000 each. Total: $2,000,000.

24 sets of alloy wheels (4 wheels to a set): $1400 each set. Total: $33,600.

5 data acquisition/engine control computers: $10,000 each. Total: $50,000.

3 on-board telemetry units: $30,000 each. Total: $90,000.

3 tractor-trailer "semis"...one for each driver's cars, one for testing: $180,000 each. Total: $540,000.

1 Newell motorcoach and adjacent tent used at the races for entertaining clients: $400,000.

1 set of machine tools at the team's permanent Albuquerque, New Mexico shop, additional tools for shops in the semis that are brought to the races: $200,000.

(Each mechanic supplies his own hand tools, an average of about $10,000 per mechanic.)

2 pickup trucks for local use: $15,000 each. Total: $30,000.

Miscellaneous gas carts, bottle carts, timing and scoring stands, fuel rigs, etc. Total: $15,000.

10 team uniforms per crew member times 32 crew members at the track: $100 each. Total: $32,000.

Miscellaneous team uniforms, shop uniforms, jackets, hats, rain suits, etc.: $15,000.

3 fireproof driving outfits—suit, gloves, shoes, underwear—times 2 drivers: $1000 each. Total $6000.

3 full-face helmets for drivers times 2 drivers: $900 each. Total: $5400.

5 fireproof Nomex outfits—suit, gloves, shoes—times 2 pit crews: $500 each. Total: $5000.

2 full-face helmets for refueling crew times 2 crews: $200 each. Total: $800.

TOTAL CAPITAL INVESTMENT: $4,672,800.

EXPENDITURES DURING THE SEASON

50,000 square foot race shop plus 6000 square foot paint shop in Albuquerque, New Mexico, leased from local racing enthusiasts at $1 per square foot: $56,000.

Race entry fees, $8000 each times 5 cars at the Indy 500, approximately $4000 at each other race times 15 races: $100,000.

Race credentials and miscellaneous fees, 32 people times 16 races times $50 each: $25,600.

Replacement of worn and damaged body and chassis parts (suspension arms, for example, are replaced every 800 miles, gearboxes are rebuilt after every race, body parts are stripped and repainted after every race): average $25,000 per car per race times two cars times 16 races. Total: $800,000.

45 engine rebuilds (engines are rebuilt every 500 miles): $15,000 to $30,000 each depending on wear and damage, average $25,000 each. Total: $1,125,000.

4 sets of Goodyear tires per car per race weekend times two cars times 16 race weekends: $1000 each set (a fraction of Goodyear's actual cost). Total: $128,000.

2 sets of Goodyear tires per test day times 30 test days per season: $1000 each set. Total: $60,000.

Replacement of sponsor decals before each race: $2000 per car times 16 races. Total: $64,000.

Dry cleaning of driver and crew uniforms and fireproof suits at $7 each use: $15,000 per season.

Meals for drivers and crew members at the races, $25 per diem times 32 people times 5 days times 16 races plus 30 test days (one car test crew): $76,000.

Hotel rooms for drivers and crew members at the races, $50 per man (double occupancy) times 32 men times 5 days times 16 races plus 30 test days (one car test crew): $152,000.

Air transportation for drivers and crew members to and from races, average of $400 per man per race times 32 people times 16 races plus 30 test days (one car test crew): $396,800.

Rental cars for trackside transportation, $30 per day times 6 cars times 5 days times 16 races plus 2 cars times 30 test days: $16,200.

Miscellaneous insurance, office supplies, legal and insurance costs, diesel fuel for the transporters at 4 mpg, etc.: $200,000.

TOTAL EXPENDITURES: $3,214,600.

PAYROLL

Galles/Kraco Racing employs approximately 50 people, year-round, not including their independent Galmer company in England, which has 9 employees building suspension pieces and doing wind-tunnel development work as outside contractors to Galles/Kraco.

Galles/Kraco Racing includes 38 technicians with various specialties (engine, fabrication, suspension, bodywork, painting), two chief mechanics, a chief engineer, a public relations/marketing manager, two public relations/marketing assistants, two secretaries, three truck drivers, a building superintendant, etc. Total monthly payroll: $125,000 (team owners Rick Galles and Maurice Kraines work for free!). Total annual payroll: $1,500,000.

2 "seat-to-wheel spacers" as wise-cracking mechanics refer to drivers, in this case Al Unser, Jr., and Bobby Rahal. Actual driver salaries are top secret, but an educated guess is about $50,000 per race, plus 40 percent of the prize money (each driver is expected to win a minimum of $1,200,000).

Salary: $850,000 (estimated) each driver, plus $774,733 for Unser and $584,983 for Rahal in prize money, or $1,624,733 for Unser and $1,434,983 for Rahal in 1990. Estimated Total: $3,059,716.

TOTAL PAYROLL: $4,559,716.
GRAND TOTAL DISBURSEMENTS: $12,447,116.

INCOME

Prize Money: $1,936,833 for Unser and $1,462,458 for Rahal over the 16-race 1990 season.

TOTAL PRIZE MONEY: $3,399,291 (includes CART CPI Fund: $10,000 per entered car per race.)

Sponsorship: Galles and Kraines won't reveal their exact sponsor arrangements for 1990, but sponsorship deals are pretty standard throughout Indy Car racing. Each car carries a "major sponsor" plus "major associate sponsors," "associate sponsors" and "decal sponsors." Drivers also rent parts of their anatomy for driving suit patches or helmet decals.

Standard Indy Car sponsorship rates, dependent on driver's fame, past wins, expected success, etc.:
Major Sponsor: $2,500,000-$5,000,000.
Major Associate: $1,000,000-$2,500,000.
Associate Sponsor: $500,000.
Decal Sponsor: $50,000 to $300,000.

Al Unser, Jr., had Valvoline as his major sponsor, Raychem, Toshiba and STP as major associates, Goodyear and Kraco as associates, Bosch as a decal sponsor. Galles Chevrolet claims Little Al's helmet.

Bobby Rahal had Kraco Industries and STP as major sponsors, Otter Pops as the major associate, Goodyear and Valvoline as associates, Bosch as a decal sponsor.

TOTAL SPONSORSHIP (estimated): $8,500,000.

RESIDUAL VALUES

Tools, transporters, shop trucks, motorcoach, office equipment and such can be depreciated at normal rates over a few years, but top-rank teams must replace these items every three years or so to preserve that "look of success." Helmets, uniforms, etc., are used up after one year or even less and must be replaced.

Nominal residual value of trucks, etc.: $250,000.

In the past, used Indy cars had almost no value at all. Today, the AIS series races cast-off Indy Cars, so a one-year-old Indy car has a value of perhaps $75,000 without an engine. Particularly successful designs can sometimes be updated for a year or two, but top-rank teams like Galles/Kraco start with all-new cars each year.

Residual value of 4 cars (assuming one total wreck): $300,000.

GRAND TOTAL INCOME AND RESIDUALS: $12,449,291.
TOTAL PROFIT (estimated): $2,175 (otherwise known to accoutants as "zip").

Rick Galles claims, "I'm never going to make money in racing. And if I did, I'd put it right back into the team. I do this because I love it. There are other things I could do to make more money, but very few people will ever have the opportunity to own a car that wins the Indianapolis 500. Or even a chance to win the Indy 500. It's an unbelievable feeling. There's more to life than money. I mean, why do people go to the moon?" ▪

(top right) **Employees of Indianapolis Power and Light salute the Pan American Games with their float in the 500 Festival parade.** (bottom right) **13.1 miles from Monument Circle to the Speedway comprise the Mini Marathon...10,000 runners make this the largest mini marathon in the country.** (below) **When your legs are only 5 inches long, even one lap of the Speedway seems like a Mini Marathon. Scotty and West Highland terriers outrace the Pipe and Drum Corps during pre-race festivities.**

your car will only pull 12,000 rpm at the same place, you make a mental note to talk to your aerodynamicist about changing the wing angles. In the second instance, this driver is telling you that the fastest lap he's turned so far took him 40.7 seconds. If you're turning 40.4s, you can feel pretty smug. If you're struggling to lap at 42 flat, you have a good reason to go back to the garage and rethink your whole set-up.

From a driver's lap time, you can tell pretty much where he'll sit on the grid come race day. Back in June of 1990, for example, one could already predict that a four-lap qualifying average of 40.0 seconds or less would probably put you on the front row of the 1991 Indy 500; anything slower than a 42.5 second average and you probably wouldn't make the field. Thousands of drivers, engineers, mechanics and sponsors spend their lives contemplating that brief 2.5 second window of opportunity.

Throughout the spring and summer, even while the teams are competing in the PPG Indy Car World Series, they continue testing at Indy. They have so much knowledge of the Speedway, it provides a relatively stable baseline for any changes they will make to their cars, even for races at other tracks.

At the same time, car designers like Nigel Bennett of Penske and Bruce Ashmore of Lola are testing their latest ideas in the wind tunnel, refining the new designs they will build for the following year. Engineers at Cosworth, Ilmor, Alfa-Romeo and Judd are simultaneously testing improvements to their engines.

With any luck at all, the new cars for next year are ready for preliminary testing before Christmas. "The team buys a car from the constructor," explains Al Unser, Jr., "and then *develops* it. My car is a Lola like everybody else's, but we run different wings, different ducting, different springs, different suspension settings, different engine details. Since the cars are all the same to start with, it's the development that's most important.

"You learn to be very sensitive to what the car is telling you. If my crew turns the adjusting plate on one front spring/shock

absorber unit half-a-turn up, I can tell. A quarter-turn? Maybe. Now the hard part about testing—and we go testing an average of one day a week, year-round, plus nearly every day at Indy during the month of May—is that every time you change something on the car, you have to change your driving to accommodate that change. You have to sort yourself out along with the car, and that can sometimes be very difficult."

What makes this development process even more confusing is that the track keeps changing, too. The settings that work at the Speedway in March may be all wrong when the temperature is 20 degrees warmer in May. Humidity, cloud cover, the amount of rubber built up on the track, how recently it has rained—the number of variables in racing is infinite. And so the teams test. They keep elaborate records of all the test conditions, so that as the time to qualify approaches, they can make minute changes to their cars to give the best performance under the prevailing conditions.

(left) Galen Fox receives a plaque of appreciation during the 1989 Drivers' Meeting the day before the Indianapolis 500. Seated behind him are the thirty-three qualifiers.

PIT STOP: SECOND 1
During the 1990 Indy 500, Doug Shierson's Domino Pizza crew prepares for eventual winner Arie Luyendyk to come in for four tires, 40 gallons of methanol and a drink of Sportmax electrolytes...all in 16 seconds. Arie is already on pit row, as you can tell from the right front tire man who has his arm raised. The crew leader's hot pink hat helps Arie find him quickly, though the crew talks the driver all the way around the oval on their two-way radios in any case. The diagram painted on the pavement not only shows Arie exactly where to park his Lola/Chevy, but positions the crew members precisely, too. See how they're all tensed in anticipation.

Throughout the year, but increasing in intensity as the 500 approaches, maintenance crews are at work on the Speedway. Each year brings some new improvement in spectactor access, in communications, in accommodations, in the race track itself. Then in March, April and May, the entire Speedway is mown, cleaned, washed or repainted to present its best face possible. By the time the crowds arrive, the famous National Historic Landmark, eighty years young, is the most pristine motor racing facility on the planet. When the Speedway officially opens on the first weekend of May, both the racers and the race track are ready for action. After all, they've been getting ready for a year.

TIME TRIALS

Before starting virtually any other race in the world, drivers are given only a few hours of practice. Then they usually have just a couple of short sessions in which to qualify for the race itself. Invariably, their position on the grid is based on their single fastest timed lap, which may or may not actually be as fast as they can go. In most road course races, for example, all the cars must qualify during the same session, so it is sometimes impossible to get a "clean" lap for qualifying because of the other cars out on the track at the same time.

Qualifying for the Indianapolis 500 is a much more serious matter. To begin with, drivers can practice just about as much as they want during the month of May leading up to the race. Qualifying takes four days, the Saturday and Sunday of the two weekends before race weekend, and there is even practice all morning before the qualifying sessions. No driver has ever complained that there is not enough time to practice before the 500, though some people have driven so many miles in practice they've just about worn out their car before the race ever starts.

It's well known that the Indy 500 draws more spectators than any other single-day sporting event. Know what is nearly as popular? Right, the first weekend of qualifying before the 500. Upwards of 200,000 die-hard fans come out to watch the unbelievably tense qualifying laps.

The Speedway uses a complicated but fair qualifying system. The evening prior to the first day of Time Trials, there is a drawing to determine the order in which the drivers will attempt to qualify. Every driver who is a "first day" qualifier is guaranteed his shot at the pole, even if the first day of qualifying is rained out or shortened.

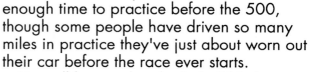

LIVING HISTORY

The entire Indianapolis Motor Speedway is one huge museum, of course, and in 1987 was designated a National Historic Landmark. But between Turns One and Two there is also the Hall of Fame Museum, chronicling seventy-five years of racing at the Speedway.

The Museum contains almost 100,000 square feet of floor space, the heart of which is devoted to showing approximately thirty different cars which have won the Indianapolis 500. The Museum's permanent collection numbers over two hundred vehicles, of which about sixty are on display at any one time. In addition, there are permanent displays of racing memorabilia of all sorts, including engines, helmets, trophies and photographs.

The most successful of the historical Indy winners displayed are Wilbur Shaw's Boyle Maserati, Mauri Rose's Blue Crown Special, Bill Vukovich's Kurtis roadster and the laydown Belond Special driven to victory by Sam Hanks and Jimmy Bryan. The oldest winning car in the Museum is Ray Harroun's famous 1911 Marmon Wasp—complete with rearview mirror. Among the others are Jimmy Murphy's Duesenberg, which won the 1921 French Grand Prix as well as the 500 in 1922, A.J. Foyt's four winners and Mark Donohue's 1972 McLaren.

The Hall of Fame Museum complex includes a gift shop, ticket office, snack bar and the Speedway's administrative offices. Tours of the track also leave from here. The not-for-profit Hall of Fame Museum is open every day except Christmas, and admission is only $1. Another dollar gets you a ride around the track. For $2 plus a hot dog, you can spend the day immersed in Indy lore. There's not a better bargain in racing. ∎

(above) The old main gate; Hall of Fame Museum outside and inside.

PIT STOP: SECOND 2
Slow! Slow! You can see the gray smoke coming off Luyendyk's right front tire as he slides to a stop. He's a couple of feet too close to the wall, which will cramp the left-side tire crew. The orange line across the foreground is the air hose for the impact wrench used by the tire changer. These impact wrenches are customized, hot-rodded to spin about four times as fast as the impact wrenches the mechanics use in your local Goodyear tire store. Each wheel is retained by a single center "knock-off" hub over which the impact wrench exactly fits. Notice that the tire men are all wearing Nomex gloves... both tire and wheel will be red hot after running 230 mph on the oval.

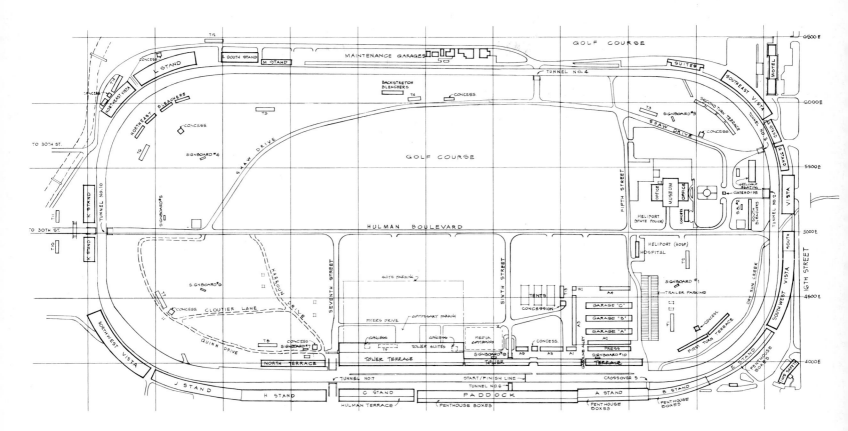

During Time Trials, each driver is allowed two warm-up laps, then four qualifying laps, then a cool-down lap. His qualifying speed is the average of all four timed laps. If something is wrong and the driver isn't going fast enough, his crew can wave him off any time before he completes his four laps. Their driver then may go to the back of the qualifying line for a second or even a third chance. As soon as he completes his group of four laps in a row, however, that average becomes his qualifying time. And no car gets more than three qualifying attempts.

After all the "first day" qualifiers have had their chance, the starting grid is made up, with the fastest qualifier on the pole, second fastest in the middle of the first row and so on back through the field. On each subsequent day, the qualifiers are lined up behind the "first day" grid. It is possible, therefore, to be the fastest

(left) An aerial view of the Speedway on Race Day, 1987 shows how elaborate a facility the Speedway has become in modern times.
(above) A plan as of May, 1990. As you can see, the track is very nearly ringed with grandstands, suites, vistas and penthouses.

PIT STOP: SECOND 3
Arie rolls to a stop on a signal from the crew leader. Fuel crew is already jumping between the wheels; the right rear tire man has already run across behind the Lola, trailing his high-pressure air line. Running over an air line is dangerous and earns penalty seconds from the stewards. Notice how the crew leader already has his impact wrench at the proper height, in the proper hand. He's also wearing knee pads for protection. Each tire is clearly marked for position, direction and pressure. They are also numbered in sets so tires can be matched as closely as possible. In the background, a Speedway pit official has turned around to watch for infractions.

THE RIGHT SET-UP

Racing is a lot more than strapping yourself into a powerful car and mashing the throttle down. For starters, it takes a team of people to field a modern racing car—each as expert at their task as the driver is at his—and they spend hundreds of private hours in testing for every public hour they spend in the race. A lot of that pre-race practice time, especially at the Indianapolis Speedway, is spent in trying to find "the right set-up." Today's cars are almost infinitely adjustable, so it takes a driver and chief engineer of rare perception to figure out which combination of adjustments is going to make their car faster than everybody else's. Their tools are no longer just wrenches and screwdrivers, but wind-tunnels, computerized data-loggers and microprocessor-generated simulations.

(below) USAC tech inspectors measure heighth, width and ground clearance on the late Billy Vukovich's Hemelgarn-Consani Lola/Judd in 1989.

And, of course, the very experienced seat of the driver's pants.

One of the best drivers at this painstaking analysis is 1986 Indianapolis 500 winner Bobby Rahal. As he says, "Our cars are now so sophisticated, you must be very cool and analytical to succeed. In the old days, you were presented with 'X' for a race car, and you made the best showing you could. Today, there are so many adjustments you can make, just in the suspension settings and the aerodynamics, that you have to deal with 'X+Infinity.'

"The secret to success in Indy car racing is now communicating with your engineers. Despite their computer printouts, the engineers don't know exactly what the car is doing. The driver is the only one who can truly tell them what it's like out there. For example, the stopwatch might say that the lap times are the same, but the car could be very different to drive. One way it might be easy to drive, the other way it might be beating you up. Only the driver can know that. Obviously, the more experience you have—the more testing you do—the better you can interpret and explain what's really happening.

"You must realize, the order of magnitude we're talking about is *very* small. For example, we might change the angle of attack on the left front aerodynamic wing by 1/10 of 1 degree. Believe it or not, the speeds are so high at Indianapolis that a tiny change like that will have an effect on the handling of the car that you can definitely feel.

"Such a tiny change might let you go around the Speedway 1/10 of a second faster. At the end of 200 laps of Indianapolis, that's a difference of 20 seconds—enough to win or lose the race. Now imagine if you could figure out enough of these minute adjustments —each one worth an additional 1/10 of 1 second—that you could gain an advantage of a full second, or even 2 seconds a lap. You'd run away with the Indy 500. That's why we do months and months of testing before the race itself.

"We have a new computer system that measures miniscule changes in the car, changes so minor that a human being can't sense them. We can measure acceleration and braking G-loads, lateral G-loads, aerodynamic downforce front and rear. All of that information helps figure out the optimum set-up. Of course, once you get the car optimized, everything changes. As the 500 goes on, more rubber gets laid down by the tires. If the day is hot, the track will be slick. If a cloud comes up, all of a sudden, you'll have tremendous grip in the corners.

"Everything at the Speedway is in constant flux; you, the car, the engine, the track, the weather. The secret is to control what you *can* control and just deal with the rest. For example, we set up the car to be affected as little as possible by changes in the track adhesion. We use cockpit-adjustable anti-roll bars that I can change as I go, and we can alter the aerodynamic settings at every pit stop.

It goes without saying that we try to put the car together so it won't change over the course of the race and upset all our careful calculations.

"The driver can't get upset, either. You can be aggressive, but you must remain emotionally cool. The more your emotions run you, the more you'll make mistakes. The driver is a vital component that must be kept in perfect adjustment just like any other part on the race car." ∎

(left) Andale Racing mechanics adjust the rear suspension geometry on Bernard Jourdain's Lola/Cosworth during qualifying in 1989. This angle gives a good view of the ground effects expansion cones which exit between the tires and transaxle. Even minute changes in suspension settings or body configuration have a dramatic effect on the car's performance, so the mechanics must be extra careful in everything they do.

PIT STOP: SECOND 4
To work! Front tire men are already loosening knock-offs, rear tire men are getting into position. Fuel hose is already connected, overflow hose is about to be connected. Notice that fuel crew must wear helmets and eye shields. Methanol fuel is less explosive than gasoline, but it burns with a colorless flame...by the time you realize it, you've already been burned. Hence the elaborate fire protection. Arie is just reaching for his Sportmax dispenser. At the same time, the crew is hitting the switch for on-board hydraulic jacks that will lift the Lola clear of the pavement for tire removal. The Indy official just walking into the photo is looking for rules infractions.

car in the Indianapolis 500, but start in the middle of the pack because you were not able to qualify on the first day.

After thirty-three cars have qualified, they start the procedure known as "bumping." If a late qualifer is faster than one of the thirty-three cars in the field, then the slowest car is "bumped" and the new qualifier is added. This goes on until the qualifying period has expired and the thirty-three fastest cars and drivers make the field. When you realize there might be sixty cars vying for those thirty-three precious spots, it's clear that even qualifying for the Indy 500 is an accomplishment of no little merit.

(below) There's no limit on the age of race fans or the ingenuity of souvenir creators; this crew of six-year-olds sports vests checkered like a flag and Pennzoil hats winged front and rear like Rick Mears' racing car.

INDIANAPOLIS 500 FESTIVITIES

Over the years, the month of May has become the focus of the Indianapolis social calendar. While the drivers and crews are straining to make the starting line-up, the rest of Indianapolis is putting on a city-wide party. Included in the Indianapolis 500 Festival are the 500 Festival Queen Beauty Pageant held in the middle of March, the month-long 500 Festival of the Arts at the Children's Museum, which starts in mid-April, the Mayor's Breakfast on Track Opening Day and the 500 Festival Mini Marathon the Friday of Race Weekend. There is also a Memorial Service the same morning at the World War Memorial. The pre-race 500 Festival culminates with the Memorial Parade the afternoon before the race.

There's also the Queen's Ball the Friday night before the race, just one of dozens of parties that weekend. Many are charity benefits. There is also a charity fashion show sponsored by CARA and featuring not only the drivers' wives and children, but most of the drivers as well. Down at Indiana University in Bloomington, the fraternities participate in the Little 500 relay race on bicycles.

At the Speedway itself, one of the most heartfelt events is Mari Hulman George's "Arnold" barbeque for the benefit of the Indiana Special Olympics. Held on the opening weekend, it brings together hundreds of drivers, car owners and all sorts

(above) Tero Palmroth has one of the most colorful helmets in racing, carefully divided among his various sponsors. The clear plastic tube is from his life-support system and supplies oxygen in case of a fire.
(left) Not many racing jackets are as fancy as this one, but nearly every spectator wears something special that relates to a favorite driver, a specific team, the Indianapolis Motor Speedway or motor racing in general.

PIT STOP: SECOND 5
Under the eyes of the Indy official, the entire crew is hard at work. The front knock-offs are already removed, the rears are coming off. Methanol is whoosing into the fuel cell, a fireman wearing Nomex is standing by behind the car with a fire extinquisher, just in case. Arie is reaching for his drink container, handed to him on a pole to save an extra person "over the wall" in the pit. The crew has already activated the on-board jacks; you can see one jack touching the pavement below the body just beneath the car's left-side wing. The jacks don't go up precisely at the same instant...you can see that the right side of the Lola is momentarily slightly higher than the left.

(above) In the 1990 pre-race parade, Vice-President Dan Quayle and his wife, Marilyn. (above right) Indianapolis Police Department Motorcycle Drill Team. (below) At Indy, even some photographers wear Nomex. (below right) Rick Mears helps out at the Special Olympics Arnold barbeque.

of other celebrities from the racing fraternity to meet hundreds of Special Olympics competitors. The Arnold barbeque has raised well over $750,000 for charity in the past decade.

The Opening Ceremonies are also held at the Speedway the first Saturday in May. Later in the month there is a charity driver's golf tournament, a Mechanic's Recognition Party during the week before the race and the annual Driver's Meeting the day before the 500. The spectacle of the Indianapolis 500 ends with the annual Victory Dinner at the downtown Convention Center the evening of Memorial Day. Of course, the ramifications of the 500 go on for months, particularly for the top-finishing drivers. "It's incredible," says Emerson Fittipaldi. "When you win the Indianapolis 500, you can't imagine how much attention it brings."

RACE WEEKEND

You really have to think of it as a "Happening" more than just another motor race. By Friday afternoon, there isn't a hotel room or rental car available anywhere between Bloomington and Lafayette. Hundreds of thousands of spectators are converging on Indianapolis from all over the world. Every blues club, pub and restaurant in downtown is crammed, while thousands of people walk the streets, a parade of their own. Sponsors and guests are to be found everywhere from the conservative Columbia Club to Rick's Cafe.

Many teams—and several drivers—have their own suite at the track. The "In Crowd" is out at the Speedway Saturday morning, having brunch with their favorite driver before he goes off to attend the Drivers' Meeting at 11:00. Then it's back to town for the 500 Festival Parade, with time for a snack and a walk around Monument Circle before dressing for that night's party. Even at midnight, there is still a steady stream of traffic being diverted around Monument Circle, which has been partially closed-off by the police to keep local teenagers from staging an Indianapolis 500 of their own.

By the time the Saturday night parties spill their happy couples onto the down-

(above left) Jim Nabors' pre-race rendition of "Back Home Again in Indiana" is a beloved tradition. (above right) Tom Carnegie has been the announcer for every Indianapolis 500 since racing resumed after World War II.

PIT STOP: SECOND 6
The hydraulic jacks are fully extended... you can see them clearly beneath the car. You can also see the radio antenna mounted on the nose. Arie is drinking from his sports dispenser, having had to open his helmet visor and snake the drinking straw past his Nomex balaclava. The two front tires are off, but the right rear tire man is having some troubles getting his impact wrench going. Notice how thick the brake pads are—thick enough to last 500 miles at Indy without needing replacement—and how the long upper and lower control arms are as delicate and streamlined as possible. That's to let as much air as possible flow past and into the square inlets for the underwings.

TIMING/SCORING

The basic timing and scoring system at the Speedway was created by Chester Ricker, Director of Timing and Scoring from 1913 until 1951 and a member of the Auto Racing's Hall of Fame. Ricker's system uses two separate groups of people, the Timers and the Scorers, each keeping separate records.

The Official Timer records the time at which each race car crosses the start/finish line on each lap, about 4500 numbers during a typical Indy 500. He also records the time for every lap during qualifying on the weekends preceding the race itself.

Ricker's clever system was used without major change up until 1980. He used a ship's chronometer manufacturered in 1876 to drive a Stewart-Warner timer which printed lap times on paper tape. In the early days, the printer was triggered by a wire strung across the track. A photocell replaced the wire in the Twenties, though the Chief Timer still had to manually push a button as each car passed start/finish. As he pressed the button, he also called out the car's number to his assistant, who wrote the number next to the time on the paper tape. Lap numbers for each car were added later.

There are thirty-three scorers—one for each car on race day—and they record the time on each lap as "their" car crosses the finish line. Starting in 1927, each scorer wore his car's number pinned to his back, and as the cars changed position on the track, the scorers changed their seats appropriately. Radio broadcasters seated behind the scorers could simply read the race order off the scorers.

(above) Drivers in 1919 time their rivals with pocket watches...left to right; Eddie O'Donnell, Eddie Pullen, Art Klein, Eddie Hearne, Roscoe Sarles. (below) The most accurate timing instrument available in the Twenties was a Hamilton Chronometer. (right) The timing crew in 1932, still using a chronometer and paper tape timer. (bottom right) The AAA timing staff in 1946. Their technology is still based on the mechanical clock and punch card tabulator, surprisingly accurate but requiring some specialized skill to run.

In 1927, the scorers also began using IBM punch cards. Each car received a punch card for each lap, which were then tabulated every ten laps by an IBM Tabulating Machine.

In 1981, timing and scoring was computerized. The Chief Timer now pushed a button each time the race leader passed, a second button as every other car passed. Times were stored in an IBM PC. The scorers were each issued electronic clip boards. With the press of a button, each car's number and lap time were recorded by the PC and displayed on the scoring pylon.

Starting in 1990, timing and scoring was completely revamped. A radio transmitter is now installed in each car's left side pod. Timing antennae are spaced around the track in grooves cut into the pavement. As each car crosses these timing lines, its number and lap time are sent to the IBM PS/2 Data Manager. The scorers still use their electronic clipboards, providing a back-up for the automated Data 1 system. This gives the Indianapolis Speedway the most up-to-date timing and scoring system in the world of motor racing, a worthy successor to Chester Ricker's famous chronometer. ■

(top left) The human-powered scoreboard employed one man for each car number. Numbers were constantly shuffled during the race as car positions changed. This is 1938.
(above) Today's digital equipment uses radar to measure speed. This is 1989.
(left) The famous Speedway scoring pylon displays laps, leader's average speed, car positions. It is updated instantly by computerized IBM equipment.

PIT STOP: SECOND 7
More of the same. Arie drinks, gas guzzles, tires are swapped. Both front tire men have already put the old tires out of their way and are ready to install the fresh rubber. Things are running behind in the rear, where the impact wrench has just been dropped and the tires are starting to come off. You can see clearly in this picture that Shierson's crew is so organized even the brake pads are individually numbered to be sure they end up in the right spot. You might think the fuel man is just standing there, but he's actually pushing as hard as he can to counteract the force of the flowing fuel and the spring-loaded fuel cell filler. You can see that his leg muscles are tensed from the strain.

TIRES FOR 240 MPH

Most people think of a tire, if they think of it at all, as something round and black that hopefully holds air. But a tire is actually the product of an incredibly-complex job of engineering. As Leo Mehl, Goodyear's Director of Competition, puts it, "At Indianapolis, the outside tires have to handle a greater load than the inside tires. So the outside tire heats up faster. When a tire heats up, it expands. These cars have gotten so sophisticated that the designers might ask us for a tire that's 0.10 inch larger for the right rear than the left rear, in order to induce what they call stagger, so the car will turn left more easily.

"We're talking about a big doughnut that's made out of rubber, that's filled with air. And these guys want it to stay the same size to 0.10 inch at 240 mph, pulling a side force of over 3.0G. This isn't something you cook up in your backyard."

The enemy of tire engineers is heat, says Mr. Mehl. To combat heat you have to mix the rubber compound from which you mold the tires for durability. But to get this necessary tire wear, you must give up some traction. So the trick in tire design is to achieve a balance between wear and traction. It's hard to discover the proper tire design without testing.

"Back in the old days," says Mr. Mehl, "tire technology was an art, not a science. We didn't have a laboratory where we could test tires. We'd make some tires and put them on some fellow's car and see what happened. Today we can do our durability testing in the laboratory, but we still must go to the track to test the performance of different tires.

"We pay different drivers so much per mile to do testing for us. We guarantee to put the car back in shape if they crash it, and we supply racing engines for them to use. We have our own engine builder, Herb Porter, who maintains our engines.

"Rick Mears, Bobby Rahal, Mario Andretti, Al Unser, Jr. They're all good test drivers. But A.J. Foyt has the best natural instincts of any driver I've ever worked with. He can figure out in three corners what might take another driver all afternoon."

(right) Gordon Johncock's 1989 Hemelgarn Racing crew brings just a few of their supplies out to pit lane before the race. They've got four sets of mounted spare tires, plus everything from helmets to drink coolers and spray wax. Their custom-built pit cart and trailer are as nicely turned-out as the race car.

Tires have become so important to the performance of an Indy car that chassis designers actually come to Goodyear during the summer to find out what the tire engineers are planning for the following season. Then they literally design their cars around the tires.

"The construction of our radial racing tires is so secret," Mr. Mehl explains, "that we put a serial number on each tire. The teams have to sign each tire in and out. We register each tire to a team, and unless all the tires come back, they don't get any more.

"We supply every team with four sets of tires for free. Beyond that they have to pay for tires. At Indianapolis, we usually have two dozen tire engineers and technicians plus about 1500 tires. Each car will use around a dozen sets of tires for practice, qualifying and the race.

"The drivers tell us that each tire has one 'fastest lap' after which that tire will never go that fast again. It depends on the driver, his car, the track conditions, the temperature. It might be the second lap on one day, the fourth lap another day. After that, those tires are useless.

"Every team has tires with the same compound, so there is no advantage or disadvantage to who gets which tire. All the tires are as identical as we can make them. We are very careful to let the teams make their own decisions about pit stops and tire changes, about the speeds they can run. We are completely neutral about who wins—as long as they're using our tires, of course.

"We can actually determine how good the race will be by the tires we supply. Since every compound is a compromise between wear and traction, if we supplied a tire with too hard a compound, the drivers wouldn't have enough traction to feel confident. If they're not confident in how the car will respond, they won't run close to each other, there will be very little passing and the race will be boring. If we give them tires that are too soft but have lots of traction, they might blister or overheat, and the drivers won't feel confident with those tires, either. Our job is to produce a tire that is safe, comfortable and predictable, that the drivers can trust. Then you end up with an exciting race, with lots of passing and repassing." ∎

(above) Chris Kneifel signs autographs for young fans. Wide tires have many unexpected uses. Among other challenges, the suspension designer has to calculate his geometry so that as the tire travels up and down over bumps, the wide tread stays parallel with the pavement. It the tire develops too much camber, it will ride on one edge rather than on the entire tread width. If that happens, the tire will lose traction.

PIT STOP: SECOND 8
Things seem like they're happening more quickly, now. Fresh front tires are on, old rear tires are finally off. Notice that the guys are careful to lay the used tires flat on the pavement so they don't go rolling into traffic. The fuel crew is getting anxious, they're ready for the overflow to show in the clear tube, which means the 40 gallon tank is full and they can disengage. Notice how carefully every detail of the Lola is sculpted...the vertical tabs on the front wings, the rearview mirrors, the openings into the underwing area. The cockpit is pulled so tightly in around the driver, it's barely wide enough for Arie's shoulders. A strap from helmet to rollcage counteracts centrifugal force.

town streets, the real action has shifted to Sixteenth Street. The west-bound lanes are closed off, and the highway for miles leading into the Speedway main gate is one huge parking lot. Or one huge party. Thousands of fans stay up all night before the race. They camp out on Sixteenth Street in cars, trucks and campers, eating and drinking until dawn.

While all this partying is going on, the drivers and crews are holed up in their homes and hotels, trying to relax and get some sleep. Even if you've been in the 500 a dozen times before, this is still one of the most nerve-wracking nights a man has to get through...thinking about all the things that can go wrong, about the car, the engine, the team, the tires, the other drivers. A million things can keep you out of Victory Lane. It's a calm man, indeed, who can get to sleep before midnight when he has to drive in the Indy 500 in the morning.

RACE DAY

Race Day always seems to dawn hot and sunny. At 5:00 am, a military bomb goes off inside the Speedway. That's the signal to open the gates. Outside on Sixteenth Street, there's a mad rush to be among the first through the Main Gate, because the first arrivals get to pick their favorite infield viewing spot along the fence. Among the most popular spots are those along the straight between Turns One and Two—a good view but near the gate to easily leave at the end of the race. By 5:30, thousands of spectators are already settled along the fence. Some are cooking breakfast, others are reading the Sunday *Indianapolis Star,* some are already opening their first beer of the day or sipping their last beer from the night before. Lawn chairs sprout like mushrooms on the Speedway lawn. The Infield crowd gets there early.

By 7:00 am, the grandstands and suites are beginning to fill up. Lucky ticket holders arrive by car, bus, taxi, motorhome. Outside the Speedway, there's pandemonium. Walls of people, all

(below) Bottled nitrogen is used to power on-board jacking systems which speed pit stops. Nitrogen is also often used to inflate tires because it does not expand when heated the way air does, helping to preserve designed-in tire parameters.

PIT STOP: SECOND 9
Arie's getting anxious, too. He's checking in the mirror to see which of his rivals are also in the pits, plus he can see the refuelers. His Nomex balaclava is still pulled down below his nose rather than up over his nose where it should be. All four new tires are in position. In the background, you can just make out the yellow flag being displayed from the starter's tower. By pitting under yellow, rather than green, Arie has saved nearly a lap compared to leader Emerson Fittipaldi, who was forced to stop under green to change some badly-blistered tires. That final green flag pit stop made all the difference and cost Fittipaldi the 1990 Indy 500.

TEAM EFFORT

Fifty or sixty years ago, a lonely genius like Wilbur Shaw could literally build a car with his own two hands, gather a few friends together and go win the Indy 500. It was like something out of an old B-movie, with Wallace Beery and Mickey Rooney. "Come on, Fellas, I can build a car and win the Big Race! I just know I can!" Not anymore, Kid.

Nowadays, even Wilbur Shaw would need at least two or three dozen highly-trained technicians—"mechanic" isn't the right word, anymore—just to get him as far as Indy practice. As for actually qualifying—or heaven forbid, *winning*—it takes an organization about on a par with the Eighth Army.

One of the best Indy generals is a graying, soft-spoken fellow named Jim McGee, who stands third on the all-time list of Indy car chief mechanics behind the legendary George Bignotti and Clint Brawner. No one could be better at explaining just what it takes to go racing at Indianapolis today.

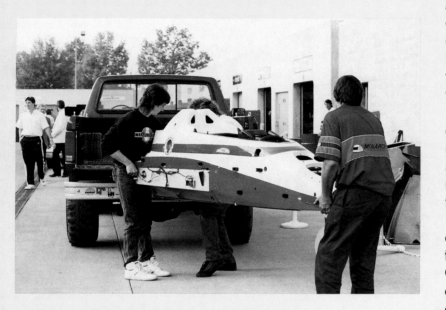

(above) Crew members from Andale Racing carry a new monocoque for Bernard Jourdain's 1989 Lola/ Cosworth. In a matter of days, this bare "tub" will be transformed into a complete car with which Jourdain will then finish ninth in the 500.

"When I started racing Indy cars in the early-Sixties," says Mr. McGee, "we would run twenty-six races during the season. We spent $200,000. That was for everything... race cars, spare parts, mechanics, food, travel, everything.

"We had the Dean Van Lines Special, and Al Dean would borrow $200,000 from the bank at the beginning of the season. On a good year, we'd have that loan paid off right after Indianapolis in May. The rest of the season, we'd run at a profit. Today, even with tremendous sponsor support, we barely break even. It costs a minimum of $6 million to run one car for the season.

"I like to compare racing to professional football. Pat Patrick is the president of Patrick Racing. He's like the the team owner and general manager of a football team. I see myself as The Coach. I get to be The Coach because I've done it so many times I can identify just about any problem.

"Over the years, I've built cars, I've built engines, I've built gearboxes. I'm getting paid for my years of experience...in knowing what's going on, in being able to hire the right people to get the job done. Part of my job is to keep the driver and the team psychologically 'up' for the Big Game. It's very easy for a team to get a little bit sideways, particularly in a losing streak. A big part of my job is just keeping the team working well together, with a positive attitude. Like The Coach.

"Our chief engineer is like the head of the offensive coaching staff. He has to have a tremendous amount of experience. He has only one job: to figure out ways to make the car go fast. Next is the chief mechanic. My chief mechanic has twelve men working for him. He is in charge of actually assembling and racing the car. He's also in charge of the five men who do fabrication and development. He also runs the machine shop and the paint shop.

"In the old days, we always built our own engines. But Chevrolet wanted to keep everything to do with the Chevrolet Indy V-8 in one location. So we hired two men who worked for us at the VDS shop in Midland, Texas, where all the Chevy Indy V-8s are built—except those for Mr. Penske. He builds his own. Then when we started using the Alfa Romeo engines last year, they supplied the engines directly to us. We just take them out of the crates and bolt them in.

"We keep twelve engines in service at any one time. They get rebuilt about every 400 to 500 miles. We also have three cars. We keep all three in race-ready condition because in June and July there are so many races there isn't time to run back to the shop and rebuild a car every time we need one. We bring two cars to every race. The third car is in the shop, ready to go. We can fly that spare car to any race track in the country in 24 hours if we need to.

"This is run just like any big business. We deal with literally hundreds of suppliers, but our immediate team starts with an office manager who has her own secretary. We have one man who does nothing but take care of ordering all the shop supplies and maintaining the shop vehicles, the two transporters and the motorhome. Another man handles all the race car parts plus hotel and travel arrangements for the team. We have our own marketing manager and a publicity manager. All together, there are over two dozen Patrick Racing employees, not counting the racing driver. The driver gets all the credit—or the blame—but he's just the visible tip of the iceberg. This is a real team effort. A team sport." ■

(above) Elaborate timing and scoring computer used by Teo Fabi's Porsche Motorsports team to keep track of his March/Porsche at Indy in 1989. Unsung crew members behind the scenes are as important to the success of a racing team as the driver.

PIT STOP: SECOND 10
The right rear tire man has now caught up; he's already reversed the drive on his impact wrench and is zipping the wheel nut back onto the hub, while the front tire men are still picking up their wrenches. The fuelers are wondering what's taking them so long; Luyendyk is wondering what's taking *everybody* so long. In his mirror, he can see the Beretta pace car come off the banking onto the main straight, lights flashing. If he gets back onto the track before the pace car comes around, Arie can catch up to the pack, only a few hundred yards behind the leaders. If he doesn't get out before the pace car, he'll be 2.5 miles behind...too much to make up this late in the race.

(above) Marilyn Quayle entertains Roger Penske, Rick and Chris Mears before the race in 1989.
(right) Jane Ellen Bizal, the 1989 500 Festival Queen, surrounded by her court.
(below) Infield crowds camp on Sixteenth Street the night before the race so they can be near the head of the line when the gates open at 5:00 am.

making their way towards the gates, run the gamut from teenagers in bathing suits and T-shirts to corporate sponsors in sports jackets and ties. The roads are bumper to bumper in every direction, while every front yard for miles around carries a sign that reads "Parking $5."

On Monument Circle, huge shuttle buses are filling up with fans who've wisely parked their cars in downtown Indianapolis, have equipped themselves with a checkerboard pattern box lunch and are waiting to be chauffeured out to the Speedway. The high rollers are still inside, enjoying the breakfast buffet at the Columbia Club. Their chauffeur-driven limousines will be along in another hour. The really high rollers stay at resorts out of town and arrive at the Speedway via helicopter. By mid-morning, there will be dozens of choppers sitting near the Speedway, waiting to take their owners home again above the crowded streets.

Team members get to Gasoline Alley early. Their cars have to be ready to race, polished within an inch of their lives, and positioned in front of their pits by 8:00 am. The drivers, unable to sleep late though it would be the best thing for them, are up early, too. Experienced drivers are relaxing in their suites or motorhomes, chatting with family and sponsors. Nervous drivers are down with their crews, staring at their cars and making everybody else nervous. Few of the drivers eat much. Aside from the discomfort of pulling 3.0G with a full stomach, having a heavy breakfast inside you can be literally lethal in case of an accident.

By 9:45, the race cars must be towed or pushed to their grid positions. Most drivers and crew members are already wearing Nomex. The stands are already full, the infield covered with cars and people. Because many Indy fans reserve their seats a year in advance, some have been sitting next to the same people for decades. It's like a party with friends you only see once a year.

Everyone has their little traditions. Some announce the race into their own tape recorders. Some keep a lap chart. Some bring a stopwatch and do their own timing and scoring, no doubt checking the Speedway's own figures. Others are content to just watch the crowds, talk with friends and enjoy the weather. The smell of sun tan lotion is heavy in the air.

Inside and outside the Speedway, an unbelievable

number of concessionaires are selling a bewildering variety of souvenirs, from inexpensive hats and shirts to expensive driving suits, books and toys. Every other stand seems to be selling food and drinks, and for every driver who foregoes breakfast, there are ten thousand fans who'll eat two. Belgian waffles, corn dogs and beer for breakfast? Why not? It's only once a year.

(below) Rick Mears uses a golf cart to cover the long distances around Gasoline Alley.

RACE HOUR

Starting at 10:00 am, there is a solid hour of pre-race ceremony. There are marching bands. There are celebrities riding on the seatbacks of convertibles. There is the 500 Festival Queen, and her court. Lately, there have been "Indiana's Own" Dan Quayle and his wife, Marilyn. There are always two or three vintage Indianapolis 500 winners normally exhibited at the Hall of Fame Museum that have been tuned up and brought out for a nostalgic moment in the sun. They're usually driven around the track by a retired winning driver.

Finally, at 10:35, the Chief Steward drives around the track in the Pace Car for one final look at everything. At 10:42, hundreds of thosands of people rise while the Purdue University Band plays the "Star Spangled Banner," then remain standing for the Invocation. Down on the track, hundreds of crew members, sponsors and photographers cluster around the cars and drivers.

At 10:46, an Armed Forces color guard presents their colors while "Taps" is hauntingly played. After "Taps," the drivers kiss their wives or girlfriends, hop into their cars and are belted in by their crews. Cool suit connections, water bottles, radios, arm restraint and helmet restraint straps; today's driver is connected to his car by more than his steering wheel and

PIT STOP: SECOND 11
Right front tire is on, left front tire is being tightened, rear tire man is just about to drop his impact wrench after tightening his wheel. The pink-hatted crew leader has to run his wrench and air hose back behind the wall before Luyendyk can leave, which is why the fastest tire-changer on the crew usually gets the prestige of doing the right front. Arie knows that this is a sign the pit stop is almost over; he's already looking ahead down pit lane. The fuel crew takes their cue from the right front corner, too. They know that when he starts his sprint across the pit that they should be almost done. So far, everybody has done his job perfectly... no time-wasting mistakes.

ARE RACING DRIVERS ATHLETES?

There are people who say racing drivers aren't athletes because obviously the car does all the work. Wrong! There is now quite a fat file of medical studies on the physiological and psychological effects of driving a racing car. And, not to put too fine a point on it, the average Grand Prix or Indy car driver is in the same class with Olympic runners or professional football players.

Indy car drivers typically have a heart rate of 60 beats per minute at rest, but 170-190 beats per minute when they're racing. They sustain this incredibly high heart rate for the length of the race, three or four hours or more. According to Dr. Jacques Dallaire of Sport Canada, this is cardiovascular performance equal to an Olympic Marathon runner.

Unlike other athletes, racing drivers not only sustain this type of performance for hours, but they must perform while undergoing cockpit temperatures of up to 150 degrees. And because of their heavy Nomex suits and full-face helmets, there is no convection body cooling such as a lightly clad runner enjoys.

Indy drivers typically lose 6 percent of their total body weight during a race, mostly due to dehydration. According to Dr. Dallaire, if you lose even 3 percent of body weight, reaction times and motor control decrease by about 20 percent. That's why out-of-shape drivers slow down near the end of the Indy 500, and why drivers in peak condition go on to win.

The race results bear this out. According to Anne Healey, exercise physiologist for the Performance Institute at Methodist Hospital in Indianapolis, two of the Indy drivers in the best condition are Emerson Fittipaldi and Arie Luyendyk, drivers who've dominated the race recently. Like Rick Mears, Danny Sullivan and other front-runners, Fittipaldi and Luyendyk work out daily with Nautilus machines and stationary bicycles. They lift weights and swim to improve their aerobic and anaerobic performance.

Alcohol and caffeine are both dehydrants. So contrary to their hell-raising reputation, serious Indy car drivers eschew not only wines and spirits, but even coffee and tea. In addition to his trainer, Emerson Fittipaldi even travels with his own health food chef.

Many current Indy car drivers were stars in other sports. Danny Sullivan was a four-letter man in prep school, Tom Sneva a college basketball star. Raul Boesel and Ed Pimm were both world-ranked horse show-jumpers. Roberto Guerrero was a ranking tennis player, while Teo Fabi and Dick Simon were ski racers.

As you'd expect, nearly every driver has excellent vision; Bobby Rahal is one of the few Indy winners to wear glasses. Indeed, many drivers have freakish vision, better than 20/5. Reaction times are typically twice as fast as normal.

According to Dr. Daniel Marisi of the North American Motor Sports Research Council, racing drivers are above normal in their ability to concentrate and to react to antici-

(below) Pancho Carter climbs carefully into his Lola/Cosworth before starting the 1989 Indianapolis 500. During the next three hours he can expect to be buffeted, pummelled and otherwise physically thrown around. He can expect to lose about 10 lbs. from his already lean 170 lb. frame. Tomorrow morning, he'll discover bruises in the oddest places, but he'll *feel* terrific.

pated phenomena. They are also superior in their ability to process information quickly. As Dr. Marisi puts it, "Drivers acquire knowledge more quickly and make decisions more quickly."

But it's the psychology of the individual, as Bertie Wooster's Jeeves would say, that's most unique. One of the most thorough psychological studies of racing drivers was done by Dr. Deborah Graham, of International Motor Sports Consultants in Costa Mesa, California. After studying hundreds of racing drivers, she has compiled a typical psychological profile of a racing driver.

According to Dr. Graham, the most decisive character trait is *dominance*. Racers try to dominate any situation in which they find themselves. This makes them assertive, competitive and persistent—which brings success on the track but doesn't always make them easy to live with.

Champion drivers are *self-sufficient*, in the sense of shrewd and calculating. They'll do almost anything to get ahead. They are also *intelligent*. Almost every racing driver tests above average in abstract thinking, and the more successful a driver, the smarter he's likely to be. The group which tests closest to racing drivers in intelligence, says Dr. Graham, is MENSA, the international organization for people with high IQs.

Drivers are *emotionally stable*. Even in the most life-threatening situation, drivers are unbelievably relaxed. Successful drivers deliberately subjugate anger, jealousy and fear. As Indy winner Bobby Rahal puts it, "Emotion is the enemy of the racing driver. The cooler you can be, the better."

Most drivers are also *introverted* and *conservative*, in the sense of believing in traditional values like hard work and honesty. Dominant, self-reliant, shrewdly intelligent, emotionally-detached, hard-working and physically fit: The typical racing driver has just those qualities you look for in a battlefield commander. Interestingly enough, if you ask most racing drivers what they'd like to be if they couldn't race, the most common reply is "Fighter Pilot." *Exactly.*

According to Dr. Marisi, drivers are logic-controlled, not emotion-controlled, independent and tough-minded. They are "sensation-seekers" addicted to stimulation from their environment, but they typically have a much healthier, more positive psychological profile than the average person. Contrary to the popular belief that drivers have a "death wish," explains Dr. Marisi, they don't race because they wish to die. Racing drivers don't believe they can get killed! ■

PIT STOP: SECOND 12
All four new tires are on, Arie's car is being lowered on its hydraulic jacks, the crew scrambles to get the used tires out of the way. Left-side tires must be lifted over the wall—each tire/wheel weighs about 40 lbs.—right-side tires must be stacked out of the way towards the rear of the car. This is the right rear tire man's job, since the crew leader has already run behind the wall. Notice the spare wheel nut dangling from his belt on a thong, handy just in case he drops the first one. Everyone, including the Indy pit official, is wondering when the fuel cell is finally going to get itself filled up. Notice Arie already has the front wheels slightly cocked to the right, ready to leave.

(opposite page) On the grid before the 1989 start.
(left) Three generations of the Hulman family in 1991. From left to right, Nancy George, Mari Hulman George, M. Josephine Krisiloff, Tony George, Mary Hulman and Kathi George. On the wall behind them is an oil painting of the late Tony Hulman, Jr.

throttle foot. For most drivers, this is when they start to feel calmer, after the nervousness of the past week. The pressure has been nearly unbearable, but now they're back in the "office," comfortable and at home, doing what they do better than any other thirty-three men in the world. Ironically, now's the time that everyone else is getting most excited.

Once they've stood for the National Anthem, nobody ever sits down again until after the start of the 500. Except, of course, those thirty-three drivers. At 10:48, it's time for Jim Nabors to sing the traditional "Back Home Again in Indiana" while thousands of balloons are released. And, at 10:51, a member of the Hulman family gives the world-famous instruction, "Gentlemen, start your engines."

Indy cars don't have on-board starters, so the crew members start the cars, make

PIT STOP: SECOND 13
Almost. The fuel crew is ready to disengage...more than ready. The left rear tire man is already behind the car, tensed to help push start it. The right rear tire man stacks tires out of the way; he'll put them behind the pit wall after Luyendyk leaves. As the fuel crew finishes, the fireman leans in with his fire extinquisher...this is the critical moment when the automatic fuel shut-off could jam and spray fuel on hot engine or brake parts. Up front, the crew leader is leaning over the wall, anxiously checking to be sure everyone and everything is out of the way before he waves Arie back on the track. Arie is no longer watching anything except the crew leader.

WHAT'S IT LIKE OUT THERE?

Not like it looks on TV. That on-board minicam ABC uses to give you "the view from the driver's seat" is mounted on a complex gyroscopic mount to hold it steady. Otherwise, all you'd see is a blur. At 240 mph, even a super-smooth track like the Speedway seems as bumpy as Tobacco Road. When you're watching the on-board camera on TV, keep your eyes on the steering wheel. You'll see the driver making constant corrections, his hands a blur. For every foot of those 500 miles, his car is pitching and tossing like a small boat in the wake of the *Queen Mary*.

It's also amazingly noisy out there. Race cars rattle, and shriek and moan. There's the tremendous rush of the wind going by with the strength of four hurricanes. There's the swish of the tires, the roar of the exhaust, the unbelievable mechanical clatter of pistons, camshafts and valves. The straight-cut gears in the transaxle howl. The bodywork squeaks and rattles, making it sound like the car is going to come apart any second.

(below) Already cool and emotionally detached, Bobby Rahal steps into his 1990 Lola/ Chevrolet Indy V-8.

Today's Indy cars can generate around 3.5 times the force of gravity in a Speedway corner. After 100 miles of that, even the strongest neck muscles are like limp dishrags and the driver's head flops helplessly onto his shoulder. Every driver's helmet now has a strap to hold his head upright and take the strain off his neck. But the rest of his body is being slammed against the side of the cockpit like a wrestler against the ropes. "The physcial buffeting really shakes you up," says Scott Pruett. "You feel like you're stuck in a vacuum cleaner."

And then there's the sheer speed of the place. Any driver who gets to Indianapolis has years of racing experience. But as Bobby Rahal says, "I don't care who you are, the first time you go to Indianapolis and go through a corner at 190 mph, it's an eye-opening experience. There is nothing else like it in racing. Even going 250 mph at LeMans doesn't prepare you. My first year at Indianapolis, I was uncomfortable all month.

"The Speedway is different. At other tracks, the driver can sometimes 'carry' an uncompetitive car by being more aggressive. Try that at Indy, and you'll end up in the wall. Those walls are right *there*."

Worst of all is the unbelievable pressure of The Greatest Spectacle in Racing. As Emerson Fittipaldi puts it, "The Indy 500 has more pressure than any other event in racing. You feel like a balloon. Every day they put more pressure in. It is very difficult to deal with so much pressure."

For a racing driver to describe "what's it like out there" is like an alien trying to describe another planet to someone who can never journey there. Legendary British driver Stirling Moss once wrote, "Racing relates to ordinary driving in about the same way as mountain climbing relates to riding up an escalator." Other drivers have called it "like driving a passenger car at 100 mph on glare ice" or "weaving through rush hour traffic on I-70, except you're all going 250 mph."

Why do they do it? Because when you do it right, there is no other feeling like it on earth. Racers don't race for the money, though they might say they do. They don't race for the fame and adulation. They race because racing can give them sensations and satisfactions which nothing else even approaches. Talk to an ex-driver like Dan Gurney, and even two decades after retirement he admits he thinks about racing, misses it, every day. Indy car drivers knowingly, willingly, go in harm's way, literally inches from destruction, with an intensity unmatched in any other sport. That makes a mark on a man that's tough to erase.

As the fictional Indy hero Stroker Ace put it in his biography, *Stand On It*, "Men race because it's a wild sensation to drive a car at speed and control it—and beat everybody else. Racing sort of burns all the other feelings out of you, and finally, you don't care for anything else but racing."

What's it *really* like out there? There's only one way to find out. ∎

(above)
Bobby Rahal #18 chases Salt Walther in #77 during early May practice. Running close together like this on the banking—at over 230 mph—is more exciting than anything most people can ever dream of experiencing. It's a thrill that pumps you up with adrenalin and leaves you trembling for a half-hour after you stop. There's no other satisfaction like the sensations you can get from racing. Glorious. Simply glorious.

PIT STOP: SECOND 14
Waiting for the fuel crew! The hydraulic jacks are still slowly lowering the Lola, the tire crew is done and ready to help push-start the car, Luyendyk is ready with the car in gear...all that's lacking is those final few gallons. Back in the old days, when the fuel was forced into the car under pressure, the crews could dump almost 10 gallons per second. The standardized gravity-feed refueling rigs used for the past two decades are much safer, but flow only about 4 gallons per second. Slower, but the same for every team, and much safer. Notice the concentration of the pit official, keeping on top of the proceedings. Like everyone else involved, he's carrying a two-way radio.

sure they're running properly, then wheel their battery carts behind the pit wall. The grid is cleared of everyone except the drivers in their cars, and at 10:52 the Pace Car leads the field three times around the Brickyard.

There is a warm up lap, a parade lap, then a pace lap, then the Pace Car pulls off into Pit Lane. And then, like clockwork, at precisely 11:00 am on the Sunday morning before Memorial Day, in front of nearly 500,000 spectators, the Indianapolis 500 starts with a wave of the green flag from the Starter's tower and a roar of thirty-three engines impossible to drown out even with the cheer that goes up from all those spectators. The Start of the Indy 500. The Greatest Moment in Sports.

Approximately three hours later, one of those thirty-three drivers will cross the finish line to a standing ovation, and his life will never be the same. He'll instantly be something special. Once you've won Indy, your self-confidence goes zooming up, along with your income. You're deluged by telegrams of congratulation from around the world, by business offers, by sponsorship. Having your face modeled on the side of the Borg-Warner Trophy marks a man, permanently. Out of the hundreds of thousands of people who've sat behind the wheel of an automobile in competition over the past century, only fifty-four have finished first·in The Greatest Spectacle in Racing.

As Danny Sullivan says, "There is a tremendous amount of pressure to win the Indianapolis 500. But once you've won it, well, they can't take that away from me. Ever. I will always be an Indy winner."

PIT STOP: SECOND 15

Finally! The two-man fuel crew disconnects in an unavoidable spray of methanol and backs quickly out of the way. They carry the fuel hose to safety behind the wall. Spring-loaded fuel shut-offs automatically close both the fuel cell filler opening and the nozzle of the fuel hose itself. The crew leader on the right is still waving Luyendyk to stay put...this can be a dangerous moment when the driver is anxious to get back into the race, but the crew members are still between the wheels and vulnerable. Arie is already looking in his mirrors for overtaking traffic in pit lane. He won't drop the clutch until he feels the tires hit the road, nor until the crew leader waves him on.

CAR OF THE FUTURE

Surprisingly enough, it's fairly easy to predict what the racing car of the future will be like: it won't be that much different from what we have today. The whole history of Indy car racing has been a steady upward progression, punctuated by the occasional revolution. Knowing that, we can pretty confidently predict that at least for the next decade, we'll probably still be using internal combustion, reciprocating engines.

According to most engine designers, the most efficient way to package an Indy engine is eight cylinders arranged in a "V." So we can expect that the car of the future will be powered by the same basic type of V-8 we have today, with at least four valves per cylinder. Some designers are already using five or six

valves per cylinder on racing engines, and that's a distinct possibility. According to Indy car engineers, a DOHC V-8 is a very efficient powerplant, which leaves room to fit the turbocharger behind the engine. This helps reduce frontal area.

There are already experimental racing engines running with ceramic and plastic components. These high-tech parts can be lighter, smaller and more efficient than the metal parts used in today's engines. Imagine an engine with a composite resin engine block fitted with a ceramic crankshaft, ceramic pistons and a ceramic turbocharger. It could be lighter and smaller than today's engines, and rev to much higher speeds. A redline at 20,000 rpm isn't out beyond reality for an engine with such lightweight moving parts.

It goes without saying that there will be bigger and more sophisticated computers on Indy cars in the future. Active suspension systems—in which the computer senses what the track surface is doing, predicts what the track is about to do and then moves the wheels individually to meet those track conditions—could be universal not only on racing cars in the future but passenger cars as well. There is no reason to think that computer-controlled ABS brakes and traction control couldn't appear on Indy cars, too. On-board telemetrics and highly sophisticated data-loggers to gather even more information about how the car and engine are performing will obviously be coming along any year now.

Since the engine will be smaller and lighter, the whole car can be smaller and lighter, too. That means it can be much more aerodynamic. The bodywork will fit much more tightly around the driver and the engine. But even though the car will be smaller, it will also be safer. In the Seventies, the driver was moved forward in the chassis so that the fuel cell could be stored between the driver and engine. In the future, the driver will be moved back from the nose and fitted into more of a safety "capsule." With the driver back out of the way, the whole nose of the car can be made lower, with consequently much better aerodynamics than today's Indy cars. So the race car of the future will be not only a safer car, but a faster car.

Of course, in the past, every time the cars have gotten too fast, there has been a rules change to slow them down. The easiest way to slow down cars in the future will be to reduce downforce. As lap speeds approach 230 mph at the Indianapolis Speedway, many people think the cars are already going too fast. Most Indy insiders predict that there will be a rules change to reduce downforce before 1995.

Indy car racing is already flush with important sponsors, but most people predict that even more large corporations—particularly passenger car companies—will become involved with Indy car racing, as Porsche and Alfa Romeo have already done. It's only logical to expect Japanese car companies to get involved with Indy cars within the next decade. America is the largest passenger car market in the world, and these manufacturers will use racing cars as a way to publicize their passenger cars. It will be like the old days, the days of Ray Harroun and Joe Dawson, when passenger car manufacturers raced at Indianapolis to prove their products to the public. That was valid in 1911. Why shouldn't it be valid in 2011? ∎

PIT STOP: SECOND 16
Go! Go! Go! The tires are already moving as the Lola hits the ground. Because of their tall first gear, it's hard to start Indy cars from rest without slipping the clutch. 750 hp can burn up even a racing clutch *like that* so the crew pushes the car up to walking speed to make it easier. They're being very careful not to bend the rear wing. The crew leader waves him out, though Arie is already looking where the car is going. Flawless pit stops like this, consistent driving, luck with yellow flags and in just 2 hours, 41 minutes and 18.4 seconds, Arie Luyendyk wins the 1990 Indy 500 at a record speed of 185.981 mph. Those six guys working the pits had a lot to do with it. A lot!

GENERAL INDEX

A

Adams, Jack 172
Aerodynamics 30, 41, 58, 75, 94, 97,109, 131, 134, 141, 151, 154-155, 168-169, 172, 174, 179, 190-191, 197, 208-209, 224, 238-239, 252-253, 277
Aerodynamicist 179
Agajanian, J.C. 117, 119
Aircraft/Technology 51, 107, 110, 133, 157, 160, 172, 233
Allison Engineering 52
Allison, Jim *17, 51*
American Airways 51
American Automobile Association (AAA) 31, 32, 65, 83-84, 89, 103, 139
American Automobile Association National Championship 31, 37, 43, 46, 57, 59, 72, 77-79, 91, 97, 109, 126, 131, 139, 180
AAA Midget National Champion 139
Ansted, Bill *234*
Ashmore, Bruce 246
Association Internationale de l'Automobile Clubs Reconnus (AIACR) 31, 89, 102
Automobile Club de France (ACF) 15, 20, 21, 31

B

Bailey, George *94*
Balestre, Jean-Marie 239
Bellamy, Ralph 209
Belond, Sandy *141*
Bennett, Gordon, Cup 18-20, 31
Bennett, Harry *114*
Bennett, James Gordon 15, 18-20
Bennett, Nigel 226, 227, 228, 246
Bicycles 28-29, 53, 60, 155-157, 254
Bignotti, George 127, 135, *162, 163, 185, 234, 235*
Binford, Tom 212
Birkigt, Marc 24
Bizal, Jane Allen 266
Bluebird 57
Blue Crown Spark Plug Company 108
"Black Box" *237, 237* See also: Computers
Bonelli Stadium 131
Bonneville Salt Flats 155, 175
Borg-Warner *111,* 274
Botany 500 Men's Wear 169
Bowen, A.J. 112
Boyle, Mike 91, 97
Brakes 32, 38, 43, 51, 58, 83, 94, 109, 121, 134
Brawner, Clint 180-181
Britton, Barbara 111

Brooklands Motor Course 21-23, 31, 35, 36, 63, 89, 142
Budgets, racing 77, 244-245

C

California racers 57, 88, 91, 97, 100, 117, 119-122, 124, 126, 155, 158-159, 205, 225
Capanna, Tony 127
Car of the future 276-277
Carburetors 60, 86; See also: engines; cars, developments in
Carnegie, Tom 257
Carrillo, Fred 185
Cars; See also: Sprint cars; Roadsters, specific makes; Pace cars; stock-blocks; Midgets; Champ Cars
Cars, cost of 43, 61, 65, 66, 77, 81, 97, 108, 127, 133, 144, 146, 171, 176, 177, 206, 210, 227, 229, 244-245, 264
Cars, developments in 12, 24-25, 30-35, 38-43, 56, 58-64, 73, 76-77, 107, 111-135, 149-176, 179-203, 205-216, 220-224, 226-238, 276-277
Cars, formulas for 15, 18, 20-21, 31-35, 43, 46-47, 58-59, 65-68, 72-73, 83-85, 89, 92-93, 101-103, 106, 139-140, 151-153, 172-173, 182-185, 190, 209, 216-217, 220-221
Cars, frame construction 155-161
Cars, oddball 112-113, *112* See also: Specific makes
Cars, passenger 12, 25, 30-31, 48, 51, 53, 59, 66, 69, 73, 107; See also: Indy 500, Race record summaries; Pace cars
Cars, single-seater 19-35, 46-47
Championship Auto Racing Teams (CART) 181, 209, 218, 220, 233, 239
Cassaroll, Gene 121
Champion, Albert 32
Champ Cars 127, 162, 181, 233
Chapman, Colin 158, *158,* 189, 190, 200, 209
Charisse, Cyd 111, *141*
Charlatans, Les 24-25, *33, 47*
Chassis 21, 24, 38, 43, 66, 77, 85, 94, 109, 118-119, 121-122, 227-228
Chinetti, Luigi 93
Chitty-Chitty-Bang-Bang 45
Clancy, Pat 113
Cleary, Michael *69*
Clemons, Fred 90

Cloutier, Joseph *216*
Cockpit 11, *73,* 92, 180, 199, 237
Cogan, Kevin, 223
Colors, national 18, 20
Commision Sportive Internationale (CSI) 89, 151-153, 183, 190, 200, 209, 210, 239
Computers 229, 237, *237,* 259, 265, 276-277
Constructors Championship 167
Conze Brothers 121
Coppuck, Gordon 177, 189, 227-228
Costin, Frank 190
Costin, Mike 200
Crosthwaite, John 155, 168

D

Dahl, Arlene 111
Daimler, Gottleib 12, 61
Dallaire, Dr. Jacques 268
Darnell, Linda 111
Daytona International Speedway 57, 141, 151, 161, 163, 180, 211
Dean, Al 180, 218, 264
DeBisschop, Bob 171
Demler, Norm 172
Depression, The Great 65, 82
Desmodromic valve gear 24
Detroit Grand Prix 200
Differential, quick-change 121
Downforce 179, 191, 200, 209, 221, 253
Drafting 238
Drake, John 192
Drivers, amputee 109
Drivers, apprenticeship of 233, 236, 238-239
Drivers, as athletes 268-269
Drivers, relief 47, 67, 79, 90
Duckworth, Keith 200
Dunlop tires 153
Dunning, Roscoe E. 90
Dzus fasteners *141*

E

Eastern Airlines 51
Ecclestone, Bernie 239
Egbert, Sherwood 175
Eldorado ice cream company 143
Engines 12, 15, 20-21, 23-25, 39-41, 49, 52-53, 60, 78, 80-81, 86-87, 89, 92-95, 111-112, 127-129, 132-134, 158-159, 195; See also: Cars, formulas for; Indy 500 race record summaries
Engines, bus 112
Engines, turbo 195, *195*
Engines, twin, 111, 112
Epperly, Quin 129, 132, 141
European racing 12, 13-15, 18-19, 30-35, 47-48, 67-68, 72, 89, 92-93, 96-97, 101-103, 111, 140-143, 151-153, 167, 182-185, 216, 239 See also: Grand Prix
Evenrude, Olie 60

F

Federation Internationale de l'Automobile (FIA) 31, 102-103, 151-153, 209, 212, 239
Federation Internationale du Sport Automobile (FISA) 239
Fires 38, *49, 95, 109, 115,* 135-136, *183,* 199
Firsts, American driver and first American car to win a major European motor race 33
Firsts, automobile with mon-ocuque chassis 160
Firsts, balloon tire 161
Firsts, disk brakes on an Indy Car 94
Firsts, CART driver to win more than $2 million for a single season (Emerson Fittipaldi) 239
Firsts, fiberglass helmet worn at Indianapolis 500 134
Firsts, gas-engine vehicle to win a race 12
Firsts, Indy builder to make body-work out of fiberglass and magnesium (A.J. Watson) 131
Firsts, dry pump oil system 24
Firsts, Indy 500 four-time winner 162-163, *162, 163,* 202-203, *202, 203*
Firsts, Indy winner 14, *27, 35,* 37
Firsts, magnesium wheels at Indy 121
Firsts, million dollar Indy purse for winning (1989) 240
Firsts, modern monocoque racing car 161
Firsts, motorcar 12
Firsts, motor race in America 12
Firsts, organized motor race 12
Firsts, quick change differential at Indy 121
Firsts, practical front-wheel drive car 52
Firsts, race at Indy 14, 35
Firsts, racer to talk to his crew on the radio 71
Firsts, roadster with engine tilted over and drivetrain run down left side (KK500A) 130
Firsts, rules for racing 15
Firsts, tubular shock absorbers at Indy 121
Firsts, wedge-shaped cars 172
Firsts, winning driver presented with Pace car (Louie Meyer) 82
Firsts, woman to qualify and race at Indy 202

Fisher, Carl 16-17, *17*, 21, 23, 31-32, 35-38, 45, 51, 105, 144
Fittipaldi, Wilson 241
Flags 18
Fleming, Ian 45
Ford, Edsel 74
Ford, Henry 74-75
Ford, Henry II 167
Formula One 31, 103, 151-153, 180, 182-183, 200, 206, 209, 211, 216, 219, 232-233; See also: Cars, formulas for
Formula One Constructors Association (FOCA) 239
Formula One World Championship 151, 159, 181, 189, 209, 238, 241
Formula Two 103, 140, 151
Formula Three 103
Four-wheel drive 94, 112, 113, 145
Fox, Galen *247*
Foyt, A.J. III *163*
Foyt, Lucy *163*
Front engine automobiles 149-150, 152, 168, 174, 176
Front-wheel drive 52, 57-58, 60-61, *61*, 75, 108, 111-112, 118, 121, 145, 168
Fuel 12, 40, 56, 59, 69, 78, 83-85, 89, 92-94, 108, *111*, 119, 134, 145, 159, 173, 204, 247, 253, *253*, 255, *255*, 261, *261*, 263, *265*, 267, 269, 271, 273
Fuel, diesel 111, 113, 118, 122
Fuel cell 173
Fuel-injection 159, 171, 231, 237
Fuel-injection, Hilborn 115-117, 121

G

Gable, Clark *175*
Galles/Kraco Racing 244
Galles, Rick 244-245
Gasoline, See; Fuel
George, Tony Hulman *105*, *271*
Giacosa, Dante 157
Gilmore Oil 91
Gilmore Stadium 147
Goetz, Harry 19
Goggles *63*
Golden Submarine *12*, 60
Graham, Dr. Deborah 269
Granatelli, Andy 159, 172, 174, 175, *175*, 180
Granatelli, Joe 175
Granatelli, Vince 175
Grand Prix 20-21, *23*, 24-25, 31-35, 46-48, 53, 58-59, 67-68, 89, 92-93, 96-97, 101-103, 111, 135, 138-139, 140, 167, 183, 206, 210, 216, 219, 233
Greer, Jane 111
Gulf Oil Company 94
Ground effects 208, 212, 221,

239 See also: Downforce

H

Halibrand, Ted 121, 173
Hall, Jim 208-209, 210
Hamilton Chronometer 258
Hanks, Alice *141*
Hawkes, Gwenda 63
Healey, Anne 268
Helmets 63, 67, 134, *134*, 179, *179*, 255
Henning, Cotton 77, 90, 97
Henry, Ernest 24-25, 47, 49
Herd, Robin 189
Hilborn, Stuart 117, 121, 133, 171
Hitler, Adolf 67
Horsepower 11, 17, 21, 23, 39, 40-41, 53, 59, 62, 68-69, 73, 76-77, 81, 86-87, 93, 97, 108, 111, 117, 120, 127, 133, 145, 153-154, 159, 171, 179, 185, 188, 193, 195, 201-202, 220, 222-223
Horton, Carl 130
Hulman Family *271*
Hulman, Anton, Jr. (Tony) 51, 91, *101*, 103, 104-105, 135, 139, *141*, 145, 151, 177-178, 202-203, *203*, *271*
Hulman, Herman 104
Hurricane Racing Association 175
Hurst, George *169*

I

Iacocca, Lee 167
Indianapolis 500; See also: Indianapolis Motor Speedway, Indy race record summaries
"Back Home Again in Indiana," Indianapolis 500 171, 257, *257*, 271
Balloons, Indianapolis 500 *257*
Borg-Warner Trophy, Indianapolis 500 99
Crews, Indianapolis 500 *98*, 99, 127, 137, 244-245, 247, 252, *253*, 255, *255*, 257, *259*, 261, *263*, 264-265, 267, 269, 271
Crown, Indianapolis 500 53, 54
Driver's Golf Tournament, Indianapolis 500 256
Driver's Meeting, Indianapolis 500 247, 256-257
Festivities, Indianapolis 500 254-257, 266-267, 270-277
Festival, Indianapolis 500 254
Festival Parade, Indianapolis 500 254, 257
Festival Queen, Indianapolis 500 254, 266
Finishes, Indianapolis 500 217, 221 See also: Indy 500; Race record summaries

"Golden anniversary 500," Indianapolis 500 150, *164*, *165*
Highland Pipe and Drum Corps, Indianapolis 500 246
Indiana Special Olympics "Arnold" barbeque, Indianapolis 500 254, 256
Indianapolis Police Department Motorcycle Drill Team, Indianapolis 500 256
Indianapolis Power and Light float, Indianapolis 500 246
Little 500 relay, Indiana University 254
Mechanic's Recognition Day, Indianapolis 500 256
Media Coverage, Indianapolis 500 *37*, *144*, 258, 272
Medical Support, Indianapolis 500 98
Milk/Victory Lane, Indianapolis 500 141, *163*
Mini-Marathon, Indianapolis 500 246, 254
Month of May, Indianapolis 500 243-277
Purdue University Band, Indianapolis 500 *165*
Qualifying, Indianapolis 500 21, 36, 69, 75, 77, 80, 122, 134, 152, 186, 189, 191, 197, 219, 234, 248, 254; See also Indy 500 race record summaries
Race Day, Indianapolis 500 263-276
Race record summaries, Indianapolis 500 14, 18, 20, 22, 28, 32, 36, 38, 42, 44, 46, 48, 52, 56, 58, 62, 64, 66, 68, 72, 76, 78, 80, 82, 84, 88, 92, 96, 100, 102, 106, 110, 116, 118, 120, 122, 124, 126, 128, 132, 138, 142, 146, 148, 150, 152, 154, 156, 160, 166, 170, 176, 178, 182, 184, 188, 192, 194, 196, 198, 202, 204, 206, 210, 212, 216, 220, 224, 226, 228, 232, 236, 240, 242
Sixteenth Street, Indianapolis 500 263, 266
Start, Indianapolis 500 21
Testing, Indianapolis 500 246-247, 248, 251
Time Trials, Indianapolis 500 248, 251
Victory Dinner, Indianapolis 500 254
Indianapolis Motor Speedway, Brickyard 16-17, 35, 83, 105, *115*, 248, *248*
Indianapolis Motor Speedway, founding of 16-17
Indianapolis Motor Speedway, Gasoline Alley 95, 99, *117*, 266
Indianapolis Motor Speedway, Hall of Fame 163, 180, 258, 267
Indianapolis Motor Speedway,

Indianapolis Motor Speedway Hall of Fame Museum 113, 135, 95, 178, 249, *249*
Indianapolis Motor Speedway, ownership of 51, 65, 91, 101, 104-105, 135, 139, *141*, 145, 151, 177-178, 202-203, *203*, 271
Indianapolis Motor Speedway, pagoda, *16*, 54, 69
Indianapolis Motor Speedway, Tech Inspectors 252, *252*
Indianapolis Motor Speedway, Timing and Scoring 13, 258, *258*, 259, *259*, 265, *265*
Indianapolis Motor Speedway, Track layout 17, *17*, 35, 83, 250, *250*, 251, *251*
International Business Machines (IBM) 258-259
International Sporting Commission 31

J

Jano, Vittorio 47
Johnny Lightning toys 235
Jones, Dick 171
Jones, Parnelli 201
Judd, John 222

K

Kaiserpreise 21
Keck, Howard 128
Kizer, Karl 91
Klein, Seth *114*
Kohlsatt, H.H. 12
Kraines, Maurice 244

L

Landis, Carole 111, *175*
Leader Cards Team 151, 165, *175*, 213
Lee, Don 111
LeMans 138-139, 161, 163, 167, 172
Lesovsky, Luiji 119, 141
Locke King, H.F. 21
Long Island Motor Parkway 19
Luyendyk, Mieke *274*
Lyon, Charlie *71*
Lubricants 38-39, 42, 43, 59, 78, 107; See also: Fuel

M

MacLaine, Shirley 111
Marisi, Dr. Daniel 268-269
Materials, advances in racing 14-15, 38-40, 43, 49, 56, 59, 107, 110, 121, 130-131, 134, 166, 229, 232-233
Matlock, Spider 68, 72
Maybach, Wilhelm 12, 41, 61
Mayo, Virginia 111
Mayer, Teddy 189
Maywood Speedway 29
McGee, Jim 264-265
Mechanics, riding 15, *19*, 20,

35, 46-47, 50, 67, *71*, 73, 75, 117
Mecom, John 166, 234
Media coverage *37*, 144, 258, 272
Mehl, Leo 193, 260- 261
Melitich, Vel 201
Michigan International Speedway 35, 179, 218, 238
Mid-engine 83, 94, 112, 131, 149-152, *153*, 154, 158, 168-169, 174, 176
Midget Cars 126, 147, 163, 233
Midgley, Thomas 56
Military Air Transport Service 51
Minyard, Hal 134
Mitchell, Billy 51
Mobil 109
Modified Cars 233
Monaco 167
Monocoque Chassis Construction 39, 94, 157-161, 190, 229
Monopostos; See: Cars, single-seaters
Montlhery 23, 63, 89
Monza Autodromo 23, 35, 89, 140, 142-143
Myers, T.E. "Pop" 32, 35

N

Nabors, Jim *257* See also: Indianapolis 500
NASA, impact on racing 233
NASCAR 220
Newby, Arthur *17*, *17*
Newman, Paul *214*
NHRA 220
Nitromethane (pop) 134
Nomex 157, 179
Notre Dame 53

O

O'Brien, Erin 111
Ontario Motor Speedway 179, 234
Outboard motor, invention of 60
Oval Tracks 21-23, 28-30, 46, 63, 77, 89, 103, 119, 140, 142, 179, 233, 238

P

Pace cars *21*, 82, 85, *187*, 267, 274; See also: Indy 500, race record summaries
Packard Proving Grounds 63
Patrick, U.E. (Pat) 239, 241, 264
Pennsylvania International Raceway 180, 218
Phillippe, Maurice 189, 190, 200-201
Pickens, Bill 23
Pikes Peak 213
Pits 12, *19*, 64, *65*, 110, 129, 139, 150, 156, 188, *188*, 194, 237, 247, *247*, 248, *248*, 251, *251*, 253, *253*, 255, *255*, 257, *257*, 259,

259, 261, *261*, 263, *263*, 265, *265*, 267, *267*, 269, *269*, 271, *271*, 273, *273*
Playa del Rey race track 29
Pocano International Raceway 35, 179, 234
Pop (nitromethane) 134
Porsche Team 223
Porter, Herb 171, 260
PPG Indy Car World Series 236, 238, 239, 241, 246
Prest-O-Lite 16, 17, 37
Prince, Jack 29
Prize Money 12-13, 17, 30, 35, 37, 45-46, 76, 105, 144, 146, 151, 179, 211, 225, 234, 239-242; See also Indy 500 race record summaries
Purdy, Ken 53

Q

Quayle, Dan *256*
Quayle, Marilyn *256*, *266*

R

Race Of Two Worlds 142-144
Radio 71
Rearview mirrors 14
Rear-wheel drive 60, 145, 149-150, 169
Rellimah Corporation 61, 77
Reventlow, Lance 183
Reynard, Adrian 226
Rickenbacker, Edward V. 22, 28, 32, 50-51, *50*, *51*, 65, 83, 86, 91, 104-105, 135
Rickenbacker Motor Company 51
Ricker, Chester 258
Rigling, Herman 77
Rigling and Henning race shop 69
Riverside International Raceway 151
Roadsters 111, 113, 119, *123*, 128, 130
Roberts, Vic 144
Rounds, Nat 112
Rounds Rocket 112-113
Ruth, Babe 45

S

Safety 12-15, 17, 21, *27*, 29, 35, 38, 40, 42, 48, 49, 53, 63, 76, 81-82, 90-93, 97, 98, 107, *109*, 112, 120, 128, 130, 134-135, *134*, 138-139, *140*, 143, 146-147, 156, 157, *157*, 158, 166-168, 170, 173, 179, *183*, 192, 199, 203-204, 211, 213, 219, 221, 224-225, 227, 235, 255, 260-261, 266, 271, 277
SCCA National Championship 219
Schell, Lucy O'Reilly 93
Schell, Harry 93
Schroeder, Gordon 119

Sebring Circuit 161, 180
Senna, Ayrton 237
Set-up, racing 235, 252-253, *252*, *253*
Shaw, Wilbur 51, 264
Shelby, Carroll 157, 169
Shore, Dinah 111
Simpson, Bill 225
Sloan, Alex 23, 59
Slobodynskj, Roman 189
Smith, Clay 117, 127, 147
Smallman, Andy 167
Snell Memorial Foundation 144
Snively, Dr. George 144
Sommers, Phil 77
Souvenirs *117*, *254*
Spectators 13, 19, 29, 32, 65, *81*, *99*, *103*, *121*, *129*, 135, 138, *254*, *255*, *266*, 274
Speed 12, 14, 17, 21, 23, 29, 31, 36, 40-42, 55, 62-63, 85, 97, 108, 111, 116-117, 119, 122, 153-155, 166, 174, 179-182, 186, 191, 197-199, 203-204, 209, 220-221, 245-246, 252-253, 277
Speed on board tracks 29
Speed records 12, 29, 53, 57, 63-64, 95, 117, 168, 172, 189, 191, 211, 277
Speedway car 127
Spoilers 208
Sponsorship 37, 43-44, 81, 103, 108-109, 126, 141, 143, 146, 158, 167, 169, 175, 177, 200, 203, 219, 235, 245, 277
Sprint cars 97, *101*, 106, 109, 116-117, 119, 126, 162
Stanwyck, Barbara 111
Stevens, Myron 77
Stimson, Henry 51
Stock-blocks 31, 69, 75, 76-78, 80-82, 127, 171-172, 222-223
Stouffer, Lissa 218
Streamlining 75
Street circuits (racing) 101
Strikes 76
Stroker Ace 273
Sunoco 219
Supercharger 52, *53*, 57, 62, 145, 171, 195
Suspension 52, 58, 75, 76, 112, 116, 119, 121

T

Telemetrics 237, 277
Temporary road courses 19, 47, 238
Thorne, Joel 86
Tires 12, 19, 20-21, *27*, 42, 56, 58, 76, *111*, 120, 134-135, 152, 155, 161, *164*, 166, 167, 193-194, 196, *215*, 249, 251, *251*, 253, *253*, 255, *255*, 257, *257*, 259, *259*, 260, *260*, 261, *261*, 263, *263*, 265, 267, *269*, 269, 271, 273, 275,

277
Trueman, Jim 228, 229
Tucker, Preston *71*, 74-75, 95, 170
Turbochargers 171

U

United States Auto Club (USAC) 105, 133, *136*, 139-144, 153, 162, 168, 173-174, 177, 183-194, 199, 201, 203, 209, 220, 233, 239
USAC National Championship 147, 162, 185, 211, 225, 234-235, 238
USAC National Dirt Championship 162
USAC Sprint Car Championship 211
USAC Stock Car Championship 162
Unser, Mom *235*
Unser, Pop *234*

V

Vanderbilt Cup 19-20, 85, 88
Vanderbilt, William K., Jr. 19, 85
Vanwall team 93, 140
Velodromes 29
Vidan, Pat *136*, *185*
Voiturette formula 46, 97, 101-103

W

Wagner, Fred *27*
Wallis, Ken 169, 172
Watkins Glen 181
Watson, A.J. 127, 131, *131*, 132-133, 137, 141, 147
Wedge-shaped cars 172, 183, *189*, *189*, *190*, *191*
Welch, Lewis 75, 87, 145
Weslake, Harry 171
Wetteroth, Curly 77
Wheeler, Frank 17, *17*
Wheeler-Schebler Carburetor 17
Wheels 12, 24-25, 38, 42, 58, 113, 121, 134, 141, 155, 193
White, Bill 80-81
Wickerbills 191
Wilke, Bob 131, 147, 213
Wilson, Marie 111
Winfield, Bud 86-87
Winfield, Ed 86-87, 112
World War I 25, 28, 31-32, 37, 44, 49, 50-51, 139
World War II 101, 106-107, 110, 135, 147, 160

Y

Young, Loretta *105*, 111
Yunick, Smokey 127, *136*, 169

Z

Zandvoort Circuit 200
Zink, John 131-132, 172, 183

CARS, ENGINE BUILDERS AND MANUFACTURERS

A

Alfa Romeo 25, 47, 59, 67, 89, 93, 103, 111, 223
Alfa Romeo Indy V-8 222
Auburn 53

B

Ballot 25, 32, 40, 49
Belanger Special *119*
Belond Special *141,* 249
Benz, Karl 149, 155
Benz Tropfenwagen 150
Blitzen Benz 12, 40
Blue Crown Special 106, *107,* 108-109, 111, 119-120, 249
Bowes Seal Fast Special 68, *91, 135*
Boyle Maserati 111, 249
BRM 93, 151, 167
Bugatti *45,* 59, 60, 67, 93
Bugatti, Ettore 49
Buick *92,* 146, 196, 198, 212, 220
Buick V-6 (engine) 223, *223*
Buick V-8 (engine) 168
Burd Special *85*

C

Cadillac 68, *187,* 192
Chaparral 209, 219
Chaparral/Cosworth 210, 215
Chevrolet (Automobile) *110, 128,* 170, 178, 204, 209 216, 219, 228, 242, 265
Chevrolet V-6 223
Chevrolet Indy V-8 155, 168, 201, 222, 223, 225
Chevrolet smallblock V-8 *127,* 168, 223
Chrysler *56, 76,* 100, 120, *154,* 232
Cisitalia 157
Cole 48
Colt/Ford *182, 184, 185,* 191
Cooper 151
Cooper, Charles 151
Cooper/Climax *149, 149,* 219
Cooper, John 151, 153, 155
Cord 53, 61, 66
Cornelian *39,* 160
Cosworth 25
Cosworth-Ford DFV 200-201
Cosworth-Ford DFX 201, 222, *223*
Cosworth-Ford DFY 200
Cosworth-Ford 200, *200,* 222
Cosworth Ford V-8 (engine) *185,* 192, 193
Coventry Climax (engine) 151
Coyote/Cosworth *207*
Coyote/Ford *163, 170, 181*
Coyote/Foyt *190, 199, 202*
Cummins Engine Company 111, 113, 118, 122, 127
Cutting *15*

D

Daimler *41*
Daimler, Gottlieb 149
Diedt, Emil 77, 118
Deidt/Offy 106, 110, 116
Delage 22, 40, 47, 59
Desoto (automobile) *132*
Desoto Hemi V-8 (engine) *127*
Dodge (automobile) *126, 184*
Double overhead cam engine (DOHC) 31, 39, 41, 49, 53, 59, 86-87, 112, 153, 201, 217, 223, 276
Drake, Dale *79,* 117, 170-171, *185,* 188
Drake/Goosen/Sparks/Offy 222
Drake, John 188
Drake/Offy 192
Duesenberg (automobile) 32-33, 35, 41, 43, 46, 48-49, *48,* 52-56, *52,* 53, 58, 60-63, 73, 249
Duesenberg, Augie 30, 48, 53, 60
Duesenberg, Fred 30, 32, 48, 53, 60, *77*

E

Eagle 189, *189,* 191
Eagle/Offy *165,* 176, 177, 192, 196, 197

F

Fageol, Lou *75,* 112, 169
Fageol Twin Coach Special *107,* 111, 112
Ferrari 103, 111, 138, 152, 180, 190
Ferrari, Enzo 96
Fiat 59
Firestone 50, 76, 89, 91, 97, 114, 134-135, 140, *141,* 155, 161, 173, 177
Flying Cloud Special (Miller) 90
Ford *12,* 55, 61, 79, 80, 124, 150, 156, 158, 167, 174, 176, 177, 180, 193, 200, *206;* See also: Miller/Ford
Ford V-8 (engine) 74, 158-159, *159,* 168, 170, 185
Foyt/Ford V-8 (engine) *185,* 193, 222
Frontenac *29, 39, 41, 42, 43,* 55

G

Garrett-AiResearch 171
Gas Turbine (engine) 172
Gilmore Special 88, *90, 91-92*
Goodyear 161, 177, 193, 196, 221, 249, *249,* 260-261
Goossen, Leo 52, 64, 77, 80, 81, 86, 108, 117, 119,

129, 133, 141, 159, 170-171, 188
Grancor Automotive 175
Grey Ghost 23
Gulf/Miller 61, 94-95, *94, 95,* 103, 112, 150

H

Hawk/Ford *178, 181*
Hawk/Offy *183*
Hispano-Suiza 24
Hudson 68, *77,* 88
Hurst Floor Shift Special (odd cars) 169, *169*

I

Inline-6 (engine) 127
Inline-8 (engine) 43, 49, 59, 60-61, 69, 73, 77, 86
Ilmor (engine) 25, 222

J

Jaguar 25, 139, 143
Judd-Honda V-8 222, *222*
Jynx Special (Miller) 90

K

Kurtis/Cummins 171
Kurtis KK500A (automobile) 128, *130,* 148
Kurtis/Miller *101, 111, 115, 118, 119, 121*
Kurtis Kraft 130-131
Kurtis/Offy *120,* 124, 126, *128,* 135
Kurtis, Frank 112-113, 116, 119, 121, 130, 141, 145, 156-157
Kurtis KK500C 130-131
Kurtis 500S *130*
Kurtis 500G 144
Kurtis KK2000 157
Kurtis KK3000 130
Kuzma/Offy 122, *122,* 141
Kuzma, Eddie 119, 129

L

Lancia 138, 160
LaSalle 51, *58, 78, 84*
"Lay-down" roadster 113, 129, 131, 138, 140-141, *141*
Leader Card Special *137*
Lencki *107*
Lesovsky/Offy 109
Lightning/Offy *203*
Lincoln *72,* 102
Lola 219, 226-228, 246
Lola/Chevy Indy V-8 242, 247, 251, 253, 255, 257, 259, 261, 263, 265, 267, 268, 269, 271, 272, 273, 275, 277
Lola/Cosworth 204, 253, 264
Lola/Ford 234, *234*

Lotus 151, *161,* 167, 190-191, 209
Lotus/Ford 158-159, *160*

M

March 226-228, 243
March/Cosworth 205, 220, 224, 226 227, *227,* 228, 229, 232, 233, 235
McLaren, Bruce 189
McLaren (automobile) 249
McLaren/Cosworth 199
McLaren/Offy *186, 188, 194, 197, 198*
McLaren M16 189, 191, 197, 227
Marmon 19, 27, 37, 38, 43, 62, 83, 249
Mason 50, 53
Maserati 91-93, *92, 93,* 96, 97, 100, *107, 109,* 111
Maserati 8CTF (engine) 97
Maxwell 29, 50, *50*
Mercedes 23, 31, 33, 41, 89, 93
Mercedes-Benz *15, 23, 28,* 68, 111, 135, 138
Mercer 40
Mercury 118, *138*
Meyer-Drake Offenhauser 25, 59, 79, 117-118, 133, *133*
Meyer, Louie 170
Miller 25, 35, 43, 44, 46, *46,* 48-49, 52-64, 56, 60, 62, 64, 66, 72, 73, 76, 77-82, 78, 79, 82, 85, 86, 101, 111, 122; See also: Gulf-Miller
Miller, 91-type 55, 59, 61, *61,* 63-64, 65, 77
Miller/Duesenberg 44
Miller/Ford 71, 73, 74-75, *74, 75,* 111, 167
Miller, Harry 30, 49, 57, 60-61, 60, 64, 74-75, 77, 79, 81, 118, 122, 159
Miller-Hartz Special *73*
Monroe *38,* 121
Moore, Lou 109, 119
Moss, Dr. Sanford 52
M/T Challenger (odd car) 168, *168*

N

Nash *106*
National Motors *17, 18, 44*
NOC-Out Special/Offy *99,* 100
Novi 75, 87, 107, 109, 110-112, 119-121, 175

O

Offenhauser (Offy) 59, 61, 78, 80, 81, 86-87, 103, 108, 112-113, *115,* 116-118, 119, 122, *131, 185,* 222
See also: Meyer-Drake-

Offenhauser
Offenhauser Engineering Co. 81
Offenhauser, Fred 60, 64, 77, 79, 80, 81, 86, 117
Offy Engine 86, 87, 133, *133*, 171
Oldsmobile *116, 148, 182, 188, 194, 202, 226, 236*

P

Packard *15, 21, 28, 36, 82*
Packard Cable 60
Parnelli Grand Prix Car 235
Paxton Products 175
Penske (automobile) 226-228
Penske/Chevrolet Indy V-8 *231, 236, 238, 240, 241*
Penske/Cosworth 199, *206, 207, 212*
Penske PC-16 225
Penske, Roger 213, 218-219, *218,* 227-228, 239, 266
Penske Corporation 218
Penske Racing 218-219, 225,

232, 235, 241
Peugeot *20, 24-25, 25, 31, 32, 33, 36,* 40, 41, 47, *50*
Plymouth *160*
Pontiac 151, *210, 224, 240*
Pope-Hartford *11*
Porsche-designed Auto Union 68, 88-89, 93, 150
Porsche, Ferdinand 94
Porsche Indy V-8 222
Pratt & Whitney Turbine 172, 174

R

Rambler 53
Renault 21
Renault, Marcel 13
Rickenbacker 8 *52*
Rover 172

S

Salih, George 129, 141, *141*
Salih/Offy *138*
Sampson Special 87
Schact *15*

Sears Allstate Special (odd car) 168, *168*
Shaw/Offy *84*
Shelby-Wallis Special (odd car) 169, *169*
Silent Sam 172, *174, 175* See also; Whooshmobile
Silver Arrow 68, 102, 103
Single Overhead Cam Engines (SOHC) 31, 41, 112
Sparks, Art 86, 185
Sparks-Goossen-Drake (engine) 188
Sparks-Thorne Engine 86, 87, 185
Simplex engine 40
Stein, Al 169
Stevens/Miller 65
Stoddard-Dayton *14, 20, 22*
STP (Scientifically Treated Petroleum) 174, 175
STP gas turbine 169-170, *174,* 176
Studebaker 64, 68, 69, *69,* 96, *122, 152, 174*
Stutz 18, *42, 57*
Sunbeam 47, 59

T

Talbot 59, 103
Texaco 203
Thorne *103,* 111, 117
Thorne, Joel *77,* 86, 102
Turbocharger *181,* 195, *195*

V

Valvoline Special (odd cars) 169, *169*

W

Watson/Offy *132, 146, 148, 150, 152, 154, 156*
Wetteroth/Miller *88*
Wetteroth/Offy *80,* 100
Whooshmobile 172, *174, 175*
Wildcat/Cosworth *207, 216*
Wildcat/DGS *203*
Winfield, Ed 130

Z

Zerex Special 219

DRIVERS

A

Ader, Walt 118
Agabashian, Fred 106, 110, 111, 113, 116, 118, 120, 122, 124, 126, 127, 128, 132, 138, 171
Aitken, Johnny 14
Alboreto, Michele 200
Allen, Leslie 66
Alley, Tom 28, 32, 36, 42, 44
Allison, Bobby 192, 196
Allison, Donnie 182, 184
Alsup, Bill 212
Amick, George 141, 142, 146, 148, *135*
Anderson, Gil 14, 18, 20, 22, 28, 32
Anderson, Les 106, 110
Andres, Emil 82, 88, 92, 96, 100, 102, 106, 110, 116
Andretti, Aldo 180
Andretti, Jeff 181
Andretti, John 181, 223, 236, 240, 242
Andretti, Mario 159, 160, 163, 166, 170, 175, 176, 178, 180-181, *180-181,* 182, 184, 188, 192, 194, 196, 198, 201, 202, 204, *207,* 209, 210, 212, 216, 219, 220, 224, 225, 226, *227, 227,* 228, 232, 233, 234, 236, 240, 242, 260
Andretti, Michael 181, 224, 226, 228, 232, 233, 236, 240, 242
Andrews, Keith 128, 132

B

Ansterberg, Ernie 48
Ardinger, Herb 78, 82, 84, 88, 92, 106
Armi, Frank 126
Arnold, Billy 62, 64, 66, 68, 72, 73
Arnold, Chuck 146
Ascari, Alberto 111, 122, 135, 180, 181
Aspen, Al 68, 72
Ates, Sonny 178
Ayulo, Manny 116, *117,* 122, 124, 126

B

Babcock, George C. 28
Bablot, Paul 36
Bagley, Tom 204, 206, 210
Bailey, George *75,* 78, 80, 84, 88, 92, *95, 95*
Baker, "Cannonball" 44
Ball, Bobby 120, 122
Banks, Henry 88, 102, 106, 118, 120, 122
Barbazza, Fabrizio 232
Barringer, George 78, 82, 92, 94, 95, 96, 100, 102, 103
Basle, Charles 14
Batten, Norman 47, *49,* 56, 58, 62
Bauman, "Dutch" 58
Beardsley, Ralph 14
Bedard, Patrick 220, 224
Behra, Jean 143
Belcher, Fred 14
Belt, C.W. 62
Bergere, Cliff 58, 62, 64, 68,

69, 72, 76, 78, 80, 82, 84, 88, 92, 96, 100, 102, 106, *107, 109*
Bettenhausen, Gary 176, 178, 182, 184, 188, 192, 194, 196, 198, 202, 204, 210, 212, 216, 221, 228, 232, 233, 240, 242
Bettenhausen, Tony 125, 106, 109, 110, 118, 120, 122, 124, 126, 128, 132, 138, 141, 142, 143, 145, 146, 148
Bettenhausen, Tony, Jr., 212, 216, 220, 221, 224, 226, 228, 232, 233, 236, 242
Bigelow, Charles 14
Bigelow, Tom 194, 196, 198, 202, 204, 206, 210, 212, 216
Billman, Mark 76
Bisch, Art 142
Boesel, Raul 223, 226, 228, 236, 240, 242, 268
Boillot, Andre 36, 38, 42
Boillot, Georges 22
Boling, John 38, 68
Bondurant, Bob 151
Bordino, Pietro 52
Borzachini, Baconi 66
Bost, Paul 68, 76
Bouillon-Levegh, Pierre 135
Boyd, Johnny 128, 132, *135,* 138, 141, 142, 146, 148, 150, 152, 154, 156, 160, 166
Boyer, Joe 36, 38, 42, 46, 47, 48

Brabham, Geoff 212, 216, 220, 224, 226, 228, 232, 242
Brabham, Jack 149, *149,* 150, 151, 153, 156, 178, 182
Bragg, Caleb 14, 20, 22
Branson, Don 146, 148, 150, 152, 154, 156, 160, 166
Brayton, Scott 212, 220, 223, 224, 226, 232, 236, 240, 242
Brett, Riley L. 42
Brisko, Frank 64, 68, 72, 76, 78, 80, 82, 84, 88, 92, 96, 100
Brock, S.F. 22
Brown, Walt 106, 118, 120
Brown, W.W. 36
Bruce-Brown, David 14, 18
Bucknum, Ronnie 176, 178, 182
Burman, Bob 14, *15,* 18, 20, 22, 28
Burton, Claude 66
Butcher, Harry 66, 68
Bryan, Jimmy 122, 124, 126, 128, 132, *135,* 138, 141, 142, 143, 146, 148, 249
Bueb, Ivor 143

C

Caccia, Joe 66
Campbell, Malcolm 57, *57*
Campbell, Ray 72, 76
Cannon, Larry 194, 198, 210
Cantlon, Shorty 66, 68, 76, 78, 80, 81, 82, 84, 88, 92,

102, 106
Cantrell, Bill 110, 116
Caracciola, Rudi 89
Carey, Bob 72
Carlson, Billy 22, 28
Carter, Duane 109, 110, 116, 118, 119, 120, 122, 124, 126, 128, 139, 146, 148, 154, 221
Carter, Pancho (Duane, Jr.) 194, 196, 198, 202, 204, 206, 210, 212, 216, 220, 221, 223, 224, 226, 228, 232, 233, 240, 242, 268, 274
Caruthers, Jimmy 188, 192, 194, 196
Chandler, Michael 212, 216, 220
Chandler, William 22, 32
Chassagne, Jean 22, 38, 42
Chassey, Steve 220, 223, 232, 236
Cheesbourg, Bill 138, 140, 141, 142, 145, 146, 150, 156, 160, 169, 172
Cheever, Eddie 242
Chevrolet, Arthur 14, 32, 41, 43
Chevrolet, Gaston 36, 38, 41, 42
Chevrolet, Louis 28, 29, 30, 32, 36, 38, 39, 41, 43
Chiron, Louis 64
Chitwood, Joie 96, 100, 102, 106, 110, 116, 118
Christiaens, Josef 22, 32
Christie, Bob 132, 138, 142, 146, 148, 150, 152, 154
Clark, George 20
Clark, Jim 151, 156, 158, 158, 159, 160, 161, 166, 170, 181, 200
Cobe, Harry 14
Cogan, Kevin 212, 216, 219, 220, 221, 223, 224, 226, 228, 232, 233, 236, 240, 242
Cole, Hal 102, 110, 116
Collins, Peter 151
Comer, Fred 48, 52, 56, 62
Congdon, Gary 166
Connor, George 80, 82, 84, 88, 92, 96, 100, 102, 106, 109, 110, 114, 116, 118, 120, 122
Cooper, Earl 22, 28, 36, 46, 52, 56, 164
Cooper, Joe 28
Corum, L.L. 44, 46, 47, 48, 56, 66, 76
Cotey, Al 58
Cox, G.C. 28
Crawford, Charles 78
Crawford, Jim 223, 226, 228, 236, 240, 242
Crawford, Ray 126, 128, 132, 143, 146
Crawford, Wes 64, 72, 76
Crockett, Larry 126
Cross, Art 122, 124, 126, 128, 129
Crowe, Allen 152, 154
Cucinotta, Letterio 66
Cummings, Bill 68, 72, 76, 78,

80, 82, 84, 88
Curtner, Jack 44

D

Dallenbach, Wally 170, 176, 178, 182, 184, 188, 192, 194, 196, 198, 202, 204, 206
Daly, Derek 220, 224, 226, 232, 236, 240
D'Alene, Wilbur 32, 36, 44
Davies, Jim 118, 120, 124, 128, 129
Davis, Don 150, 152
Davis, Floyd 47, 84, 92, 96, 100, 108
Dawson, Joe 14, 15, 18, 22, 47
Daywalt, Jimmy 123, 124, 126, 128, 132, 138, 146, 150, 152
de Alzaga, Martin 46
Decker, Rick 64, 66, 76, 78
de Cystria, Prince 46
Delaney, Ernest 14
Denver, Bill 66
DePalma, John 28
DePalma, Ralph 14, 15, 18, 20, 23, 28, 29, 30, 32, 36, 38, 41, 42, 44, 46, 52
DePaolo, Peter 44, 47, 48, 52, 53, 56, 58, 60, 64, 66, 85, 89, 90, 164
DeVigne, Jules 32
de Viscaya, Pierre 46
DeVore, Billy 84, 88, 92, 96, 100, 102, 110, 113
DeVore, Earl 52, 62, 58, 62
Dickson, Larry 166, 170, 176, 178, 184, 204, 206, 212
Dingley, Bert 18
Dinsmore, Duke 102, 106, 116, 117, 118, 120, 132
Dion, Comte de 12
Disbrow, Louis 11, 14, 18, 20, 22
Dobson, Dominic 236, 240, 242
Dodge, Horace 53
Donohue, Mark 178, 182, 184, 186, 188, 192, 197, 219, 249
Dreyfus, Rene 89, 93
Duff, John 56
Duman, Ronnie 156, 157, 160, 166, 170, 176
Duncan, Len 126
Durant, Cliff 36, 44, 46, 48, 56, 62
Durant, Louis 102
Duray, Arthur 22
Duray, Leon 44, 46, 52, 56, 58, 59, 62, 63, 64, 68, 77, 90
Duryea, Frank 12

E

Ecclestone, Bernie 151
Edmunds, Don 138
Elisian, Ed 126, 128, 132, 138, 140, 142
Eldridge, E.A.D. 56

Ellingboe, Jules 42, 44, 48, 52, 56, 58
Elliott, Frank 44, 46, 48, 52, 56, 58
Ellis, Fred 14
Endicott, Bill 14, 18, 20
Endicott, Harry 14, 20
Engelhart, Bill 210
Evans, Dave 58, 62, 66, 68, 76, 77, 78
Evans, Robert 20

F

Fabi, Teo 220, 223, 224, 236, 240, 242, 268
Fahrnow, Dusty 78
Fairman, Jack 143
Fangio, Juan Manuel 143, 144, 144
Fankhouser, Milt 106
Farina, Nino 144
Farmer, Frank 64, 66, 68
Faulkner, Walt 118, 120, 124, 128, 134
Fengler, Harlan 46
Ferguson, Dick 210
Fetterman, I.P. 44
Fillip, Chet 216, 220
Firestone, Dennis 210, 212, 216, 220, 224
Fittipaldi, Emerson 181, 216, 219, 224, 226, 228, 229, 232, 233, 236, 238-239, 239, 240, 241, 241, 242, 243, 256, 268, 273
Fittipaldi, Wilson, Jr. 241
Flaherty, Pat 118, 124, 128, 131, 131, 132, 146, 175, 175
Fohr, Myron 116, 117, 118
Follmer, George 178, 182, 184
Fonder, George 116, 122
Fontaine, Louis 42
Forberg, Carl 120
Force, Gene 120, 148
Ford, Percy 42
Foster, Bill 160, 166
Fowler, Ken 84, 106
Fox, Frank 14
Fox, Malcolm 72, 76
Fox, Stan 232, 236, 242
Foyt, A.J. 142, 143, 146, 148, 150, 151, 152, 154, 156, 159, 160, 162-163, 162-163, 166, 170, 176, 178, 180, 181, 181, 182, 184, 188, 190, 192, 193, 194, 196, 198, 199, 199, 202, 203, 204, 206, 207, 210, 211, 212, 216, 220, 224, 225, 226, 228, 232, 233, 234, 234, 235, 236, 240, 242, 249, 260
Frame, Fred 58, 62, 64, 68, 72, 76, 77, 80, 82
Franchi, Aldo 32
Frayer, Lee 14, 18, 50
Free, Roland 66, 106
Freeland, Don 124, 126, 128, 132, 138, 142, 143, 146, 148
Friedrich, Ernest 22

G

Ganassi, Chip 216, 220, 224, 226, 228
Gardner, Chet "Speed" 64, 66, 68, 76, 78, 80, 82, 84, 88
Garrett, Billy 132, 142
Garza, Josele 212, 216, 220, 224, 226, 228, 232, 233
Gaudino, Juan 72
Gehlhausen, Spike 198, 204, 206, 210, 224
George, Elmer 138, 152, 154
Gilhooley, Ray 22
Ginther, Richie 172, 190
Gleason, Jimmy 62, 64, 66, 68, 90
Gloy, Tom 224
Goldsmith, Paul 140, 141, 142, 146, 148, 150, 152, 154, 161
Goodyear, Scott 242
Gordon, Al 72, 78, 80, 81
Goux, Jules 20, 22, 24, 30, 33, 36, 38, 44, 223
Grant, Harry 14, 20, 22, 28
Grant, Jerry 160, 166, 170, 176, 182, 188, 192, 194, 196, 198
Green, Cecil 118, 120
Gregory, Masten 143, 160
Greiner, Arthur 14
Griffith, Cliff 120, 122, 132, 150
Grim, Bobby 146, 148, 150, 152, 154, 156, 166, 170, 176
Guerrero, Roberto 223, 224, 226, 228, 232, 236, 242, 243, 268
Gulotta, Tony 56, 58, 62, 64, 66, 68, 72, 76, 78, 80, 84, 85, 88, 92
Gurney, Dan 32, 151, 152, 154, 156, 158, 159, 160, 161, 163, 166, 170, 171, 178, 181, 182, 185, 189, 223, 233, 273
Guthrie, Janet 202, 203, 204, 206
Guyot, Albert 20, 22, 36, 42, 56

H

Haibe, Ora 32, 36, 42, 44, 48
Hall, Dean 242
Hall, Howard 14
Hall, Ira 62, 72, 76, 88, 92
Hall, Norm 150, 156
Halsmer, Pete 212, 216
Hanks, Sam 96, 100, 102, 105, 110, 116, 118, 120, 122, 124, 126, 128, 129, 132, 134, 138, 139, 141, 141, 151, 221, 249
Hansen, Mel 92, 96, 100, 101, 102, 106, 110
Hansgen, Walt 156, 160
Harder, Fred 48
Harkey, Bob 156, 184, 192, 194, 196, 198
Harroun, Ray 14, 19, 26-27, 29, 35, 42, 43, 47, 164, 249

Hartley, Gene 118, 122, 124, 126, 132, 138, 146, 150, 152
Hartz, Harry 44, 46, 48, 52, 56, 57, 58, 73
Haupt, Willie 20, 22, 28, 38
Haustein, Gene 68, 76, 78
Hawkes, W. Douglas 44, 56
Hawthorn, Mike 139, 143
Haywood, Hurley 210
Hearne, Eddie 14, 18, 36, 38, 42, 44, 46, 48, 58, *258*
Heath, George 19
Heimrath, Ludwig, Jr. 232, 236, 240
Hellings, Mack 110, 116, 118, 120
Henderson, Pete 32, 38
Hepburn, Ralph 52, 56, 58, 62, 64, 68, 76, 78, 80, 82, 84, *89*, 92, 96, 100, 102, *107*
Herman, Al 128, 132, 138, 146, 148
Herr, Don 20, 47
Hickey, Denny 36
Hickman, Jim 216
Hill, Bennett 38, 42, 46, 48, 52, 56, 58, 76
Hill, George 28
Hill, Graham 159, 166, *167*, 170, 172, 174, 176, 181, 190, 239
Hill, Jim 58
Hill, Phil 143, 152, 181
Hinnershitz, Tommy 96, 100, 110
Hiss, Mike 188, 192, 194, 196
Hitke, Kurt 36
Hobbs, David 184, 192, 194, 198
Holbert, Al 224
Holland, Bill 106, *108*, 109, 110, 116, 118, *119*, 124
Holmes, Howdy 206, 216, 220, 224, 226, 236
Holmes, Jackie 116, 118
Homeier, Bill 126, 129, 148
Horan, Joe 18
Horn, Ted 70-71, 75, *75*, 80, 82, 84, 88, *89*, 92, 96, 100, 102, 103, 106, *107*, 110
Householder, Ronney 77, 84, 88
Houser, Norm 116, *117*
Houser, Thane 48, 56
Howard, C. Glenn 44
Howard, Ray 36, 38
Howie, George 68
Hoyt, Jerry 118, 124, 126, 128
Hucul, Cliff 202, 204, 206
Huff, Joe 66, 68, 72
Hughes, Hughie 14, 18
Hulme, Denis *169*, 170, 176, 178, 184
Hulse, Chuck 152, 154, 166, 170
Hunt, Bill 48
Hurtubise, Jim 145, 148, 150, 152, 154, 156, 160, 166, 176, 188, 194

I

Insinger, Harris 80

J

Jackson, Jimmy 102, 106, 110, 116, 118
Jagersberger, Joe *11*, 14
James, Joe 120, 122, 127
Jenkins, Johnny 18, 20
Jones, Bubby 202
Jones, Davy 232, 240
Jones, John 240
Johncock, Gordon 160, 166, 170, 176, 178, 182, 184, 188, 192, 194, 196, 198, 202, 204, 206, 210, 211, 212, 216, *217*, 220, 221, 224, 232, 240
Johns, Bobby 160, *169*, 178
Johnson, Art 32
Johnson, Eddie 122, 128, 132, 138, 142, 146, 148, 150, 152, 154, 156, 160, 166, 168
Johnson, Herm 216, 223, 224, 268
Johnson, Luther 68, 72, 76
Jones, Ben 56
Jones, Herbert 52
Jones, M.C. 52
Jones, Parnelli 148, 150, 151, 152, 153, 154, 156, 158, 159, 160, 163, 166, 170, 172, *174*, *175*, 181
Jones, Will *11*, 14
Jourdain, Bernard 240, *253*

K

Karl, Jerry 192, 194, 196, 204, 210, 212
Karnatz, Albert 64
Keech, Ray 57, 62, *63*, 64
Keene, Charles 22
Keller, Al 128, 132, 138, 142, 146, 150
Keneally, Mel 66
Kenyon, Mel 166, 170, 176, 178, 182, 184, 188, 192
Kimberly, Jim 153
Kinser, Sheldon 196, 198, 202, 204, 206, 212
Kirkpatrick, Charles 36
Kladis, Danny 102
Klausler, Tom 212
Klein, Art 22, 28, 36, 38, 44, *258*
Kneifel, Chris 220, 224, *261*
Knepper, Arnie 160, 166, 170, 176, 178
Knight, Harry 14, 18
Knipper, Billy 14, 20, 22
Kohlert, Henry 62
Kreiger, Johnny 72
Kreis, Peter 52, 56, 57, 58, 62, 64, 72, 76
Krisiloff, Steve 184, 188, 192, 196, 198, 202, 204, 206, 212, 220
Krueger, Phil 228, 236
Kunzman, Lee 188, 192, 202, 206

L

Lanier, Randy 228
Larson, Jud 142, 146
Lautenschlager, C. 46
Lazler, Bob 212
Lecklider, Fred 56, 58
LeCocq, Louis 36
Leffler, Greg 210
Leonard, Joe 160, 166, 170, 174, 176, 178, 182, 184, 188, 192
Levassor, Emile 15
Levrett, Bayliss 116, 118
Lewis, Dave 52, 56, 58
Lewis, Randy 232, 236, 240, 242
Liesaw, Billy 18, 20
Lindau, Bill 64
Linden, Andy 120, 122, 124, 126, 128, 129, 132, 138, 143
Litz, Deacon 62, 64, 66, 68, 72, 76, 78, 80, 82, 84, 92, 100
Lockhart, Frank 56, 57, *57*, 58, 64, 239
Loquasto, Al 198, 202
Luyendyk, Arie 226, 228, 232, 233, 236, 240, 241, 242, 249, 251, 253, 255, 257, 259, 261, 263, 265, 267, 268, 269, 271, 273, 274, 275, 277
Lynch, George 116
Lytle, Herbert 14

M

McCarver, Jack 56
McCluskey, Roger 150, 152, 154, 160, 166, 170, 176, 178, 182, 184, 188, 192, 194, 196, 198, 202, 204, 206
McCoy, Ernie 124, 126
McCoy, J.J. 36
McCoy, Larry 196, 198
McDonald, J.C. 66
McDonough, Bob 48, 52, 64, 72
McDougall, Bon 56
McDowell, Johnny 116, 118, 120, 122
McElreath, Jim 145, 152, 154, 156, 160, 166, 170, 176, 178, 182, *183*, 192, 194, 202, 204, 206, 210
McGrath, Jack 110, 116, 118, 120, *121*, 122, *123*, 124, 126, 128
McGurk, Frank 82
McLaren, Bruce 151, *169*
McQuinn, Harry 78, 80, 82, 84, 88, 92, 96, 100, 102, 110
McRae, Graham 192
McWithey, Jim 146, 148
MacDonald, Dave 156, *157*, 168
MacKenzie, Doc 72, 76, 78, 80, 82
MacPherson, Jeff 232
Mackey, Bill 120

Magill, Mike 138, 142, 146
Mahler, John 188, 202, 204, 206
Mais, John A. 28
Malloy, Jim 176, 178, 182, 184
Malone, Art 145, 154, 156
Mantz, Johnny 110, 116
Marchese, Carl 64
Marquette, Mel 14, 18
Marshall, Cy 66, 106
Marshman, Bobby 150, 152, 154, 156, 159
Martin, John 188, 192, 194, 196, 198
Mason, George 22
Mathouser, Bob 156, 168
Mauro, Johnny 110
Mays, Rex 78, 80, *81*, 82, 84, 86, 88, *89*, 92, 96, *97*, 100, 102, 106, 110, 116
Mears, Rick, *163*, *193*, *195*, 204, 206, 210, 212, 216, *217*, *219*, 219, 220, 221, 224, 225, *225*, 226, 228, 230-231, 232, 236, 240, 242, 256, 260, 266, *267*, 268
Mears, Roger 216, 220, 221, 225
Melcher, Al 58
Merz, Charlie 14, 18, 20, 32
Meyer, Eddie, Jr. 79
Meyer, Louie 54-55, 62, 64, 65, 66, 68, 72, 76, 78, 79, 79, 80, *81*, 82, 84, 85, 88, 91, 92, 108, 117
Meyer, Zeke 66, 72, 76, 82
Miller, Al 72, 76, 78, 80, 82, 84, 88, 92, 95, 96, 100, 106
Miller, Al 154, 160, 166, 170
Miller, Chet 66, 68, 72, 76, 77, 78, 80, 82, 84, 88, 92, 96, 100, 102, 110, 111, 120, 122
Miller, Eddie 42
Milton, Tommy 36, 38, 42, *43*, 44, 46, 47, 48, 52, 53, 56, 58, 90
Moore, Lou 62, 64, 66, 68, 72, 76, 78, 80, 82, 85, 106, 108-109, *108*, 110, 119
Moran, Charles 66
Moran, Rocky 236, 240, 242
Moreno, Roberto 228
Moriceau, Jules 64
Morton, Wade 52, 58
Mosley, Mike 176, 178, 182, 184, 188, 192, 194, 196, 198, 202, 204, 206, 210, 212, 220
Moss, Alfred E. 48
Moss, Stirling 143, 151, 273
Mourre, Antoine 48
Mulford, Ralph 14, 18, 20, 22, 28, 32, 36, 38, 42, 44
Murphy, Jimmy 32, 33, 35, 38, 42, 44, 48, 249
Musso, Luigi 143
Muther, Rick 182, 184, 194

N

Nalon, Duke 88, 96, 100, 102, 106, *109*, 110, 111, 116, 120, 121, *121*, 122, 124
Nazaruk, Mike 120, 124, 126
Nemesh, Steve 56
Niday, Cal 124, 126, 128
Nikrent, Joe 20
Nuvolari, Tazio 85, 89, *89*, 93

O

O'Connor, Pat 126, 128, 132, 138, *140*, 142, 143
O'Donnell, Eddie 28, 36, 38, *258*
Oldfield, Barney *12*, 22, 23, 32, *40*, 60
Olivero, Bobby 202
Ongais, Danny 202, 204, 206, 210, 212, 216, 224, 226, 228, 235
Opperman, Jan 194, 198
Ormsby, Len 18
Orr, Tom 28

P

Palmroth, Tero 236, 240, 242, *255*
Pardee, Phil 68, 90
Parsons, Johnnie *114-115*, 116, 118, 119, *119*, 120, 122, 124, 126, 128, 129, 130, 132, 138, 142, 143, 221
Parsons, Johnny 194, 196, 198, 202, 204, 206, 210, 216, 220, 221, 226, 228
Patschke, Cyrus 47
Paul, John, Jr. 226, 242
Penske, Roger 151, 219
Petticord, Jack 58
Petillo, Kelly 72, 76, 78, 80, 81, 84, 88, 90, 92, 96, 100
Petty, Richard 151
Phillips, Overton 100
Pilette, Theodore 20
Pimm, Ed 226, 228, 232, 268
Pixley, Ray 82
Pollard, Art 170, 174, 176, 178, 182, 184, *190*
Porporato, Jean 28, 38
Posey, Sam 188
Prentiss, Willard 76
Pruett, Scott 240, 272
Pullen, Eddie *258*
Puterbaugh, Bill 196, 198, 202
Putnam, Al 88, 96, 100, 102

Q

Quinn, Francis 68

R

Rager, Roger 210
Rahal, Bobby 216, 220, 221, 223, 224, 226, 228, 229, 232, 233, 236, 240, 241, 242, 244, 252, 260, 268, 269, 272, 272, *273*
Rasmussen, Eldon 196, 202, 206
Rathmann, Dick 118, 132, 140,
142, 146, 148, 150, 152, 154, 156
Rathmann, Jim 116, 118, 122, 124, 126, 128, 132, 138, 142, 143, *143*, 146, 148, 150, 152, 154, 163, 175
Rebaque, Hector 216
Reece, Jimmy 122, 126, 128, 132, 138, *140*, 142, 143
Regazzoni, Clay 202
Resta, Dario 28, 29, *31*, 32, 46, 239
Revson, Peter 178, 182, 184, 188, 189, *189*, 191, 192, 197, 198
Rice, Larry 204, 206
Richmond, Tim 210, 212
Riganti, Raoul 46, 76, *93*, 96
Rigsby, Jim 122
Rindt, Jochen 170, 176, 189, 190
Roberts, Floyd 80, *81*, 82, 84, 88, *89*, 91, 92, 108
Robson, George 96, 100, 102, *103*, 111
Robson, Hal 102, 106, 110
Rodee, Chuck 152, 160
Rodriquez, Pedro *153*
Romcevich, Pete 106
Rooney, Tom 32
Rose, Ebb 150, 152, 154
Rose, Mauri 47, 76, 78, 80, 82, 84, 85, *85*, 88, 92, 96, 100, 102, 106, *107*, 108, 109 110, 116, 118, 120, *175*, 249
Rosemeyer, Bernd 88
Ross, Sam 62, 68
Ruby, Lloyd 148, 150, 152, 154, 156, 160, 166, 170, 176, 178, 182, 184, 188, 192, 194, 196, 198, 202
Rupp, Mick 160
Russo, Eddie 128, 138, 148
Russo, Joe 68, 72, 76, 78
Russo, Paul 96, 100, 102, 106, *107*, 110, 111, 112, 116, 118, 124, 126, 132, 138, 142, 143, 145, 146, 152
Rutherford, Johnny 154, 156, 160, 170, 176, 178, 182, 184, 188, 192, 194, 196, *197*, 198, 199, 202, 206, 210, 211, *211*, 212, 213, *215*, 216, 222, 224, 226, 228, 232, 233, 236
Ruttman, Troy 116, 118, 119, *119*, 120, 122, 126, 131, 132, 138, 143, 148, 150, 152, 154, 156

S

Sachs, Eddie 138, 142, 143, 146, 148, 150, 152, 153, 154, 156, *157*, 164, *173*
Sailer, Max 46
Salay, Mike 110
Saldana, Joe 204, 206
Sall, Bob 80
Sarles, Roscoe 36, 38, 42, 44, *258*
Saulpaugh, Bryan 72
Savage, Swede 188, 192, 199
Sawyer, Johnny 76, 78

Saylor, Everett 100
Schindler, Bill 118, 120, 122
Schneider, Louis 58, 62, 66, 68, 72, 76
Schrader, Gus 72
Schuppan, Vern 198, 206, 212
Schurch, Herman 64, 68
Scott, Billy 198
Scott, Bob 122, 124
Scarborough Carl, 120, 124
Seaman, Dick 88
Sessions, Sam 176, 178, 182, 184, 188, 192, 196
Seymour, Johnny 62, 64, 66, 78, 80, 82
Shafer, Phil 46, 52, 56, 64, 66, 68, 72, 78
Shannon, Elmer T. 36
Shattuc, Dr. W.E. 52, 56, 58
Shaw, Wilbur 58, 62, 66, 67, 72, 76, 78, 79, 80, 82, 84, 85, 88, 89, *89*, 90-91, *90-91*, 92, 96, 97, 100, 103, 105, 111, 131, 249, 264
Sheffler, Bill 102, 110, 116
Shepherd, A.J. 150
Shoaff, Benny 53, 58, 62
Simon, Dick 182, 184, 188, 192, 194, 196, 197, 198, 202, 204, 206, 210, 220, 224, 226, 228, 232, 236, 268
Simpson, Bill 194
Smiley, Gordon 210, 212
Sneva, Jerry 202, 204, 206, 210, 216, 221
Sneva, Tom 194, 196, 198, 199, 201, 202, 204, 206, 210, 212, 216, 219, 220, 221, 224, 226, 228, 232, 236, 240, 242, 268
Snider, George 160, 166, 170, 176, 178, 182, 184, 188, 192, 194, 196, 198, 202, 204, 206, 210, 216, 220, 224, 226, 228, 232
Snowberger, Russ 62, 64, 66, 68, 72, 76, 78, 80, 84, 88, 92, 96, 100, 102, 106
Snyder, Jimmy 80, 82, 84, 86, 88, 92
Souders, George 58, 62
Spangler, Lester 76
Spence, Bill 64
Stapp, Babe 58, 62, 64, 66, 68, 76, 80, 82, 84, 88, 92, 96
Stevens, Myron 68
Stevenson, Chuck 120, 122, 124, 126, 147, 148, 150, 154, 156, 160
Stewart, Jackie 166, 170
Strang, Lewis *13*, 14, 17, *17*
Stubblefield, Stubby 68, 72, 76, 78
Sullivan, Danny 216, 218, *219*, 219, 220, 223, 224, 226, *227*, 228, 232, 233, 236, 240, 242, 268, 274
Sutton, Len *140*, 142, 146, 148, 150, 151, 152, 156, 160
Swanson, Bob 84, 87, 92, 96
Sweikert, Bob 122, 124, 126, 128, 131, 132

Szisz, Ferenc 21

T

Teague, Marshall 124, 138
Templeman, Shorty 128, 142, 148, 150, 152
Tetzlaff, Teddy 14, 18, 20, 22
Theys, Didier 240, 242
Thomas, Joe 38, 42, 44
Thomas, Rene 22, 36, 38, 42
Thompson, Mickey 154, *155*
Thomson, Johnny 124, 126, 128, 132, 138, *140*, 142, 143, 146, 148, 163
Thorne, Joel 86, 88, 89, 92, 96, 100
Threshie, Phil 204, 206
Thurman, Arthur 36
Tingelstad, Bud 148, 152, 154, 156, 160, 166, 170, 176, 178, 184
Toft, Omar 36
Tolan, Johnnie 132, 138, *140*, 142
Tomei, Louis 80, 82, 84, 88, 92, 96, 100, 102
Tower, Jack 14, 20
Trexler, Marion 66
Trintignant, Maurice 143, 151
Triplett, Ernie 64, 66, 68, 72, 76
Trucco, Vincenzo 20
Turner, Jack 132, 138, 142, 146, 150, 152
Turner, W.H. "Jack" 14

U

Unser, Al 35, 160, 166, 170, 176, 182, 184, *185*, 188, 189, 191, *191*, 192, 194, 196, 197, 198, 201, 202, 204, *205*, 206, 210, 212, 213, 216, 219, *219*, 220, 222, 223, 224, 225, 226, 228, 232, 233, *233*, 234-235, *234-235*, 236, 240, 242
Unser, Al, Jr. 213, 220, 224, 226, 228, 232, 233, 235, 236, 240, 241, 242, 244, 246, 260
Unser, Bobby 145, *145*, 154, 156, 160, *165*, 166, 170, 171, 176, *177*, 178, 182, 184, 188, 191, 192, 194, 196, *197*, 198, 202, 204, 206, *207*, 210, 211, 212, 213, *213*, 219, 234
Unser, Jerry 142, 213, 234
Unser, Louis 213, 234

V

Vail, Ira 36, 42, 44, 48, 52
VanAcker, Charles 106, 110, 116
VanRaalte, Noel 28
VanRanst, Cornelius 41, 42
Veith, Bob 132, 138, 142, 143, 146, 148, 152, 154, 156, 160, 170, 176
Villeneuve, Jacques 228
Villoresi, Gigi 102